Developing Power

Developing Power

How Women Transformed International Development

Edited by
Arvonne S. Fraser
and Irene Tinker

The Feminist Press
at The City University of New York
New York

Published by the Feminist Press at the City University of New York
The Graduate Center
365 Fifth Avenue
New York, NY 10016
www.feministpress.org

First Feminist Press edition, 2004

Library of Congress Cataloging-in-Publication Data

Developing power : how women transformed international development / edited by Arvonne S. Fraser and Irene Tinker.— 1st Feminist Press ed.
    p. cm.
  Includes bibliographical references and index.
  ISBN 1-55861-484-2 (hardcover : alk. paper) — ISBN 1-55861-485-0 (pbk. : alk. paper)
  1. Women in development. 2. United Nations. 3. Women in development—International cooperation. 4. Women in politics. 5. Women's rights. I. Fraser, Arvonne S. II. Tinker, Irene. III. Title.

HQ1240.D48 2004
305.42—dc22

                                                    2004019268

Text and cover design by Dayna Navaro
Printed in the U.S.A. on acid-free paper by McNaughton & Gunn, Inc.

09 08 07 06 05 04   5 4 3 2 1

Contents

part III
In and Out of Government

part IV
Influencing Development Policy

part V
Education and Development

Preface

After the 1995 United Nations Fourth World Conference on Women held in Beijing, China, a few of us with over two decades of experience in the international women in development (WID) movement decided it was time to document what had been accomplished and how the movement had affected our lives. As researchers, scholars, and activists, we had seen tremendous change since the idea of considering women's interests in the development process began to grasp imaginations and inspire agitation in the early 1970s. From 1975 to 1995, we had watched participation in the world women's conferences more than quadruple. We had encouraged, participated in, and witnessed the proliferation and increased effectiveness of nongovernmental organizations (NGOs), and we had instigated policy changes at national and international levels. Little did we realize in the 1970s how enriched our lives would be by this experience.

Although the WID acronym was adopted quickly, it was always difficult to define exactly what WID was because "women" and "development" are such complex and broad categories. The origins of WID are often traced to United Nations resolutions about integrating women in the development of the non-industrialized countries when economic development was the focus of both industrialized and developing countries. But as the chapters in this book reveal, the WID idea was conceptualized by women working within the United Nations system, refined by women scholars and practitioners, and implemented in many different ways by women in nongovernmental organizations (NGOs), in the WID offices established by donor countries, and by governments, albeit reluctantly. A good working definition of WID is simply the taking of women into account, improving their status, and increasing their participation in the economic, social, and political development of communities, nations, and the world.

This book is a series of memoirs describing how the WID idea was put into practice. We chose to write history via memoir because women's lives are much more multifaceted than men's. Universally women have and tend the children, take care of homes, and too often are thought to do only that. A major purpose of this book and of the WID movement was to dispel that myth. We also thought it important to show younger women and men how work and family can be integrated. Most of the contributors to this volume are—or were—married and have children. Many were mid-career women when they began working internationally. Some moved in and out of government and UN positions and organized new NGOs when they saw a need. Others created organizations that linked women internationally and publicized not only their activities but what governments and the UN were doing—or not doing.

Virtually all of the contributors refer to the United Nations world conferences on women, without which the WID movement could not have been successful nor the truly international women's movement created. Some of the contributors were government delegates to UN world conferences and also worked in grassroots women's organizations. This book illustrates the interaction between those inside government and those who worked in NGOs to influence governments directly or in the programs governments established and funded. The book is the story of only a few women who participated in this movement from the 1970s to the beginning of the twenty-first century. We intentionally mention others with whom we worked and who contributed immensely to the movement. One chapter deals almost exclusively with an early WID organization operated in an industrialized country to protect the activist women in less democratic countries—a need that continues to this day. That particular organization, however, now operates in locations around the world.

Our intention is that this book will stimulate others to write. Too often women's contributions to history are overlooked because women do not take the time to write of their accomplishments or are too modest, conforming to social norms that inhibit their telling the full story. The reader may find remnants of these constraints in this book. Cultural norms still dictate that women should disguise their accomplishments as luck or serendipity and minimize their successes. Even feminists find it hard to overcome constraints reinforced over a lifetime. For far too long history has been his-story. Too many of our foremothers did not write her-story. Yet they formed international organizations in the early days of the twentieth century, got an "equal rights of men and women" mandate in the UN charter, floated the idea of an international women's conference when the United Nations was formed, and established the UN Commission on the Status of Women almost immediately thereafter. Their accomplishments undergirded our work. The WID movement and this book would not have been possible without their foresight and courage.

We began this book as an American story. In late 1998 three of us who were then living in the mid-western part of the United States convened at Martha Lewis's farm. Kathleen Cloud and Martha Lewis were especially concerned that some of the histories being written were portraying women as victims rather than as agents of change. Elsa Chaney, who could not join our gathering because she was attending a Latin American conference, sent a tape of her ideas and was a wellspring of enthusiasm for the book until her death in 2000. We all wanted, as Irene Tinker reiterated after she joined the project, to express agency, to show that women can and have made a difference internationally. The 1995 Beijing conference had convinced us that a quiet revolution was underway. We felt there was a rich and rather unique history to be written to show younger people, especially those interested in international affairs, what had transpired for, about, and with women during the last three decades of the twentieth century. Because many of us are living examples of the idea that international careers can be combined with family life—a view that not all feminists of our day shared—we decided to write a combination memoir-history.

Around Martha Lewis's farmhouse table and over drinks on the porch, we made a long list of potential contributors to the book and hoped to interest Irene Tinker in serving as co-editor because of her involvement in the movement and her skills as a researcher and analyst with an international reputation. We breathed a collective sigh of relief when she agreed. Because of time, money, and communications limitations we decided, at first, to limit our contributors to those who lived and worked within the United States. Our hope was that this would encourage our colleagues abroad to write as well. But we were wisely encouraged by Florence Howe of the Feminist Press to rethink the volume and include contributors from the Global South. We agree that the book would have been incomplete without voices of activist women—practitioners, scholars, and researchers—from around the world. The rapid development of e-mail made this possible, just as relatively inexpensive air travel made possible increased participation of women in the UN world conferences and the thousands of WID meetings in all parts of the globe. Still, there are many voices yet to be heard and we look forward to the many volumes still to come.

Our greatest hope for this book is that it show that "development" means more than economic development and that "human rights" refers to more than civil and political rights. The unique contribution of the WID movement was that it challenged and taught both men and women in and out of government to think and act differently in virtually all fields of endeavor.

This book would not have been possible without the many donors—international development agencies, foundations, and individuals—who supported WID programs and projects. Some are identified in the essays. I am confident that I speak for virtually all the contributors by especially thanking the Nordic country development agencies and the Ford Foundation for their support. I am personally grateful to Genevieve Vaughn, Catharine Cram, Judge Earl R. Larson, Jill Sheffield, and Harlan Cleveland, all of whom made my transitions from government to NGO work possible. President Jimmy Carter, Vice President Walter Mondale, Richard Moe, and Mary King are first among the many who made my service as head of the Women in Development office at the United States

Agency for International Development (USAID) possible. I am also grateful to President Bill Clinton, who appointed me ambassador to the UN Commission on the Status of Women as the commission was preparing for the Beijing conference. Marsha Freeman, my successor at the International Women's Rights Action Watch (IWRAW), Sally Kenney, director of the Center on Women and Public Policy, and my research assistants at the Humphrey Institute of Public Affairs, University of Minnesota, not only tolerated me in uncertain times but made academic life productive and fun.

Irene Tinker and I are especially grateful to the contributors who gave generously of their time and talents and bore with us over the years that it took to produce this book. We also thank our spouses and networks of colleagues and friends for their moral and logistical computer support. Florence Howe expressed interest in having the Feminist Press publish this combined memoir and movement history before she saw a single chapter. As she and Mariam Chamberlain, founding president of the National Council for Research on Women and Feminist Press board member, read over early submissions, they cautioned us to limit the use of development jargon so that this important story of women changing the world would interest the broadest possible audience. We are most grateful for their advice and encouragement. At the Feminist Press, Jean Casella, Stacy Malyil, and Jocelyn Burrell supported the book and its co-editors through the many stages of publication and deserve more thanks than this space allows.

Finally, as every chapter author acknowledges, and as the contributors' lives and world events testify, the revolution is not over. There remain mammoth challenges. It is the hope of the contributors and editors that readers will take to heart the idea that the whole world is still—and always will be—developing and that men and women are partners, not antagonists, in our global society.

Arvonne S. Fraser
Minneapolis, Minnesota
October 2003

Introduction

Ideas into Action

Irene Tinker

The 1970s were heady days for the incipient global women's movement. The energy and turmoil fueling the reassertion of women's rights in the United States provided greater visibility to the growing demands for equality by women around the world. Women at the United Nations struggled to be heard in patriarchal institutions, women in newly independent countries challenged male predominance, and women scholars challenged the assumption that international development benefited everyone. Instead of reversing the inroads that colonialism had made on women's traditional rights, the new economic development programs were in fact reinforcing women's subordination. Resistance to these policies grew as women put their ideas into action.

Individual women wielded great influence through their ideas. But the upheaval of gender relationships globally has been the result of women becoming organized at every level. The paradigm shift in development aid was precipitated by efforts of women's groups in Washington to ensure that the flow of funding to developing countries and their rural poor also reached women. UN women organized to demand greater equity in pay and assignments for themselves while working for women's equality abroad. Around the world, organized women protested against laws that enshrined prevailing roles assigned to women. Brought together through the series of UN World Conferences on Women and the parallel Nongovernmental Forums, these women have coalesced into the global women's movement, which has changed the lives of women and men throughout the world. Women instrumental in leading this amazing transformation recall, in this book, how they converted their ideas to action.

The World Fifty Years Ago

Recall the worldview at the time. The United States had led the world to victory over Germany and Japan and then had initiated a major recovery package for Europe, the Marshall Plan. Certain that their approach was universal, economists projected this model of economic development onto the newly independent countries of Asia and Africa. This male view of the world hardly mentioned women except to opine that often women's religious views made them resist change. If pressed, economists noted that women and children were subsumed under the household, where their happiness and goals would be projected by the benevolent patriarch, an assumption since demolished by gender-sensitive economists.[1]

During the 1960s, new UN members from formerly colonial countries had become a majority in the international body and brought with them a heightened concern for economic development. While the industrialized countries—the Global North—who were donors of development assistance modeled progress on their own experiences, the developing countries—the Global South—agitated for changes in the international policies and treaties relating to, among other things, trade and industrialization. These debates continue. The donor countries introduced new types of agricultural technologies and crops, urged a slowing of the birth rate, and promoted literacy and health. That such programs affected women differently than men was not recognized, much less considered. Worse, because development projects were using northern models, they were perpetuating the unequal gender relationships against which the women's movement was rebelling.

The women in development movement altered both international and bilateral development policies. Resources flowed to women to organize, implement, and study programs for women. The UN conferences enabled and empowered women everywhere. Looking back from the new century, the accomplishments of women over the past four decades are truly phenomenal. How women influenced, and profoundly changed, international development policy, how they altered the concept of human rights to encompass women, how they gave voice to women and for women's issues, is a story that must be preserved. That is the purpose of this book.

The contributors are women from around the world who have played a significant role in global change. In their essays they describe their personal backgrounds and why and how they became involved in the global women's movements, what actions they took, and how their actions expanded their own horizons and capabilities. To accomplish their goals, most of these women have been at one time or another activist, practitioner, and scholar.[2] Few had anticipated that they would act on the international stage. They reflect diverse backgrounds and different perspectives on the specifics of international development and women, but all describe an unusual confluence of circumstances that made possible their contributions to this extraordinary movement.

None of these individual accomplishments would have been possible without the power of women's organizations that have challenged the cultural prescriptions that both protect and support them. The women of these organizations have come together in women-only groups, as women's sections of larger associations, or as integral members of political parties and nongovernmental organizations. This proliferation of women's groups in village, town, and capital city around the world has been astounding. The consistent goal of the women in these groups is active participation in issues and events that concern them as their countries industrialize.

These women espouse many ideologies, diverse approaches, and distinct feminism.[3] In some countries, feminist organizations, perceived as elitist, are distinguished from women's groups whose interests are closer to the poor. Such class and national variations have prompted scholars to utilize the term "gender" in order to emphasize that every individual—woman and man—is socially constructed. In the 1990s, Gender and Development (GAD) was rapidly adopted by the developmental agencies in preference to the use of WID. Not everyone is happy with this switch; contributors to this volume reflect a range of views. Most agree that the analytical power of the term has been compromised by its use as a substitute for the word "woman," a use that obfuscates the need to consider men as well. Those involved in field projects report how the term often confuses them because gender is a complex idea and difficult to translate; further, several women stress the need to continue women-only projects while introducing programs for men and those based on gender analysis. Others, like myself, see the replacement of women by gender as a political attack on the power of the women's movement by men and women uncomfortable with the growing empowerment of women. Overall, the introduction of gender concepts has enriched the understanding of obstacles for achieving equity for women and men in this tumultuous era of socio-economic transformation.

Women Influencing the United Nations

Global networking and organizing were greatly enhanced by the four United Nations World Conferences on Women, which were held in Mexico City in 1975, Copenhagen in 1980, Nairobi in 1985, and Beijing in 1995.[4] Preparations for these conferences were the responsibility of the United Nations Commission on the Status of Women (CSW), which was set up in 1946 as the result of lobbying especially by women from Latin America who had been active in a similar body of the Organization of American States. These women were joined by organizations set up to promote suffrage, such as the International Council of Women, the International Association of University Women, the International Alliance of Women, and Country Women of the World, all of which immediately applied for nongovernmental status at the United Nations.[5]

During the nationalist struggles for independence from colonial powers, women activists from such groups also demonstrated and organized; many were rewarded with significant governmental positions in their newly independent governments. During the 1950s, most former colonial countries in Asia became independent and joined the United Nations; African countries followed in the 1960s. Often women from these nations, such as Vijaya Lakshmi Pandit from India and Annie Jiaggie from Ghana, held more visible positions in the UN or in their country delegations than did women from the industrialized world. Such women provided exemplary leadership at the United Nations and the women's world conferences.

The Commission on the Status of Women

When the United Nations was formed in 1945, women and their rights were little discussed, but women delegates were able to add to the charter's preamble a provision calling for equal rights of men and women. Continued agitation led the Economic and Social Council of the UN (ECOSOC) to create a subcommittee on women to the Human Rights Commission in 1946; in the following year, the Commission on the Status of Women became a separate entity.

Under the leadership of Margaret Bruce from the United Kingdom, the CSW focused during its early years on women's legal rights and education. Despite a limited budget and staff, the commission, supported by international women's organizations participating at the UN, was successful in steering through the UN General Assembly a series of measures on women's rights relating to citizenship, employment, and family law. In contrast, the delegates from the communist bloc saw no need for such rights because, they argued, such issues were irrelevant, since women and men were equal in their countries. For these delegates to the commission the significant issue for women was peace. When themes for International Women's Year 1975 were proposed, peace was included along with equality and development. The symbol of the year was a dove of peace whose wings enclosed an equals sign and whose body held the sign for female.

Gradually other topics were introduced into the CSW. In 1963 Aziza Hussein, delegate from Egypt and the first Arab member of the CSW, "dared to raise the issue of family planning as a relevant agenda item, particularly as regards countries suffering from excessive population growth. . . . The effect of [her] words thundered like an explosion." Other contested issues that Aziza writes about in her essay in this volume include women's status in Islam and women's rights in occupied territories.

Less controversial within the commission was language for the Declaration on the Elimination of Discrimination Against Women, which was drafted by the CSW beginning in 1965 and adopted by the UN General Assembly in 1967. After the Mexico City conference in 1975, the CSW revisited the issue, and in spite of weak support from Western countries, a Philippine draft formed the basis of the Convention on the Elimination of All Forms of Discrimination Against Women (CEDAW). Leticia Shahani recounts in this volume the fascinating tale of the unorthodox approach she took in ensuring the debate on this draft. CEDAW was subsequently adopted and presented for government signatures at the Copenhagen conference in 1980; by the following year twenty member states had ratified the convention, giving it the status of a treaty. Women, for the first time, had a UN body to which they could appeal. Clearly CEDAW is one of the most critical successes of the global women's movement.

Ratification is supposed to mean that the convention has the force of law in the particular country, but ratification does not always mean implementation. Thus women's groups often present "shadow" reports to the UN committee that monitors implementation when they believe governments are not complying with the convention. Nonetheless, the existence of CEDAW and other UN documents exerts strong pressures on governments to expand women's rights. In 1985, Arvonne Fraser helped set up the International Women's Rights Action Watch (IWRAW) to give attention to the problems of implementation globally, and to encourage governments such as the United States to ratify CEDAW.

Putting Women into Economic Development

During the 1950s, as more formerly colonial countries became independent and joined the UN, they lobbied the General Assembly for greater focus throughout the system on development issues. The First Development Decade 1960–70 had emphasized infrastructure and industrial projects. This approach to development resulted in an increasing inequality between rich and poor. As a result the UN Economic and Social Council urged greater attention to social issues in development. A 1969 report of an experts' meeting in Stockholm reiterated that under the capitalist approach to development social indicators were ignored, as were women's economic roles. The report stressed the importance of "integrating women in development," a phrase Gloria Scott conceived. In her essay in this volume she recalls her efforts in 1972 to convene a second experts' meeting, this time to explore the relationships between women and development, and to draw CSW into cosponsorship.

Ester Boserup's Impact on the Debate

The rapporteur of the meeting, and member of the UN Development Planning Committee, was Ester Boserup, whose landmark book *Woman's Role in Economic Development* had been published in 1970. In describing her role in that meeting, Boserup writes that the CSW secretariat "saw it as a means to get members of the Commission to change their focus from the generally unpopular subject of abstract women's rights to the popular one of economic development."[6]

Boserup had found that even in countries with a large participation of women in agriculture, women were nonetheless classified as housewives or "nonactive" persons. To challenge these data categories, Boserup assembled case studies from Asian and African countries that provided hours worked by women and men in both paid and unpaid work, including agricultural work, household enterprises, and the fetching of fuel and water. Women's work varies by agricultural system; in Africa south of the Sahara, women are the primary farmers while men assist in clearing the fields and protecting their homes. The plow changed agricultural techniques and required men to work in the fields as well but gave men control over new technologies, to women's disadvantage. Boserup believed that population increase drove the technological change that in turn altered women's roles. In addition, she noted that male migration to cities is easier where women are farmers, as in Africa; female migration has predominated in Latin America where women have had little agricultural role.

Boserup criticized European colonial policies that imposed Western models that were not adapted to the local cultures and led to the loss of women's status. Two of her points stand out: first, the promotion of land ownership deprived women of use rights in areas of Africa and Southeast Asia, and second, the belief that men were superior farmers encouraged the introduction of technology and cash crops to men, especially in Africa, thus leaving women to continue using traditional low-yield methods for growing subsistence crops. Such policies ignored women's essential and often predominant agricultural roles while undercutting their ability to grow food to feed their families.[7]

Boserup's insights challenged many prevailing economic development theories regarding not only women but also agriculture, technology, and population. Her book on women provided the intellectual foundation for the women in development movement; as its guru, she is more often quoted than read. Her research sparked a tremendous interest among women's scholars in producing further case studies to corroborate or challenge her evolutionary presentation.

Changing Donor Policies

Other women, traveling abroad for research or to supervise donor assistance, also noted the cultural dissonance created by economic development policies and determined to change the approach. The first country to alter its programs to include women was Sweden, in 1964, persuaded by Inga Thorsson, an active politician and cabinet minister who later joined the UN. A grant from the Swedish government funded the women's position at the UN Economic Commission for Africa; Snyder discusses Thorsson's impressive efforts to set up that pathbreaking office.

In Washington, D.C., a group of young scholars, influenced by the rising voices of U.S. women, observed in their research abroad that development projects were exporting the very stereotypes about women's work against which they were demonstrating at home. In my essay in this volume, I recount how I organized a women's caucus within the Society for International Development to document these observations. Testimony at the Department of State and before congressional hearings led to an amendment to the Foreign Assistance Act of 1973 that mandated women's inclusion in programs designed to alleviate poverty abroad. Known for the U.S. senator who introduced it, the Percy Amendment became a model for resolutions within the UN system as well as among bilateral development agencies that mandated efforts to integrate women into development. The insights into the adverse impact of development on women illustrated in Boserup's book and instilled into bilateral programs influenced the agenda at the first UN World Conference on Women in 1975.

The United Nations World Conferences and Women

The growing strength and visibility of the reinvigorated women's movement influenced the UN staff in New York City. Women within various departments began to demand an end of discrimination against women at work and for promotion. Both Gloria Scott and Kristen Timothy describe in their essays the chilly climates within which they operated. When the *New York Times* ran a story on how the UN, with its claim to support equality, discriminated against women in their hiring policies, the secretary-general hastened to appoint Helvi Sipila as the first woman assistant secretary-general.

Sipila's first task was to organize events and a conference to mark International Women's Year in 1975. The General Assembly proclaimed the themes for the year as "equality, development, and peace," reflecting the primary preoccupations of the three ideological blocs: the communist East, the industrialized West (now the Global North), and the developing Third World (or now the Global South) The World Conference for International Women's Year was held in Mexico City in June 1975.

Patterns and Politics at World Conferences

Starting in 1972 with the Environment Conference in Stockholm, the UN began to convene world conferences on topics relating to development that either had not been included in the original UN charter or needed updating. As had been the case with previous UN conferences, member governments, UN agencies, and NGOs in consultative status with the UN were expected to send delegates. But in 1972 the "green" movement was already an important political force in Europe. Members of these environmental organizations demanded to be heard and camped out at the airport to put pressure on the UN to accommodate them.

Ever since, at major UN world conferences, accredited nongovernmental organizations with a stake in the outcome of the particular conference have organized a parallel event, the NGO Forum, which is open to interested organizations and people. These meetings combine professional panels with the gaiety of a fair; they provide a way to disseminate new ideas and research both to UN delegates and to the growing NGO community. Most of all they provide an opportunity for activists from around the world to meet and set up formal or informal organizations and networks. Participants at the parallel NGO conferences often exceed the number of official delegates and draw most of the media coverage.

While the NGOs with official consultative status at the UN are steeped in UN procedure and understand how to influence the system, most activists attending the UN forums do not. Once they arrive at the conference site they begin to realize that any input they might have should have taken place much earlier in the process. The almost inevitable result has been a march on the official meeting, unless the country where the conference is taking place—such as Romania, Kenya, or China—has an authoritarian government. Official UN conference documents are typically the subject of many rounds of debates in regional meetings and in preparatory committees, and the language is freighted with global debates of the day. Final revisions are made during the two-week official conferences, and over time women activists have learned how to insert phrases and paragraphs throughout the process so that the final documents adopted at the conference reflect issues of concern raised by women's organizations and research centers. Although official UN documents lack the force of law, their political and moral power is considerable, and consequently they provide activists in individual countries and internationally, as well as the UN system, with powerful tools for change.[8]

During the 1970s, tensions grew between North and South and were reflected at these major world conferences. Whatever the official conference topic, discussions referenced the continual contentious debates over the appropriate priorities for and direction of economic development as envisioned and funded by the North. The North-South differences affected both agenda items and the final documents of the conferences, and never more than at the women's conferences; generally women lacked the political power needed to influence negotiations over such political posturing. In other world conferences, the old-boy networks had soothed the debate and facilitated compromise.

Today the sites of this contention have shifted from UN conferences, where the North does not dominate, to meetings of the World Trade Organization or those of the leaders of the industrialized world (G-7 in UN parlance), which are dominated by the champions of unfettered globalization. Thus the South finds itself with fewer methods of influencing the world debate in these forums. Nor have the conveners of these meetings created adequate mechanisms for consultation with the NGO community, which itself has grown more diverse and disruptive. Without some open and official way for moderate NGOs to engage the world meetings in debate, as in the forums provided by the UN world conferences, the fissures between the North and South, between governments and civil society, become ever more fractious.

These opposing perspectives were starkly evident at the second major consciousness-raising conference, the Population Conference in Bucharest in 1974. The North argued that, for economic development to succeed, countries had to adopt methods of population control; in contrast, the South believed that economic development would in turn lower fertility rates and so demanded development first. Both official sides tended to see women as objects, not people. In contrast, at the NGO Forum, emphasis on cultural factors that influenced women's fertility choice underscored the weakness of the then-prevalent population policy emphasizing distribution of contraceptives.

Twenty years later, at the Third Population Conference in Cairo in 1994, this approach was dramatically reversed. Women's access to health and education were promoted as the preferable method of reducing population. A woman's right to control her own body, a fundamental goal of the women's movement, was also championed. Many contributors to this collection have been active in family planning groups as well as women's organizations.[9]

Four UN World Conferences on Women

The patterns discussed above were clearly visible during the four women's conferences, although some differences were distinct. The range of women's interests are all-encompassing and include those discussed in the separate UN conferences on food, population, environment, and technology. Women demanded a place on the official delegations and railed at the predilection of governments for sending men as the delegation heads while including wives of high officials as tokens. Some women were convinced that the governments used women's conferences as a proxy for global debate, recognizing that many women delegates had no alternative to following the political line.[10]

Indeed, the specific concerns of both women delegates and women's organizations often diverged from the political interests of their own governments. As agenda items increasingly reflected this divergence between specific women's issues and global debates over economic and political issues, views among women themselves diverged. Many women of the North preferred to separate "women's issues" from "global issues" and to question the usefulness of spending time at women's meetings attempting to influence policies that would ultimately be decided by the General Assembly. Those who favored limiting the debate to issues of gender equality made the fundamental assumption that being a woman conditions one's status and role in a given context more than does class or ethnicity or the structure of the international economy. They believed that women could agree on actions to ameliorate the lives of women worldwide and feared the divisiveness of a broader agenda.

By contrast, many Third World women felt that the poverty and power-lessness of women cannot be addressed by looking at gender alone but must be seen as a consequence of the Third World's economic dependency on the industrialized North. They argued that women of the North benefit from the existing international distribution of power and are therefore unlikely to be highly critical of it. Further, these women of the South argued that racism cannot be dismissed as a domestic problem but must be regarded as an international issue, a legacy of colonialism, that affects the economic and power relations among states.

Perspectives on what is a woman's issue clearly shifted from 1975 to 1995 as the interconnection between macro-economic policy and local practice became obvious and the interaction between decisions about trade, debt, industrialization, and women's livelihood was documented. This debate about what constitutes "women's issues" is addressed by many contributors to this volume.[11]

The NGO Forums have been particularly instrumental in enlarging the scope of debate and in shaping a global women's movement. The number of women and the few men attending NGO activities at women's world conferences has risen steadily from 6,000 at Mexico City to over 25,000 at Beijing. Many more had registered to attend the NGO Forum in Huairou but were unable to obtain visas or secure funding, thus confounding statistics on actual participation. China continues to use the number who registered in 35,000 as the official total, which reflects only foreign participants, not Chinese. Official delegates to the UN conference represent member nations, UN agencies, media, and NGOs in consultative status. Since all delegates must fit into an assembly hall, the size of the official UN conferences has grown only slowly, to about 5,000.

Mexico City, 1975

The planning phase for the UN conference for International Women's Year was abysmally short. Neither the UN bureaucracy nor most member countries were enthusiastic about the conference, but they were pressured by women's organizations and supportive NGOs. The official document, called the Plan of Action, was not reviewed by regional preparatory committees, as is now the practice before a UN conference, but many of the ideas from meetings of women before the population conference were incorporated. Much of the agenda was based on previous work of the CSW dealing with equality. But the General Assembly, by adding development and peace to the conference themes, opened the conference to the unresolved conflicts within that body. In 1975 the most contentious issues concerned restructuring the international economic system, determining the fate of the Palestinians, and dismantling apartheid.

During the discussions at Mexico City, Zionism was for the first time in any UN document identified as a cause of underdevelopment, along with colonialism, imperialism, and racism. Debate on this issue so diverted the conference that there was no time to discuss several sections of the Plan of Action. Nonetheless, under pressure from the women delegates, the plan was passed unanimously. The more controversial positions were issued separately as the Declaration of Mexico City, with eighty-nine countries voting in favor of it, three against (the United States, Israel, and Canada), and eighteen abstaining.

Substantively, the Mexico City conference endorsed the demand for legal equality for women, which encompassed the rights of divorce, custody of children, property, credit, education, voting, and other citizenship rights. Governments agreed to set up special offices, or national machineries, for women to monitor and support changes in programs and policies that would benefit women. The difficulties of this endeavor are evident in Dorienne Rowan-Campbell's discussion in this volume of her efforts to coordinate this work with governments of the Commonwealth.

Development was a relatively new topic for women to discuss. Ideas for new projects emerged at a pre-conference seminar on women in development attended by many delegates and advisers. Because I convened this seminar under the aegis of the American Association for the Advancement of Science and its Mexican counterpart, the discussions and recommendations carried academic respectability important for international acceptance. The idea for Women's World Banking was germinated at the seminar; Michaela Walsh traces in her essay the subsequent expansion of that unique organization.

Two new UN institutions were established at the world conference to deal with major issues of development. The International Research and Training Institute for the Advancement of Women (INSTRAW) was set up to encourage and coordinate research on women around the world; among our contributors, Aziza Hussein and I served on its first board and Daniela Colomba was later a member and chair. The Fund for Women, later renamed UNIFEM, was provided with funds for grants to women's organizations at the local level. Margaret Snyder became UNIFEM's first director; she describes in her essay her efforts to create a viable agency.

The NGO Forum, called the Tribune in Mexico City and organized by Mildred Persinger with advice from Rosalind Harris, was relatively unstructured, with many rooms for impromptu meetings. U.S. feminists, certain that they had the keys to achieving women's equality, enraged many women from Latin America with their views about global dependency and class warfare; the ethnocentrism of many Northern feminists continues to be a source of contention in development programs as well as at global meetings.

More positively, the Tribune spawned the International Women's Tribune Center (IWTC) to provide an interchange among the many women and women's groups that were present in Mexico. IWTC has maintained and expanded its communication reach around the world and has held events at all subsequent women's conferences; Anne Walker relates the saga of these activities in her essay in this volume.

Copenhagen, 1980

The upsurge of support exhibited in Mexico City for further exploration of women's changing status led the UN to declare the Decade for Women 1976–85 and to hold both a mid-decade conference in Copenhagen, Denmark, in 1980 and an end-of-the-decade conference in Nairobi, Kenya, in 1985. Global political events, as aptly described by Vivian Derryck in her essay, dominated the Copenhagen meeting even more than they had the first women's conference. For example, the selection of Denmark for the second conference resulted from the abrupt change of government in Iran, since Tehran had originally been designated as the site for the second women's conference. The overthrow of the shah exacerbated the tensions in the Middle East and sharpened the debate about Israel. The contentiousness displayed at the NGO Forum itself was emblematic of the global dissension. Delegates not only marched from the Forum to the UN official meeting but invaded the floor and demanded to be heard. The fracas resulted in the United States withdrawing its funding for UNIFEM and INSTRAW.

Condemnation of Zionism was actually included in the conference document, the Programme of Action. The United States, Australia, Britain, and Canada voted against the document because they could not accept language opposing Zionism, favoring the Palestine Liberation Organization, and blaming the West for Third World underdevelopment. This vote embarrassed the women in the U.S. delegation and upset U.S. feminists.

Despite the political static, the Copenhagen conference produced the best researched documents of the decade. The secretary-general of the conference and later the first woman to be named a deputy secretary-general at the United Nations, Lucille Mair, engaged women scholars primarily from the South to write on topics relating to women's work and development; their work became the basis for paragraphs in the Programme of Action. Regional meetings were convened to ensure input from women around the world. Emphasis was given to the importance of rural women's income to family survival; solutions included adopting appropriate technology to reduce their daily drudgery of fetching water, carrying firewood, and pounding and processing food to eat. Other paragraphs called for improving their access to education and productive employment.

At the NGO Forum, organized by Elizabeth Palmer, a gathering place was set up by the International Women's Tribune Center where women could congregate and network. Panels included new topics, such as women's health—as distinct from maternal health, which had long been the sole focus. The volatile issue of domestic violence was discussed as a result of pressures by ISIS, among others; Ana Maria Portugal discusses this in her essay. Panels on women's studies, organized by Florence Howe and Mariam Chamberlain, were for the first time part of the forum. Networking during those panels provided the Feminist Press with new authors and produced the ongoing International Interdisciplinary Conference for Women.

Nairobi, 1985

As plans for the 1985 World Conference to Review and Appraise the Achievements of the UN Decade for Women moved forward, everyone feared a repeat of the confrontation in Copenhagen. At the official UN level, Leticia Shahani was named secretary-general of the Nairobi conference. Like Helvi Sipila, she had long been active in the CSW and sought ways to ameliorate the situation. Her efforts to ensure that consensus was reached on the conference document called the Forward-Looking Strategies are recounted in her essay.

U.S. feminists feared that the U.S. delegation, recalling the contentious conference in Copenhagen, might decide not to attend. Some observers believe that only when Maureen Reagan, the U.S. President's daughter, arranged to head the U.S. delegation was U.S. attendance assured. Still, the United States was adamantly opposed to agreeing to the wording concerning Zionism in the conference document. The Kenya government, with support from other African countries, pushed for a compromise in language in the early hours of the final debate, and the document was adopted unanimously.

The international NGO committee, under the leadership of Dame Nita Barrow, began planning the Forum two years ahead in order to minimize confrontation. Chairing the Kenya committee for Forum 85 was Eddah Gachukia, who writes in this volume about her several roles and distinct observations in this and previous women's conferences. The Kenya government was also determined to avoid disruptions at the Forum; police checked passes at each gate to the university campus where the NGO Forum took place, effectively controlling egress. Women in Kenya were apprehensive about the reach of their government in controlling the Kenya delegation that was planning the conference.

Seeking ways to reduce tension among NGO participants, however, the committee agreed with the Kenya government's suggestions to start the Forum mid-week, before the official conference, thus limiting the overlap of the two meetings to a week. Many excursions to game parks and villages were set up to distract the participants.

Several significant activities also reduced friction. The IWTC sponsored an appropriate technology fair that was particularly intriguing to the many Kenyan women who attended the Forum. Another was the Peace Tent, an innovative space where informal debates over Zionism, the Iranian revolution, and apartheid took place. Emotional diatribes often gave way to embraces and tears. (See Walker, this volume)

A newly formed group of women scholars from the South, called DAWN—Development Alternatives with Women for a New Era launched a report that has helped reframe the discourse of women and development. The report, and the panels in which the members of DAWN discussed perspectives from the developing countries, gave voice and visibility to the distinctions between and the similarities of women's struggles around the world. Questioning the emphasis on individualism among Northern feminists, these scholars reasserted the importance of family and community. At the macro level, they illustrated the connection between the feminization of poverty and international economic policies. Devaki Jain traces the origins of DAWN in her essay in this collection; Peggy Antrobus presents some of DAWN's more recent activities in her essay.

A series of panels emphasized the role of women in the environment; another documented the importance of housing for women, especially in urban squatter settlements. Population panels reflected a reversal of attitudes, with the South declaring family planning a right and the conservative U.S. administration reversing its policy presented at the 1984 Population Conference in Mexico City.

Beijing, 1995

Women's organizations locally and globally continued to lobby their governments about the importance of having another world conference to evaluate the progress achieved on the strategies proposed in Nairobi, and the fourth world women's conference was set for Beijing in 1995. Once again the host government, in this case China, became apprehensive at the thought of thousands of feminists converging on the capital and influencing the country's women. Kristin Timothy was one of the major UN officials responsible for the Beijing meeting and recounts in her essay the political maneuvering with China over details of the NGO Forum.

When Chinese efforts to send the Forum to another country failed, the Chinese concocted other means of control. Participants were required to register months in advance and pay a fifty-dollar fee to cover the cost of a dog-tag they were required to wear; a visa was issued only if the participant was successfully registered from her own country. The location of the NGO Forum was shifted to a muddy site sixty miles outside Beijing in Huairou; many buildings were unfinished when the meetings took place. Attendance by Chinese women was severely restricted, and each panel was assigned a Chinese observer expected to report to their government. Despite the rain and mud and surveillance, Huairou was an extraordinary experience. Not only did more women attend than at previous forums, but they represented the spectrum of women of all classes and education, from Indian dalit to Hillary Clinton.

In the decade between Nairobi and Beijing, four major world conferences had been held in which women's presence and issues were significant: environment in 1992, human rights in 1993, population in 1994, and social summit in 1995. Most critical for women were the resolutions declaring that women's rights are human rights—inside the family as well as without—and that education and health care for women are the preferred approaches to slowing population growth.[12] Conservative efforts to restrict the scope of these resolutions were not successful at Beijing; rather, the mantra "women's rights are human rights" has been indelibly etched on the world's consciousness.

Beijing + 5

The NGO community has sought the continuation of the mega conferences, but the cost and unruliness that have characterized many global meetings have made both the UN and member governments chary of these events. Instead, five-year reporting meetings have been introduced. Coupled with the shift away from the UN toward the international financial meetings, the plus-five meetings have tended to focus on topical rather than political issues. Beijing + 5 was held in June 2000 in New York City. NGO events were scattered around the city, reducing opportunities for networking and effectively limiting opportunities for demonstrations.

Years of experience, however, have taught the women's movement effective methods of implementing their goals. UN conferences were critical in raising women's issues globally and promoting networking. The psychological dimensions of this mobilization process should not be underestimated. The four world women's conferences and the many events that surrounded them legitimated women's agendas and united women across ideological and national boundaries. Jacqueline Pitanguy, in her essay in this volume, demonstrates how these women's conferences encouraged Brazilian women to organize.

Influencing Policies of Development Agencies

The resolutions passed at the Mexico City conference in 1975 provided women with legitimacy when they lobbied for new offices within donor agencies to respond to the need for considering women's concerns in all programs. Resolutions also stressed the importance of a women's office or bureau, called a national machinery in UN parlance, within each country's governmental structure. Women's organizations pressed for such changes, often staffed these offices for a time, then returned to continue their efforts to influence policy through action research.

Economic development assistance flowed from UN agencies and bilateral aid from industrialized countries and foundations. Many contributors to this book discuss their efforts, both working within the institutions and lobbying from without, to change development policies. All argue that development programs as originally conceived were having an adverse impact on women by ignoring their economic contributions to their families and countries. Like many powerful ideas, the insight that development was undermining rather than advancing women's status was simple to explain once the right questions were asked.

The stereotype of woman as housewife supported by a caring husband is largely a middle-class myth; once women were considered citizens and workers in their own right, their economic contributions to family and country became obvious. Documentation was essential; many contributors to this book pursued research in their own and new areas. Some discuss how they created new programs and secured grants to carry them out. Others recount their efforts to convince development assistance agencies and non-governmental organizations to recognize that women are, worldwide, the caretakers of children.

Within the UN, the two new agencies set up at the Mexico City conference, UNIFEM and INSTRAW, were dependent upon voluntary contributions for their establishment and survival. Only recently has UNIFEM achieved a visibility commensurate with its mandate. Meanwhile, the UN Development Programme maintained its small women's office, the International Labour Organization commissioned studies on rural women, and the World Bank established an office with Gloria Scott as its first director. Supporting women's issues within a sectoral division was still challenging, as Marilyn Hoskins demonstrates in her account of going to work for the Food and Agricultural Organization.

Donor agencies set up new offices to initiate projects for women and to monitor overall programs. This dual function of establishing separate programs and mainstreaming women and gender is both difficult to manage and essential for successful implementation of activities designed to improve opportunities for poor women or those marginalized by religion, ethnicity, or customary practices. Debates on how to balance these functions are discussed by several contributors to this volume as they recall their work within bilateral agencies. Arvonne Fraser, Jane Jaquette, Elsa Chaney, and Kathleen Staudt write about the working at the United States Agency for International Development (USAID) Office for Women in Development; Geertje Lycklama reflects on the different approach that led to her posting at The Netherlands Ministry of Foreign Affairs. For many years the Ford Foundation distributed as much or more funds than many countries, focusing on innovative or demonstration projects; Cornelia Flora discusses her work as staff for Ford in Latin America.

Governments installed a variety of offices for women; many of our contributors observe this process and how country offices were supported by UN regional offices and also the cross-regional Commonwealth. The challenges of coordinating women's issues within the Commonwealth, with its mix of developing and industrialized countries, are presented by Dorienne Rowan-Campbell.

Researching Women's Global Issues

The challenge to produce studies and data to support changes in international development policy led to the establishment of research centers in many countries, some attached to government centers or state universities, others freestanding. Perhaps the first was the International Center for Research on Women, which I founded in 1976. Devaki Jain focused on women's issues in her Institute for Social Sciences. The Women and Development Unit (WAND) offices in Jamaica produced textured work on the Caribbean under Peggy Antrobus's direction (see her essay). All faced the problem of summarizing academic studies so that the findings were accessible to policy makers. To bridge the gap between practitioners and scholars, I later established the Equity Policy Center, which worked with practitioners who were carrying out projects. Daniela Colombo built on her media experience to promote women's international development and then set up AIDoS, an action-research center in Rome. Other organizations were awarded funds to carry out USAID projects. Elise Smith recalls in her essay efforts of the Overseas Education Fund, and then of Winrock International, to implement such projects. Martha Lewis tells of her experiences leading up to her work with Partners for the Americas.

On U.S. university campuses, especially those land-grant institutions that received large USAID funding for agricultural development, WID offices were set up to ensure that women's concerns were integrated into such projects. Kathleen Cloud led such an effort at the University of Arizona, and then spearheaded a national effort. Jane Knowles portrays in her essay the intensity of resistance to including women in international development programs found on many campuses. Teaching about WID soon followed in the United States because, in contrast to the central control of curriculum within the higher education system in many countries, universities in the United States are free to introduce new courses. An early advocate of such courses was Elsa Chaney. Like many of our contributors, she returned to academia after her action years, as did Cornelia Flora, Jane Jaquette, Geertje Lycklama, Kathy Staudt, and myself. Two contributors became senators: Leticia Shahani in the Philippines and Geertje Lycklama in the Netherlands.

Conclusion

In this book one can see the complex interrelationships among many of these early WID leaders and the vast number of roles each of them has played. We asked each of our contributors to emphasize a few of the most significant actions she undertook, in order to trace the expansion of the women and international development initiatives. But few have stopped with one or two efforts; rather, they continue to write and research and lead in many distinct ways and in a wide variety of venues. What each author has revealed—and what should intrigue the reader—is when and how she reached that "a-ha" moment when disparate facts and ideas crystallized into a new path for thought and action.

PART I

At the United Nations

The Absence of Women from the Curriculum and Scholarship

Aziza Hussein

Educated at the French Mère de Dieu, the American College for Girls, and American University in Cairo (B.A. 1942), Aziza Hussein has lectured and published extensively. In 1954 she was designated by the Egyptian government as its first woman representative in the UN General Assembly. During the 1960s she was an active member of the UN Commission on the Status of Women, served as a member of a UN expert committee on the role of women in development and of a UN advisory mission on family planning to Pakistan. In 1974 she headed the Egyptian delegation to an international forum on women, population, and development and in 1978 was elected to the first board of trustees of the International Research and Training Institute for the Advancement of Women (INSTRAW).

From 1977 to 1983 she was president of the International Planned Parenthood Federation (IPPF) and is a founder and president of the Cairo Family Planning Association. She has been a delegate or NGO participant in a long list of world conferences and in 1994 chaired the Egyptian NGO Commission co-hosting the NGO Forum for the International Conference on Population and Development in Cairo. During the 1990s she served on the board of the Population Council in New York, and in 2000 received the IPPF award for her pioneering work organizing family planning groups and supporting social marketing of contraceptives in Egypt and internationally.

The Archon Award that she received from the Honor Society of Nursing, Sigma Theta Tau International, in 1999, says: "Aziza Hussein's career is notable for its impressive array of pioneering initiatives . . . establishing the first rural nursery school in Egypt, the first non-governmental family planning program which paved the way for governmental initiatives and the first project aimed at eradication of unhealthy traditional practices such as female genital mutilation."

Crossroads for Women at the UN

In 1961 I was nominated to represent Egypt on the UN Commission on the Status of Women. This was the first time that a volunteer had been designated by the Egyptian government for an official international position. I felt prepared for this post through my multicultural background, built on a Western educational orientation in school, a modern Islamic ideology at home, and an involvement with women's welfare in volunteer activities on the grassroots level, which gave me a special perspective on women's issues.[1] During my years on the commission (1962–77), I expounded to the rest of the world those issues that had defined my work with women in Egypt—a concern for women in the Islamic family, including rights to family planning.[2]

Prior to taking up the post, I attended the Conference of the International Alliance of Women in Dublin, where I was initiated into current feminist issues and perceptions worldwide.[3] On the agenda were the familiar themes calling for political, educational, and economic equality between men and women. Noting that in Egypt the taboo on family planning had already been lifted, I timidly proposed this topic for possible consideration as a woman's right. I was instantly rebuked in deference to the Catholic hosts for whom family planning was an anathema. Little did I realize that this issue was going to top many feminist agendas in the future and that the Commission on the Status of Women itself would also make it one of its major concerns.

Scared stiff by the harsh reactions to my dissenting views in Dublin, when I arrived in New York in 1962, I asked one of the leading NGOs to orient me to the method of work of the Commission on the Status of Women and my role in it, both as a government representative and of an NGO. No one from either Egypt or any other part of the Arab world had been a member of this commission before. Israel had occupied the chair allocated to the countries of the Middle East for the previous nine years, at the end of which its representative had been elected chairperson of the commission.[4]

The Relevance of the Commission on the Status of Women

My first intervention in 1962 reflected the gossip overheard in some UN corridors: "Does not the existence of a special body dealing with women as a separate group contribute to further division of humanity into camps and poles based on sex, and does this not aggravate already existing human dissension?" I told the commission that this remark would have dampened my enthusiasm for the Commission on the Status of Women had I not further reflected and come to the conclusion that this was perhaps one of the least divisive of the divisions. I told the commission that "as the family, man, woman, and child, is an indivisible unit, the woman in this commission does not represent her sex, but humanity, on the level of its most tender relationships. The woman in this capacity will not dream of fighting her husband, brother or son, but in fact will be looking after their basic human interest by trying to give them a happier and a more adequate wife, mother and daughter." After expounding, as a newcomer to the commission, my idyllic view of the family, I realized that the family institution was considered by the diehard feminists as a major obstacle to women's liberation from traditional subjugation. In fact, feminist arguments for equality have usually foundered on the rock of the primacy placed on the role of the family, its sacredness and indispensability, for which women have usually paid the price.

Addressing Islam and the Status of Women

My first interest on the commission was to promote a good image of my country and its women. I started by expounding the status of women in Islam as applied in Egypt within the context of the UN principles of human rights and women's rights. Drawing on the modern interpretation of Muslim Sharia as propounded by the educated theologians of Al Azhar University, I covered women's rights in the family, such as marriage, polygamy, divorce, and parental rights and duties. What I said must have sounded like a revelation to many non-Muslims and Muslims alike, including representatives of such Muslim countries as Iran.

At subsequent sessions of the commission I expanded on this new interpretation. In 1965 in Tehran I spoke about divorce and noted that, in Islam, marriage is based on mutual consent of the couple who agree to a marriage contract that details rights and obligations. The marriage contract could include conditions enabling the woman to initiate divorce, but not many couples take advantage of this provision. In both modern Egyptian law and the Sharia, divorce is initiated by the man; but in fact provisions exist that aim to mitigate the effects of divorce.

Later, in New York, I made the case that according to the true interpretation of Islam, polygamy should be abolished; this interpretation refers to a saying of the prophet, "If you cannot be fair to them, then only one." It is a big burden for a man to assume responsibility for more than one wife. In Egypt polygamy is considered a disgrace among the educated elite but is engaged in by other classes where the combination of wealth with ignorance facilitates its practice.

Certain laws inspired by religion are more advanced and egalitarian than some existing laws in Egypt derived from the Napoleonic code. For example, the penal code dealing with adultery in Islam treats offending men and women on equal terms, whereas the modern penal code discriminates between men and women. Under the latter code, the woman offender is punished on all counts, while the man is punished only if adultery takes place in the matrimonial residence.

Muslim Sharia law is frequently interpreted differently according to the country; efforts have been exerted, particularly by the League of Arab States, to reach a unified interpretation that brings the law closer to the universal human rights principles, particularly regarding the family. On the other hand, Islam has its own rules of human rights that in essence treat men and women equally as independent persons in terms of legal capacity and property rights. In the Koran there is always reference to men and women as being created from one source. In the case of equal rights and responsibilities within the family, Islam opts for equivalence and equity rather than equality because roles of men and women in the family represent a complementary relationship rather than an equal or identical one. This applies to inheritance rights; the man's privileges in inheritance are balanced by his additional responsibilities for the maintenance of his close family members as well as those in the extended family. Because of this stance regarding the family, Muslim governments find it difficult to accept all the articles in Convention on the Elimination of All Forms of Discrimination Against Women (CEDAW) and most of them express reservations on the articles on the family on religious grounds.

Three Initiatives

During my tenure the commission took several important initiatives that extended its role beyond the one defined in its initial mandate and brought it face-to-face with new realities in the areas of population, humanitarian laws applicable to women in armed conflict (the Geneva Convention), and intergovernmental politics.

Population

At the 1963 commission meeting I dared to raise the subject of family planning as a relevant agenda item, particularly as regards countries suffering from excessive population growth. I had just come from an international population conference held in Singapore by the International Planned Parenthood Federation (IPPF) to launch the oral pill; thus began my long association with that organization. My position was supported by my government and national and international NGOs.[5] The effect of my words thundered like an explosion. "You have, in your mild manner, exploded a bomb," the French delegate told me in the corridors. "No one has ever dared to approach this subject, which is so crucial for the status of women. Some of us would go to jail over it." The representative of Colombia said that she could not go back to her country if she had mentioned the subject of family planning. Yet, within ten years, Colombia became one of the most successful countries in the family planning field. As for me, I was treated as a heroine by the international and some U.S.-based NGOs, who honored me with special celebrations.

At the commission's 1965 session in Tehran, Egypt co-sponsored a resolution asking the secretary-general to provide the commission with information about the possible interrelationship between the status of women and family planning in countries suffering from overpopulation. Half of the commission members abstained from voting on this resolution. Later, more countries joined in and population became perhaps the most important issue in many development agendas for years to come. The Commission on the Status of Women was commended for being the first UN body to introduce the subject of family planning in the world body.

In 1968 Helvi Sipila, the Finnish member of the commission, was nominated as special rapporteur for the Status of Women and Family Planning Project. Her mandate was to study the question in depth by launching studies and seminars on the subject, nationally, regionally, and internationally. Also in 1968, the Human Rights Conference, held in Tehran, declared family planning as a human right at the initiative of the Egyptian delegation. These activities culminated with an international seminar held in Istanbul in 1972, which I attended as representative of the League of Arab States.

With interest in family planning spreading in the world, the commission, in cooperation with a population NGO, convened a global forum, Women Population and Development, in April 1974. The inauguration was held in the hall of the General Assembly to symbolize the importance of the forum, and subsequent sessions were held in Airlie House in Virginia in deference to the co-sponsor. Helvi Sipila acted as the secretary-general. I represented Egypt on the forum, but also acted as a bridge between the Commission on the Status of Women, the IPPF, and the Egyptian Family Planning Association. I felt myself treading on familiar ground during the forum deliberations as I exerted efforts to establish a documented link between family planning and women's development. I was happy at the prospect of gaining new advocates for our cause among forum representatives from various countries and the prospect of reinforcing old alliances. The forum also included experts, one of whom was my sister, Prof. Laila Hamamsy, who had been my adviser on evaluation of the research work of the Cairo Family Planning Association, which I founded in 1967 and remain president of to this day. The forum issued a set of recommendations that were endorsed by the commission and then incorporated into the conference documents of the World Population Conference, which was held in Bucharest in July 1974. This was the first time that the UN Population Commission, which was the coordinator of the Bucharest conference, had taken note of the link between the status of women and population. Strangely enough, this issue eventually gained general consensus in the conference, by contrast with the divisive question of which came first, development or population control.

Research worldwide suggests an inverse relationship between the stage of social and economic development and population growth, as well as a direct relationship between the social and economic stage of development and the status of women. Hence multi-sided, integrated development seems to be the answer to both problems. This equation came out clearly at the Bucharest conference, despite the polarization between those who promoted setting up demographic targets through contraceptive delivery as a priority in facing the population explosion and those who argued that "factories," meaning economic development, "were the best contraceptives." I represented IPPF at the Bucharest conference and chaired one of the panels held by the NGO tribune, which discussed voluntary family planning as a human right and the importance of tailoring services to respond to women's perspectives and needs. After the conference, the IPPF secretariat set up a special women's department to give the organization a stronger feminist orientation. I was the vice-chairman of the IPPF governing body and served as president of IPPF from 1977 to 1983. Most IPPF affiliates began to launch women's projects with a demographic objective. However, unmet needs in contraceptive services continue to plague demographic efforts in developed as well as developing countries. Fertility surveys have shown a big gap between desire to practice family planning and actual prevalence, owing to inadequacy of services, particularly for adolescents. (For additional discussion of the 1974 World Population Conference see Gloria Scott's chapter in this volume.)

Efforts in Egypt

As the planned parenthood movement slowly moved away from the concept of supplying contraceptives as a means of achieving demographic targets to the development-oriented concept of demand creation through women's economic empowerment, among other interventions, pilot studies were needed. Egypt was one of the first countries where a case study on the subject was carried out, in one of the local governorates.[6] Results proved that the economic independence of women working outside their homes as industrial workers prompted changes in social structure and a conflict between women's employment and childbearing that strongly influenced the women's decision to practice family planning and opt for a small family. Years later, the area where this study was carried out was still enjoying a comparably lower birth rate.

Another intervention on the link between the status of women and family planning was a project undertaken by the Cairo Family Planning Association regarding the legal security of women in the family and its effect on women's decisions to practice family planning. From the beginning our aim has been to secure equality of treatment in the rights of husband and wife to marry and divorce, an effort that thus far has failed. Nonetheless, our advocacy campaign resulted in a 1979 amendment to family law that made it more difficult for a man to divorce his wife or to remarry. Subsequent struggles in parliament negated and then reinstated provisions of the amendment; ultimately changes made to the law in 2000 give women more freedom in making major decisions affecting their life. The newly established National Council of Women, under the leadership of Suzanne Mubarak, is laying much stress on the role of law in empowering women to make decisions in various aspects of their lives, including reproduction.[7]

Humanitarian Laws Applicable to Women in Armed Conflicts

In the early 1970s the Egyptian delegation under my leadership brought up the question of the protection of women and children in emergency and armed struggle in the occupied territories. Noting the escalating never-ending conflict between Israel and the inhabitants of the occupied territories due to an unequal and unjust power relationship, I emphasized that women and children were the prime victims. Some members questioned the relevance of this issue to the terms of reference of the commission on the ground that the protection of women and children could not be tackled in isolation from the protection of civilians at large. They argued that the Red Cross, with its Geneva Convention, was exclusively entrusted with this task and that the UN deals with human rights in peacetime, not with humanitarian laws in times of conflict.

The arguments of these members were eventually refuted, since we had taken pains to introduce the subject on humanitarian grounds in order to avoid being accused of politicizing the commission. We had contacted the Red Cross representative and learned that, in its formulation of the Geneva Convention, the Red Cross had from the start reserved a special place for the protection of women and children. Indeed, the organization wanted to do more and was especially interested in the initiative taken by the commission which noted that the Geneva Convention was not fully implemented in the territories occupied by Israel. The UN had, in 1971, endorsed the convening by the Red Cross of a governmental meeting of experts calling for the continuation of efforts aimed at the reaffirmation of humanitarian laws in armed conflicts. In 1972 a draft protocol was developed that was added to Article 3 of the Geneva Convention of 1949, which supplemented "the rules applicable to non-international armed conflict with a view to providing combatants and non-combatants with basic humanitarian protection. This includes measures for the benefit of children, mothers of infants, women having the custody of infants and expectant mothers."

The result of the commission's deliberations was the framing of an international instrument, the Convention on the Protection of Women and Children in Times of Emergency and Armed Conflict, which was later endorsed by the UN General Assembly. Although this convention is applicable to many situations where civilians, particularly women and children, are at great risk in armed conflict, the situation in the Middle East remains especially inflammable because Israel has never signed the Convention. Hence, it has not had the intended effect in the Middle East.

The Red Cross supported this initiative and intimated that the convention was of immense value to the pursuit of its own humanitarian work. Likewise, UNESCO gave its support and the secretary-general gave attention to the question of the protection of women and children in his report to the General Assembly on Human Rights in Armed Conflict.

Concerted International Action

A third initiative that left its mark on the work of the commission during my time there was the designation of the year 1975 as International Woman's Year (IWY). The International Federation of Women and other NGOs had lobbied with the official delegations to pass a resolution on the year, establishing the themes of equality, development, and peace. The resolution was co-sponsored by Egypt and a number of other delegations, and it passed unanimously. The commission's success in mobilizing all governments of the world to attend the First World Conference on Women, in Mexico City in 1975, raised its political profile. The aftereffect of the conference was staggering and long lasting. It is still engaging the world community, men and women, to this day.

The Plan of Action, adopted at the conference, represented a kind of globalization and consolidation of earlier efforts of the commission that had, since 1968, led member countries to formulate the Unified Long-Term Programs for the Advancement of Women. To help implement and monitor these programs, national and regional mechanisms were to be set up. This agenda item gave me a chance to introduce the Arab Women's Commission of the Arab League, which had been established in 1971 and was composed of eighteen countries.[8] It was the first regional commission for women outside of the UN system to be established since the creation of the United Nations; its terms of reference had been borrowed from the 1967 UN Declaration on the Elimination of Discrimination Against Women.

I attended the Mexico City women's conference as an observer, heading the IPPF delegation and delivering a speech on behalf of my organization. At the NGO Tribune I chaired a panel that underlined the relationship between family planning concerns and the status of women. At the time I was still a member of the Commission on the Status of Women and maintained a close relationship with the Egyptian delegation, headed by Jihan Sadat, for whom I wrote a speech. Hence, there was more than one way for me to influence the conference.

Through my participation I could see that the commission's strong links with NGOs was at the back of its remarkable demonstration of power at the Mexico conference and in its aftermath. The fact that most of the representatives to the commission were basically activists devoted to the cause of women, rather than government executives, strengthened this connection. Commission members were united until a political issue popped up, in which case government instructions became imperative and male advisers suddenly filled the room. This often happened when the subject of Israel and the Arabs was raised.

Going Ahead with CEDAW

Besides supporting the World Plan of Action for the International Women's Decade, the conference agreed to support the Convention on the Elimination of All Forms of Discrimination Against Women (CEDAW) and to create the International Research and Training Institute for the Advancement of Women (INSTRAW). The decision to go ahead with the formulation of a convention put an end to the stalemate encountered during prior deliberation of the subject at the 1974 meeting of the commission. As the rapporteur of the expert working group, mandated to lay the groundwork for the convention, I had reported the two largely irreconcilable options produced by the working group. Commission members had been split between those who endorsed the idea of a comprehensive convention and those who feared that it would undermine already existing specialized conventions that were in operation under the aegis of various bodies, including the commission, the ILO, and UNESCO. It seemed to me that the latter group was trying to sabotage the effort to achieve consensus. Further discussions aggravated the split and it became a stalemate. Finally the conference endorsed the drafting of a comprehensive convention, thus putting an end to the stalemate and spurring the commission on to work on a comprehensive draft convention.

Nobody knew how important the convention was going to be until it was finalized a few years later through the assiduous work of the commission, supported by ECOSOC and the General Assembly. The convention was based on the framework of the Declaration on the Elimination of Discrimination Against Women passed in 1967. After finalization and endorsement by governments in the UN General Assembly, CEDAW was opened for signatures at the 1980 mid-decade World Conference on Women in Copenhagen. It is still engaging the world as a watchdog for the status of women worldwide and as a morale booster for feminist activities.

I worked hard to ensure that the convention incorporated four separate provisions on the rights of women to family planning. The inclusion of these provisions indicated a drastic, if not revolutionary, change of attitude from the time of the 1967 declaration, when family planning was taboo and all that could be mentioned in this regard was "that women had a right to ensure the health and welfare of their families," as the 1967 declaration read. I was especially pleased that we had included a section on the rights of rural women giving them equal rights of participation on all levels of development. Article 14 mentions the significant role that women play in the economic survival of their families and recommends ensuring the right of access to agricultural credit and loans, marketing of facilities, appropriate technology, and equal treatment in land and agrarian reform. Besides reflecting the personal interest of some of the members like me, it also reflected new, concrete developmental concerns being placed on the commission's agenda as a result of the IWY themes of equality, development, and peace.

In 1981 I had the chance to witness demonstrations in Japan, led by Japanese women, calling on their government to sign CEDAW. Any skepticism I might have had until then about the relevance or value of UN conventions was soon dispelled, giving way to a new sense of fulfillment and gratification that I had participated in the drafting of this convention.

CEDAW has since had a monitoring committee that keeps governments and NGOs on their toes; Mervat El Tellawi of Egypt was the chairperson of this committee for some years. I have heard some NGO members say that CEDAW was the single most important achievement of the Commission on the Status of Women. (For additional discussion of CEDAW see Leticia Ramos Shahani's and Arvonne S. Fraser's essays in this volume.)

Reflections on NGOs and the UN

My NGO orientation has dominated my vision throughout my life. For two decades I participated in NGO meetings at local, national, and international levels, including those convened by IPPF, the commission, INSTRAW, and many ad hoc committees of the UN on population and women's economic development. Experiencing these different perspectives enabled me to act as a bridge between these various institutions. Hence, I was quite aware of the interactive relationship between the dynamics of NGOs and those of the UN, particularly in the field of women and population.

For example, the UN picked up the family planning angle from IPPF, then pioneered a new strategy linking family planning to the status of women and launching it throughout the world. This initiative in turn influenced the NGO family planning movement worldwide, and IPPF itself began to center its attention on the role of women as a focal entry point in its programs and for the first time established its own women's department. I believe that the pioneering and advocacy role played by the population and women's NGOs, in which I played a modest role, climaxed into the official mobilization of governments and the UN, spurring them on to launch global conferences. Conversely, the outcome of UN decisions in these conferences has had an important effect on the thinking and direction taken by NGOs in Egypt and worldwide, by virtue of the moral weight and authority that they carry with governments and NGOs alike.

The UN Conference on Population and Development, which convened in Cairo in 1994, invigorated the spirit and morale of Egyptian NGOs and emboldened them to call for changes in the restrictive Egyptians laws on NGOs, thus creating a new reality for civil society as a whole. The NGO Committee on Population and Development, which I have chaired since 1993, produced an Egyptian NGO platform document that adapted and translated global ideas and principles into the language of people's everyday concerns. This helped integrate views and perceptions on different levels of society and for different categories of people: men and women, the elderly and youth, the religious and the secular.

In many ways, this conference brought together the many concerns I have held throughout my career: Egyptian and global NGOs; women's rights especially to family planning and to development; and UN activities. The final conference Programme of Action gives precedence to reproductive health as a broad mandate in place of the limited contraceptive practice concern of the previous decades. Priority is also given to the concept of the empowerment of women and to the elimination of practices promoting violence against women and female children, including combating the customs and traditions that perpetuate them.

Gloria Scott

Gloria Scott was a pioneer in social planning at the United Nations before becoming the first director of the women's program at the World Bank. Born and educated in Jamaica, she attended the London School of Economics, majoring in economics and sociology. Returning to Jamaica, she served as assistant under-secretary in the Ministry of Development, the highest post held by a woman, before joining the United Nations in 1966 to head its new social planning unit. Utilizing the action research project called Women, Development and Population, which she directed, she convened preparatory regional seminars for the UN First World Conference on Women in 1975. Reports and plans of action from these seminars were influential in shaping the UN's Decade for Women agenda.

In 1977 Scott joined the World Bank as adviser on women in development, a new post set up following the conference of 1975 to advance understanding of how women affected and were affected by bank-financed projects and policies. There she developed ways to incorporate women's concerns by identifying issues relevant to the sectors, countries, and particular loan activities of the bank and found ways to present the issues in a manner fitting the bank's culture. As World Bank spokesperson on women in development issues, she collaborated with individuals and organizations on state-of-the-art women's issues and methodological development.

Scott left the bank in 1986. Since then she has worked for international and national agencies and nongovernmental organizations as a consultant on women and rural poverty, sustainable development, health, population, and aging.

Breaking New Ground at the UN and the World Bank

Like many professional women, I have tended to be silent about my life history, but since this is my story on WID it is important to include some personal details that contributed to my thinking and orientation. Many factors influenced the decision I made in 1966 to leave a comfortable life in Jamaica and move to New York to become an international civil servant. The move posed special challenges as well because it meant leaving my husband in Jamaica and taking my three dependent children. In one step I became a single mother with a new job in a new place.

I grew up in Jamaica in a household that was materially well off, in an environment that encouraged high moral values, discussion, tolerance, and respect for the views of others, and sharing what we had. My mother was strict and capable, and even though there were servants to do everything, she insisted that my sister and I do assigned chores. My father, a dentist, was a gentle man. I never heard him raise his voice or speak a harsh word; when we did wrong he would talk through our folly with us. My sister and I went to a good boarding school and were sent to England for higher education. I wanted to do dentistry but my father felt it was too strenuous a career for a woman. More important, since the dental education available in the United States was the most highly regarded, I would have had to study there, and my father would not expose me to the segregation he had experienced at Howard University. So I ended up studying economics at the London School of Economics and Political Science (LSE). After graduation I went back to Jamaica and worked with the government in four different jobs, each a promotion and each a brand new job that no one had done before.

While working with the Jamaican government, I became used to being the sole professional woman at my level, and there were none above me. I was always dealing with men as equals, and the idea of discrimination never entered my consciousness. As I prepared to return to the LSE for graduate work, I had a rude awakening. My husband was in England and in order to take our children there I had to get his written permission to obtain passports and buy air tickets. Although my civil service rank entitled me to passage to England for myself, my spouse, and my children, because I was a woman the passage for my children was denied. When I returned from England I wrote a brief on the situation and my minister agreed to take the matter to the cabinet, which overturned the personnel decision. By precedent, I ensured the future entitlement for women at my rank. This was my first victory over inequality. Some years later I got another shock. I was denied promotion to the only grade remaining for me in the civil service, not because I was not the best candidate, but because I was a woman. My anger at this injustice spurred me to accept a repeated invitation to join the Secretariat of the United Nations in New York.

At the United Nations I laid the groundwork for what later became known as women in development, or WID. At the UN and later at the World Bank, I focused increasingly on both aspects of women's situation in development: how they contribute to, and are affected by, development, as participants and beneficiaries in development. Because I come from a developing country I have a different and broader perspective than women from the North. Working on WID in the early days was a lonely enterprise that challenged women's capacity for negotiation in strikingly male establishments. As a result, my colleagues and I sought intellectual stimulation and support outside our particular organization.

At the United Nations: Social Development

As chief of the new social planning section in the Department of Economic and Social Affairs (ESA), I set up the section to incorporate the social aspects of development into national economic development planning. I well remember my first day at the UN, many times worse than a first day at school. One positive feature was that I was officially welcomed by the director of the population division, who was clueless about me and the new function. Discussing my background and what I expected to do in the new job was an opportunity to focus on its relation to population issues. This gave me a useful entrée as I established myself at the UN.

The Economic and Social Council (ECOSOC), the governing body of my department, was meeting in Geneva and all the senior staff were there. I had to take decisions and reply to requests for information from Geneva on things I did not even know where to find. In Geneva they were dealing with a resolution on development and utilization of human resources, for which I had to draft substantive background. Using my Jamaican experience, I emphasized age and sex differences as well as location and market issues as needing to be incorporated into national policies.

When they heard my title—chief of social planning—many people outside the UN thought that I was planning the secretary-general's parties. It was not always easy to explain what social planning was because in many respects it was a default, what was left out of economic development planning. The resolution establishing the new section of which I was selected to be chief indicated that the aim was to speed up social progress, clarify the function of social factors in development, and help governments assess social needs and establish feasible social objectives in development plans. An important dimension of our work was making links between sectors and showing the several interrelated activities required to attain objectives. Our work program included issues such as distribution of income, social aspects of industrial development, the utilization of human resources, and urbanization. Questions of equity and efficiency ran throughout.

Seven different nationalities were represented in my section. Two staff members had worked elsewhere within the UN, but the rest had little or no knowledge of how the UN operated. Getting together as a team presented all sorts of comi-tragic challenges aggravated by serious language differences and deficiencies. One challenge, which sticks in my mind as an example of effective innovation, was a report on employment issues drafted in English by a staff member with minimal understanding of the language. We had no time to have the report rewritten before the deadline. And so, sentence by sentence in a Central European language—not an official UN language—the author explained his thoughts to another staff member, who put the phrases into understandable English and checked substantive issues with me. In spite of the three-way report writing, it ended up a good report. Cultural differences and resentment at being supervised by a woman from a small developing country were sometimes just below the surface. Except for such instances, being a woman at the UN was not a challenge, as there were professional women in the organization and in my department. The challenge was penetrating the male cliques.

The UN often convenes an expert group to test new ideas and get a peer review of substantive work. I organized such a group on social development planning in 1972. Funded by the Swedish International Development Cooperative Agency (SIDA), the group met in Stockholm and was chaired by the eminent sociologist Gunnar Myrdal. Perhaps because he had recently finished his book *Asian Drama*, with its focus on equality, the political issues of changing institutions, and the human dimensions of these changes, women emerged clearly as an issue, although the meeting focused on planning to accommodate socioeconomic disparities. In the expert group report to the social development commission, I inserted the phrase "integration of women in development." This often-misinterpreted term was thereafter included in the international development decade strategies and subsequent UN resolutions.

To colleagues in other parts of the Social Development Division I was an anomaly. They were trained in and dealt with discrete social areas; I dealt with multisectoral issues. I was an economist focusing on social aspects of economic development. I had to identify the economic implications of social policies, which forced me to comment on—and interfere in—their work. When I was instructed to collaborate with the status of women division under Margaret Bruce and the social welfare section headed by Aida Gindy in planning a working group on women and welfare, none of us was happy.

Emboldened by the endorsement of economists in the expert group, I was outspoken in insisting that welfare and status were empty concepts without development. I suggested an expert group with a noted economist as chair. My former LSE professor, Sir Arthur Lewis, accepted the challenge (his words). He was well known in UN circles and his acceptance raised my status; thereafter, I was included in planning agendas and identifying invitees. Ester Boserup, who, like Lewis, was a member of the UN Development Planning Committee, served as rapporteur. The Interregional Meeting of Experts on the Integration of Women in Development, as we called it, ensured a development focus in discussions about women. I regard this as one of my significant achievements at the UN.

To retain this focus required continuing efforts, however, and pushed me increasingly toward seeing women as a distinct element in my work. For example, in work on social policy and income distribution, specific policies clearly were needed to ensure that women retained or obtained an equitable share of income. In studying social aspects of industrialization it was apparent that special policies were needed to facilitate women's access to jobs, protect the conditions under which they worked, and ensure that their sources of income were not destroyed by industrialization.

The report of the expert group was submitted to both the Commissions on Social Development and on the Status of Women, and eventually to ECOSOC. At each stage recommendations or resolutions were passed giving direction on integrating women in development into the UN system. Especially important was the collaborative process of preparing, discussing, and approving the resolutions. This educated the representatives of the countries participating and fed into their national policies.

At the time, few universities had courses on social development planning. I sensed the need for skilled people to further social planning at various levels of national and international planning. This need was also emphasized in the political discussions leading to the establishment of the UN social planning function. With funding from SIDA, I devised a project for a correspondence training course for developing country planning staff. Inga Thorsson, a former Swedish cabinet minister, was then director of the Social Development Division. The correspondence project enrolled some forty participants each year from 1970 to 1972. We wrote the course material, which covered methodology and information for planning and showed links between sectors, the impact of changes in one sector on others, and the frequently unforeseen consequences that should be considered in planning. Methods to identify social prerequisites, impediments, and social costs of development were presented with illustrations of ways to incorporate these issues in planning and implementation processes. Social and economic policies relating to participation in development were emphasized. The study guides and assignments emphasized the importance of using specific information from the participants' countries.

Most women, including me, have experienced discrimination, serious or mild, at some stage in their career. Although I didn't recognize it at the time, I experienced an affirmative action early in my UN career. The under-secretary, Philippe DeSeynes, asked me to come to his office. (This was like a summons from God.) Raul Prebisch, under-secretary of the UN Commission on Trade and Development (UNCTAD), whom I knew from my Jamaica service, was there. After greetings and pleasantries I was asked if I would go to New Delhi, India, for two months as secretary of the Third Committee of UNCTAD. Colleagues later told me that because that committee was notoriously troublesome, and the agenda included many items that were controversial for the Group of 77 developing countries, Prebisch wanted a woman from a developing country who was substantively competent and had experience dealing with men. In fact the committee ran quite smoothly and only once did we have to take out the ballot box, the bane of every committee secretary's life. This was an UNCTAD record. I never considered the possibility that I was being set up; two men in whom I had confidence selected me for the assignment, and I accepted because I knew I was competent. It was not necessarily easy to insert myself into an established organization with its particular culture, but the staff, like their boss, wanted the conference to succeed, and gave me their support. The only discrimination I experienced in New Delhi was from the male Indian stenographer assigned to me, who, until firmly reprimanded by my male UNCTAD assistants, found it difficult to accept that I was the boss.

In 1973 there was a major reorganization of the Department of Economic and Social Affairs, among other purposes, to create a cabinet for Helvi Sipila, the first female assistant secretary-general at the UN. I was summoned again by DeSeynes, who outlined his vision for the reorganized department. Social planning, by now established and respectable, could be merged with economic development planning. He saw the need for a senior adviser to Sipila and asked me to take the job. Anticipating the 1974 International Population Conference, we secured extra-budgetary funding for a project to do policy-related research and broaden the relevant database on women, development, and population. Elise Boulding, then at Colorado University Institute of Behavioral Science, was hired as a consultant to break down data in the UN Statistical Yearbooks and to compile a report on women. This report, along with data assembled by the staff, was much used in preparing for International Women's Year.

But the draft plan of action for the 1974 Population Conference referred to women only twice, neither reference having much to do with women's reproductive function. The wording read as if countries had babies, and Sipila agreed that this was not acceptable. Given the time pressure, the most realistic proposal for improving the draft plan was to organize a large-scale international forum. This would get media attention and give special prominence to questions concerning population, the status of women, and women's integration into the total development effort.

The International Forum on the Role of Women in Population and

Development was held from 25 February to 1 March 1974, and attended by high level women, including politicians, wives of heads of state, leaders of women's organizations, and civil servants, together representing 111 countries, including six nonmember states. Organizing the forum demanded a superhuman effort. The lead time was less than three months and the funding came from a hodgepodge of sources, each having its own administrative requirements and wanting a say in the planning. The forum was held in the General Assembly Hall at the UN, a first. Participants examined the draft plan of action, made specific proposals for highlighting women's interests in population dynamics more adequately, and for mobilizing public opinion to support population issues. The messages of the forum were taken home by participants and were included in briefings for the 1974 Bucharest Population Conference, and as a result, a much more satisfactory plan of action emerged from the conference. (For additional discussion of the 1974 World Population Conference see Aziza Hussein's essay in this volume.)

The 1975 Mexico City Conference

The Women, Development, and Population Project also funded three regional meetings in Asia, Africa, and Latin America, which served as regional preparatory meetings for the 1975 First World Conference on Women in Mexico City. These meetings produced regional plans of action, which together formed the draft Plan of Action for Mexico.[1] The first seminar, in the Asia and Pacific Region (ESCAP) was a wake-up call for the region, both countries and organizations, and the experience helped the planning of the other seminars. For the Africa meeting, Margaret Snyder, of the Economic Commission for Africa, and Jean Ritchie, seconded by the Food and Agriculture Organization (FAO) to that commission, prepared a useful African women's database. The Latin American meeting, held in Venezuela, was the most politicized. Representatives on some delegations came with instructions on preparing a declaration to be promulgated in Mexico. This had not been anticipated and there was considerable tension between delegations and sub-regional groupings. This politicization continued, resulting in the Declaration of Mexico City.[2]

Since the Mexico City conference derived from resolutions of the Commission on the Status of Women, it was not part of my responsibilities, and I was happy not to be involved. Few resources had been allocated to the conference, compared with other international conferences. The preparations seemed chaotic and unprofessional, with inadequate supervision and much of the work farmed out to consultants. A couple of months before the conference my happy isolation ended. I was handed two impossible drafts of the paper on the "Integration of Women in the Development Process as Equal Partners with Men" (item 10 of the provisional agenda) and assigned the tasks of writing the paper and introducing it to the conference. Thus I became a full member of the conference secretariat, which I resented at first; but soon I got caught up by the excitement and the crises. Once inside I saw the serious problems with which the staff had to cope, and in the end I felt privileged to be part of an earth-moving event.

The conference was held in a beautiful palace and I fantasized about gliding down the elegant staircase. All the staff were overworked, did not eat properly, and got stomach problems. The committee rapporteur and I had just finished the report in my office when I passed out, regaining consciousness as I heard the doctor worrying that after twenty minutes he still couldn't revive me. My fantasy was turned around as I was taken down the stairs on a stretcher with TV lights glaring, and I spent four days in the hospital.

I recently read that report again. It touched on international development strategies and key issues concerning integrating women in development; it attempted a definition of the concept and meaning of development and its implications for women. It examined women's participation in their national economies and their share in the benefits of social progress and development, highlighting strategies for improving both. The paper has stood up well since 1975. Writing it was an opportunity to document some of the work we had done in social planning.

The Mexico Plan of Action contained many resolutions and recommendations that had to be implemented. Among the resolutions on my plate was the establishment of the International Research and Training Institute for the Advancement of Women (INSTRAW). A great deal of preparatory work had been done with Princess Ashraf Pahlavi and her team in Iran, which was to host the institute. In the summer of 1976, Helvi Sipila and I visited Tehran to finalize the arrangements, but the coup against the Government of Iran, which banished the Shah and his family, overtook all previous planning and the institute was nearly lost in the shuffle. The first institute board was appointed in 1979 and INSTRAW was temporarily housed at UN headquarters. That same year Iran withdrew its offer, but eventually, in August 1983, INSTRAW was established in the Dominican Republic. When I returned to New York from Iran in 1976, following a much-needed vacation with my two daughters, I found messages from the World Bank inviting me to come to Washington to be interviewed for the new position they had created to sensitize bank staff and member countries about development for women.

At the World Bank

In January 1977 I joined the World Bank as adviser on women in development. My function was to increase staff and borrowers' understanding of how women affected, or were affected by, bank-financed activities. The challenge was to bring this information into the bank's policy, sector, and loan work. Within the central projects staff of the bank, there were project advisers on several subjects, posts usually created to introduce a new topic into bank work. Each adviser had to convince the rest of the bank of the importance and relevance of the new issues, and of the need to consider them. While each adviser was a separate entity, we did try to reinforce each other and share experiences and information.

The World Bank at that time was a decidedly white male establishment. Unlike appointments at the UN, bank appointments are not controlled by geographical representation, that is, a fixed quota of staff for each member country. There seemed to be a preponderance of ex-colonials at the bank. I knew the job was not going to be easy. As I tried to spread the WID word I often felt as if I were trying to push the world uphill. My task was made more difficult by many female staff who felt that the purpose of the post was to improve the status of women in the bank. It took a lot of energy to convince them otherwise.

As with the other brand new jobs I had held, I had to develop the concepts and modus operandi, identify appropriate points of intervention, and establish priorities. The first priority was to learn how the bank worked. To introduce myself and learn the interests of different departments in the bank, I spoke at many staff meetings. In preparation for these meetings I would select a few projects from the staff's portfolio, in different sectors and countries and at different stages of preparation or implementation, and I would base my illustration of women's issues on them. But I was always prepared to answer questions on projects in the portfolio that I had not selected, and often met with staff to follow up.

The first to invite me to his staff meeting was Greg Votaw, director of the Asia region. This encouraged other directors to follow suit. In the formal bank atmosphere these first meetings were important, and knowledge I had gained at the UN was invaluable. I had a respectable library that I took with me to the bank so that I could reinforce my comments with material written by others. During my first year I again realized how important it was to build up and organize a database. My research assistant, Alcione Amos, collected information incorporated later into the bank's sector library, where staff could find WID data for project analyses.

Given the size of the bank, and the meagerness of the resources attached to my office, I needed to find ways of wholesaling my advice. One of the early tools I prepared was a framework for project analysis. Project analysis and design is the basis of a great deal of the bank's work, and Robert McNamara, the bank president, had insisted that WID issues be integrated within the framework of each project. My framework showed by sector and activity the kinds of questions that should be asked to find out what related activities women did, how the project would affect them, and how women's contributions to the success of the project could be improved. While equity was a concern, questions had to be framed in terms of efficiency.

I was anxious to get WID issues documented in terms of the bank's own experience. The bank's Status of Women Working Group had been involved with preparations for the Mexico conference and had a vested interest in publicizing my new post. The group suggested holding a symposium on women in development. My response was much more modest than that but also more efficient. McNamara approved my program, including resources for consultants to do case studies of WID issues based on bank projects and for holding a three-day seminar outside the bank to discuss and refine the case studies and thus contribute to the conceptualization of the bank's WID approach. I worked with the bank's training department, but felt it would be politically beneficial to have outside trainers.

I approached Jim Anderson of the Harvard International Institute for Development, who had done staff training for the bank's agriculture and rural development department, a "hard" sector with many implications for women. He organized a training team that included Mary Anderson, Cathy Overholt, and Kathleen Cloud. There was a lot of high-level interest in the seminar, and while the preparations and execution were not without dramas, it was deemed quite successful and entrenched WID activities in the bank. Ester Boserup gave a keynote address and the few other outsiders invited included Marilyn Carr from the Intermediate Technology Group in London, with whom I was collaborating on women and technology issues in Bangladesh. We ran six other seminars, each for between fifteen and twenty bank staff. Relative to the size of the bank staff, the numbers were small and far from a critical mass, but they were fairly well spread to provide some leaven.

Publicizing the bank's WID work to other multinational and bilateral agencies, NGOs, universities, and professional societies was demanding. This effort included a seminar, initiated by Margaret McNamara, the president's wife, for spouses of bank governors at annual meetings held in Washington. The theme of the first seminar, in 1977, was "Changing Patterns of Employment." We invited WID practitioners from outside the bank as panelists and commentators to present their thinking and research findings. Not many of the bank's governors attended these seminars, but the hope was that their spouses did share some of the information.

For several months, Arvonne Fraser and I repeatedly were interviewed together on radio and TV, until we began to feel like the Mutt and Jeff of WID. Balancing these public appearances with work inside the bank was always challenging, but they contributed substantively to my work. A director once made a snide remark about them, but was silenced by my report on the work and hours involved and by support from outside the bank. Early in my career I learned the importance of documenting my time and tasks, invaluable in this instance. Other early lessons honed by experience were the value of saving my comments at meetings till they would have an impact and then getting directly to the point, and adhering to the absolute correctness required of a woman in a male establishment, which was frequently exhausting but critical for survival.

The most direct way to influence national development policy was through contributions to country, sector, and project work, especially when I went to the field and illustrated what we talked about in Washington. Few officials in the countries had seriously considered WID issues and they had little contact with women's groups or research programs. On country missions I made a special effort to visit these groups, especially grassroots women, bringing information back to government officials. When possible, I facilitated meetings between the women and the officials.

I also allocated resources to identifying WID issues in hard sectors, not just in the traditional sectors associated with women. Resultant case studies reported on irrigation projects in Indonesia, industrialization in El Salvador, rural roads in Kenya, tourism in Mexico, and rural technology in Bangladesh. I also got WID issues into the annual World Development Report. For example, the significance of improving women's status for reducing fertility was emphasized in the 1984 report on population and development. Another significant way to influence policy was to review projects in the portfolio of an upcoming AID consortium (donors group), pointing out WID and cross-cutting issues donors could discuss with the national officials involved.

Interagency collaboration within the UN system was critical to ensure implementation of resolutions passed by the several women's conferences. Ulla Olin at the United Nations Development Programme (UNDP) led the effort, which produced an action-oriented assessment of rural women's participation in development (Evaluation Study no. 3, June 1980). Our mutual support strengthened our individual efforts to insert WID issues into national policy. Within the Organization for Economic Cooperation and Development, the bank collaborated with the Center for Development Studies under Winifred Weekes-Vagliani, the Development Assistance Committee, and the Working Party on the Role of Women in the Economy.

The bank was generous in allowing me to support the efforts of others. I worked with Magda Pollard, the WID officer of CARICOM, the Caribbean regional organization, to help enhance Caribbean participation in the 1985 women's conference in Nairobi. I collaborated with Dorienne Wilson-Smiley (now Rowan-Campbell), WID director at the Commonwealth secretariat, in a two-week workshop in India for forty Commonwealth officers to expose them to WID concepts and approaches by addressing the issue of women's employment from the policy level rather than the prevalent income-generation approach. For the bank's report for the Copenhagen women's conference, I identified issues for women by sector and showed how bank activities were addressing them. Journalists have a knack for extracting key phrases to catch attention. Peter Muncie in the bank's publication department gave the report its title, "Recognizing the

Invisible Woman in Development." During my years at the bank and since, I have strived to lessen that invisibility.

Life After the Bank

Since leaving the bank, I have continued to plough the WID fields and scatter ideas around the world, though with the passing years I have restricted the areas of the world in which I will physically work. Many of us who traveled a lot equipped ourselves to make our missions as comfortable as possible. I learned early about the "medicinal" bottle of scotch, water-purifying tablets, light bulbs (hotel rooms invariably are equipped with fifteen-watt bulbs), and both electric and ear plugs. Other essentials included medicines against tropical bites and illnesses and electric kettles or immersion heaters for making soup or tea. In hotel rooms all over the world we have strategized with other women, drafted resolutions, learned about conditions in our countries, and shared our problems, hopes, and fears. A nice cup of tea or a remedy from my pharmaceutical supplies has rescued many a colleague, and my little Sony traveling kettle is still the first item I pack for a trip.

In 1993 Torild Skard, assistant secretary-general for development cooperation in the Norwegian Ministry of Foreign Affairs, organized a consultation, inviting three former WID officers: Ingrid Eide of UNDP, Ruth Finney Hayward of FAO, and me. In a session entitled "A look from the past on the situation today and tomorrow regarding the contribution of the UN system to the advancement of women," we discussed our experiences supporting WID in male bureaucracies. It was a great luxury not to have to fly an agency flag or have a bureaucratic role. From current WID officers we heard about increased resources, rationalization of WID mechanisms, improved access to power, enhanced databases, better networks within and between agencies, and debates about the best administrative location for WID offices. I heard many success stories but also some of the same discouragement I experienced at the bank: isolation, limited access to information, and the need to watch one's back constantly and be a little superhuman.

Without a doubt, women have become a political force, and WID issues are firmly planted on important agendas. But many women working on WID are still marginalized in their agencies and few understand how to work the system and its internal and external linkages. Most senior staff are still men who have informal ways of exchanging information to which women are not privy because they do not share washrooms with vice presidents. Still, all of us have tried to share our experiences over the years, to support colleagues and groom our successors. We ourselves have had support from large numbers of male and female colleagues, many of whom went out on a limb to take up WID issues in the early stages. With us those people can take pride in the survival and progress of WID.

Leticia Ramos Shahani

Leticia Ramos Shahani has had a varied career in education, culture, foreign affairs, and agriculture, but one theme has held her life together: service to individuals; her country, the Philippines; and the international community. Educated in elementary and secondary schools in the Philippines, she received her bachelor's degree from Wellesley College and her Ph.D. from the University of Paris. She entered the Philippines Foreign Service, reaching the highest rank of ambassador, at which rank she served in the German Democratic Republic and Australia (1975–81). She served in the United Nations for nine years and was named assistant secretary-general for Social Development and Humanitarian Affairs (1981–86). As secretary-general of the UN Third World Conference on Women in 1985, she led the important breakthrough that made women's issues legitimate global concerns at the UN.

Returning to her country in 1986 as undersecretary of foreign affairs, she ran for senator during President Corazon Aquino's administration. In her twelve years in the Senate (1987–98) she sponsored landmark legislation on women including the Anti-Rape Act, the Gender and Development provision in the annual Government Appropriations Act, and the Act Defining Discrimination Against Women in the area of equal pay for work of equal value. Under the administration of President Gloria Macapagal Arroyo, she served as presidential adviser on culture.

A widow and single parent since 1968, she raised three children while pursuing her career. She has also paid attention to the development of her personal life, which in her view should shape her outer life.

The UN, Women, and Development: The World Conferences on Women

As a young girl growing up in a middle-class family in the Philippines—I was born in 1929—I hardly noticed or experienced blatant discrimination against women in my immediate surroundings. My mother, a charming and attractive woman, was a teacher of English in high school and later in college. She was loved and respected by her students and colleagues, males included. She was also my father's best political campaigner in his five successful runs for office and a valued partner in his fifteen-year career as a member of Congress. Because she was an early feminist, I began to read pamphlets and magazines on women's rights and activities written by leading women leaders in our province. I cite my mother's life because most women are influenced by their mothers in their attitudes towards themselves and feminism. I was fortunate to have a wonderful role model. Mother often talked about her own mother, Crispina. Although she died at an early age and I never saw her, I felt close to my grandmother in spirit, mainly because she was a mother of eight children as well as a teacher and a pioneer in a colonial era. She was trained as a teacher by Americans who arrived in the Philippines at the turn of the twentieth century to teach English.

From an early age I felt equal to boys and I don't think that my experience was unusual in the Philippines. The Philippines, fortunately, is one country where the heavy hand of tradition, which discriminates against women, has not flourished. In my view, what has caused discrimination against women in our country is poverty and lack of opportunities rather than custom and tradition.

Living and studying abroad also influenced my outlook on women's issues. My father was appointed to the diplomatic service when the Philippines became independent in 1946 and we lived in Washington, D.C. I also attended Wellesley College in the United States, which trains women to be independent and self-reliant human beings. These early influences in my life were extremely important in shaping and directing my commitment and dedication to the women's movement with which I was to be closely identified at certain periods.

At the United Nations

I entered the Secretariat of the United Nations in 1964, and in 1967. I transferred to the Section on the Status of Women under the Division of Human Rights, which at that time was located in New York. Thus began my formal introduction to the women's movement at the international level, in particular, the conflicts that influenced women's issues, such as the Cold War confrontation between East and West and the economic gap between the rich and the poor countries. I also had the opportunity to work under the first head of the Section on the Status on Women, an able professional from the United Kingdom, Margaret K. Bruce, who impressed on her Secretariat staff the need to be objective and impartial. Women's issues during the early days of the UN, as part of its legacy from the League of Nations, came under the classification of human rights. As a member of the secretariat, I was introduced to the inner workings of the Commission on the Status of Women (CSW) because the secretariat prepared the commission's annual meetings and, particularly, its documentation and program of work.

During the 1960s the priorities of the UN were focused on human rights in the Western sense of the phrase, meaning civil and political rights, and on anti-colonialism. Development was just beginning to gain attention as a priority. These trends were reflected in the work of the CSW, which at that period was concentrating on drafting legal instruments, such as the Convention on the Political Rights of Women, the Convention on the Nationality of Married Women, and the Convention on Consent to Marriage, Minimum Age of Marriage and Registration of Marriages. The most active and vocal members of the commission during my time in the secretariat were the French, the Poles, the Russians, the Africans, and some Asians.

The Cold War, which was then at its height, naturally influenced the proceedings of the commission. A constant topic of debate in the commission between those who came from the East and their Western counterparts was the superiority of women's status in the Socialist bloc as against the advantages of women in market-oriented economies. The challenge of development to bridge the gap between the rich and the poor countries was not yet well articulated by women leaders coming from the South. They were not yet aware of the international dimensions of the women's movement. Since the United Nations becomes hostage to the political trends experienced by its members, it therefore moves slowly toward reform, but once ideas are supported by the general population and NGOs and are actively espoused by governments, these movements within the institution rapidly take on a life of their own.

As a member of the section on the status of women, I learned how to draft UN documents that avoided controversial or offensive remarks (the reason that they make dull reading). I also was trained to help delegations with their needs for information and documentation at meetings while being careful at all times not to express partisan views. Through this training I gained an understanding of the dynamics of political, economic, and social forces at the UN. At the same time I learned how to help push ideas deemed useful by governments and nongovernmental organizations through the circumscribed but focused work of the secretariat.

The demand from the developing countries for emphasis on development issues at the UN slowly brought more focus on women. The Western emphasis on human rights—that is, civil and political rights—was not adequate to convince the poor countries that this was the main issue for women. In order for human rights to be realized and exercised, observed those in developing countries, the proper economic and social conditions—such as the rights to education, employment, and freedom of expression—had to be created and put in place. Development would create these conditions. For instance, the debate on population made delegations realize the need to educate and employ women to help them plan their families. Women's issues began to evolve in the direction of development. Before I left the secretariat in 1968, I prepared one of the first reports on development for the commission, titled "Community Development and the Status of Women."

Planning the Mexico City Conference

At the sudden passing of my husband in 1968, I decided to resign from the UN Secretariat and return to the Philippines with my three small children. Fortunately, I had previously passed the career examination for our foreign service and had a job waiting for me in which I could also pursue my deepening interest in the feminist movement. I was assigned to the United Nations Office in the Department of Foreign Affairs in 1969 and became the Philippine representative to the Commission on the Status of Women. I had come full circle, from international to national. At that time, there were only twenty-three members of the CSW and obtaining a seat at the commission was not as fiercely competitive as it is now. I was fortunate to represent the Philippines at the commission for several years.

In 1974 I served as chairperson of the commission to prepare for the first international conference on women, to be held in Mexico City in 1975, which had been declared International Women's Year by the UN General Assembly. It was a fascinating experience, as a former member of the UN secretariat, to be at the head of a functional commission of the UN. I saw first hand the political and social forces at work as delegates pronounced their points of view and as the secretariat took notes for the basis of nonpartisan reports. The commission at that time was not as powerful as it is now. The organization of the series of global conferences on women forced governments to take the women's issue seriously and gave NGOs all over the world unprecedented support at all levels for their efforts. Although the word "networking" was not officially adopted until the Nairobi conference in 1985, the ease and speed with which women communicated with each other along informal and flexible lines had already been discovered and put in motion in the 1970s. The phenomenon of networking by and among women was born then.

The idea of holding an international conference on women had been brought before the commission around 1973. There was general enthusiasm for it among the NGOs but little interest among the permanent representatives and the professional diplomats of the permanent missions, most of whom were men. They scoffed at the idea of placing women in the international agenda alongside "more serious" issues like disarmament, the non-proliferation treaty, the new international economic order, and gross violation of human rights. At that time, the women's issue was a marginalized topic that came under the sector of social welfare in the view of governments and the private sector. But the international conference all the same figured in the agenda of the 1974 session of the CSW.

The Soviet Union, under the leadership of a dynamic woman leader, Tatiana Nikolaeva, at the 1974 CSW session opposed the resolution to hold the conference and, with its allies, filibustered until nine o'clock at night to prevent passage of the resolution for transmission to the Economic and Social Council (ECOSOC) and the General Assembly. New as I was to UN politics, I could not, at that time, fully understand why the Soviets were against it. I finally realized that by making the women's issue truly international through a UN conference where not only the socialist countries but also the capitalist and the Third World countries could participate and shape the women's movement, the Soviet Union would weaken its grip on the women's issue among its allies and thus lose a powerful tool of control and propaganda. The Soviets did not succeed in their efforts to stop the conference and arrangements were straightaway made to prepare for Mexico.

The First World Conference on Women, held in Mexico, did not have the elaborate preparation that the succeeding women's conferences had. Prep-aration for each succeeding conference took two years and included meetings in all of the regions of the world and two or three at UN headquarters in New York or Vienna. The draft of the Mexico Plan of Action was quickly prepared by the drafting groups of delegations and the UN Secretariat and submitted directly to the Mexico City conference. This explains the general tone of the document, which lacks specific and concrete detail. However, the plan was adopted by consensus. A shorter and more controversial document approved at the conference was the Declaration of Mexico, which became conveniently forgotten. The fact that the plan was adopted by consensus satisfied everybody. The two controversial statements were "Zionism is a form of racial discrimination" and "women have sovereignty over their bodies." These were destined to be debated over and over again in the next two world conferences and in other UN meetings.

Two institutions were born at the Mexico City conference: the United Nations Voluntary Fund for Women, now known as UNIFEM, and the International Research and Training Institute for Women, or INSTRAW. At Mexico governments finally accepted women's issues as their legitimate concerns, and as a source of international cooperation and fierce debate as well.

Drafting CEDAW

After the Mexico City conference, the UN General Assembly proclaimed the period 1976–85 as the UN Decade for Women: Equality, Development and Peace. After Mexico work in the commission was intensified to come up with the Convention on the Elimination of All Forms of Discrimination Against Women (CEDAW). The Declaration on the Elimination of Discrimination Against Women had been adopted by the United Nations General Assembly in 1967. After that, several countries, mainly from the developing world, pressed for a convention on the same topic, stressing that only a convention would make the national legislation of member-states binding on the standards set up by an international convention to eliminate discrimination against women.

Western countries, especially the United States and the United Kingdom, were lukewarm about this initiative, saying that their own law-making processes did not automatically follow UN conventions and that they did not regard UN conventions to which they were not parties legally binding. Eventually the commission agreed to start the drafting of the convention and I belonged to the drafting group. All regions of the world were represented in the working group, including the Soviet Union, its allies, and the United States and Western European allies, thus reflecting the political and economic divisions within the UN. The question before the drafting group was who would prepare the text of the draft convention. The members of the Secretariat said it was not within their mandate to do so and none of the delegations were ready to take the responsibility. We returned to our own countries unable to make any commitments.

In preparing for the next annual meeting of the CSW, I saw that the absence of a working draft would be a major stumbling block. At that time the rules about the origin of working drafts were far stricter than they are now. As the assistant secretary for the UN and international organizations of the Department of Foreign Affairs in Manila, I took it upon myself to prepare a draft convention without making it a Philippine submission. I enlisted the help of a bright young lawyer on my staff, Minerva Falcon, who has now served as our ambassador and consul-general to several countries. We used the Declaration on the Elimination of Discrimination Against Women to guide us on the various sectors where discrimination had to be removed.

With a complete draft of the convention in hand, I went to New York to attend the annual session of the commission. At the working group meeting, the problem of the nonexistence of a working draft became an issue. Wanting to help find a solution, I quietly approached the Soviet delegate, Tatiana Nikolaeva, to ask whether she was willing to join me in submitting a draft. At that time our two countries had no diplomatic relations, but women could be ahead of their times. Since she did not always ask for instructions and was ready to take initiatives, Nikolaeva readily said, "Yes." For my part, I knew I was taking a risk, for I had not cleared the draft with my government. But I justified my initiative by saying that it was just a draft working paper and did not reflect the Philippine government position. However, some colleagues of mine in the Philippine Permanent Mission to the UN reported my actions to the secretary of foreign affairs, the well-known and respected diplomat, Carlos P. Romulo. The next day I received a telegram from my foreign secretary reprimanding me for not having sought the permission of the government to present the draft paper, which contained several topics not yet resolved nor reflected in our national laws.

I knew, however, that if I had gone through the intricate process of clearing the draft with the many requisite government agencies, I would never have finished it on time for the session of the commission. I explained my dilemma to the working group and out of consideration for the delicate situation in which we found ourselves, the group put aside its usual objections and decided to adopt the draft as a basic working paper without attributing it to any individual delegation. This is how the first draft of the Convention on the Elimination of All Forms of Discrimination Against Women was formulated. Often I wondered whether I had taken the right step. In retrospect I believe I made the right decision. Had we waited for a formal submission of a working draft, much precious time would have been lost and the shape of the convention could have been quite different from the present one. (For additional discussion of CEDAW see Aziza Hussein's and Arvonne S. Fraser's essays in this volume.)

Controversy at Copenhagen

I was able to attend all of the women's world conferences up to the year 2000, including one that was not so well-known, the second world women's conference held in Copenhagen in 1980, officially titled the World Conference of the United Nations Decade for Women 1980: Copenhagen, and often referred to as the Mid-Decade Conference. I served as one of the several vice presidents of this event. The world situation was still tense then. The protagonists of the Cold War were active in confronting each other and the Israeli-Palestinian issue was increasingly violent. One of the leading personalities who attended this conference was the Palestinian superactivist, Leila Khalid, who was idolized by some of the feminists of the Third World.

The final document of the conference, the Copenhagen Programme of Action, had many good features but it ran into controversy because of the inclusion of Zionism as a form of racial discrimination and other controversial resolutions condemning the Western group of nations. The techniques of negotiation, back-channeling, and consensus were not yet well developed among the feminists. The Copenhagen Programme of Action failed to be adopted by consensus and the conference, rocked by controversy, was not considered a success.

The women had not yet learned to be masters of their own conferences; the male diplomats were still in command. This was a disappointment to the host, the Danish government, as well as to Lisle Ostergaard, the conference president, and Lucille Mair, the secretary-general, who was from Jamaica. The one bright feature of the conference was the opening of the Convention on the Elimination of All Forms of Discrimination Against Women for signature by member nations. Fifty-seven countries signed the convention, a milestone in the work of the UN for the rights of women.[1]

The Nairobi Conference and the Forward-Looking Strategies

My involvement at the international level on the women's issue gained another important dimension when in 1981 I was appointed UN Assistant Secretary-General to head the Centre for Social Development and Humanitarian Affairs based in Vienna. I succeeded a long-time colleague, Helvi Sipila of Finland. The structure of the centre is interesting, for it reflected in the 1980s where the women's issue was placed within the UN Secretariat. Because the women's issue was considered part of social development, it was placed in the same Centre alongside programs on social welfare, the disabled, youth, the aging, and crime prevention. Fortunately, in 1996, after the Beijing conference, the Branch for the Advancement of Women was elevated structurally and placed within the Department of Economic and Social Affairs under the supervision of Angela King, the special adviser on gender issues and the advancement of women.

In 1983, the two-year preparations for the Nairobi conference began and I was named the conference's secretary-general. Having observed the other conferences on women at close range, I vowed to work hard to bring about consensus on the final document, "The Forward-Looking Strategies for the Advancement of Women" (FLS). This was a most ambitious dream, shared by many other women, who had seen previous efforts fail as a result of the power of male diplomats or political forces inimical to women's concerns. In 1985 the world situation was still precarious; although the Soviet Union was beginning to break apart, apartheid still held sway in South Africa and the Arab-Israeli situation remained as intractable as it had ever been. Yet at this time women better understood the mechanics of preparing for a global conference with the aim of reaching consensus than they did in 1975 and 1980.

Much care was given by the secretariat, governments, and NGOs to prepare draft plans of action at the regional level, which could be adopted by consensus. But the political problems of the world, which had now become more thoroughly enmeshed with women's issues, threatened the consensus that we, the majority of delegates, and Javier Perez de Cuellar, the UN secretary-general, wanted to achieve. At the third and final preparatory conference for Nairobi the FLS still contained many paragraphs in square brackets, that is, still not agreed upon. The preparatory conference needed to arrange an extra meeting before we could go to Nairobi. I flew to New York to report to the secretary-general that the collapse of the conference was imminent, given that we were still far from consensus on the final draft document. Secretary-General Javier Perez de Cuellar acted quickly and a fourth preparatory meeting was organized. This time there were no interpreters or official documents because the meeting was supposed to be informal and was not funded from the regular budget. By the time we went to Nairobi the major nuts and bolts were in place, albeit loosely screwed together. However, until the very last night of the conference, no one was sure that the final document would be adopted by consensus, as the method then was to vote on each paragraph separately. As at Copenhagen in 1980, the issue of Zionism as a form of racial discrimination was causing the lack of consensus. The Americans bluntly said they would walk out if the word "Zionism" appeared in the Forward-Looking Strategies. The Africans and the Arab groups also threatened to break up the conference if the word was deleted.

Late in the evening of the day of adjournment, 26 July 1985, a small group of us met. The group represented the major stakeholders of the conference: the Kenya government as the host government, the Russians, the Americans, the Palestinians, the Western European groups, and the United Nations Secretariat. We had to decide whether we wanted the conference to succeed or not. We all agreed that it should; otherwise, we asked, what was the UN for? We decided, therefore, that the word "Zionism" would be deleted, with the phrase "all forms of racial discrimination" substituted for it, and that no explanation of vote would be given to the effect that all forms of discrimination could mean Zionism. With that understanding, we went back to the main conference hall and began to vote paragraph by paragraph on the Forward-Looking Strategies for the Advancement of Women.

The FLS could be one of the last major documents of a UN conference to be voted upon paragraph by paragraph. After Nairobi the procedure was to adopt separate paragraphs by consensus. The voting by paragraphs at Nairobi was accompanied by joyous dancing, clapping, and singing led by the Africans. The Forward-Looking Strategies was finally adopted by consensus at four o'clock in the morning of 28 July. What a beautiful victory. The struggle at the Nairobi conference was to integrate women's concerns into the major economic and political issues already accepted by the UN. The Nairobi conference ensured that women's causes would not be classified merely as social issues. It laid the groundwork for gender mainstreaming and paved the way for the Beijing conference ten years later, making it easier to adopt the Beijing Platform for Action.[2]

The Beijing Conference Platform for Action and Beijing + 5

I was the head of the Philippine delegation when we went to Beijing for the Fourth World Conference on Women in 1995. I was particularly elated at heading the delegation since, by that time, I was also a senator in the Philippine legislature and had served for several years as the chairman of the Senate Committee on Women and Family Relations. Being at Beijing meant seeing old friends of the feminist network and working with them again for a common cause. In the Philippine delegation were several distinguished colleagues with whom I had previously worked in our national machinery women's bureau, the National Commission on the Role of Filipino Women, which we had created in 1974. The chair of the main committee at Beijing was also someone from the Philippines, Dr. Patricia Licuanan, and the secretary-general of the conference was an old friend of mine, Gertrude Mongella, from Tanzania.

The Beijing conference was held under more auspicious circumstances than those we experienced in Nairobi. The Cold War was over, apartheid had ended in South Africa, and the peace process for the Israeli-Palestine problem promised, in 1995, to have lasting results. The emphasis on human rights was more readily accepted by the Global South. An important feature of Beijing was the extensive coverage by CNN as well as other international media. During the Nairobi conference the world did not hear much of our struggles, and those who did hear of them did not quite understand them. Those of us who participated both in Nairobi and Beijing felt a deep sense of satisfaction and a sense of continuity. The work accomplished in Nairobi made possible the comprehensive Platform for Action adopted by consensus in Beijing, which contained many useful concrete proposals and details for implementation.

I also attended the Beijing + 5 conference in 2000 in New York as a member of the Philippine delegation. Some participants felt that this conference did not go beyond the Beijing Platform for Action and was more a semantic exercise than a reporting on achievements. Five years is too short a time to assess achievements, especially in the women's field. However, Beijing + 5 did help push the women's issue as crucial to the lives of millions of women and as a concern of government for human-centered development.

Having retired from politics after twelve years in the Senate, I remain active in women's issues at both the national and village level. Much remains to be done, from giving impoverished women access to microcredit to helping to empower women to compete in the ruthless world of globalization. I consider myself fortunate to have had a mother and a grandmother who prepared me to be part of the international women's movement and yet remain rooted in my national base. It will take time before the rich, the emerging, and the poor countries will accept their individual and collective responsibilities to live together in peace and justice. Despite the roller-coaster ride on which the world seems to be caught, and despite the disadvantaged position of women from developing countries, I am confident there will be steadying and liberating influences coming from women and men the world over who fully understand the major role women can now play in creating a more humane and just world.

Leticia Ramos Shahani donated her papers to the Library of the University of the Philippines as well as to the Women's Studies Center, University of the Philippines, Diliman, Quezon City, Philippines.

Margaret Snyder

A graduate of the College of New Rochelle and the Catholic University of America, Margaret Snyder received her Ph.D. in sociology from the University of Dar es Salaam in Tanzania. She lived and worked a total of fifteen years in Africa, and has on several occasions been an international election observer there.

She was a regional adviser at the UN Economic Commission for Africa (1971–78), where she headed the Voluntary Agencies Bureau and was co-founder of the African Centre for Women. During the same period she was a member of the Committee to Organize Women's World Banking. She is founding director of the United Nations Development Fund for Women (UNIFEM) (1978–89). After leaving the UN she became a visiting fellow at the Woodrow Wilson School at Princeton University in 1992–93, then a Fulbright Scholar at the Department of Women and Gender Studies of Makerere University, Uganda, in 1995–96. She is the author of the three books, a monograph, a bibliographic essay, and numerous other publications.

Her awards and honors include Ford and Rockefeller Foundation grants, an honorary Ph.D. from LeMoyne College, a Woman of Conscience award from the National Council of Women of the United States, and recognition for promoting women in agriculture and education in Africa. She has been a trustee for NGOs in Africa and the United States and holds memberships in a number of development and women's organizations.

Walking My Own Road:
How a Sabbatical Year Led to a
United Nations Career

The majestic slopes of Mount Kilimanjaro and the sharp peaks of Mount Kenya poked through the clouds as our plane touched down at dawn. It was Nairobi, 1961. My career and life were about to be transformed. Seven years of work at a male-run college had sharpened my awareness of women's exclusion from decision making in many institutions, and volunteer work at a foundation dedicated to black migrants had aroused my desire to spend a sabbatical year working in Africa. As I arrived in Kenya, the winds of change were carrying political colonialism into history. Women were seeking ways to share in shaping their new nations, initiatives that would later be called the women in development movement.

My early years in Africa would confirm my conviction that a critical strategy for reaching common goals is to strengthen or create institutions that ensure a movement's long life. Mine is thus a story of institution building for women's empowerment. I tell it in the spirit of Albertina Sisulu of South Africa, who says, "We are required to walk our own road—and then stop, assess what we have learned and share it with others. We can do no more than tell our story. [The next generation] must do with it what they will."[1]

First Encounters with Women and Development, Kenya and Tanzania, 1961

After seven years establishing the office of dean of women at the young LeMoyne College, which had a faculty of one hundred men and no women, it was time to move on. Inspired by African visitors to the United States, I had become fascinated with that vast continent's people; but making connections for a sabbatical year there proved daunting. President John F. Kennedy's brand new Peace Corps turned me away with the statement, "We just opened. No typewriters. Please come back later." Finally, the Women's Africa Committee of the African-American Institute made contacts in Kenya on my behalf; five members of the LeMoyne College Board of Regents and my undergraduate alma mater, the College of New Rochelle, financed my year.

Kenya women—my first mentors on the subject of women and development—convinced me that the movement is indigenous. As parliamentarian Phoebe Asiyo said recently, "The issue was here. . . . You can't remove the dates." When she was a community development officer, I journeyed with Asiyo to Lake Victoria, where farm women came on foot to a small school-house on a still and steamy afternoon and sat in the building's shade. Their first question was startling: "How will Sputnik change our lives?" Awed that village women knew of that Russian satellite, I had my first lesson on women and development; it means much more than male-female equality.

Capable, serious, and gifted, with a disarming sense of humor, Margaret Kenyatta, whose father, Jomo, was imprisoned but would soon be Kenya's first president, taught me how "women keep democracy going." By the early 1960s Kenya women had organized 5,000 nursery centers across the country—under a tree, in a community center, in a backyard—and had sent hundreds of their sons and daughters off to American colleges with ululations that nearly overwhelmed the roar of jet airplanes. By the 1990s, 16,000 women's groups were affiliated with churches, women's organizations such as Maendeleo ya Wanawake (progress of women), and government community development programs.

As the momentum for independence built, in 1962 Margaret and Phoebe called community leaders to the first nationwide Kenya Women's Seminar, entitled "The Roles of African Women: Past, Present and Future." Volunteers interpreted Swahili and local languages in order that the voices of rural women could be heard. So democratic were those women that at one stage the whole organizing committee resigned, leaving me to conduct a formal election. As the movement spread through Uganda and Tanganyika with East African seminars, what was new was not women's organizing—they had done that for generations—but their belief that they had a right and responsibility to prepare themselves to build their new nations side by side with men.

Invited to stay another year in Kenya, I returned my contract to LeMoyne unsigned. Then neighboring Tanganyika (later renamed Tanzania) asked me to advise its national women's organization, Umoja wa Wanawake wa Tanganyika, or United Tanganyika Women (UWT), led by the formidable Bibi Titi Mohamed, a short, stocky professional singer and key leader in the independence movement from the 1950s. She had mobilized hundreds of mostly Muslim coastal and upcountry women in pursuit of their goal: better lives for everyone. Educated women, both nationals and expatriates, were also risk takers for their fellow women and men in the policy and practice of building the nation. Their lives bear witness to the meaning of development as their president, Julius Nyerere, defined it: "increasing peoples' freedom and well-being." If we accept that definition, women and development becomes a concept and a movement "whose long-range goal is the well-being of society, the community of men, women and children."[2]

A Model Regional Institution in the United Nations

After some years at the African studies program at Syracuse University and as coordinator of its graduate research in Tanzania, I made a long-term move to the United Nations. An exceptional opportunity arose when in the late 1960s the Swedish International Development Cooperative Agency (SIDA) financed two senior positions at the United Nations Economic Commission for Africa (ECA), with the responsibility to transform the resolutions of regionwide women's conferences into a program that ECA would carry out. The person who convinced SIDA to finance those posts remains an unrecognized hero of the global women's movement. Inga Thorsson persuaded the Swedish Parliament to mandate government support for women in its foreign assistance programs in 1964, a full nine years before the U.S. Congress passed the similar Percy Amendment.

I was convinced by Tanzanian colleague Martha Bulengo to "take the job at ECA and work for all of us women." Arriving at the ECA headquarters in Addis Ababa early in 1971, I found the role and participation of women in national development had been an agenda item for ECA since 1969, with the approval of the United Nations Economic and Social Council (ECOSOC). An Africa regional meeting, also in 1969, on "The Role of Women in National Development" had called for studies on trade, business, industry, and agriculture. It was to be followed in 1971 by another conference, "Factors Affecting Education, Training and Work Opportunities for Girls and Women Within the Context of Development." My first assignment was to draft the basic document for the conference. Reflecting on the concerns of those years, I am ever more aware that Africa's women and development movement arose from its own African roots.

The fledgling ECA Women's Programme needed a strategic plan. I assigned a young research assistant to draw up forty-nine country womanpower studies as baseline information on the status and situation of women, their education, health, organizations, parliamentary participation, and so forth. Meanwhile I looked for common themes in the reports of five conferences in the 1960s sponsored by ECA and the UN Secretariat acting for the Commission on the Status of Women. Based on that information, and on visits to member states to discuss their priorities, we produced the Five Year Programme (1972–76) for training girls and women for full participation in development, which ECA would execute and use to enrich its mainstream programs.

Because it was at the cutting edge of the international women and development movement, and thanks to Margaret Bruce and Aida Gindy of the UN Secretariat, the Five Year Programme was appended to the working document for the UN's expert group meeting on women and economic development held in 1972. I represented ECA at that global women and development meeting, which was the first to be convened by the UN or any other organization. Its influence would be powerful.

At ECA, more innovation was to come. Information from our country studies underlay "The Data Base for Discussion on the Interrelations between the Integration of Women in Development, Their Situation and Population Factors in Africa." It was another first for Africa and the world, the first document for a whole geographic region that was both quantitative and qualitative. It followed on "Women, the Neglected Human Resources for National Development" published in 1972. Its popular version, "Women of Africa Today and Tomorrow," was in great demand. None of us was aware at the time how those documents would help fuel a revolution.

Beating the Drum

Implementing the five-year program brought many new experiences, including confronting customs officers in apartheid South Africa who did not welcome the diversity of our itinerant training team—a Ghanaian, an Ethiopian, a Scot and an American—and so detained us at the Johannesburg airport overnight. Our rural training teams traveled to twenty-eight countries, always transforming UN practice and its underlying policies by combining government and NGO workers in a single training course. Thanks to a grant from the United States Agency for International Development (USAID) obtained through the intervention of Kay Wallace, Mary Hilton, and Clara Beyer of the U.S. Department of Labor, other itinerant teams of African women parliamentarians and American and Canadian representatives of women's bureaus held three-day national seminars on "national machineries," government-based policy and action institutions, such as women's bureaus. By 1993, thirty-three African countries had national machineries whose policy-making power was admittedly mixed. Yet, as F. Joka-Bangura, an evaluator with the United Nations Development Fund for Women (UNIFEM), said, "Without them . . . no one else would have taken up" the question of government resources benefiting women.[3]

Wherever our teams went, women took us to their presidents or parliamentarians to tell them what the UN was saying about women. Of course those same women had been government delegates at regional conferences that designed the very policies we would discuss. These women wanted a center of their own, and the final push for it came from participants in a Zambia rural training course. The top officials of ECA—executive secretary R. K. A. Gardener and division chief James Riby-Williams, both Ghanaians—responded to the women's desire to institutionalize their concerns by creating the African Centre for Women (ACW) on 31 March 1975.

1975: A Year for the World's Women

We went proudly to Mexico City in 1975 to celebrate International

Women's Year. Africa had its women's centre—a model for the world. At the pre-conference seminar initiated by Irene Tinker and sponsored by the American Association for the Advancement of Science, African creativity again shone when Ghanaian entrepreneur Esther Ocloo, concerned about women's lack of investment capital, announced impatiently, "What we need is a women's bank." "Yes," another participant said. "A women's world bank!" Four of us drafted a resolution, whose principal author was Virginia Saurwein of the UN, and we plotted its introduction at the government conference, preparing the way for Women's World Banking (WWB). Delegate Justice Annie Jiaggie, flush with success in creating Africa's first national machinery, the Ghana National Council on Women and Development, recalled our visit to her hotel room: "We agreed that women all over the world should join together on this question of access to capital because women don't have the collateral the banks require and they have to go to moneylenders who charge 100-percent interest." Organizers and sponsors of the resolution in Mexico were joined in New York by banker Michaela Walsh, development specialist Caroline Pezzullo, filmmaker Martha Stuart, and others to form the Committee to Organize WWB.

The question of the scope of women's issues caused a serious rift among delegates at Mexico City. The major concern of women of the North, where feminism was taking hold, was male-female relations and opportunities. For women of the South, fresh from colonial domination, issues such as apartheid, the global economy, and Palestinian rights were integral to improving the status and situation of women. "If apartheid keeps a whole people down, how can women advance?" they asked. Developing countries called for a New International Economic Order (NIEO), their first of a quarter-century effort to transform global trade and finance that would culminate in Seattle in 2000. In response, we prepared another pathbreaking ECA publication, "The NIEO: What Roles for Women?" for the 1977 Nouakchatt African regional conference. Working with ECA's statistics division, we estimated women's contributions to the gross domestic product (GDP) of their countries. Lucille Mair, from Jamaica, the first woman to be a UN under-secretary, complimented Africa as "the first of the world's regions to discuss the meaning of the NIEO for women."[4]

These social and economic justice matters, which were found incompatible with Northern interpretations of the concept of women's issues, were put into the Declaration of Mexico so that the conference's Plan of Action could be passed unanimously. But they would remain divisive for a decade, erupting at Copenhagen in 1980, then subsiding at the Nairobi conference in 1985 when Northern women's experience with economic setbacks and the opportunity to visit Kenyan women's groups in the countryside enhanced their understanding of global issues and broadened their concept of women's issues. In a complementary way, women of the South began to articulate gender-relations issues that were prominent in the North, such as violence against women and equal rights. A truly global movement was maturing.

ACW: Too Much Success?

As word of the success of the African Centre for Women spread worldwide, some powerful ECA officials tried to relocate it to an individual African country, out of ECA and out of the UN. To stall for time, we suggested that a review team composed of government, donor, and UN representatives evaluate our work. A prescient comment of one team member about the would-be internal coup reflects the view of many: "The problem, I fear, is that the Centre has quietly and almost entirely on its own resources, gone about its business rather more effectively than its fraternal partners in other divisions." Commenting on the vastness of the continent served, and the multiplicity of languages, customs, political systems, and levels of economic development of its forty-nine countries, the team paid tribute to the "extraordinary versatility, skills, and commitment of [ACW] staff to the development, implementation and evaluation of programs."[5] Those comments set the stage for the centre lawyer, Nellie Okello of Kenya, to devise a face-saving strategy for initiators of the center's would-be expulsion from ECA; ECA, a United Nations organization, must not compete with the plans of a political body, the Organization of African Unity (OAU), for a center for women. ACW remained at ECA. An exceptional team had passed its first major test.

Unique Partnerships

The roster of investors in the ACW multiplied, making it "the only genuine interagency partnership in the UN system," according to Marilyn Care of ITDG.[6] For its research and training, ACW could draw on the experience of the UN specialized agencies, thanks to the vision of Jean Delaney and Jean Ritchie of the Food and Agriculture Organization (FAO); Aida Gindy, formerly at UN headquarters; and Virginia Hazzard of the United Nations Children's Emergency Fund (UNICEF), who assigned staff and helped finance our activities. Encouraged by a U.S. grant, additional bilateral donors—Karin Himmelstrand for Sweden, Geertje Thomas (now Geertje Lycklama) for the Netherlands—assisted both staffing and programs. Even NGOs invested; the Intermediate Technology Development Group (ITDG) supported Marilyn Carr to introduce technologies for the food cycle and the Ford Foundation sponsored the compilation of national bibliographies. Zonta International assisted an exchange of businesswomen, the German Foundation for Developing Countries paid conference costs, and the World YWCA and the International Co-operative Alliance helped with training programs. The centre, with seventeen staff, was thus the precursor of UN multi-agency efforts of the 1990s such as UNAIDS, the joint work against the AIDS pandemic.

After seven years the time came for me to move on again, to become UNIFEM's first director. Years later in 1998, as ECA's special guest at its fortieth anniversary celebration electronic roundtable and seminar, "Developing African Economies: The Role of Women," I felt proud to have assisted the establishment of the centre a quarter-century earlier. I recalled how, in the early 1970s, we knocked on doors of African embassies in Addis Ababa to bring out enough delegates to produce a quorum for a meeting. Those days passed quickly. Today, ACW is taking its rightful place in the policy and program activities of ECA. ACW pioneered a most unlikely and radical UN procedure: government and NGO delegates sat side by side at Africa-wide meetings in 1998 and at ECA's fortieth anniversary celebration.

A Fund for the World's Women

During the 1960s women benefited from UNICEF as wives and mothers, but they remained outside major economic and social programs because they were labeled "farmers' wives" and "unpaid family labor" rather than the own-account farmers, merchants, and entrepreneurs they actually were. A fund of their own would give women clout to transform major —"mainstream" in current parlance—policies and programs. They got it in 1975 at Mexico City, where delegates to the International Women's Year Conference, influenced by financial pledges from Shirley Summerskill of the United Kingdom and Princess Ashraf Pahlavi of Iran, decided to create a fund for the world's poorest women. Using as its initial capital the money saved after conference costs were paid, the Voluntary Fund for the UN Decade for Women (VFDW, later renamed UNIFEM, the term I use here) was formally established by UN General Assembly resolution 31/133. Its administration rested with the Office Responsible for the Advancement of Women, headed by the indomitable Finnish lawyer and first woman to become an assistant secretary-general in the UN, Helvi Sipila.

Our requests to UNIFEM from the ACW in Addis Ababa had languished at UN headquarters. If the new fund were to function, its intergovernmental consultative committee said, someone had to be paid from its own resources to "love it full-time." I was invited by committee members Lucille Mair (Jamaican representative and lawyer), Leticia Shahani (Philippine representative, who would succeed Sipila), and Terese Spens (UK representative and development specialist) to be that person. My objective was to help build a lasting institution for women's empowerment. Success would be more elusive than at ECA, where we were blessed with top-level policy support from two men who understood the women and development imperative and were willing to bend the bureaucracy. I soon learned how to get policy made in an international organization; one builds constituencies through a tripartite coalition of UN civil servants, government delegates from both industrial and developing countries, and NGO representatives. Such a coalition was key to making UNIFEM a lasting institution; acting in harmony, coalition members could influence the major players in UN policy arenas.

The political consultative committee was already our greatest ally; international NGOs rallied around, and we gradually gained the support of women and men in the UN Secretariat. Kristen Timothy, for example, ensured my invitation as co-keynote speaker with Senator Charles Percy at the first conference of the Association for Women in Development (AWID) in 1979. Chief of Administration Kofi Annan, later UN secretary-general, endorsed an internal evaluation that determined the fund's future status. A capable team from the UN regional commissions extended our outreach. The team included Daw Aye of Burma for Asia-Pacific, Vivian Mota of the Dominican Republic for Latin America-Caribbean, Thoraya Obaid of Saudi Arabia for Western Asia, and Mary Tadesse of Ethiopia for Africa. That collaboration in turn pressured the commissions to build their own women's programs.

Women Transform UN Development Policies

Reaching poor women in developing countries necessitated reaching their voluntary groups, but bureaucrats resisted. "We cannot sign agreements with or transfer money to NGOs because the UN is an intergovernmental organization and we transfer to governments," I was reminded by finance officials. "But to reach women we must assist their village groups and savings societies," I countered. After many meetings we negotiated a policy compromise and, by 1985, 50 percent of UNIFEM's partners were NGOs of their own nations.

The finance officials' impatience was compounded after I was told by a young field worker, Dumsile Shiba, that in Swaziland what women needed most was start-up capital for their small businesses, and that a community revolving credit fund they could manage themselves would be an ideal "renewable" form of assistance. In other words, the women would become agents of change rather than victims of circumstance. "We can buy vehicles and pay for experts as we have always done; that is how the UN works," the finance officers said. That issue, too, was resolved, a new administrative policy was put in place; the United Nations Development Programme (UNDP) itself quickly adopted the approach. Today micro-credit funds are a common form of assistance.

Investing in Peoples' Freedom and Well-Being

UNIFEM invested in increasing the freedom and well-being of women worldwide to enrich their families and countries. In Peru, for example, early assistance to the *comedores populares* (community kitchens) that mushroomed in the shanty towns of Lima as women's survival mechanisms against the impact of the global recession and poor national policies attracted other investors despite the assassination of one of its leaders, Maria Elena Moyano. Factory workers became trade union leaders and rural women created networks, mobilized by the Flora Tristan NGO, led by Virginia Vargas. The Peruvian mothers' clubs movement, assisted technically by the local affiliate of ITDG, introduced food-processing technologies and business skills to preserve foods during times of abundance and market them at times of scarcity, an activity soon expanded to neighboring countries with World Bank financing.

UNIFEM cooperated with women who would become world leaders, such as Ela Bhatt, the gentle but steel-strong founder of India's Self Employed Women's Association (SEWA), a remarkable instrument for poor women that is now more than twenty-five years old and spreading worldwide. Ela Bhatt tells how members of their trade union who roll cigarettes, carry headloads, and make pots and pans from scrap, said, "Commercial banks do not want us, so we must have a bank of our own." "How can we own a bank when we are so poor?" she asked. "Because we are so many!" the women replied, in a phrase that should echo in the ears of every feminist. Forty thousand mostly illiterate women soon owned a bank, signing their names with thumbprints until they got plastic "gold cards" with their pictures for identification.

Another world leader with whom UNIFEM cooperated is Wangari Maathai, Africa's foremost environmentalist and founder of the Green Belt Movement, which received its first major financial grant from UNIFEM in 1981. Eight years later, Maathai stood up against the threatened loss of Kenya's urban park, and protested ethnic cleansing in her country. She paid a personal price by being beaten and put in jail because, according to Maathai, organizing ordinary people, poor people, and telling them they can cause positive change in their environment, and they can do it on their own, may appear threatening to the status quo.[7]

UNIFEM also assisted women in strengthening their influence on multi-country economic groups, such as the Southern African Development Community (SADC), starting with their own priority, food security, and supporting technical seminars and policy-oriented women staff within its secretariat. Those actions were the first of what became women's strong political and economic influence in that sub-region.

The Battle of Vienna

Once the money was moving to viable activities in low-income countries, the second policy step was to ensure that the fund remained transparent to representatives of UN member states that either financed or used its resources.

Annual, formal reporting to the General Assembly was not enough; the fund had to stay visible in New York, where all UN member countries have offices. We also needed ready access to the finance offices that transferred out money and to UNDP's and UNICEF's technical expertise. Even though there was just one professional officer (me) at the time, when the UN's Branch for the Advancement of Women was shifted to Vienna, UNIFEM's continuance in New York disturbed some high officials who were determined either to control its grants or to see it dismantled entirely at the end of the Decade for Women. Austria, the East-West buffer state, was angered; it had never made a single contribution to the fund but was determined to fill all its newly constructed Vienna international center offices. As fund director (that title would come later, but I use it here for identification purposes) I came under fire. One bureaucratic tactic to annoy and occupy the time of dissidents like me is to authorize audits and evaluations of their offices; I was seldom free from such time-consuming inspections.

Supported by my wonderfully capable deputy director, Olubanke King-Akerele of Liberia, and our assistant, Kyo Naka of Japan, a third major administrative policy step was taken. UNIFEM's mandate to exist was extended indefinitely and it was moved from the UN proper to the development agency, UNDP, with the intention to remain there until its voluntary contributions were large enough, say $30 million annually, to allow complete autonomy. The move maximized the fund's independence and enabled use of UNDP offices in every developing country. After many late-night sessions, the General Assembly approved the "autonomous association" with UNDP in 1984 in its resolution 39/125, a legal document that to this day is considered exceptionally precise and effective. UNIFEM staff attended the Nairobi conference the following year without fear of fierce fighting over the fund's future. We honored representatives of partner groups at an awards ceremony, the first of many occasions when we brought ordinary rural and poor urban women into the limelight.

Political Violence Against Poor Women

Those internal controversies pale in light of the controversy that made poor women political pawns. The divisiveness over the meaning of "women's issues" that was fended off with the Declaration of Mexico resurfaced in confrontations over whether apartheid and the Israeli-Palestinian issue ought to be discussed at the Second World Conference on Women in Copenhagen in 1980. UNIFEM was yanked into American politics as the scapegoat of those who disapproved of discussing such topics and who pressured the U.S. Congress to cease its voluntary contributions. The United States had initially been the fund's largest donor, thanks to leaders such as the chief U.S. delegate to the Mexico City conference, Pat Hutar, and diplomat and NGO leader Virginia Allen. The fund was guilty by association with the UN, despite the fact that it had not financed the Copenhagen conference and even though, in politically sensitive areas of the world, UNIFEM always co-sponsored activities with UNICEF, which was not selected for punishment. American ambassador to the UN Jeane Kirkpatrick initially urged continuing U.S. contributions, then lost her courage and said, "Our position is to have no position"—hardly a neutral stance by the most powerful country in the world. Hutar, along with NGO representatives Mildred Robbins Leet, Carol Liemas, Norma Levitt, and women leaders from the Jewish community, all of whom disagreed with the U.S. position to withhold contributions on the basis of the discussions of Palestinian issues at Copenhagen, worked tirelessly to reverse the unjust punishment inflicted on the fund and the poor women it served. A congressional contribution to UNIFEM was eventually restored, but at a low level.

That the activities we financed and the views of grassroots women we promoted influenced national, regional, and organizational policies is evident from the six monthly reports we expected, and most often received, on our hundreds of investments. We developed "the UNIFEM system" to generate economic growth while improving peoples' lives through investing in the women who make major contributions to their countries' GDP, that is, the women who create wealth rather than simply demanding its redistribution. We implemented strategies to systematize the inclusion of women and their concerns in the allocation of national resources. We faced the futile and distracting debate over women-specific versus integrated (mainstreaming) activities and institutions by recognizing that both types of investment are needed and that situations must dictate the choice. A seldom-recognized contribution to mainstreaming women's concerns came through the transfer of experienced UNIFEM staff to other organizations, where they become resident coordinators (country chiefs of mission) or senior officers for UNDP and other organizations. They contribute what can sometimes be more important than policy—practical methods for involving women in all activities.

The "Fifth Freedom"—From Bureaucracy

It was time for me to move on once more. I was on my own, grateful for my UN years, but delighted to be free of bureaucratic constraints after nearly four decades of institution building. In Addis Ababa and at UNIFEM I had sensed that we were pioneers of a new global movement, and so I had set aside duplicates of important documents. I was convinced that in a world dominated by communications media controlled by affluent countries, we who were pioneers of that new global movement are obliged to share our experiences, to make its geographically diverse pre-1970s origins known.[8] Mary Tadesse and I wrote the story of the ACW and I wrote the history of UNIFEM's first fifteen years; both volumes tell of the institutions' pioneering influence on policy and action and of the conflicts that arise in the human struggle for power when the system is challenged with new ideas.[9] I went on to share those experiences and learn again from African women as a Fulbright lecturer at the new Department of Women and Gender Studies of the venerable seventy-five-year-old Makerere University in Uganda. The many interviews I did of women in business there are recorded in my most recent book.[10] I am also a member of the African Women and Peace Support Group which produced a book on that tumbled country.

The UN: Guardian and Advocate of the Global Women's Movement

Africa of the 1960s was the start of my own road, an enriching international career. I am in awe of what a few strategically placed persons can accomplish, as the international civil service pioneers of the women's movement did. We helped create a revolution that made women a force, development a women's issue, and the United Nations the guardian and advocate of the global women's movement. Yet I am saddened by my own country's failure to meet its obligations to the UN and by its uncritical promotion of forms of globalization that shatter health care systems, leave little girls standing outside school doors, and stifle fledgling local industries in developing countries. I believe that strong women-specific groups and institutions, such as ACW, UNIFEM, and Women's World Banking, continue to be essential, not only to empower women but also to generate policies and public and private actions to eliminate poverty, foster peace, and promote economic and social justice, for people's freedom and well-being.

The archives of Margaret C. Snyder have been placed with the Public Policy Papers of the Seeley G. Mudd Manuscript Library of Princeton University, Princeton, NJ. These archives include papers on the history of UNIFEM, the UN Development Fund for Women, the African Training and Research Centre for Women of the UN Economic Commission for Africa, and East African Women's Seminars.

Kristen Timothy

Kristen Timothy received a B.A. in political science from Tufts University (1965). She then earned an M.A. in African studies from Makerere University (1968) and an M.P.A. from Harvard's Kennedy School of Government (1980).

Subsequently, she had a thirty-year career at the United Nations, where she combined research on socio-economic development and women's issues with policy making and management. From 1990 to 1992 she was senior program adviser at the UN Development Program (UNDP) in Bangkok, where she helped design a long-term program of technical assistance for Thailand. On returning to the UNDP in New York, she managed a $1 million project development fund. From 1994 to 1999 Timothy served as deputy director of the UN Division for the Advancement of Women and was a key organizer of the UN Fourth World Conference on Women at Beijing in 1995. Her efforts and diplomatic skills helped to ensure participation at the Beijing gathering of over 5,000 women representing NGOs worldwide. Subsequently, she oversaw the adoption of an optional protocol to the Convention on the Elimination of All Forms of Discrimination Against Women (CEDAW), the international women's human rights treaty. In 1999 Timothy joined the National Council for Research on Women as a research scholar, overseeing preparation of a CD-ROM on the United Nations and the international women's movement.

She is a senior consultant with CKL Associates. A member of the Council on Foreign Relations and former president of the Association for Women in Development,

Timothy has published articles and contributed to several books on women rights, development, and the United Nations.

Walking on Eggshells at the UN

Pursuing a dream to see the world, I took Robert Frost's advice and chose what in the 1960s seemed like "the road less traveled by." My journey began in Cheyenne, Wyoming, where, during my senior year, the national high school debate topic was "How to strengthen the United Nations." My debate partner and I developed a case for an international lottery to raise money for the United Nations. We argued that this would give people as well as governments more say in the world organization. We won the Rocky Mountain regional debate championship. We never expected that a similar proposal would be tabled by an African representative in the UN General Assembly two decades later. When I visited the UN as a reward for writing an essay about it for another contest, I decided I wanted to work for this magnificent world organization. But I did not believe then that this part of my dream would come true.

Leaving the security of life on the prairie, I enrolled at Tufts University in Boston, where the civil rights movement captured my interest. I tutored black children in Roxbury and participated in protests in and around Boston. Having had little contact with black Americans while growing up, I was profoundly affected by these experiences. The day I heard a speech by James Robinson, founder of Operation Crossroads Africa, I decided I wanted to go to Africa and work alongside young Africans to build the future for that continent.

In the summer of 1963 I went to Malawi (then Nyasaland), a place many of my friends and family could visualize only as Joseph Conrad's "heart of darkness." My Crossroads group consisted of twelve college students assigned to help construct a secondary school in the birthplace of Nyasaland's president, Kamuzu Banda. Working with local Malawian students, we made bricks out of mud and straw to construct a classroom at what later became the site of a university founded by President Banda.

In our travels in Malawi, we saw women carrying heavy burdens on their heads and babies on their backs, hoeing for long hours in the fields, and selling food in the local markets and at rural clinics and schools. But none of us took more than a passing interest in the special plight of the country's female population. Our group and most Westerners in Malawi focused on economic development. This was in keeping with the dominant paradigm for development in the 1960s, that is, a market-driven economy modeled after an industrial state in which the nuclear family was reinforced by the income structure, with paid labor being performed largely by men. Only later did it become apparent to me that this model assumed that women worked primarily in the home and in subsistence agriculture and that development assistance should be targeted primarily to men.

In 1964 I met David Rubadiri, newly appointed ambassador of Malawi to the United Nations following Malawi's admittance to the UN after independence. A graduate of Makerere University in Uganda, one of Africa's best universities, he encouraged me to enroll in Makerere's master's program in African studies. Filled with idealism and with only a small stipend in my pocket, I went to Uganda and moved into the women's dormitory at Makerere, nicknamed "The Box" because of its architecture. Women students, most of whom had gone to missionary-run secondary schools in Uganda and surrounding countries, constituted only about one-third of the student body.

The interdisciplinary African Studies Program devoted little if any attention to gender. My thesis research focused on the intersections between local-level politics and emerging Ugandan nationalism in the Kigezi district in southern Uganda, where I had excellent access to political leaders at both the local and national levels. As an educated white woman, I was treated as something of a neuter, not subject to the traditional attitudes that defined life for African women. This made it easier for me to gather information on political leadership, including an interview with Prime Minister Milton Obote.

Uganda's colonial experience had not been as violent as the experience in neighboring Kenya. Whites were sought after to contribute to Uganda's modernization process, particularly as teachers, and I sought a job as a secondary school teacher to support myself while I did my thesis research. I went to the ministry of education expecting to meet with a personnel officer; instead I was ushered into the office of the minister, who personally helped find me a job at Kinyansano Boys' Secondary School in Rukungiri, Kigezi.

My interlocutors were local political leaders, all men. Women appeared behind huts and in dusky rooms, tending to fires, pots, and barefoot children who stared shyly at me through the doors or ran after my car as I maneuvered the dusty tracks in the African bush. I was unaware that in neighboring Kenya women were starting to organize themselves and expand their efforts into other countries in the region. It was only my close women friends at Makerere, such as Esther Kimweli, who gave me insights into what it was like to be female in postcolonial East Africa.

I spent three remarkable years in Uganda and then took a job as an associate at the Institute of Social Studies in The Hague while I finished writing my thesis. One of my thesis advisers, Martin Doornbos, had also done research on political development in Uganda. My students at the Institute were middle-level civil servants from developing countries, mainly men; men also constituted the majority of the teaching staff. We examined social development policies and practices, but with little attention to gender.

In 1968 I decided it was time to return to the United States, and in Palo Alto, California, I was drawn into the anti–Vietnam War movement that was tearing the country apart. Working on an underground newspaper, *The Plain Wrapper*, I soon realized that many of the male activists in the movement took women for granted. They expected us to clean, cook, and shop, and gave us low-level jobs on the newspaper—copyediting and copy-pasting. Soon we decided to form a women's collective to organize women factory workers, much to the surprise of many of our liberal anti-war compatriots.

Joining the United Nations

During this period of disenchantment with the male chauvinism and growing militancy of the anti-war movement, I was offered a job at the United Nations. I was seduced by the idea of following my earlier dream, but worried about "selling out," about becoming an insider in a large multilateral bureaucracy, albeit one that stood for social justice and equality. After much soul-searching I decided to take the job, if only for one year. Little did I realize that I would spend thirty years at the UN, become an acknowledged feminist, and help to sustain a place where women could lobby for better treatment and equal rights.

In the Social Affairs Division of the Secretariat I helped design and conduct a correspondence course on social planning for middle-level civil servants from developing countries under the initial leadership of Gloria Scott. We focused on balancing economic planning with social development policies to counter prevailing models that relied primarily on stimulating economic growth without attention to social equity issues. The UN Commission for Social Development (CSD) had begun focusing on social justice in the distribution of resources and opportunities, emphasizing that the benefits of economic growth were not automatically trickling down to the poor as had been predicted by many economists.

In 1972 the interest of the Social Development Commission in social justice converged with the growing focus on women in development at the UN Commission on the Status of Women. Spurred on by members of the Secretariat, such as Margaret Bruce from the United Kingdom, the two commissions sponsored an expert meeting on women in development that stressed the low status of women, especially in developing countries, was as a major factor in global concerns such as poverty, rapid population growth, illiteracy, forced urbanization, and poor nutrition and health conditions. Ester Boserup, the Danish economist, had prepared the background paper for the meeting. She argued that women were being marginalized by advanced agricultural technology and that investment in women would increase the overall efficiency of development efforts. The expert meeting was able to draw on data collected by the CSW in the late 1960s concerning the role of women in socio-economic development plans of UN member states. The research indicated that most governments assumed economic progress would improve women's as well as men's lives. Boserup's research and the results of the expert meeting challenged this assumption.

This new interest in development with social justice led us to deconstruct development beneficiary groups to better understand the needs of different income groups. Our aim was to counter the prevailing tendency to lump together all the targets of development into undifferentiated categories with no regard for gender roles, class interests, or cultural factors—indicators of development that went beyond GNP (gross national product). Other traditional indicators of growth were being developed by scholars such as Irma Adelman and Cynthia Morris.[1] We found this research valuable for exploring the socio-economic and political characteristics of countries and for discussing policy remedies for under development, but we were still handicapped by a dearth of data disaggregated by sex.

In the late 1970s a basic needs approach to development was introduced by the International Labour Organization. This helped focus global attention on the poorest of the poor, a large share of whom were women and girls. It also emphasized the limited benefits from modernization accruing to the poor. Women and poverty was a major topic at the first world conference on women held in Mexico City in 1975, but developing countries objected to the basic needs approach. Those seeking funds for large-scale infrastructure projects giving lower priority to social programs were particularly resistant. The basic needs approach was shelved, disappointing those of us focusing on social justice and equity.

In 1979, discouraged by these developments and the slow pace at which the UN was addressing social issues, I took a study leave and went to the Kennedy School of Government at Harvard, where I was especially interested in the intersections between macro- and microeconomics for socio-economic policy formulation in developing countries. At Harvard I met Kathleen Cloud and Natalie Hahn, both at the Graduate School of Education. A shared feeling of isolation motivated us to find others who were interested in women in development and we started the Harvard-MIT Women in Development Group to put pressure on Harvard's development institute and other parts of the university to devote attention to women.

The success of the Harvard-MIT group helped to inspire the founding in 1982 of the Association for Women in Development (AWID). After returning to the UN Division for the Advancement of Women in 1980, I served on the AWID board and was elected president in 1987. As president, my goal was to transform AWID from a volunteer organization into one with staff and a viable budget. Spurred on by board members Joyce Moock of the Rockefeller Foundation and Adrienne Germain of the International Women's Health Coalition, we developed a financial plan, hired paid employees, and instituted a forum series, beginning with a discussion of the pros and cons of gender mainstreaming that took place not long after the concept surfaced at the international level.

The supportive atmosphere of AWID helped in my UN research on women and in coming to grips with sex discrimination at the UN, where sexual harassment was widespread. I once told Barbara Crossette, a reporter for the *New York Times,* that working at the United Nations was like walking on eggshells. Women professionals were very much in the minority when I went to work for the organization and this did not change quickly. Women constituted only 20 percent of the professional staff as late as 1988, an increase of only 3.6 per cent over 1984 levels. Between the early 1970s, when the first surveys of women in the UN were carried out, and 1984, women had remained at around seventeen percent of the professional staff. We had to deal with the male chauvinisms of the world, from countries as diverse as Iran and France. We grumbled about harassment, but found little institutional recourse until October 1992, when the extent of the problem was acknowledged and an administrative instruction was circulated, laying out procedures for recourse. The multicultural and ethnic mix at the UN, and the sensitive nature of issues, made even the use of humor to deflect tension difficult. It required treading with extreme care, and having both a thick skin and endless patience.

Like many working women of my generation, I have been torn between my professional and private lives. UN jobs require frequent travel and long hours, often incompatible with sustaining personal relationships and family life. Among UN women professionals the divorce rate is high, with many women opting to remain single. My first marriage in 1970 ended in divorce, but in 1984 I married a colleague, Charles Lankester, who worked for the UN Development Program and was sensitive to the demands of a UN career. In 1985, just months before the third United Nations Conference on Women, our daughter Kathryn was born. Anne Walker, director of the International Women's Tribune Center, proclaimed her our mini-feminist on a T-shirt produced for the occasion. Little touches like that sustain UN women.

But role models for young professional women at the UN in the 1970s on handling family-work challenges and on getting ahead in the organization were few. No women had held senior positions above the level of director until Secretary-General Kurt Waldheim appointed Helvi Sipila as assistant secretary-general in 1972. Sipila helped raise the profile of women at the UN. She pressed for International Women's Year and for a conference to mark the year.

Global Women's Conferences

In 1980, in preparation for the Copenhagen Conference, I went straight from the Kennedy School to work with the conference committee that negotiated the final agreement on language in the conference document on women refugees and witnessed the lengthy debates on the inclusion of the words "sexism" and "Zionism" the final agreement. A few years later, in preparation for the Third World Conference on Women in Nairobi, I worked on the draft of Forward-Looking Strategies for the Advancement of Women to the Year 2000 (FLS). One of the dilemmas during this drafting was how to treat specific groups of women—the disabled, migrants, abused women, and young and elderly women. Leticia Shahani of the Philippines, secretary-general for the conference, proposed a section called "Areas of Special Concern" that became the focus for interest groups trying to incorporate language on behalf of special groups of women. This resulted in one hundred additional paragraphs in the negotiating text. (See Leticia Shahani's essay in this volume.)

At Nairobi in 1985 I worked with Ambassador Rosario Manalo of the Philippines, who was chairperson of the committee where the "Areas of Special Concern," introductory chapters, and the section on international and regional cooperation were negotiated. The committee was sequestered in the basement of the Kenyatta International Conference Center, where it went through the draft text paragraph by paragraph, eventually resolving everything except references to the Declaration of Mexico, which had references to Zionism as racism.

Early in the negotiations, which were conducted in an open-ended working group with all delegates having the same right to contribute, it was clear that the negotiating blocs were facing grave difficulties in arriving at consensus on a number of issues. It seemed that women's issues did not easily lend themselves to the same type of negotiating structures as did other issues at the UN. The developing country bloc, called the Group of 77, sought to break the impasse by informally meeting in smaller, regional groups in hopes of reaching agreement on controversial women's issues. The hope was that countries with similar cultural and political interests might be able to find common ground.

As the last day of the conference approached, there was serious concern that political issues would undermine the women's agenda. Key paragraphs were still in brackets and some countries, including the United States, were threatening to block consensus on the document as a whole. Determined to avert a crisis and an inconclusive ending, I invited a number of delegates to breakfast to discuss strategy. Committed women, such as Maureen O'Neil of Canada and Laetitia Van Den Assum from the Netherlands, were equally concerned about a potential failure. We agreed to mobilize women delegates in a last ditch effort to prevent the conference from being held hostage to wider political disputes.

That night, as the conference was due to end, the tension in the plenary was palpable. At nine o'clock, with no agreement in sight on the contentious paragraph where the term "Zionism" had been included as in reference to one of the obstacles to the advancement of women, the chairperson, Margaret Kenyatta, suspended the meeting. In the interim Kenyan officials, members of the UN Secretariat, and key delegations kept the telephone lines humming and the back rooms buzzing as they tried to find a way around the stalemate. When delegates reconvened several hours later, Kenyatta called for the vote on paragraph 94, deleting "Zionism" from the text and substituting "all other forms of racism and racial discrimination." Quickly surveying the room, Kenyatta brought down her gavel before any objections could be raised.

We left Nairobi filled with the realization that the truly global feminist movement which had been born during the Decade for Women was christened at Nairobi. Nearly 15,000 women came from all regions of the world, including an estimated 5,000 from Africa. Until the Nairobi conference, the term "feminism" was rarely heard at international governmental meetings. It was associated with bra-burning Western feminists with whom women and men from developing countries had not identified. But thanks to groups like Development Alternatives Women for a New Era (DAWN), women from developing countries had also been asserting their own brand of feminism and were prepared to join a global feminist movement that also articulated their views. (For additional information on DAWN see Peggy Antrobus's essay in this volume.)

Inspired by the Nairobi experience but frustrated by the obstacles to breaking into the senior ranks at the UN, I successfully sought election as president of the Group on Equal Rights for Women (previously known as the Ad Hoc Group for Women) in 1989. The group is an informal staff lobbying group for affirmative action inside the Secretariat that has been a critical pressure group since Patricia Tsien founded it in 1971. At its outset, the group advocated for 25 percent professional women in the UN ranks and promotion of more women into high-level positions. One of the group's most significant achievements was winning agreement to override seniority requirements when deciding on promotions for women, that is, letting women jump the queue if they had languished for a long time at one level. This opened up possibilities for promoting women at a pace comparable to the rate for men.

In 1990 I wanted a chance to serve the organization outside of its New York headquarters. In a rare two-career move, I was assigned to the UN Development Programme (UNDP) Office for Thailand as a senior program adviser and my husband was seconded by UNDP to head up the Mekong River Basin secretariat. While in Bangkok, I was able to put WID principles into action. In formulating the five-year program of UNDP assistance for Thailand, I worked closely with UNIFEM's representative based there, Linda Miranda of the Philippines, to ensure that gender was integrated into UNDP's five-year funding for Thailand.

After my husband and I returned to New York I joined, in 1993, the newly formed secretariat for the Fourth World Conference on Women scheduled for Beijing. Secretary-General Boutros Boutros-Ghali had appointed Ambassador Gertrude Mongella from Tanzania to head up conference preparations. One of our tasks was to prepare a draft text for the Commission on the Status of Women to review as a first step toward the Beijing Platform for Action.

Mongella and I organized a roundtable discussion in October at the end of the AWID conference, inviting about fifteen conference participants from various regions to give their thoughts on what should go into this draft text. It was our idea to develop a logical framework for the negotiating text that would draw on the latest research on women's issues and on experience with concrete strategies to achieve gender mainstreaming and equal rights for women. A second brainstorming was held in early December. Caroline Moser of the World Bank had published a book in 1993 on gender planning in which she examined ways to develop policies to address both the practical and strategic needs of women.[2] We invited Moser, along with a number of other experts on gender, including Wafas Ofosu-Amaah of Ghana, and Rose Arungu-Olende of Kenya, to meet with our staff. Also invited by Mongella were Roxanna Carillo from UNIFEM, Abraham Joseph from the UN Secretariat, and Mallika Vajrathon from the UN Fund for Population Activities.

At this meeting we discussed ways to structure the initial draft of the Platform for Action, taking into account the suggestions made by the Commission on the Status of Women earlier that year. In addition to identifying eight critical areas of concern, the CSW had created five slogans or titles of campaigns: share power equally; full access to the means of development; overcome poverty; promote peace and defend women's human rights; and inspire a new generation of women and men working together for equality. We envisioned an approach that would portray women not as victims but as empowered actors. We recognized that the slogans represented a combination of women's practical and strategic needs. But the slogans did not in the end receive sustained support in the CSW as preparations moved forward. Some countries did not endorse the idea of campaigns. They were considered too narrow to address all of the actions required to achieve women's equality. Countries at different stages in improving the lives of women and girls preferred to address a wide variety of problems, ranging, for example, from female genital mutilation to female feticide, from equal wages to recognition of sexual preferences and women in decision making.

When I joined the conference secretariat, I was told that the draft negotiating text would be only about ten pages long and limited to eight areas of concern. Before we finished, there were twelve critical areas of concern and a negotiating text of more than 300 paragraphs covering every aspect of women's lives from cradle to grave.

The CSW looked at the draft of the negotiating text for the Platform for Action for the first time in January 1994 in New York and this meeting was tempestuous. The draft did not reflect the results of the early secretariat brainstorming sessions but rather came out of later consultations chaired personally by Mongella. The CSW working group was not satisfied with the results of those meetings and requested that a new draft be prepared for the full CSW meeting in March, giving little guidance on content. Tension around the draft Platform for Action continued throughout the preparations for the conference as different groups, ranging from radical feminist to the religious right, tried to influence it.

The text that was eventually agreed to at the conference by consensus was adopted by some countries with serious reservations. A number of countries, along with the Vatican, recorded their reservations on matters such as women's right to control their sexuality, parental rights, and the use of the term "gender." Some delegations objected to language on sexual identity and language that conflicted with the Islamic Sharia. Still others objected to text on women's right to own and inherit land. Such reservations led to further disagreement.

While other members of the conference secretariat assisted the negotiations on the draft text during the conference, I was responsible for NGO access and for the side events—panels and roundtables on topics relevant to the conference—organized for delegates and NGOs by the UN specialized agencies and programs. Additional funds for space and interpretation arranged with the cooperation of Arthur Holcombe, the UNDP representative in China, with whom we worked closely, made these events possible.

The immense interest and participation in the Beijing conference and its preparations came as a surprise to many senior UN officials. At early meetings Mongella and I were often met with disbelief when we suggested that the conference was likely to attract more participants than any other UN event up to that time. The staggering numbers also came as a surprise to the NGO organizing committee, and more important, to the Chinese hosts. The conference and its parallel NGO Forum '95 held at Huairou, just outside Beijing, attracted nearly 50,000 persons, primarily women, from all regions of the world. Thousands more were active in regional and other preparatory meetings, or followed the conference on the Internet. The conference also offered a rare chance for many to visit China. For opponents of Chinese policies, notably its one-child policy, its policies on Tibet and Taiwan, and its human rights record, the conference provided an excuse to engage in China bashing. Petitions of all kinds were directed to the UN objecting to Chinese policies and to issues before the conference, such as abortion and sexual orientation. Most of these petitions ended up in my office.

From the beginning, I was committed to making the conference as open and accessible as possible. I believed that it was important to create a sense of ownership, not only by governments, but also by NGOs. The women's movement had started as a grassroots movement and women's NGOs had grown in numbers and influence over the twenty years since the Mexico City conference. The goal to ensure the widest possible participation by women NGOs in the official government conference was carried out at the expense of many sleepless nights.

One of my tasks was to oversee the accreditation of nongovernmental organizations to the government conference. This proved to be a highly politicized exercise in which resistance to certain NGO groups was pitted against arguments for universal access. More than just the women's confer ence was at stake. Governments were concerned about the broader question of NGO participation in the work of the UN in general, and each global conference tested the possibilities in this regard. Accreditation to the women's conference was particularly complex because of the diverse nature of the constituency. Women are not a homogeneous group, but represent a wide spectrum of political and religious views as well as race, ethnicity, and class.

In the end, 4,000 representatives of 2,500 organizations participated at the official conference, representing diverse interests and perspectives. This was achieved only after many backroom meetings of a small contact group of the Commission on the Status of Women, followed by meetings at the Economic and Social Council under the skilled chairmanship of Ambassador Ahmad Kamal of Pakistan. It was at the council that what I call a "devil's pact" on accreditation of NGOs was made. Trading off the interests of such countries as China, Iran, and the United States, members of the Economic and Social Council voted on which NGOs could be accredited. In the end, all countries participating in these negotiations seemed equally unhappy; only then was it possible to agree on the final list of NGOs.

Turnout at the conference would not have been so great without the energy, commitment, and perseverance of the NGOs themselves and the desire of our Chinese hosts for a successful event. In the end, the Beijing conference went a long way toward advancing the women's movement and raised the profile of the United Nations among women worldwide.

In 1995, after recovering from the exhaustion brought on by the confer-ence, I began working energetically on the follow up to increase accountabil-ity and develop alliances between and among the secretariat, government delegates, and NGOs to help put the Beijing recommendations into practice both inside and outside the UN. For example, I worked to ensure the regu-larization of the interagency group on women under the Administrative

Committee on Coordination (ACC), a valuable network of focal points on women and gender from the specialized agencies and other parts of the UN system. This interagency group had been relegated to the status of an ad hoc group of the ACC for over twenty years. After considerable effort it was made a standing committee of the ACC in 1996, a decision precipitated by pressure from the Beijing conference.

The new information technologies were important in the success of the Beijing conference and demonstrated the potential of the Internet in providing timely information about the UN and its efforts to advance the international agenda for women in development and women's rights. Under my supervision, and with the enthusiasm of Oliva Acosta of Spain, the Web site, WomenWatch (www.un.org/womenwatch), was initiated as a joint undertaking of the UN Division for the Advancement of Women (DAW), UNIFEM, and the International Research and Training Institute for the Advancement of Women (INSTRAW). We also succeeded in retaining within the division the servicing of the committee monitoring the Convention on the Elimination of All Forms of Discrimination Against Women (CEDAW).

The Beijing platform had succeeded in linking separate movements, that is, women in development and women's human rights. I felt it was critical to bring these movements closer together, and saw an opportunity to do so by keeping the CEDAW committee under the UN Division for the Advancement of Women, which also dealt with women in development through the Commission on the Status of Women. That meant derailing a proposal to transfer CEDAW to the High Commission for Human Rights in Geneva, a move that would have risked untying important threads in the Platform for Action and would have been a missed opportunity for the international women's movement.

Privileged during my career to have touched the lives of many women in developed and developing countries alike, I am proud to have contributed toward advancing the cause of women in development and achieving worldwide recognition of the need for gender equality.

PART II

New Ideas, New Organizations

Irene Tinker

Irene Tinker has divided her career between university teaching and action-research with nonprofit organizations. She was on the faculty of Howard University, Federal City College, American University, and the University of California at Berkeley. To date she has conducted research in fifty-six countries and lectured in thirty-six.

Tinker was director of the Office of International Science at the American Association for the Advancement of Science, where Margaret Mead taught her about lobbying the United Nations. She co-founded the Wellesley Center for Research on Women and founded the International Center for Research on Women and the Equity Policy Center.

Ultimately, she seeks to influence policy. She began her political education by giving out campaign literature when she was nine, and ran unsuccessfully for the Maryland state legislature in 1966. After holding a presidential appointment during the Carter administration, she decided she could influence policy better from outside the government.

She studied government at Radcliffe College and the London School of Economics, writing her doctoral dissertation on the first general elections in India. Tinker drove from London to New Delhi with colleagues, then drove back with her recently acquired husband through Africa. From 1957–59, she studied elections in Indonesia, where their son was born. They also have two daughters. In 2002 she and her husband celebrated their fiftieth wedding anniversary in New Delhi, where they had married.

Challenging Wisdom, Changing Policies: The Women in Development Movement

Women's "yellow pages" listed nearly 300 women's groups in Washington, D.C., in the early 1970s, more than in any other city in the world. The ferment stirred up by the second wave of the women's movement brought professional women together into a myriad of new organizations and networks. In New York City, feminist writers and artists promoted separate spheres for women to counter patriarchy in magazines, radio, and television. In contrast, we women in Washington worked with the government to change laws and regulations to improve the lives of women.

The first national Women's Commission, convened by President John F. Kennedy in 1961 and headed by Esther Peterson, identified causes of inequality in the states. We lobbied Congress for change, testified at hearings despite the lack of good data, and marched in support of the Equal Rights Amendment to the U.S. Constitution.[1] Issues we addressed included equal pay, equal access to professional schools, part-time work, and training programs for "displaced housewives" who had bought into the myth of male support in marriage. Groups were formed to demand funding for rape counseling centers and to advocate improved health services.[2]

We felt empowered. During those halcyon days, equality of women under the law moved closer to reality. The women's movement spread throughout the United States as states and some cities set up their own commissions on the status of women. Press coverage of women's events, which began as derisive, became more sympathetic and soon even the international press was reporting about the accomplishments of the newly energized women's movement.

Back to Asia

During much of this time, I was teaching comparative government at two predominantly black colleges, Howard University and Federal City College (now the University of the District of Columbia), and managing my household of three young children and their father with considerable help from my mother-in-law. Choosing to work in these institutions reflected my commitment to civil rights, but also the limited opportunities for women in university departments of political science. The ingrained prejudices my black colleagues endured forced me to examine my own status of white educated female and to understand both the privileges and limitations of that background. While the black bourgeoisie welcomed me, the black nationalists made it clear that I had no place in their revolution.[3]

I needed to update my international skills if I were to teach elsewhere. Economic development assistance for the developing countries was at its height; projects were expected to raise the gross domestic product of the country, with improved livelihood trickling down to the poor. My earlier research in India (1952) and Indonesia (1957–59) had focused on elections and legislatures. It was time to study the impact of development on the lives of the people. So in 1972 I returned to Indonesia to investigate its rapid urbanization and the explosion of squatter settlements.

While in Jakarta I was asked to talk about the U.S. women's movement. In order to set our change in context, I needed to relate it to women in Indonesia. Yet almost nothing was written about women outside anthropological ethnographies. I began quizzing the Indonesian professional women I met about their own experiences; I began to talk to wives at receptions, something I had usually avoided on the assumption that housewives were not interesting. What I learned was that independence had brought a period of expanding opportunities for women that was increasingly being narrowed as the growing middle class demanded jobs for its sons. Soon the Indonesian government was promoting motherhood as the ideal female occupation, despite the traditional roles of women as entrepreneurs and farmers. This conservative attitude toward women was being legitimized by actions of the development community that was exporting the same belief system we women at home were trying to change.

Was modernization actually hurting women? Was the promise of progress being turned on its head? I had grown up in a scientific family where progress and technology were considered unquestionably good, so to me the realization that development was having an adverse impact on women was incendiary and it has shaped my life ever since. Indeed, the movement called women in development (WID) brought together into a single focus key strands of my life: my predilection to organize friends for a purpose, my conviction all that people are equal, my belief that ideas could influence actions, and my curiosity about the world.

Uniting the Strands of My Life

By the age of eight I was organizing kids in the neighborhood to form an acting group when the boys told me I could no longer play softball with them. At twelve, when the Girl Scout leader refused to start a Sea Scout troop so we could sail on the Delaware River, I found a sympathetic woman to head the new troop. Before my junior year in high school, we moved to Wilmington, Delaware. The public school system was segregated and weak, offering little academic challenge, so I reorganized student government elections and arranged school dances for the teenaged service men home on leave during World War II. More controversial was the social I organized for students from the four "Ys": the YWCA, YMCA, YMHA, and the

Colored Y. My photo made the front pages of the local newspaper. This commitment to civil rights stayed with me when teaching at two predominantly black colleges in Washington, D.C, and participating in the 1963 Mississippi summer voter registration campaign.

My college years at Radcliffe were an intellectual treat; the choral society was an inspiration, and I met talented poets and writers when we started a co-ed literary magazine. To raise money for it, I even organized a fashion show for *Mademoiselle* magazine the fall after I was one of their college editors. Only Spanish class gave me trouble. Despite having done badly on my college board exam, I had insisted on taking second-year Spanish; only the good will of the teacher allowed me to pass. By then I had learned you could pass the language requirements for graduation by taking a test. So after working for two months as a waitress at Stouffer's in New York City, where I had worked the summer before, I took a bus and a train to Mexico City. Several marriage proposals later I bussed home again, memorizing word cards on the way, and passed the test.

This Mexican foray underscored my ignorance about the rest of the world. Harvard offered few courses dealing with contemporary foreign countries outside Europe. In Rupert Emerson's course on nationalism we read Nehru's *Autobiography;* five years later Nehru granted me a Sunday morning interview in New Delhi. A new course students called "rice paddies" introduced me to China and Japan; only many years later did I visit Shanghai, where my husband was born. When Harold Laski, a frequent visitor at the home of my mentor, Perry Miller, urged me to come to the London School of Economics (LSE) for graduate work, I went.

The international atmosphere in London was intoxicating; my lack of knowledge about the non-Western world was palpable. Politics were also exciting. I planned to study elections and the British Parliament; when the second postwar elections were called for the spring of 1950, LSE emptied as we all campaigned. Laski caught pneumonia and died; without his dominant presence, political science at LSE lost its edge. Besides, finding a new angle for my dissertation was difficult. Why not study how British institutions functioned in India? For a year I immersed myself in Indian history and politics while arranging, with two colleagues, to drive a tiny Ford Anglia to New Delhi across the Middle East in order to experience life in the countries we passed through. The atmosphere in those countries is uncannily reflected in many contemporary crises: unrest in Macedonia, tension in Jerusalem, international fights over oil, a nationalist government in Iran, and fighters on the streets of Kabul.

In India I followed election commissioners around the country from north to south as they held elections state by state; I observed and studied the great democratic experience of India's first general elections of 1952. Running low on money, I began looking for a job, but instead found a husband, Millidge Walker, who was working at the U.S. embassy. In the summer of 1953 we returned to London via Africa, driving in a new Austin from Mombasa around East Africa, then north to Cairo and across the desert to Tunis before taking a ferry to Italy. Colonial Africa was stirring; I met many leaders through my reporting for the Calcutta *Statesman*. Roads were worse than in the Middle East, and violence was simmering everywhere. Driving that route would be impossible today.

After receiving my doctoral degree from LSE, we drove the Austin through France, Spain, and Morocco and then from New York to Berkeley, California, where I worked with the Modern India Project while my husband studied for his doctorate. His research took us to Indonesia for two years; in 1960 his teaching position at the American University moved us to Washington, D.C. In 1965, three kids in tow, we revisited South and Southeast Asia.

Despite all this exposure to developing countries, I hardly thought about women as women; we are all equal, are we not? I had interviewed women members of parliament and leaders of political organizations, including Indira Gandhi. These were strong elite women, active in their independence movements. Gradually such women were eased out as the more conservative middle-class culture with its traditional view of women's roles, exploited nationalism to gain political power. Today, women are finding their own turf by founding women's organizations.

Origins of Women in Development

When I returned to Washington in 1972, I brought together women who had also been in the field to discuss this detrimental impact of development on women; we formed a women's caucus of the Society for International Development (SID) called Women in Development. Pushpa Schwartz and Patricia Blair, editors of the *Development Digest*, decided to publish summaries of the growing literature on the topic, including Ester Boserup's book, *Woman's Role in Economic Development*, which had just become available in the United States. Her work, and works of other authors, substantiated our belief that Western forms of development, whether colonial or aid programming, were undercutting women's traditional economic activities.

Boserup traced the impact of increased population on agricultural technology, which in turn altered agricultural systems in which women and men played distinct roles, and fashioned an historical theory of stages of economic development. Our activist group focused on changing the way economic development projects were undercutting women's livelihoods. The concept of women in development, once you think about it, is simple. It recognizes that globally most women, especially poor women, work. But this economic value of women's work was overlooked because subsistence and farming activities, such as fetching water or fuelwood, working in the fields, or processing food, are not paid and so are not included in national accounts. In cities, women selling street foods or working as domestic servants are not counted either, though they do earn money. So the economists looked at statistical data that made women's work invisible, and they focused their economic assistance projects entirely on men. Too often these programs also undercut women's ability to work and provide for their families. We set out to challenge this conventional wisdom and change international development policies.

The WID group organized a series of panels at the 1973 Costa Rica meeting of SID. Because we had missed the official application process for presentations, our three panels were scheduled at night. This turned out to be a benefit since no other panels competed with ours. Men as well as women attended, and once they realized that development programs affected women and men differently, the audience was convinced of the need for new approaches and projects that reached women specifically.

The Percy Amendment

The next major event, in the fall of 1973, was at the Department of State. Virginia Allan, then the highest-ranking woman in the Department of State, convened a briefing on International Women's Year in her capacity as the deputy assistant secretary of state for public affairs. This was routine, but not the fact that she added leaders of women's organizations around the country to the usual list of academics and journalists concerned with international affairs. Typical of such meetings, State Department officials lectured us about the United Nations, U.S. foreign policy, and the UN's International Women's Year and conference with its three themes: equality, development, and peace. The audience grew restless. Women in these new egalitarian organizations were used to interacting and criticizing; leadership was suspect. Finally, a woman from out of town, rejecting the niceties of the setting, blurted out her complaint, punctuated with four letter words, that State was putting us on, that there would be no time for discussion. The shock of her words was palpable. Allan rose to the occasion, saying that everyone who wished to talk would be able to; the meeting would continue several hours beyond the scheduled close and would meet again at 8:00 a.m. if necessary. The next morning my turn came to expound on the "detrimental impact of development on women."

Meeting with Allan later that day were Mildred Marcy, head of the U.S. Information Agency women's programs, and Clara Beyer, a venerable civil servant on loan to State from the Labor Department. Aware that Congress was at that moment debating a foreign assistance bill that would refocus development policy from infrastructure development toward basic human needs of people, Beyer asked Marcy if something about women could not be added to the bill. This germ of an idea eventually became law in a manner I now recognize as typical but which did not fit anything I had been taught in political science textbooks. Marcy, encouraged by her husband, the chief of staff for the Senate Foreign Relations Committee, drafted an appropriate paragraph requiring that women should be integrated into all the new basic needs programs detailed in the foreign assistance bill, then considered which Republican senator (since a Republican administration was in power) might be willing to introduce an amendment and spoke to Scott Cohen, Senator Charles Percy's foreign relations assistant. It was Cohen who reminded Percy, as he was rushing for a plane on Friday, October 2, 1973, that he had promised to introduce the amendment. His colleagues, aware that no appropriations were called for and perceiving the bill as a gesture to women, passed the amendment by voice vote.

The entire foreign assistance bill was passed later in the day and was sent to conference committee. The Percy Amendment was not in the House of Representatives version. To publicize the need for the amendment, Arvonne Fraser, a committed feminist and activist who had been at the State Department briefing, convinced her husband, Representative Donald Fraser, head of the House Foreign Affairs Subcommittee on International Organizations and Movements, to add a session on the status of women to a series of hearings he had already scheduled on the international protection of human rights. The speaker who preceded me, the head of the Department of Labor's Women's Bureau, Carmen Maymi, had just returned from a tour of Africa and was appalled that official statistics showed that only 5 percent of women there were in the labor force. The contrast between such national data, counting only women working in the formal labor force, and the reality of African women subsistence farmers, who raise some 80 percent of the food for the continent, clearly illustrated the need for the amendment, as I quickly pointed out.

The conference committee, thinking of the amendment as "apple pie and motherhood," threw it out. Two types of lobbying saved it: political pressure and information. Mildred Marcy alerted Virginia Allan, then in Hawaii at a convention of the Business and Professional Women, who encouraged these BPW women from all over the country to deluge Congress with telegrams. Marcy herself was active in the League of Women Voters and stirred up more support. That these were mainstream women's organizations was critical as they were harder to ignore than the more strident newer women's groups who were already busy trying to defeat the Hyde amendment that prohibited the use of USAID funds for abortion use abroad. Lower key, but critical to increasing support for the amendment, were the calls I made to staff of every member of the conference committee to explain how current policies were unfair to women while the amendment would make foreign assistance programs more equitable. All this lobbying was successful; the amendment was reinstated, and Senator Percy became a staunch supporter of WID. In 1974 he introduced a similar resolution into the UN General Assembly and headed the delegation to the first UN conference for women in Mexico City in 1975.

He assigned one of his staff, Julia Chang Bloch, to oversee the implementation of the amendment in USAID; subsequently, when Bloch held high-level posts in USAID and served as U.S. ambassador to Nepal, she remained a strong WID advocate.

Going International

In January 1974 I was appointed a U.S. delegate to the UN Commission on the Status of Women meeting in New York City as an adviser specializing in development. Arvonne Fraser was also an adviser but on domestic issues. We were quickly immersed both in the planning for the 1975 International Women's Year (IWY) and conference as well as in UN politics and procedures.[4] The clarity of the WID argument, buttressed by the Expert Committee Report of 1972 on women and economic development that Gloria Scott had organized, not only influenced the Plan of Action for the IWY conference but also resulted in resolutions for integrating women into development programs being introduced into working plans of most of the UN agencies in addition to the General Assembly. (See Scott, this volume)

At both UN world conferences held in 1974, one on population and one on food, women formed ad hoc groups to draft and lobby for additional paragraphs about women in the respective Plans of Action. At every subsequent world conference, women with increasing sophistication inserted language concerning women's work and responsibilities into the appropriate sections; I personally attended three of these conferences: on population in 1974, on science and technology in 1979, and on new and renewable energy in 1981. I was also an NGO representative at all the four UN world conferences for women (1975, 1980, 1985, and 1995). At all seven conferences I participated in panels at the NGO Forums and lobbied delegates at the official conferences.

In direct policy terms, I believe that women's concerns are most readily accepted by the global political establishment when arguments are made in specific terms. Energy and environmental specialists understood the critical activities of women in collecting and burning firewood and responded with new forestry plans and new types of cookstoves. Agriculturalists began to introduce new crop varieties to women. In contrast, debates on women's concerns at women's conferences were often manipulated by the male power structure pursuing a political agenda.[5] However, women's conferences, especially the NGO Forums, provided a marvelous space to meet and exchange ideas with women from every country in the world. The networks formed at these meetings promoted the global women's movement that has influenced all levels of society more profoundly than any other social movement in the twentieth century.

AAAS Seminar in Mexico City

In 1972 I became the first director of international science at the American Association for the Advancement of Science (AAAS). Working with a committee of eminent scholars headed by Margaret Mead, we produced a report on the cultural aspects of population change for the population conference that influenced population policy and research for many years. Mead took me with her to Bucharest to help present the findings at the UN conference and NGO forum, projecting a vivid illustration of the power of ideas.

This experience convinced me that AAAS should produce a similar report for the International Women's Year conference. Compared with the extensive literature available on population, there was a dearth of data on the impact of development on women for the staff to review. To add to this literature, I proposed that AAAS sponsor a pre-conference seminar on WID for which we would produce an annotated bibliography and the idea was enthusiastically supported by Mead, then president of AAAS.[6]

Seeking funding for the seminar, I turned for advice to the few women staff members of major foundations in New York City. Joan Dunlop at the John D. Rockefeller Fund organized a gathering of funders where I could meet them all at one time. These women were marvelously supportive; many attended and contributed to the seminar. The United Nations Development Programme and the United Nations Institute for Training and Research became co-sponsors of the seminar and provided both recent studies on women and invaluable advice. They rightly insisted that the seminar must have simultaneous interpretation, despite the cost, and—warning of inevitable political posturing—suggested tight scheduling, especially for the final plenary meeting. Their suggestions helped the Seminar on Women in Development avoid the acrimony that characterized many subsequent meetings on the topic. Sponsorship by AAAS, a well-known international scientific organization, added to the prestige of the seminar; the AAAS counterpart in Mexico, the Mexican National Council of Science and Technology, assisted in local arrangements.

In Washington I hired a Danish scholar, Michéle Bo Bramson, to head the project. She in turn gathered a team of recent graduates to collect and summarize all available literature. Lead researcher Mayra Buvinic prepared the annotations for publication. Once the project was over, this invaluable collection was moved to the International Center for Research on Women (ICRW), which I had founded in 1976 to monitor the implementation of the Percy Amendment.[7] Buvinic also joined the ICRW, where she provided outstanding leadership as director for twenty years.

What is hard to comprehend in this day of instant communications is the difficulty we had in identifying participants for the seminar, whom we wished to be representative of all regions of the world. Michéle and I contacted women's organizations, professional associations, foundations, and government agencies as well as our funders and co-sponsors for names and addresses. We cross-checked names as many references consisted only of a name. The official invitation was sent by mail; the letter stated that each participant was expected to provide a five-page case study that would then be translated for distribution in French, Spanish, and English; several eminent scholars wrote background papers to lead the discussions. Eventually, ninety-eight women and men from fifty-five countries arrived in Mexico City to attend the seminar held during the week preceding the UN's First World Conference for Women in 1975.

Influencing Policy

The impact of the seminar was immediate. Background papers and workshop reports were distributed at both the official UN conference and the NGO Tribune. Ten of the participants were on official delegations while over thirty gave presentations at the Tribune. Several recommendations of the workshops were incorporated in the World Plan of Action, the official document of the conference. Notable among these were provisions concerning women's access to credit, a concept now at the heart of most poverty alleviation programs worldwide. Esther Ocloo, a dynamic businesswoman from Ghana whom I called the "marmalade queen" because she began selling orange squash and marmalade, was a passionate advocate of the need for credit and became a founding board member of Women's World Banking. The provision that the number of women in national delegations to the UN and other international forums be increased was quickly implemented, but another critical provision stressing the importance of incorporating women's needs into urban and housing plans still requires much greater support. The seminar made delegates aware of the need for further research on women and they established the International Research and Training Instituted for the Advancement of Women (INSTRAW). A fund for women, later named the United Nations Development Fund for Women (UNIFEM), was also set up to provide funding for women's organizations at the local level. UNIFEM has become a major center for international women's activity and documentation. (For additional discussion of UNIFEM see the essay by Margaret Snyder in this volume.)

Because raising funds for research is less compelling than assisting poor women, INSTRAW has struggled to find its place in the UN hierarchy, despite that fact that it is the only women's organization with a seat in the General Assembly. I was a member of the first board of directors and have continued to consult with that organization. Some years later I set up the U.S. Council for INSTRAW to publicize its activities and increase its funding from the US government.

Influencing Development Programming

To this point in my life I had acted as journalist and scholar—interviewing, studying, writing. I thought that if bureaucrats were provided with significant information about how their projects were adversely affecting women, they would immediately alter their approach and change their projects. A brief stint in government as a presidential appointee under President Jimmy Carter, serving as assistant administrator for research at ACTION, the US Agency for Voluntary Service, convinced me otherwise. As committed as I am to incorporating women's concerns into policies and projects, I had great difficulty in influencing policies in this small agency that then encompassed the Peace Corps, Volunteers in Service to America (VISTA), and other volunteer activities. Convinced that my comparative advantage was working outside government, I resigned and set up an action-research center, the Equity Policy Center (EPOC), designed to consider the needs of men as well as women and to be involved in evaluating and implementing projects.

At EPOC we followed the vicissitudes of development policy. Demands for short-term results led many development agencies to pursue the "flavor of the month" trying to find new solutions for new issues. The various UN world conferences often supplied these new issues. Wherever possible we supplied a women's viewpoint—to technology or energy, to health or housing—presenting papers and reports at UN and scholarly meetings, inserting paragraphs about women at the topical UN world conferences and consulting on actual projects dealing with these issues. Underlying most of women's needs for appropriate technology or improved cookstoves is their shortage of time; women everywhere work a double day, working for money or subsistence and then coming home to their household responsibilities. Many add to the strain on their time by caring for the elderly or organizing for community improvement. Efforts by many nongovernmental organizations (NGOs) abroad to increase women's income were based on sewing or knitting skills perhaps appropriate in the West but unknown to African farmers or Asian rice growers. These craft activities seldom provided adequate income return for the time worked.

So I determined to study how women were actually making money. Selling food in public places was ubiquitous in developing countries, but such "snack" food was disregarded as income. I coined a new term, and started a fifteen-year study of Street Foods.

Street Foods

Once again, I challenged conventional wisdom, and significantly changed policies at the municipal, state, and international levels through the Street Food project. This study, which EPOC carried out in seven countries and consulted in two more, examined the entire process of who makes, sells, and eats food on the streets. The goal of this action-research project was to identify possible interventions that could improve the income of the vendors or improve the safety of the food sold. Ten years later I visited the study sites to learn about the impact of these interventions. [8]

Despite our original plan to identify income activities by women, we found that street food vending was a cooperative family activity in Indonesia, Thailand, Philippines, Bangladesh, India, and Egypt. In contrast, women vendors in Nigeria and Senegal worked independently from men, though they had support from other women family members, and controlled their own money. In Nigeria and Thailand, over 90 percent of the vendors were women. In conservative Bangladesh, a few women were visible on the streets but they supplied foods for a third of all vendors. Long before the idea of gender was popularized, our study analyzed the spectrum of socially determined roles by women and men.

The street food study documented the importance of these foods in the diet, especially of the poor. Equally important was our data showing the income earned by the vendors and their suppliers. Indeed, many vendors earned more than bureaucrats. As a result, many municipalities reversed their policies of harassment and began to provide space and clean water to vendors. FAO (Food and Agriculture Organization) began to train vendors in safe food practices instead of lobbying for their abolition.

Implications of our data influenced the debate over the permanence of the informal sector by showing that vendors were not temporary workers waiting for formal sector jobs. The study also challenged the assumption made by the development community that offering credit is the best way to help micro-entrepreneurs. Rather, vendors blamed government harassment for impeding their investment in the enterprise. Credit was sought within families who were often repaid with unsold food. Indebtedness was avoided as dangerous to the longevity of the enterprise.

Challenging the Academic Community

Activism comes with a cost. As a former presidential appointee, I was blacklisted by the Reagan administration for U.S. government discretionary grants. Foundations seldom include general operating costs in their funds. Rather than dilute the clarity of EPOC's vision by competing for sectoral projects, I returned to teaching, first at American University and then at the University of California at Berkeley.

Academia lags well behind the development community in its incorporation of women's perspectives into all aspects of research and planning. Challenging the way courses are taught, I created new courses and accelerated my writing. [9] In the early days of WID, I mined scholarly research for policy pronouncements; now I reversed the order and based my lectures on publication on WID experience.

My students, male and female alike, are committed feminists who will adhere to the concepts of equity and social justice throughout their careers. But it saddens me that most university students and faculty are still confined to readings that present the traditional male standpoint. More courses should intertwine national and international issues, and present the differential perspectives of women and men. My students are already doing this.

My ideas on challenging the received wisdom continue to flow. Currently I am writing about the demand, articulated at the Beijing conference, that women should be granted thirty percent of all seats in elected legislatures. The questions I asked in my dissertation research on the first Indian elections resurface: who should be represented, and how?[10] I think about my own political aspirations from giving out voter lists as an eight year old to running for the Maryland House of Delegates. And I compare the opportunities for women then and now, and realize how amazing the change is. By challenging the wisdom of the day we indeed changed policies that neglected or constrained women worldwide.

Irene Tinker's personal papers as well as the EPOC library collection are in a special collection at the University of Illinois Champaign-Urbana library.

Daniela Colombo

B orn in Rovigo, a small town in northern Italy, Daniela Colombo graduated in political science from the University of Padua in 1965 and then did graduate studies in development economics at the University of California at Los Angeles. She moved to Rome in 1968; got married; worked as a special assistant to the president of Lepetit, an Italian pharmaceutical company; and became involved in the feminist movement.

In 1973 she was one of the founders, and later chief editor, of the magazine *Effe*, the main voice of the Italian women's movement, and also started doing radio and television programs on women's condition. During the 1970s she traveled with her husband in Asia and Africa and also worked as a development economist for an Italian consulting firm, mainly in West Africa.

In 1981 she founded the Italian Association for Women in Development (AIDoS) and has been its president for the last twenty years. She served as an expert on women in development for the Italian government in 1985–86 and for many years represented AIDoS in the National Equality Commission. She has been a consultant for the European Commission and several UN agencies as well as a board member of Society for International Development (SID), the International Research and Training Institute for the Advancement of Women (INSTRAW), Worldview International Foundation (WIF), and Women in Development Europe (WIDE). At present she is a member of The Human Rights Committee of the Italian Ministry of Foreign Affairs.

She often lectures at Italian universities and abroad. Editor of *AIDoSnews*, she is the author of several essays on the condition of women in developing countries. Her most recent article is "The Fight for Reproductive Rights in Italy," for a book titled *Advocating for Abortion Access*.

Striding Forward: An Italian NGO in the Developing Nations

In December 1981 a group of Italian women established the Italian Association for Women in Development (AIDoS), an action-research organization concerned with women in international development. Nearly twenty-five years later, AIDoS had become the largest women in development (WID) nongovernmental organization (NGO) in Europe, with chapters in several Italian towns, collaborating with women's organizations and institutions on all continents.

Where It All Began

It was the summer of 1981 and I was walking along the beach in Lerici with my husband and a friend of his. Both university professors of international relations, they were discussing the new development cooperation law passed by the Italian government that was opening up new perspectives for an institute of international studies on whose board they sat. I was enjoying the sun and sea when it suddenly occurred to me that this was also probably the right time to start an Italian NGO to work on women and development.

Development was not a new field for me. After graduating in political science from the University of Padua, I had attended graduate courses in economic and social development at the University of California at Los Angeles (UCLA) and in the 1970s had worked as a development economist for a consulting firm in West Africa. In 1975 I had been asked by the Food and Agricultural Organization (FAO) to write a document for the Mexico conference on women and development, which I entitled "The Missing Half." In doing so I discovered a whole new field that would allow me to put together my interest in the lot of women and my knowledge of development issues.

The idea of founding a women's development NGO had been floating in my mind for quite some time, but I had never found the right occasion to do so. In July 1980, I had attended the NGO Forum in Copenhagen on behalf of the Italian feminist magazine *Effe*, "F" in Italian, and also to prepare two programs for Italian television, one on women living under apartheid and one on the fight against female genital mutilation (FGM). I had come back from Copenhagen, as had other friends who attended the forum and the conference, with a great enthusiasm for the possibilities offered by the international women's movement. We wanted to find new ways of achieving peace among nations through more equitable development that took into account aspirations for equality not only among classes but also between men and women. We were anxious to continue networking and to create solidarity by working together with women from different parts of the world.

Meanwhile, the feminist movement in Italy was undergoing a major change. The movement, which had been very successful, had been co-opted by the political parties, the trade unions, and the mass organizations of women. Feminist clubs were empty and had begun closing down. In the autumn of 1981 we also decided to close *Effe*. Many of us felt that we had accomplished our mission and that a new phase of the women's movement was needed.

In the spring of 1981, during the campaign against the referendum called by Catholic forces to cancel the law legalizing abortion, two colleagues and I prepared a video for the weekly TV show "Si dice donna" on the feminist movement's ten-year struggle for the abortion law. The video was considered too far on the feminist side because it criticized the law for not giving complete freedom of choice to women. All the political parties, right and left, were angry and so "Si dice donna" was stopped. Since I had been working for the program as a freelance producer, I was left without a job.

The Founding and Evolution of AIDoS

So, that summer I started AIDoS with no money, no office, and no experts, just the goal of fighting for the rights, the dignity, and the freedom of choice of women. I brought together a few friends who had been in Copenhagen in 1980 and a few new university graduates who shared an interest in feminism and international affairs; they had little experience in development issues, but a lot of enthusiasm. After a few meetings to decide the aims of the association, we registered AIDoS as a nonprofit organization and started self-training sessions, reading and discussing all the material we could put our hands on, beginning with Ester Boserup's book, *Woman's Role in Economic Development*. We were given a small office, a telephone, and a part-time secretary by a male friend who was supportive of our work.

In the autumn of 1982 I received a grant from the German Marshall Fund to study the work of state and federal commissions charged with advancing equality in the United States. I had become a member of the Commission on Family at the Ministry of Labor, representing the Socialist Party, and had decided to study how such commissions worked in other countries. I left my daughter with my mother, a marvelous woman, and spent a couple of months in the United States, first with the New York State Division of Human Rights and then with the Equal Employment Opportunity Commission in Washington, D.C. This gave me the chance to connect with the UN system for women, particularly with Peg Snyder, director of the United Nations Development Fund for Women (UNIFEM), and Dunja Pastizzi Ferencic, who was at that time starting up the International Research and Training Institute for the Advancement of Women (INSTRAW). In Washington I met with Irene Tinker, the director of the Equity Policy Center, and Arvonne Fraser, head of the Women in Development Office at the United States

Agency for International Development. At the time, the first Association for Women in Development conference was being held in Washington and the organizers asked me to present the work of AIDoS. There was not really much to present except our ideas, but the conference enabled me to expand my ideas and networks. Irene asked me to help organize a seminar on women in agriculture in Europe at the Rockefeller Center in Bellagio as a follow-up to similar EPOC seminars in Latin America and the United States.

In April 1983 AIDoS received some funds from the Italian Ministry of Foreign Affairs to hold an international conference on WID at the Houses of Parliament in Rome. The heads of the WID offices of the main UN agencies and bilateral donors were invited, together with the most renowned experts from developing countries. Our connections with some of our closest supporters in the UN system date back from this conference.

Little by little AIDoS took shape. From the beginning we had a flexible structure, with a small group of permanent staff (at present we have twelve) and a roster of technical experts specializing in those sectors in which we had decided to work. Our mission and role became better defined as a few research projects were begun in collaboration with international organizations in Rome. Being the coordinator of the international group at the Equality Commission that had meanwhile been created, I served as a member of the Italian delegation to the Commission on the Status of Women for three years: 1992–94.

From the beginning, AIDoS supported its basic costs through membership fees and voluntary contributions. Income from donor organizations are tied exclusively to the implementation of specific projects; however, income from consultancy contracts on an individual and team basis from United Nations agencies and from the European Union goes to AIDoS's general budget. The fact that AIDoS has never asked for or received institutional fees for management costs—that is, overhead expenses—sets us apart from many action-research groups elsewhere. The organization has kept growing through the years, revisiting, however, the idea of enlarging too much when AIDoS started becoming very successful.

Expanding Our Goals and Policies

Created after the passage of a new law on cooperation with developing countries, AIDoS's initial objectives were to ensure that Italian development cooperation addressed women's needs in its programs and projects and that the activities of the Italian government benefited the poorest of the poor, notably women. Thus, the first several years were spent lobbying the Italian government on development cooperation programs and serving as the technical reference point for the Ministry of Foreign Affairs. Utilizing the contacts we had made during earlier feminist militancy, AIDoS reached out to Italian women's organizations and the general public to inform them about problems facing women in developing countries, but also about their strength, their creativity, their strategies for survival.

In 1984 the European Commission asked AIDoS to analyze the women and development policies of member states, an analysis we have since done several times. The parameters were expanded in 1994 to include an assessment of the member states' gender policies and programs and to develop recommendations for the definition of a common gender policy and action plan. This experience in influencing policy on a European scale led AIDoS to apply for and obtain special consultative status with the United Nations Economic and Social Council, (ECOSOC), where we have global reach. Since 1997 we have been in charge of the launching in Italy of the State of the World Population Report of the United Nations Population Fund (UNFPA). We also work closely with several UNFPA country offices as well as with other UN agencies.

Running Projects in Developing Countries

I worked for a year and a half within the government in the office of the Undersecretary of State in charge of the Italian aid fund. I was appointed to strengthen implementation of women in development projects. As the WID officer I was able to finance projects of several NGOs. For example, AIDoS received funds for a pilot project on female genital mutilation in Somalia. This experience helped me understand the constraints of government bureaucracy whether at home or in the countries where AIDoS was working. After I resigned in 1986 to return full time to AIDoS, another member of AIDoS, Bianca Maria Pomeranzi, took the WID post at the Department for Development Cooperation and still holds it.

Following the Third World Conference on Women at Nairobi in 1985, AIDoS—influenced by the pilot project in Somalia—expanded its objectives and activities to include women's empowerment and to work directly with women in developing countries. AIDoS has always had what might be called a feminist bent, seeking women's equality with men not only because it was expedient for economic and social development, but also because it was a positive thing in and of itself. Therefore, when the international development community was moving from women in development approaches to gender and development approaches, we carefully studied the issues. We opted to continue with some women-specific projects in areas where women are particularly disadvantaged because of past and present discrimination and where the projects are women-specific by their nature, while fully working for the inclusion and methodical consideration of the gender variable in the design of all development interventions.

Our approach from that time has been to implement activities at three levels: field projects, research and training, and advocacy. The lines between the levels are not always neatly drawn, and with good reason. We have found over the years that just as the sectors in which we work are interdependent and mutually reinforcing, so too are our field projects and research and training activities. All of our research and field experiences offer opportunities for formal and informal advocacy activities also in Italy, in Europe, and at international level, which at present are taking most of my time.

AIDoS carries out field projects only at the request of, and in collaboration with, local organizations; thus all our projects are designed to meet the needs articulated by the partner organizations and target beneficiaries. I believe that several underlying factors have made AIDoS's role as executing agency particularly effective. First, we try to elaborate strategies and implement pilot projects that not only offer the chance to go beyond improving conditions for this or that group of women but also have the potential to initiate changes in development intervention policies. Second, our pilots are designed and implemented as model projects that can be duplicated in other areas of the same country and, with adaptation, in other countries and on a larger scale. Thus, the models must be flexible and capable of changing as new information is received or as needs change. Finally, by working closely with our local partners, training them in administration and data collection, we empower these women to continue the work on their own once AIDoS is out of the picture.

This type of development model project also becomes a political tool, the proof that certain needs really exist and that women are able to organize themselves and improve their own lives when they are given the means to do so. Once they realize their own strength, the women can lobby their own government, asking them to create appropriate laws and structures for women's advancement.

At AIDoS we are convinced of the importance of carrying out formal impact evaluations that measure the success of our projects in meeting objectives in terms of easily identifiable, concrete indicators. Such studies are invaluable to test and formally document some of the assumptions underlying most projects that involve women, and are essential to the successful replicability of the projects. Further, the results of such evaluations are vital inputs to the international debate on the importance of mainstreaming women and including a gender perspective in all projects and programs.

The Primacy of Research

Research continues to be the base upon which our other activities are predicated. To manage our collection of documents we reviewed the classification and cataloging systems used by other organizations and decided on the most appropriate choices for our projects. More recently we developed our own two-language application for UNESCO's CDS-Isis documentation center software and prepared a specialized dual-language thesaurus on women in development with a particular focus on women's rights.

Over the years we have conducted research and produced reports for international agencies. These and academic publications are consulted before we begin new activities. AIDoS includes a research phase in all project proposals and feasibility studies to provide baseline data against which to measure progress at the various evaluation stages. Such information also contributes to ongoing methodological improvements and innovations at the international level.

Frequently the information gathered for such contracts identifies the need for new programs and projects. For example, in 1990 AIDoS prepared a series of country profiles on the condition of women in ten countries given priority status for Italian aid assistance. These profiles included specific recommendations on how Italian development cooperation should intervene in each country to promote the integration of women. Research is also a vital first step in the development of our training methodologies and materials.

Training and Education

Training plays a critical role in combating lack of gender awareness and in providing tools and concepts that allow development practitioners and policy makers to translate gender awareness into practice. This applies equally to staff in the Italian Foreign Affairs Ministry, Italian NGOs, and to our partners abroad. Particularly important have been the training activities on FGM (Female Genital Mutilation). In collaboration with local experts and the ILO training center in Turin, AIDoS has produced multimedia training manuals and given training of trainers courses for teams of program officers, trainers, communication experts, and graphic designers belonging to the national committees of the Inter-African Committee on traditional practices affecting the health of women and children.

In the field of reproductive health and rights we are particularly proud of the training manual developed in collaboration with the Women's Health Project of the University of Witwatesrand in South Africa, under a EC/UNFPA funded program, in which AIDoS was the lead agency for providing gender training to 64 Asian NGOs. The manual has a very participatory methodology and is based on a human rights and quality of care approach. With our guidance it has been translated and adapted in several Asian countries, including Iran. This has been one of the projects I have followed personally. Last year I was invited to Iran as a consultant for UNFPA country office in order to adapt AIDoS's manual to local conditions and conduct a training of trainers workshop of two weeks. It has been one of the most rewarding experiences of my professional life. For the first time I was able to give gender training at the highest level, with the directors of the schools of medicine, the directors of the family planning clinics, the WID officials of the various Ministries, and the directors of several women's NGOs. The TOT (Training of Trainers) was very successful and I was particularly pleased to see the logo of AIDoS, our green and light blue knot, on the banner under which the group photo was taken. That meant the recognition of the organization's efforts behind my work and acknowledgment of AIDoS as the first international women NGO to work in Iran. We are at present organizing a study tour in Italy for a high level group of policy makers and activists who will be studying our legislation and programs on gender based violence.

At AIDoS we are also committed to training the next generation of development experts. University students conducting research for their thesis projects regularly use our documentation center. We often help these students to develop their thesis topics more fully in areas that would be most interesting for them and most relevant for development work in general. Most recently, AIDoS facilitated the travel of a young photographer to Gaza to document the activities of the Business Service Center there as part of reportage to satisfy the requirements of her degree. Her reportage then grew into an exhibition promoted by AIDoS.

Each year we also host two graduate student interns from the master's program in development of the Instituto Orientale of Naples. During their internships, students are put to work preparing a mock project proposal. When possible we send them to the field to conduct first-hand research with guidance from the program officer responsible for projects in that area. Our motives are not purely altruistic, as the students often provide AIDoS with valuable assistance and ideas and several interns have returned to AIDoS once their degrees were completed.

Field Projects

Since the beginning AIDoS decided to work in those sectors in which the experience of the Italian women's movement had been most successful, and where we could rely on a pool of experts: women's rights, reproductive health and sexual and reproductive rights, economic empowerment and the education of girls. Together they make the largest impact on the overall status of women.

In the field of women's rights, underlying all of AIDoS's interventions is our basic commitment to the promotion and protection of women's rights as worthy in itself from an equity and empowerment point of view, but also as an integral and necessary part of the development process. We have assisted local women's organizations, mainly in the Arab world, Russia and Tanzania, to create national or regional women's documentation and information centers that are connected among themselves and that together can serve as springboards for other women's organizations. We have also financed their communication activities and publications. AIDoS generally includes a documentation center component in all of its projects so that our local partners can build up a readily available collection of information on the condition of women and can learn how to package information on their own activities for information and advocacy purposes.

An early focus of AIDoS projects concerning women's reproductive health and rights was on female genital mutilation (FGM). Since 1986 we have been working with African partner organizations in several African countries, to develop and implement model training and information campaigns aimed at the eradication of FGM. Approaches and methodologies for working in this field have changed over time. In the last two years we have been instrumental in the creation of a network of NGOs and CBOs in Europe working on this issue. We are also collaborating with other international NGOs and the various donors, to coordinate programs and avoid duplication of efforts. AIDoS has launched the first web portal to stop FGM in English, French and Arabic that can be fed directly on line and off line by eight partner organizations in Africa.

In the sector of reproductive health and rights, the first challenge was to establish model reproductive health counseling centers for women and adolescent girls, based on the feminist approaches of the early 1970s. Now we are engaged in upgrading the traditional MCH (Maternal and Child Health) and family planning centers and transform them into community based centers with an integrated, holistic approach to reproductive and sexual health, providing—besides all the clinical services—counseling and social, legal, and psychological assistance, including a special program on male involvement and on helping women victims of gender based violence.

Our enthusiastic team of consultants brings new methodologies to the projects and insists on teamwork and quality of care. It is rewarding to see women in Gaza and Jordan entering the delivery room by helping themselves with belly dancing, or see the Nepali women of Kirtipur helping one another through pregnancy with yoga and reflexology, which are part of their tradition but had not been used for this purpose.

In the micro and small entrepreneurship sector, AIDoS initiated a new research approach, in collaboration with the International Labor Organization, by looking at the entrepreneur as opposed to the enterprise as the unit of analysis. This study conducted in several countries identified the economic and social constraints faced by women entrepreneurs and suggested location-specific interventions to overcome those constraints. At the field level, AIDoS's involvement has focused mainly in promoting projects aimed at offering women income-generating activities that are compatible with their family and social roles, but that also start to challenge the old division of labor and system of resource allocation. In the Arab world we have assisted local NGOs to establish business service centers able to identify those women who have an enterprise idea and help them to become successful entrepreneurs by giving all the necessary technical, managerial assistance and access to credit. In this sector also we are at present experimenting with a new approach: "the village business incubator model" in order to assist women to create enterprises not only dealing with agriculture, food processing, animal husbandry, and handicraft but also laundromats, kindergartens, and other service providing enterprises.

When addressing the issue of girls' education, we have committed ourselves to changing the lives of a relatively low number of particularly disadvantaged girls in a very concrete way. By setting up education funds that are channeled to local NGOs for management, we have enabled Indian girls in one of the slums of Calcutta and Afghan girls living in Pakistan to attend good schools, sometimes private. Besides paying for all the expenses, we also provide funds to compensate the families for the loss of income from the girls' work. Contributions for these education funds are collected in a variety of ways, including pairing the girl with foster parents or schools. The first two Indian girls and the first four Afghan girls have been admitted to college.

AIDoS has worked in many regions of the world. Their selection has been based more on the nature of projects being considered and the potential of the partners with whom we would work than on any a priori decision to focus on particular geographical areas. Many of our projects have evolved from our contacts made at international conferences or at the field level, while others have grown out of exchanges of correspondence. While AIDoS has a special interest in working with women's organizations in developing countries, we also collaborate with a variety of other types of public and private organizations whose interests and objectives correspond to our own. In Tanzania, for example, our partner has been a government ministry.

We prefer to continue to work with the same organization in a given country if our collaboration has been successful, which is why so many of our projects are followed up with a more ambitious second phase. We will only consider working in a new country if one of our staff members or close consultants has had extensive experience there or in the region and if we speak one or more of the national languages.

The main thing that has kept AIDoS going through the years has been the recognition that, however slowly and incrementally, the work that we have undertaken together with our partners has had an impact. Equally important has been the role our projects have played in strengthening our partner organizations. Most organizations with which AIDoS has worked through the years have grown and increased their expertise. Some have moved from being predominantly volunteer organizations to having paid professional staff with management and fund-raising capabilities. Others have increased their visibility and become sought-after partners by international cooperation agencies in new development interventions. All of them have emerged from their collaboration with AIDoS significantly strengthened in terms of project management and technical expertise.

Challenges Faced

In its twenty years of operation, AIDoS has faced its share of challenges. We have carried out our work in remote villages, crowded metropolises, and impersonal conference halls all over the world. We have had successes and disappointments; we have been encouraged, disheartened, and often successful. There have been moments of financial crisis and low morale when we asked ourselves if we would be able to continue. For twenty years the answer has always been yes.

Probably one of our greatest challenges lies in the often inflexible nature of the project system itself. We find that it can be difficult to cover every contingency in the design of a project and that sometimes a project would be more efficient if it could be adapted according to problems raised in early implementation. We have also found that the long lag time between the presentation of some projects and their final approval has sometimes meant that conditions have changed and modifications in the design are necessary.

Everyone at AIDoS has been challenged by the different conception of time held by different cultures. We have slowly learned that imposing our own work rhythm has costs, both in terms of the project and our relationship with our partners. More generally, we have had to learn not to be so quick to judge other cultures and ways of doing things. Each of us has had wake-up calls, not all of them pleasant, which have led us to review some of our basic assumptions and values. We have found that just as our partners learn from us, so too do we learn from them. The list of logistical challenges we have faced in our twenty years of operation is long and includes experiences ranging from the laughable to the tragic. We have carried books and equipment ourselves while going on mission to various countries. We have carried huge sums of money on our persons when the banking systems in a country were not dependable enough to wire the money there. We have spent sleepless nights at airports, have flown on military transport planes, and have been turned back mid-flight because of coup attempts in our countries of destination. We have even bought passports to save some of our local staff. The president of the Somali women's organization once told me, "You have to suffer over projects," and this we have done with large doses of camaraderie and humor.

What Lies Ahead

AIDoS has earned recognition of its expertise at both the national and international levels. Since 1985 it has been the focal point in Italy for INSTRAW and UNIFEM, adding to our numerous networks. In 1991 we obtained the "recognition of suitability" status from the Ministry of Foreign Affairs, a status that allows us to present projects to the ministry for co-financing and implement ministry projects that are already approved and financed. By the year 2000, the total budget of AIDoS had reached 2.5 million dollars.

Despite this expansion, AIDoS has remained in the same four-room office in central Rome for which we pay a small rent. We do not open offices where we work and we remain committed to the use of predominantly local staff in our projects. While there have been changes in the number and qualifications of staff members, our organizational style, which includes the maintenance of a small expert staff specialized in each of AIDoS's main areas and a roster of technical experts who can be contracted on an ad hoc basis, has remained the same. Teamwork and staff commitment to an ongoing updating of skills and knowledge of theory and practice in development circles through training and research are other characteristics that have remained constant. AIDoS continues to fill a niche that is unique. No other NGO in Italy and probably all of Europe has a similar institution-building philosophy supported by such a strong mixture of scholarship and practical experience. We are constantly experimenting with new programs and models. In a sector that has become increasingly competitive, we retain our interest in collaborating with other organizations. We also provide information to a variety of actors from students, to the press, to development workers in both the government, and nongovernmental sectors.

Our ultimate objective is to make organizations such as AIDoS obsolete and unneeded. We hope that development cooperation with a gender perspective becomes the norm. We hope that organizations in the South become strong enough to be their own advocates and that the development agencies in the North become more willing listeners. We hope that women's rights become respected within the framework of human rights for everyone, male and female. Finally, we hope that economic and social development itself will become a reality and that the idea of assistance is replaced with the key concepts of cooperation and collaboration.

The excitement and satisfaction I have derived from my work with AIDoS has been exhilarating. As we train women to take over leadership abroad, we are incorporating a new generation of Italian women to perpetuate the feminist perspective that has defined AIDoS. Certainly these women will further adapt the association and redirect its efforts as new challenges arise to ensure that AIDoS will continue to stride forward.

Anne S. Walker

Anne S. Walker became the executive director of the International Women's Tribune Centre (IWTC) at its inception in 1976 following the two International Women's Year (IWY) meetings held in Mexico City the year before. In the ensuing twenty-six years, the IWTC constituency has swelled to 26,000 women and women's groups in more than 160 countries. A feminist activist, educator, artist, photographer, and writer, Anne spearheaded IWTC's efforts to support the initiatives of women, primarily in Asia and the Pacific, Latin America and the Caribbean, Africa, and the Middle East, with a program of communication, networking, technical assistance and training, collaborative projects, skill sharing, and the collection, production, and dissemination of information on a wide range of women and development issues.

A native of Melbourne, Australia, she lived in Fiji in the South Pacific for eleven years, working throughout that time with a local group of Fiji women to start the programs of the Fiji Young Women's Christian Association (YWCA). She left Fiji to undertake graduate studies in education and development communications at Indiana University, completing a Ph.D. in education (specializing in instructional systems technology) in 1976.

She has participated actively in all four UN World Conferences on Women, along with the four parallel NGO Forums on Women, in 1975 (Mexico City), 1980 (Copenhagen), 1985 (Nairobi), and 1995 (Beijing). She continues to work with the IWTC team to provide follow-up information about and support for implementation to women worldwide, and is currently the IWTC Special Projects Coordinator, with a focus on projects in Africa with and for rural women, using new information communication technologies.

The International Women's Tribune Centre: Expanding the Struggle for Women's Rights at the UN

The global women's movement has seen several groundswells of action, and International Women's Year (IWY) in 1975 marked the beginnings of one that emerged from the UN with the strong support of women activists worldwide. During IWY I was fortunate enough to be at the IWY World Conference and the parallel IWY Tribune of nongovernmental organizations (NGOs), both in Mexico City. My participation came about through an invitation to participate as part of a Fiji group that went to Mexico City to speak about and fight for a nuclear-free Pacific. I had been a part of this peace movement during the 1960s when I worked with the Fiji YWCA. The invitation came from Mildred Persinger, the convener of the IWY Tribune.

Described as the largest consciousness-raising session ever held, the IWY Tribune triggered a chain of events that few could have foreseen. With its hundreds of seemingly spontaneous workshops organized around a series of plenaries, the Tribune became the format for succeeding NGO forums of women. I moved from workshop to plenary, demonstration to exhibition, always with camera in hand and notebook at the ready. The slides taken were to become the first of many slide-tape sets prepared about the international women's movement on the move.

Having returned to complete my studies at Indiana University in June 1976 I received another call from Mildred, this time to come to New York for a week "to help set up a follow-up process to the IWY Tribune." The NGO IWY Committee in New York was being deluged with requests for information, support, finance, and technical assistance from many of the 6,000 women who had participated in the IWY Tribune the year before.

Strategies for Moving Forward

In New York I was greeted by thousands of opened letters and packages, heaped and spilling from desks, shelves, chairs, and boxes. I began to read the mail. Piles began forming around me, one pile with requests for information on how to contact someone they had met at the IWY Tribune, another from those with project proposals, one with requests for technical assistance and training, yet another with stories about what various participants had been doing since the Tribune, and so on. We needed a strategy that would allow us to somehow respond to this spontaneous outpouring.

The idea for a women's regional resource kit began to emerge. It was decided that I should go to an international conference of social workers then underway in Puerto Rico, where the majority of delegates would be women. At the meeting I met Peggy Antrobus, director of the Women's Bureau in Jamaica, who had led the Jamaican delegation at the IWY World Conference in Mexico City. We talked briefly. Peggy felt that women in the Caribbean could develop a regional resource book by themselves. The tentative plans to begin the development of a Caribbean regional resource kit for women were put on a back burner.

Six months later Peggy wrote to me in New York: "I have rethought your idea of a Caribbean resource kit for women and wonder if you could come to a regional meeting here in Kingston, Jamaica. We could talk again about the resource kit, and then begin making plans for collecting information from around the region."

By May 1977, we were a small team of three. Vicki Semler, a fellow graduate student from Indiana University, had joined Mildred Persinger, the coordinator of the IWY Tribune, and myself. Then in July 1997 Martita Midence began working with us to build an international resource center. Together we had produced two issues of *The Tribune,* a small, twelve-page, cut-and-paste newsletter that featured news and information from the individuals and groups who continued to write. We had also put together a fledgling resource database of project information, publications, names, and addresses received from IWY Tribune participants. And we were beginning to understand more clearly the workings of the United Nations and the ways in which NGOs had access.

Networking with Regional Women and Development Groups

Working with Peggy Antrobus and other women in the Caribbean, we began the process of developing regional resource kits for women involved in development activities, a project that absorbed the fledgling International Women's Tribune Centre (IWTC)—the name we had chosen—for the next five years. Working with national and regional groups, in many cases new groups that had developed since the IWY Conference and Tribune of 1975, strong networking linkages with activists in every world region were formed. The Caribbean women' resource kit became a template for others that followed for Asia and the Pacific, Africa, and Latin America.

The staff training and sharing that accompanied the development and production of each resource kit proved invaluable for global, regional, and national organizations. The process provided opportunities for researching and organizing information, for reaching out to groups in each region and country, and for structuring a way for communication and resource sharing.

Developing Highly Visual Materials for Community Activists

From the beginning, IWTC publications used graphics and "spoken language" to reach women community activists in the Global South. The graphics consisted of simple line drawings to facilitate easy contact; they have become the hallmark of IWTC newsletters, resource kits, manuals, workbooks, posters, and postcards. With a clear focus on reaching low-income women, both rural and urban, in Africa, Asia, the Pacific, Latin America, the Caribbean, and the Middle East, IWTC has worked with community leaders to develop techniques for adapting and translating these materials into new information tools.

Parallel to these activities, IWTC continued its commitment to skill training through a series of workshops in Africa, Asia, the Pacific, Latin America, and the Caribbean. In those early years, the small IWTC team was rarely together in the New York office. One person would be in Kenya running a media workshop for YWCA leaders, while another would be in Bangkok working with family planning communicators, with yet another in Colombia undertaking a financial planning workshop.

Despite our efforts to share fund-raising skills with others, our own financial resources were constantly stretched and we were frequently on the verge of going under. The need to develop project proposals was a constant concern and we would often find ourselves traveling to one part of the world to run a workshop and writing a proposal for an upcoming project on the plane.

The UN Second World Conference on Women, 1980

The UN Mid-Decade Conference of Women drew 10,000 women to Copenhagen in June 1980, the majority of whom participated in the accompanying NGO Forum. The secretary-general of the conference was Lucille Mair of Jamaica. Elizabeth Palmer (formerly general secretary of the World YWCA) was the convener of the NGO Forum.

One of Elizabeth's first actions as convener was asking IWTC to spearhead the information networking activities before, during, and after the Forum. With this in mind, Vicki and I accompanied her to Copenhagen early in 1980 to look over the planned Forum site at Amager University and to select a place for a central resource center. Out of this came VIVENCIA!, a center within the Forum to bring people together, provide spaces for organizing, and generally support networking activities. By this time IWTC had begun developing and producing all its publications and materials in Spanish as well as English. Vicky Mejia from Colombia had joined our staff and was key in making VIVENCIA! the focus of activities for Spanish-speaking women at the forum.

The Copenhagen event became known as "the networking conference" because several major new women's networks resulted from meetings at the NGO Forum. VIVENCIA! was a major assist in bringing these networks together. IWTC taped large sheets of paper along a wall, each titled with a major issue area. Women added their names and contact information under each title. A special issue of *The Tribune* covering all of the new networks formed in Copenhagen was later produced and disseminated worldwide.

The organizing for what became known as Domitilla's March from the Forum to the official conference also took place in VIVENCIA! Domitilla, the tireless activist who fought for miner's rights in Bolivia, held the floor for days surrounded by crowds of women painting banners, T-shirts, posters, and whatever else was needed for the march across Copenhagen to the Convention Centre where the UN conference was being held.

The day of the march was unforgettable. Tiny Domitilla led the way in full Bolivian attire, holding high a banner demanding human rights for miners in Bolivia. Thousands of women streamed behind her, singing, chanting, waving banners. Demands had been expanded to include women's human rights, labor rights, calls for nuclear disarmament, and more in the document being forged at the conference. At the Convention Centre we were met by heavily armed police and militia. Scuffling broke out as the police and militia attempted to stop the marchers from reaching the doors of the Convention Centre. Then Lucille Mair appeared before the crowd and finally agreed that Domitilla and two or three others could go into the plenary meeting and place our demands before the delegates.

It was a major step in forging a greater role for civil society in global decision making. It followed in the tradition established in 1975 when women NGOs, led by U.S. feminist writer Betty Friedan, marched across Mexico City to the IWY Conference to demand more participation by NGOs in the conference.

From Copenhagen to Nairobi, 1980–85

The years between Copenhagen and the End of the Decade Conference in Nairobi were filled with a flood of new ideas, tools, technologies, and contacts. Bridges were built between communities of women activists and those of women scientists and engineers. These were exciting years that led us into many new paths and opportunities. During these years, the growth in women's networks and women and development activities in general took an enormous leap forward.

From Copenhagen we had brought a message that practical solutions were needed to ease the workload of women as key community workers and family providers. We began working with the Intermediate Technology Development Group, the World YWCA, and the Appropriate Technology Council of Kenya to develop links with women and groups who were working in this arena. These activities and contacts burgeoned into Tech and

Tools, an appropriate technology for women event at the NGO Forum in Nairobi in 1985.

The NGO Forum of 1985 once again was organized by the NGO International Women's Year Committee, now known as the Decade for Women Committee. In 1983 Nita Barrow of Barbados was chosen as the NGO Forum convener. Nita came from a nursing background in the Caribbean and moved into international policy making when she became director of the Christian Medical Commission of the World Council of Churches based in Geneva. There, Nita became part of the executive board of the World YWCA and later was president for a record eight years. She had led the YWCA into a new era of progressive thinking and policy around racial diversity and program outreach.

Key to the success of the Forum in 1985 was Nita's ability to extend support and encouragement to networks and organizations that came up with new initiatives and ideas for the Forum program. She was particularly excited about Tech and Tools and worked with us at IWTC to see that we had the support we needed. Nita also strongly supported the idea of a Peace Tent, an idea put forward and implemented by the Women's International League for Peace and Freedom (WILPF) led by Edith Ballantyne in Geneva, with financial support from Genevieve Vaughn. When situations arose at the Forum that seemed particularly hostile or that were developing rapidly into a crisis, Nita would take the various parties to the Peace Tent to talk through their concerns. In this way, explosive issues such as the Palestinian and Israeli situation and the censorship of women's films by Kenyan authorities were discussed and mostly resolved.

The Nairobi NGO Forum was above all else an African event, with women from all parts of Africa filling the halls, classrooms, and open spaces at the University of Nairobi, the site of the forum. There was a sense of excitement that was palpable as Africans on their home turf met with women from Asia, the Middle East, Europe, North America, the Pacific, and Caribbean and Latin America, and shared experiences in workshops, plenaries, and joined in a great deal of dancing and singing.

The president of Kenya was brought to the Tech and Tools event in the second week, and via radio and TV the word spread that he was delighted with what he saw. Busloads of village women began to appear, women who wanted to see smokeless stoves, water pumps, drum ovens, beehives, hand washing machines, solar ovens and cookers, and more. The end of each day saw women leaving with stoves and solar cookers balanced on their heads as they made their way to the waiting buses and back to their villages.

The official outcome of the Nairobi World Conference, under Secretary-General Leticia Shahani of the Philippines, was the "Forward-Looking Strategies for the Advancement of Women to the Year 2000" (FLS). An action-oriented document, the FLS was fully supported by NGOs worldwide. Building solidly on the two preceding documents that were the outcomes from the world conferences in 1975 and 1980, the FLS outlined strategies for addressing the needs of women in very specific areas. In the NGO world, the 1985 Forum in Nairobi became known as the Action Forum, with a focus of action strategies, appropriate technology that would ease the burden on rural women, and legal rights for women.

World Conferences from 1992 to 2000

During the 1990s, women activists at the UN, following the lead of Bella Abzug (former U.S. Representative), developed more focused political strategies in getting their issues before the UN by setting up caucuses and issue-specific task forces during a series of UN World Conferences. This was a decade of many UN world conferences, and making gender an integral part of each became the battle cry. IWTC, with its growing track record of information outreach and networking, found itself immersed in the plans and preparations for each conference. We worked hard to open up the planning and decision-making processes for each conference, sharing information with and from women in their home countries and regions who would not otherwise have had the opportunity of participating. In this way women worldwide were to become an integral part of the agenda setting, decision-making and subsequent implementation of the plans of action developed at each conference.

The Miami Meeting and the Earth Summit

The World Women's Congress for a Healthy Planet was held in Miami, Florida, November 8-12, 1991, organized by the Women's International Policy Action Committee (IPAC), which subsequently became the Women's Environment and Development Organization (WEDO). IWTC offered its offices as the initial meeting place, and here Bella planned this meeting with the organizing help of Rosalind Harris, one of the group of women who have spent more than fifty years as NGO activists at the UN.

The 1,800 women from eighty-nine countries who attended were charged with three tasks. First, to produce a *Women's Action Agenda* for the decade to be presented to those involved in the June 1992 Earth Summit (officially known as the United Nations Conference on Environment and Development (UNCED) and held in Rio de Janeiro in June 1992). Second, to ensure that all governmental and non-governmental delegations to the Earth Summit were gender balanced, so that no delegation had more than sixty percent of either sex. Third, to build an international network of women acting in solidarity to ensure a strong women's voice on all issues pertaining to environment and development.

The Miami Conference was an important event in the history of women organizing internationally. It resulted in a strong international network and the Women's Action Agenda 21 policy document, which were used to catalyze a strong lobbying effort at the UNCED preparatory meetings and the Earth summit itself.

World Conference on Human Rights 1993

The growing interest in women's human rights and the ratification of the Convention on the Elimination of All Forms of Discrimination (CEDAW) in 1981 had focused the activism of the global women's movement on strategies to pass legislation that would protect and support women in their local communities. In the early 1990s a group of activists from the New York–New Jersey area under the leadership of the Center for Women's Global Leadership began meeting to discuss ways of combining efforts around women's human rights issues and concerns. As a founding member of this group, IWTC was particularly concerned about increasing information networking around women's human rights issues, and more specifically on violence against women. With the UN World Conference on Human Rights planned for 1993 in Vienna, the group began to focus on ways to make women's human rights a central issue on the world's agenda.

IWTC proposed to circulate worldwide a petition and gather signatures of women that would encourage groups to organize at the local, national, and regional level. The petition carried with it a simple resolution that called for all countries to take action against violence against women, and to pass legislation that would ensure that all women could be assured of their basic human rights.

The petition took off immediately. Signatures began to pour in via mail, fax, and personal delivery. As the numbers began to rise, it became clear that something important was underway. Hundreds turned to thousands, and a preliminary "drop" of signed petitions was planned in New York. Using a wheelbarrow to hold the piles of petitions, a small group of women wheeled the first 500,000 signatures across UN Plaza to the UN and handed them over to the president of the Security Council.

Before the World Conference, women's human rights groups in Asia-Pacific, Africa, Latin America, Europe, and North America held tribunals on women's human rights. From these national and regional tribunals, representative testimonies were selected and brought to Vienna in June 1993 to present at a Global Tribunal on Women's Human Rights. Much of this testimony was televised on monitors placed throughout the forum which was held on the floor immediately below the conference, thus conveying a powerful message to the delegates who often visited the forum.

At IWTC we produced posters and visual information bulletins for the World Conference and Forum that could also be sent worldwide to our ever-growing constituency. The three years leading up to the Vienna conference were years of outreach and of building communication strategies that would give a new generation of activists from every region of the world access to human rights information.

By the time of the World Conference on Human Rights and the parallel NGO Forum in Vienna in 1993, IWTC had collected a million signatures. IWTC also organized a Rights Place for Women at the Forum, where we could all display posters and publications and continue the fight to focus delegates' attention on women's rights.

Preparing for the Fourth World Conference on Women

The politicization of NGO advocacy at the UN was given a boost by the 1991 women's NGO summit in Miami, the Global Forum at UNCED in 1992, and the activism of women worldwide at the human rights conference at Vienna in 1993. Women were now more skilled in developing task forces on each specific issue and in preparing caucus statements to hand to delegates at UN meetings. As we approached the first of the Preparatory Committee (PrepCom) meetings at the UN for the Fourth World Conference on Women to be held at Beijing in 1995, women began to strategize around the most effective ways of lobbying and providing input into the planned Platform for Action.

At IWTC we developed a series of information bulletins to build "information bridges" between the various activist groups and the delegates. Known as "Preview 95," the bulletins were sent to the IWTC mailing list of more than 26,000 women's groups and individuals in every world region and handed out free to both NGO participants and government delegates at preparatory meetings. Produced in English, Spanish, and French, these highly visual bulletins covered much of the planning and preparations for the Fourth World Conference on Women and expanded the opportunities for women worldwide to be part of the agenda setting for Beijing.

Information Communication Technologies were becoming vital to the development of this new global women's movement, and in the year leading up to the fourth world conference in 1995, there was an enormous change in the way information was shared and disseminated. An example of this comes from the final PrepCom before Beijing. News came that the Chinese government was moving the NGO Forum from Beijing to Huairou, a town forty miles from the city center. At IWTC we felt it was important that this news be sent out to women worldwide. We faxed a short message to WomenNet, a fax network of twenty-eight women's media groups that had been set up in 1992 at a women and media conference in Barbados organized by the Development of Alternatives for Women in a New Era (DAWN) network. By the next morning, IWTC was flooded with letters demanding action. We developed a draft letter of protest and faxed that to the network. Within twenty-four hours, thousands of protest faxes were pouring into the offices of the UN secretary-general in New York and the

China Organizing Committee in Beijing.

We did not succeed in bringing the NGO Forum back to Beijing. But we did help bring improvements to the site in Huairou and we certainly got the attention of the world's media. Also, our fax campaign launched a new international women's bulletin network that we named Women's Global FaxNet. Before long, however, the IWTC fax machine was breaking down under the enormous load and so we needed to find another method of "instant" communication. We turned to the newly emerging world of e-mail and added an e-mail edition of the bulletin, which we called Women's GlobalNet. Within a month, the Women's Global Faxnet and Women's GlobalNet lists had grown to 1,500 multiplier groups. These were groups that took the information from our fax and e-mail bulletins and sent it on to their own networks, multiplying our outreach by tens of thousands.

During all this organizing and outreach, IWTC joined forces with UNIFEM, the United Nations Development Fund for Women, to launch a new women and development publications service known as Women, Ink. Through this service we began marketing the cutting-edge writings of women from both the Global North and Global South.

The Fourth World Conference on Women and NGO Forum, 1995

In 1995, 50,000 women gathered at Beijing for the Fourth World Conference on Women, where government delegates and official observers lobbied and debated over a Platform for Action. After its adoption by the Conference, it was generally recognized as a document owing more to the activities, advocacy, and lobbying of the global women's movement than any previous UN document.

At the NGO Forum approximately 35,000 women participated in a once-in-a-lifetime opportunity to gather and organize, discuss and strategize, assess and mobilize.[2] IWTC, working with a coalition of more than sixty women's science and technology groups, was part of the Once and Future Pavilion. The pavilion featured an Alternative Media Space; Women, Ink; a Women's Bookstore; appropriate technology exhibits; science and technology demonstrations; and more. Women from every region came and shared their discoveries, their publications and writings, their hopes and dreams for the future. Meanwhile, in the official media building next door, women learned about the Internet, sent e-mails home, and explored the World Wide Web. The Association for Progressive Communications (APC), through its Women's Networking Support Program (WNSP) trained hundreds of women in computer skills.

The IWTC biweekly electronic bulletin and its Women's FaxNet in both English and Spanish versions, continued after the Conference and went on to become a network of close to 3,000 multiplier groups. The ability to reach women with breaking news almost instantaneously has dramatically changed the way women organize and strategize.

IWTC celebrated its first twenty years of work at a lunch and ceremony at the UN in 1996 by honoring nine women who have advocated for women's rights at the UN for fifty years. The nine women are: Mildred Persinger, convener of the 1975 IWY Tribune in Mexico City and World YWCA delegate to the UN; Rosalind Harris, UN representative for International Social Service and president of the Conference of NGOs at the UN (CONGO) at the time of the 1975 conference; Jane Evans, one of the official consultants to the U.S. delegation in San Francisco in 1945; Kaye Fraleigh, UN representative of the International Alliance of Women and part of the planning committees for the NGO forums for all four UN world women's conferences; Esther Hymer, representative of the International Business and Professional Women's Federation at every meeting of the Commission on the Status of Women since 1947; Alba Zizzamia, member of the Interim Committee which established CONGO in 1947; Alicia Paolozzi, active in UN activities, programs and pursuits since her first UNICEF mission to Northern Greece for food distribution in 1948; Frances Sawyer, one of the NGO representatives who set up Women United for the UN in 1946; and Margaret (Molly) Bruce, who joined the UN Secretariat in London in 1945 and served on the UN Commission on Human Rights during Eleanor Roosevelt's time.

Second Know-How Conference and Isis, 1998

At the second Know-How Conference on Women's Knowledge held at the International Archives for the Women's Movement in Amsterdam in 1998, IWTC sat down with the three Isis groups: Isis International in Manila, Philippines; Isis Internaçional in Santiago, Chile; and Isis WICCE (Women's International Cross Cultural Exchange) in Kampala, Uganda— sister media networks that stemmed from the work of Jane Cottingham and Marilee Karl, the founders with Judy Siddens of Isis International in 1974. (For additional discussion of Isis see Ana Maria Portugal's essay in this volume.) During three intense days of meetings, we devised a women's global NGO communications plan of action that combines and supports the strengths of each of the four networks. This plan became the basis for an expanded project that emerged six months later.

Over the years IWTC and the Isis networks have worked together as women's media networks, developing strategies to reach out and support the work of women activists world wide. IWTC and the three Isis groups, recently joined by the APC Women's Network Support Programme, have become the glue that has held the global women's movement together, especially through the past twenty-five years of UN world conferences and NGO forums.

Beijing + 5, 2000

At the first Preparatory Committee meeting in March 1999 for the UN General Assembly special session to be held five years after Beijing—officially called Women 2000: Gender Equality, Development, and Peace for the Twenty-First Century and unofficially known as Beijing + 5—an expanded network of women's media groups met to discuss ways of improving communication outreach for the gathering in 2000 that would assess progress since the Beijing conference. Building on the work done by the three Isis groups and IWTC in Amsterdam the year before, the network formed Women-Action 2000, an NGO Women's Global Communications Network.

Co-coordinated by IWTC and APC-WNSP, WomenAction first developed a global Web site, followed soon after by regional Web sites in Africa along with the Asia-Pacific, Latin America-Caribbean, and Europe and North America regions. In October 1999 we undertook a workshop at the Asia Pacific Women's Information Networking Center in Seoul, Korea. Forty women came for training in Web construction and regional online dialogue facilitation, returning to their regions to train others. Within the space of a year, a dynamic, interactive network was formed, stimulating the development of NGO alternative reports in every region, informal regional meetings around issue areas, and the growth of regularly maintained Web resource spaces.

At Beijing + 5 in June 2000, WomenAction conducted an unprecedented level of media activities, including two daily newspapers—one with a focus on Africa, one global—plus an Internet café, radio and TV Web casts, and a daily media caucus. The two daily newspapers were uploaded to the Web for regional focal points to print and disseminate. All of these activities were organized over the Internet via e-mail conferences, listservs, and one-on-one online dialogues. The complexity and degree of detail involved in each activity gave added credibility to the notion that the world of women's organizing has been dramatically strengthened and changed with the coming of the Internet.

Out of the Beijing + 5 came a document simply entitled the Outcomes Document, whose purpose was to review, strengthen, and expand efforts to implement the actions called for in the Beijing Platform for Action. Whether this goal was achieved is a matter of dispute. Regardless, IWTC has continued to focus its efforts on opening access to relevant and appropriate information for women worldwide, especially rural and urban low-income women in the Global South, so that they will have the resources to work towards the empowerment of women in their home countries.

Women worldwide continue to support and reach out to each other in many different ways. The energy, dedication, and downright doggedness of women, whether activists and advocates at the UN, women's human rights leaders in their own country and/or region, or working within international women's rights groups, is cause for a book all by itself. Women activists and advocates have exhibited a remarkable level of energy, dedication, and determination in the face of seemingly impossible odds, yet have not given up the struggle for a world that is just, gender equitable, sustainable, and at peace.

The IWTC archives, including the archives from the four NGO Forums that can parallel to the four UN World Conferences on Women, are held at the Sophia Smith Collection at Smith College in Northampton, Massachusetts.

Ana María Portugal

Ana María Portugal is a Peruvian journalist who worked in the editorial section of the Lima newspapers *Correo, Crónica,* and *Ulima Hora* from 1970 to 1976. She was a correspondent for the Agencia Informativa Latinoamericana de la Mujer (Latin American Information Agency for Women), also called FEM-PRESS. She was a member of Peru's first feminist group, Acción para la Liberación de la Mujer Peruana (ALIMUPER; Action for the Liberation of Peruvian Women) and was a founding member of the Centro de la Mujer Peruana Flora Tristán (Flora Tristan Center for the Peruvian Woman). She is currently coordinator of the Communications and Publications Program of Isis International, based in Santiago, Chile.

She is a co-author, with Esther Andradi, of two editions of *Ser Mujer en el Perú* (To Be a Woman in Peru), published in 1978 and 1979. She has written an editorial on sexuality and abortion in Latin America, published by Catholics for Free Choice in the U.S. She authored *Veinte años de historia no contada (Twenty Years of Untold History)* and *Las olvidadas del milenio (The Forgotten Women of the Millennium),* published in 1985 and 2001, respectively, by Isis International.

Isis International: A Latin American Perspective

In the midst of an explosive political climate—1984 is remembered in Chile as the year of protests that preceded the end of the Pinochet regime—two women took a small office in the stock market building in downtown Santiago, the Chilean capital, to set up Isis International-Santiago. They had been part of the Spanish-language program in the Isis office in Rome, staffed by a group of Latin American women, mostly Chileans, living in exile in Italy. Isis had been formed a decade earlier by North American and English expatriates living in Europe, Marilee Karl in Rome, and Jane Cottingham and Judy Siddens in Geneva, Switzerland, who decided that the international mass media was not giving a fair picture of the new international women's movement and that an alternative women's media and documentation and communications centre was needed. Between 1974 and 1983 Isis's work in Europe was primarily aimed at creating networks and in initiating exchanges of information and experiences among women's groups in various countries and regions of the world through publication and distribution (primarily by mail) of Isis Bulletins and other materials-based information from around the world received at the documentation center.

In many Latin American countries the early 1980s marked a period of sustained activities linked to broader social movements and the creation of feminist NGOs. As the network of contacts between the Rome office and women's groups in Latin America grew, so did the demand for information in Spanish. This led to the decision to create a program for Latin American and Caribbean women.

Though I had been linked with Isis and its successor, Isis International, earlier, I joined Isis International-Santiago as coordinator of its Communications and Publications Program in 1993. As a journalist in Lima, Peru, during the 1970s, I was a member of Peru's first feminist group, called the Acción para la Liberación de la Mujer Peruana (Action for the Liberation of Peruvian Women) and also helped found the Centro de la Mujer Peruana Flora Tristan (Flora Tristan Center for the Peruvian Women). In 1978 and 1979 two editions of a book on women I co-authored with Esther Andradi were published in Lima. I was a correspondent for the Latin American Information Agency for Women, or Agencia Informativa Latinoamericana de la Mujer, called FEMPRESS.

During this same period, Arvonne Fraser was watching these developments while head of the Women in Development Office at USAID. After receiving the first Isis bulletin, she became a subscriber. She was impressed both by the content of the bulletins—dealing with issues that the donor community had not yet acknowledged—and by Isis's contacts with new women's groups in the South that were unknown to WID agencies and aid donors. After visiting the Geneva and Rome offices of Isis, she was convinced that the organization was a crucial link between the incipient international women's movement and the women in development idea. In early 2000 Fraser visited Ximena Charnes in the Isis International-Santiago office and asked if she would write a history of Isis from a Latin American perspective. Ximena turned to me. (For other historical or current information see Isis International-Manila Website at *www.isiswomen.org* or Isis International-Santiago at *www.isis.cl*. The latter Website is in Spanish.)

The Formation of Isis

The early foundational years of Isis were heroic and filled with enthusiasm. In the early 1970s, Marilee Karl, who still serves on the board of Isis International (one segment of the original Isis), worked in Rome at the International Documentation and Communication Centre, which was linked with progressive Third World groups. Jane Cottingham and Judy Siddens were associated with international church groups headquartered in Geneva. All three were concerned that while the international media were giving press coverage to the new feminist movement in Europe and the United States—albeit often in disparaging terms—they were ignoring activities among women of the South. They recognized "the common elements and diversity of women's oppression as intertwined with class, race, and economic, political and cultural situations."[1] In this formative period when Karl was working in Rome and Cottingham and Seddens in Geneva on their proposed center—eventually named Isis—they decided that it would be activist and feminist-oriented, despite the fact that women of the South did not always like the word "feminist" because of the way the media portrayed it. They also decided that their center would link women of the North and South "and be a means for them to share their ideas and experiences internationally, without the distortion of the male dominated transnational-controlled press."[2]

Development of such a center was encouraged by attendees at the First International Feminist Conference held in Frankfurt, Germany, in November 1974. Back in Rome and Geneva, the three women and volunteers from African and Latin American countries, studying in Europe or working for development agencies, began, after regular work hours, to organize the materials they had collected. Among their first contacts were women who later made their mark internationally, including Virginia

Vargas, Roxanna Carrillo, Anita Anand, Kumari Jayawardena, and Nita Barrow. Siddens returned to the United States and eventually was able to raise $2,500 from women's church groups.

With this money and the efforts of the volunteers working in Rome and Geneva, often in the kitchens of Karl and Cottingham, the first issue of the *Women's International Bulletin* was published in 1976 in English, French, and Italian. It was a response to the mass media's poor coverage of the First International Tribunal for Crimes Against Women, held in Brussels, where Simone de Beauvoir gave the welcome address to over 2,000 women from 40 different countries. The *Bulletin* featured sessions of the tribunal that highlighted the problem of domestic violence and other forms of violence against women such as rape and incest.

In the meantime, the United Nations had proclaimed 1975 International Women's Year and government delegations and NGOs from around the world gathered in Mexico City for the first world conference on women, and the feminist movement in Latin America and the Caribbean was taking its first tentative steps. Isis's bulletins were a part of what would eventually be called women's alternative media, including newsletters, mimeographed pamphlets, silk-screened posters, and so on, produced in small quantities and distributed by and among the earliest feminist groups. In Latin and North America as well as Europe, this alternative media had its roots in the work of a few daring 19th-century women writers such as Flora Tristan of France and Peru, and the teachers, suffragists and revolutionaries of North America and Europe who founded newspapers and magazines, operated presses, and laid the groundwork for future generations.

The first Isis bulletin produced enough funds from subscribers and from other groups to sustain further publication. Subsequent Isis bulletins dealt with topics such as the image of women in the media, reproductive rights and alternative medicine, women in southern Africa and apartheid, women and work, and land and food production. Although printed in small quantities, the bulletins were recirculated among new groups and information from them was reproduced in the alternative media of the South and North. Isis's activities would become known among the donor community as evidence of an international women's movement.

During the first UN world conference on women held in Mexico City, feminism was often associated by the media and many governments with the North and with white, educated, middle-class women. It was demonized by the international media which effectively ignored the demands of the women present, as articulated in the Plan of Action adopted at the conference. Later, this attitude changed.

New challenges and many new slogans were raised at the second UN world conference on women held at Copenhagen in 1980, midway through the UN Decade for Women. Latin American women won a first, decisive battle with a referendum at the parallel NGO Forum. It defined the nature of the First Latin American and Caribbean Feminist Encounter held the following year as a "feminist" and not a "women's" encounter. This decision was ratified by the Colombian hosts of the First Encounter, the historic meeting out of which Latin American feminism emerged as a movement and a new political force. One of the first accords taken at the meeting established November 25 as the Day of No Violence Against Women in memory of the heroic Mirabal sisters, who were assassinated by the Trujillo dictatorship in the Dominican Republic on November 25, 1960.

Women militants in Latin American political parties and movements refused to be seduced any longer into playing the supportive role of camp followers who served coffee and earned the money to keep their homes together while their male comrades went out to change the world. By 1984 feminism was no longer a foreign concept in Latin American reality, at least to a broad range of liberal and leftist intellectuals.

Isis Becomes Three Organizations

The enormous amount of work and the corresponding growth of both European offices led to a split in the late 1980s in Isis and its transformation into three sister organizations: Isis International, with offices in Rome, Isis International in Santiago, Chile, and Isis-WICCE (Women's Cross Cultural Exchange Programme), based in Geneva and later in Uganda. In 1991 the activities and programs of the Rome office were transferred to Manila in the Philippines. The concept of information and its use is the key to the continuity of all the Isis International programs. All Isis International programs and activities are based on the premise that women's empowerment and the development of their organizations depend largely on their ability to produce, process, transmit, receive, and utilize information and knowledge that they can creatively apply to their diverse realities in order to overcome discrimination. As Isis International-Santiago's *Annual Report* for 2000 states, "We realize that the information we need to prioritize, document, file, and distribute is not neutral. It is directly related to the changes we want to bring about to achieve women's full participation in society."[3]

While earlier Isis publications were modest efforts that reflected the incipience of the feminist movement, in the 1990s Isis International embarked on a process of modernization and professionalization of its editorial staff with the goal of practicing specialized journalism that would not be limited to women's issues. Rather, it would infuse the range of issues covered by the international press with a gender perspective.

With this goal in mind *Mujeres en Acción* (Mothers in Action), the Spanish-language newsletter launched in Santiago in 1984 along with an English edition in Rome, was redesigned as a quarterly magazine in 1991. This and other Isis International publications were reconceptualized to cover a variety of issues from a gender perspective and provide sources, testimonies, statistics, data, opinions, history, and social and political contexts to make known the reality of women's experience in a consistent and professional way. This approach expressed support for women's demands while avoiding the language of protests and slogans. It marked a significant shift from the strategy initiated in 1974, when Isis made denouncing discrimination against women a priority, along with making the women's movement agenda visible and raising women's demands in the public sphere.

Isis International-Santiago

Against this background, Isis International-Santiago organized its work into four program areas: Communication and Publications, Violence Against Women, Women and Health, and the Information and Documentation Center (Centro de Información y Documentación, or CIDOC). CIDOC was set up to serve as the foundation for the other programs, a repository to retain the collective memory of women's experience, to provide information to meet the needs of a variety of users, and to motivate the generation and distribution of such information. CIDOC staff collects, processes, classifies, and analyzes a great variety of print documents in a solid resource base. CIDOC users include students, researchers, women's organizations, social organizations, legislators, NGOs, and government agencies.

In 1986 CIDOC began converting to an electronic, computer-based system that facilitated storage and retrieval of information and enabled staff to respond more efficiently to requests for information and assistance. With installation of the CDS/Isis system, developed by UNESCO, specialized databases were created for bibliographic entries, organizations, periodical publications, and descriptors. These databases have been regularly updated and information about them published. A major task for the CIDOC staff was development of a conceptual framework for creating an information system on the subject of women. Analytical categories had to be established for managing the data and each category needed to be identified by a key word or phrase, called a descriptor. The result was a tool that not only facilitates retrieval of data but also establishes a common criteria for storing data while highlighting the terms that best express women's reality. As new information technologies have become available, CIDOC has taken on the challenge of offering its services via e-mail and a website.

Another of Isis International-Santiago's major early activities during the 1980s was participating in the NGO Forum at the third world conference on women at Nairobi, Kenya, in 1985 that marked the closing of the UN Decade for Women. The Nairobi conference exceeded all expectations. It was attended by 14,000 women from different countries, speaking different languages, and representing many different races and ethnic groups. It was also the first conference attended by a critical mass of Latin American women. Isis International-Santiago co-sponsored a Latin American and

Caribbean Women's Health Network workshop and contributed to an *Audiovisual Resource Guide for Women*. Together with a European network of resources for development and the Philippine women's organization GABRIELA, Isis International organized a series of four groundbreaking workshops on development, participatory power, and solidarity. The first two focused on the problem of multinational corporations and free trade zones, international trade, and the worldwide foreign debt crisis, all of which became major issues of concern for women in the 1990s. The other two workshops focused on women and on alternative development and the importance of networking.

Networks and Publications

In 1986 Marilee Karl had clearly defined Isis International's role in the formation of networks as a contribution to the global women's movement. Isis's presence at the First International Tribunal for Crimes against Women in 1976 had been a key factor in the development of international feminism. It led to the formation of the International Feminist Network (IFN) in March of that same year with the objective of mobilizing global support and solidarity for women who were affected by acts of violence or found themselves in violent situations anywhere in the world. At the request of activists, Isis took responsibility for coordinating the IFN for several years and was able to measure the impact of its work by the tremendous volume of mail it received.

During the first three years, Isis distributed information about fifty different cases, from rape to women's labor struggles, to acts of resistance by women political prisoners, to campaigns in favor of legalizing abortion, against forced sterilization, and demanding the recall of harmful contraceptives. By the mid-1980s the number of similar initiatives involving women had broadened enormously the range of solidarity actions. New networks arose to replace the historic IFN and assure the continuity of its work.

In 1984 the regional women's movement asked the newly founded Isis International-Santiago to coordinate the Latin American and Caribbean Women's Health Network (LACWHN), born in an agreement made during the First Regional Women's Health Meeting held in Tenza, Colombia. The network needed an institutional coordinator that could unify activities carried out by different groups around common objectives, such as promoting women's health rights, distributing information, and organizing international campaigns. Initially, coordination of LACWHN consisted of responding to requests for information received from groups in different countries and organizing regional campaigns, such as International Women's Health Day on May 28 and the Day of Action for the Decriminalization of Abortion in Latin America on September 28. The joint work of LACWHN and Isis International-Santiago resulted in the publication of the first *Boletín de Salud* (*Bulletin of Health*) in 1985; a twin English edition was added in 1987. In 1990 both publications were redesigned in magazine format under the direction of an editorial committee headed by a professional journalist. LACWHN also worked closely with the CIDOC staff on creating the bilingual databases published as the Directory of the Latin American and Caribbean Women's Health Network (1992) and Bibliographic Information on Women's Health (1996). The joint work continued to 1995, when LACWHN separated from Isis International to become an independent organization.

Following the First Latin American and Caribbean Feminist Encounter in 1981, the various initiatives aimed at denouncing violence against women reached unprecedented proportions as governments and their agencies acknowledged the importance of generating policies to confront the problem. In 1988, Isis International-Santiago initiated the Violence Against Women in Latin America and the Caribbean Project, aimed initially at assessing the dimensions of this phenomenon in the region. About 109 institutions in 22 countries responded to the first questionnaire distributed by the program to women's NGOs, government agencies, and social organizations. The results of the project were published in 1990 in the *Bibliographic Catalogue on Violence Against Women in Latin America and the Caribbean,* containing 350 entries, with an abstract for each. This information was updated in 1996 with the publication of the *Women's Database: Directory of Groups and Institutions,* containing 241 entries corresponding to groups and institutions working on the issue in some capacity throughout the region.

Between 1982 and 1990 a broad spectrum of women's social organizations, feminist NGOs, and national networks of women activists were concerned with the violence issue. The time was ripe to link them together. In August 1992 at Olinda, Brazil, representatives from twenty-one countries gathered at the first meeting of the Latin American and Caribbean Feminist Network against Sexual and Domestic Violence. Once again, Isis International-Santiago was asked to take responsibility for coordinating the network's communication and information activities. This involved producing a quarterly newsletter and overseeing the campaigns called the November 25th Day of No Violence Against Women and the Sixteen Days of Activism Against Violence Against Women.

Just as Isis in Rome had invited one of the Colombian organizers of the First Feminist Encounter to collaborate on a publication that would commemorate it, Isis International-Santiago invited an organizer of the Second Encounter, held at Lima, Peru, in 1983, to collaborate on a similar publication about that event. This became the first volume of the Ediciones de las Mujeres book series, replacing the historic *Boletín Internacional de las Mujeres.* Since then, the series has become two volumes per year, usually in the form of anthologies that reflect the development of feminist thought in

Latin America and the Caribbean and current issues about which women have significant contributions to make. Each volume in the series is carefully edited by a team of professionals in each aspect of production, from conceptualization to printing. The result is a high-quality publication in both form and content.

By the 1990s our approach needed refinement. The process of modernization and professionalization was a response to the influence of communications systems in an ever more globalized world, which demand that traditional approaches to information be reoriented toward maintaining an effective presence in the public sphere. Isis International-Santiago also saw the need to reorient its publications to keep up with the expansion of feminist ideas and the growth of women's social movements throughout the region. By 1994 the different tendencies within Latin American and Caribbean feminism, along with the diversity of the women's movement, reflected women's undeniable presence in the public sphere. Their strength was evident as their demands were raised in the political sphere.

In 1994 the Isis International staff was actively involved in preparations for the Fourth World Conference on Women held at Beijing, China, in 1995, but it was also a year of reflection and evaluation. A special 120-page anniversary issue of *Mujeres en Acción* issued in 1994 offered a retrospective look at the organization's work since the origins of Isis, along with an overview of important events in the history of global feminism in a chronology titled "The Untold Story." The issue also included contributions by a number of leading feminists from around the world who discussed the influence feminist ideas had had on the political and cultural changes in the world since 1974. The publication celebrated the presence of women in the production of knowledge and the expression of their experiences in their own words in books (fiction and nonfiction), magazines, films, and other forms.

From Beijing Onward

The year 1995 marked the end of one phase as the international women's movement faced the challenges of the Fourth World Conference on Women, the last of the twentieth century. Adoption of the Beijing Platform for Action was a great achievement because in doing so, governments and international agencies committed themselves to complying with the accords spelled out in the Platform.

In Latin America and the Caribbean, the single experience that marked the new direction taken by the feminist movement was the initiative of a group of regional NGOs to demand that the regional representative to the preparatory Conference Facilitating Committee be elected by the women's movement. This demand was met and Virginia Vargas, a long-standing feminist leader from Peru, was elected by consensus. In addition, a Latin

American and Caribbean Regional NGO Coordinating Committee, made up of numerous feminist organizations and networks and women's social movements, succeeded in mobilizing thousands of women. Isis International-Santiago served as a focal point for information and produced a pre-conference newsletter, *Hacia Beijing 95* (Toward Beijing 95), in collaboration with FEMPRESS.

Following the Beijing Conference, Isis International-Santiago stepped back to evaluate its work. The expansion and diversity of initiatives, the emergence of new voices and new demands from different sectors of the feminist movement, was probably the phenomenon that made the greatest impact at the Beijing conference. Isis International-Santiago was forced to ask itself how to respond to this challenge at a time when, contradictorily, international cooperation agencies were beginning to reduce funding to NGOs in Latin America.

One of the most immediate consequences of this situation was the closing of the magazine *Mujeres en Acción* after twelve years of publication. The final, 1995 issue was a special ninety-two page edition wholly dedicated to the repercussions of the Beijing Conference. Feminist activists and leaders in Latin America were asked to give their assessment of the state of the movement.

While bringing closure to one phase, Isis International-Santiago prepared to begin another, consistent with the challenges posed by Beijing. It began perfecting and expanding its use of new information technologies and extending Isis's presence beyond the women's groups that had been the habitual users of its services. It also took responsibility for responding to the multiple demands generated by the impact produced by Beijing from a variety of sectors, including government, the mass media, educational institutions, political parties, churches, professional organizations, labor unions, and others.

Thus, Isis International-Santiago created a Website and posted its publications, which dealt primarily with the various Platform for Action follow-up initiatives in the wake of the Beijing conference. The dossiers *Perspectives* and *Agenda Salud* were designed along these lines, as were the electronic publications *Inter-Redes*, containing information about the work of the groups and organizations in the Latin American and Caribbean Network against Domestic and Sexual Violence, and *En la Mira*, a newsletter for women journalists and communications networks in Latin America and the Caribbean.

When the Spanish-language *Boletín* was first launched in 1979, it extended the bridge with Latin America to the rest of the world. For the first feminist collectives in Latin America, which appeared in that decade, the 1970s, the *Boletín* was a valuable source of knowledge and information about the international feminist movement. At that time, Isis was giving priority to denouncing the imbalance in the flow of information by and about women and advocating media democratization. An editorial in the *Women's International Bulletin* of December 1980, titled "Women and the Communications Media," had warned that "the feminist movement needed to examine all mainstream media, to show how it neglected coverage of women, to develop new media forms with a feminist outlook, and to join the movement for a New Information Order (then being proposed at the UN by the group of 77 non-Western nations) and assure that women are part of that order." The editorial went on to advocate the creation of feminist networks and publications.

The creation in the early 1990s of networks of women journalists working in the mass media, as well as in specialized news agencies linked to feminist organizations, are among the most apt fulfillments of Isis's initial purpose. Similar pioneering efforts included the establishment of FEM-PRESS and CIMAC (Comunicación y Información de la Mujer, en Mexico or Communication and Information About Women in Mexico. Within this new spectrum of communication initiatives, Isis International-Santiago currently plays a supporting role through the creation of networks of professional women journalists, by establishing links for disseminating and exchanging information among women journalists' networks in Bolivia, Brazil, Costa Rica, and Mexico, among other countries, and by producing special publications and offering training in new information technologies. From 1997 to 2002 Isis International coordinated the Southern Women Journalists Group, made up of women journalists working with NGOs and the mass media in Argentina, Chile, Bolivia, Brazil, Mexico, Uruguay, and Paraguay.

In each phase of the women's movement, Isis International-Santiago has maintained its primary objectives. These are to provide channels for expressing the diversity of the movement and for geographically balanced coverage of varying political positions and opinions; to give visibility to organizations with less access to information; to link women from different regions and cultures and act as a facilitator of contacts and disseminator of resources; to serve as a repository and recorder of women's historical memory; and to distribute the results of research and analysis produced by Latin American women researchers, historians, and political scientists.

To ensure that women's interests, visions, and aspirations are taken into account and that they make a significant impact on society, Isis International-Santiago is utilizing the technological developments that have opened up new avenues in the field of communications. People who have been consumers of information can now generate and disseminate their ideas in a process of dialogue and exchange. The new information technologies have an important role to play in shaping the emerging global structure and in the consolidation of democracies with the participation of informed citizens. Through new channels of communication we can better understand the phenomenon of globalization and be better equipped to identify issues of particular concern to women throughout the world. The new technologies also have the potential of reducing continuing inequities. However, limited access to such technologies must first be overcome.

We consider easily accessible information fundamental because it enables all people, but especially women, to express their needs and interests, and to communicate their experiences in order to improve their lives and more fully participate in economic, social, political and cultural development.

During all these years, we in Isis International-Santiago have witnessed how. To quote our 2001 Annual Report,

> women have accumulated a wealth of data and knowledge about their own situation and status. They have learned to use information to advocate for public policy proposals, gain greater autonomy, reinforce the issue of gender, and influence knowledge and decision-making. They have experimented with and constructed systems for meetings and networking; they have managed to permeate certain power structures; and they have changed discriminatory laws. These achievements have not come about evenly.[4]

Nor have they come easily. And much still must be done.

Michaela Walsh

Michaela Walsh combines a career in investment strategies, both professional and pro bono. In the 1960s and 1970s she broke gender barriers as the first woman manager at Merrill Lynch International and the first woman partner at Boettcher Company. She helped formulate the Rockefeller Brothers Fund's strategy to encourage innovative and small-scale sustainable projects and served in the U.S. Congressional Office of Technology Assessment of Technology for Local Development. She helped launch several venture capital funds linking financial management and marketing assistance for small-to-medium-scale businesses in emerging markets. In addition to founding Women's Asset Management, she is director of the Global Students Leadership Program at Manhattanville College.

Her proudest accomplishment is as founding president of Women's World Banking, a unique institution providing low-income women with access to credit and financing. It was formed at a time when there were few women bankers anywhere in the world and when women, even those of substantial means, were systematically denied financial services in their own right.

Active in numerous national and international associations, she has spoken before groups ranging from the U.S. Senate's Foreign Relations Committee to the Swedish Parliament. She is the recipient of the Paul G. Hoffman award for outstanding work in development.

Born and schooled in Kansas City, Missouri, she was bitten by the political and social justice bug because of her father's and grandfather's involvement in legal, social, and political circles throughout the twentieth century.

Women's World Banking

I began my career on Wall Street in the 1950s, when I saw money as the form of empowerment. Since at that time women were not hired into Wall Street training programs, I attended the New York Institute of Finance at night to become a registered stockbroker and was hired by Merrill Lynch/New York. There, I was appointed New York liaison with Merrill Lynch's international offices. Being in a man's world was flattering, despite the obvious U.S. gender bias in the workplace. In 1960 I was invited to join Merrill Lynch International/Beirut. Since I was the first woman to work abroad for the corporation, it had no administrative system to handle the process. Men traveled on a company expense account; I paid for my own travel. Yet what seems a ridiculous process today was a thrilling experience for me. As a young woman from the Midwest who had never traveled outside the United States, living and working in a totally strange culture, among people from all over the world, taught me to understand that the American way was not the only way. Listening to and learning other languages and traditions gave me the confidence and ability to learn and share with others that remains with me to this day.

After three years in Beirut and two in the London office, I returned to New York in 1966, only to learn that opportunities in sales—my goal—still were not open to women. I left Merrill Lynch and joined another company to help set up its first mutual fund trading desk on Wall Street. Later, I became the first woman partner of a New York Stock Exchange member firm, the third woman to attain that level of recognition. The thrill this carried for me also brought me face-to-face with what we now understand to be gender discrimination and sexual harassment. The older, senior partners were excited about my appointment, but many of my younger colleagues were not. Old friendships became strained; the workplace changed. Then one day I was asked to assume responsibility for some trades that challenged my personal ethics. I refused. The illusory images of prestige and respect built on money faded, leaving me with a desire to clarify my personal values and understand the connections between money as a source of empowerment and money as an end in itself.

In the early 1970s most women had no access to the formal economy. Bank accounts under their sole signatures were beyond their imagination. Only a small percentage of U.S. women received credit cards in their own names. In other cultures it was often worse for women. This was also the era of the civil rights and early appropriate technology movements and the time when Rachel Carson's *Silent Spring* and E. F. Schumacher's *Small is Beautiful,* with their concerns about the environment, were influential. Women were beginning to raise their voices against inequality. In this environment I joined the Rockefeller Brothers Fund. Thanks to the encouragement of President Bill Dietel and colleague Joan Dunlop, I attended the United Nations first world conference on women at Mexico City in 1975. One of the main issues discussed there was the need for economic development, particularly the need for access to credit. At the American Association for the Advancement of Science seminar preceding the conference, Esther Ocloo of Ghana explained that the lack of credit was a real handicap to women farmers, who were the backbone of sustainable food production in most African countries. Before the end of the UN meeting, this denial of credit became a universal complaint and an international issue.

Several prominent Americans, including Betty Friedan, Bella Abzug, and Gloria Steinem, were major voices in Mexico City. I had been a part of the new U.S. women's movement since its inception. But Mexico City revealed the extent of deprivation for women worldwide, the degree to which I had not been sensitive. The diversity of people at the meetings and the impact of thousands of women, many in colorful Asian saris and African headdresses, was unprecedented. In the presence of every nationality, language, culture, skin color, and religion, the word "minority" suddenly lost its meaning. I thought to myself, "The world is never going to be the same."

During the conference, a group of women—Caroline Pezzulo, Lucille Mair, Zoreh Tabatabai, Martha Stuart, and Esther Ocloo, among others, along with the organizers Virginia Saurwein and Margaret Snyder—began promoting a UN resolution to create a new world development bank for women. I was introduced to Virginia Saurwein and Margaret Snyder, who shared a long UN history and respect among peers in development work. Like most women at that time, they had little knowledge of international banking and finance, but I was struck by their idea of a women's development bank. It would be an opportunity to use money to help women gain greater access to the benefits of economic development, the key to their empowerment. A developing economy simply could not develop when more than half the productive population did not have access to financial resources. Through a global movement, I thought it would be possible to force decision makers within governments and the banking systems of most countries to guarantee women equitable access to financial resources, thus strengthening women's economic and political impact.

Initiating a Development Bank for Women

I was sufficiently persuaded about the potential for a women's development bank that I spent the next three years working with the initial organizers. We researched the creation and management of the International Monetary Fund, the World Bank and regional banks. We defined an agenda to raise capital for a completely new concept: a global financial organization owned and managed by women for women. It was clear that professional credibility is often determined by others' perception of, and trust in, the professional wisdom of prestigious names that are linked to new ideas. We had to create a legal structure and financial system that could be endorsed by top professionals and supported by governments, individuals, and banks. That was the beginning of my dreams for what we titled Women's World Banking (WWB).

I had stepped out of a safe environment to start down an unknown path. The most profound struggle for me during the next few years was to get other members of the organizing group to understand and accept my strategies, unclear dreams, and ideas. Although our differences began over decisions about a legal structure, on a broader scale the question was to identify the real issues for women in development. Most of the organizers, familiar with the UN, wanted the WWB to be a UN project providing credit to women. I envisioned a totally independent entity, able to function through the formal banking systems of all countries. My belief was that the title we created, Women's World Banking—coined over lunch by Charles Johnston, an international banker from Chase Manhattan Bank—signified an intention to empower ourselves and other women with new access to money and finance, information services, and the decision-making skills needed for operating businesses. Many of the other women, however, did not want to be identified with banks and financial institutions in the for-profit world.

Designing New Banking Concepts

In the late 1970s and early 1980s, "for profit" and "not-for-profit" were perceived as two different worlds. Many in the international development world saw for-profit businesses as corrupt and overpowering. I was seen by many as "that Wall Street type who does not understand development." But without major collateral, I believed WWB would have to work through national and local banks to get access to information and assistance about how to evaluate loans for its clients. This would make WWB unable to meet the UN's or governments' project criteria and management. I knew WWB had to be an independent, global financial institution.

Equally important were the new concepts in structural design in the proposal for WWB. These were radically different from the traditional male-designed, pyramidal institutional structures and manifested my belief that women in development meant unity through relationship building. The Mexico City conference presented a paradigm shift. WWB represented a new commitment by women to take responsibility for local ownership and leadership rather than to continue their dependence on outside charities. This was the relationship that would ultimately distinguish WWB from other institutions and lead to its success.

I thought of the concept of a wheel. It was a visualization of the "think global, act local" idea. The axis of the wheel represented the administrative and communications center; each spoke of the wheel a local member affiliate, and the rim the clients. This imagery differed from the pyramidal organization where "rookies," if lucky, climbed the corporate and bureaucratic ladder for years before their opinions meant anything to anyone. In our model every member of WWB would participate. All would serve equally important functions under the wheel-like structure. WWB, using the wheel concept, needed to function as a single unit to run properly. It required a new level of trust in each person's talents and skills—a new global trust among women.

One of my colleagues from the Rockefeller Brothers Fund put me in contact with two important lawyers who would help shape WWB's legal design and its future success: Sylvia Chin, a partner of White and Case, a leading international New York law firm, and Floris Bannier, a partner in one of the leading international law firms in the Netherlands. I still wonder about my first meeting with Floris in 1978 in his Amsterdam office. He must have thought I was off the wall as I explained my ideas. Somehow moved by my determination and later reinforced by the power of women he met at our first meeting in 1979 in Amsterdam, he agreed to help us identify and register a unique legal structure under Dutch law called a "*stichting*" that allowed us to have dual status as both a for-profit and not-for-profit institution. We were approved for operation in 1979 as Stichting Women's World Banking, a financial institution. It took another three years before WWB received the Netherlands Central Bank's full blessing as Stichting to Promote Women's World Banking, a crucial ruling that qualified us as both a financial institution and an educational foundation. While status as a banking institution opened the doors of the formal economy to WWB and its clients, the educational status allowed WWB to receive all-important government and private-sector support. Sylvia Chin was instrumental in registering the legal fundraising arm for the United States, called Friends of WWB, USA, and has been WWB's "legal eagle" throughout its life.

We sought start-up operating support from the United Nations Development Program (UNDP). Director Bradford Morse had been supportive of my excitement and belief in the WWB dream and after a lengthy meeting we received a $250,000 grant in 1978. We were to introduce the idea behind WWB in five regions of the world in order to prove its viability as a strategy for obtaining credit for women. Those who opposed the idea of an independent WWB tried to restrict the grant. Prior to the first regional meeting, held in Amsterdam in 1979, I received a telephone call from a UNDP officer with a request to send observers. My reply was unhesitating and direct: "There have already been overwhelming numbers of requests for observers. If we comply, we would have more UN observers than participants. Since we consider this a small meeting for experienced banking professionals, we are not including observers." I was immediately reminded that the UN had provided monetary support for the meeting. I acknowledged their support with grateful thanks but explained that WWB was an independent organization and offered to return the UNDP money. The director quickly declined my offer. From then on, the warning that "Michaela Walsh is one tough lady" spread throughout UNDP. That reputation was well earned. That telephone call was a very profound lesson.

With the help of Gretchen Maynes, an independent development consultant, members of the Committee to Organize WWB planned our first regional meeting in Amsterdam. We brought together a group of women in finance and banking from twenty countries interested in helping define the operating principles and loan criteria needed to set up a global network of local financial institutions, controlled and owned by women in different countries and affiliated with a global institution. Since our goal was to raise women out of economic dependency, not to build a bank, it was concluded that a central agency was to act not as a headquarters but as a communications center to encourage open, equal, and honest communication between the center and affiliates and among the affiliates. The energy at that first meeting, coupled with challenging advice, valid skepticism, and valued encouragement set our determination to move ahead. Many of the original attendees, such as Deanna Rosenzweig, Sara Stuart, and Mary Houghton, remain valued advisers to this day.

Our strategy to carry WWB through its first ten years involved building a uniquely designed independent global banking institution with dual for-profit and not-for-profit legal status. While WWB is a financial institution, it is, at the same time, an educational organization whose purpose is to serve and educate low-income women about financing their for-profit businesses. Our focus was on building and strengthening local financial service centers that would in turn work with local women to legitimize women's small businesses.

In the past, women had always been relegated to charities and other types of not-for-profit institutions. I pushed for opening the formal economy to women to break this image and to increase productivity and profitability. To accomplish this, it would be essential for WWB to build a woman-run, broad-based decision-making structure and a source of independent capital and income; government and foundation support, however, would be crucial to WWB's success in building its sustainability and its clients' businesses.

Challenges of Leadership

At that first 1979 meeting, there was a bitter struggle among members of the Committee to Organize WWB. I won the title of acting president. I had never considered myself a competitive person, one who fought to win. Yet at the meeting something took hold of me, an unexplainable force that would shape my life for the next decade. Very few people really understood the vision I had for WWB's development as an independent global fund for women.

I finally realized that on all levels of creative and pragmatic decision making that there was no one else capable of the job. I fought to the point where I lost the collaboration of colleagues whom I had grown to respect and with whom I had been working for five years. While I greatly respected and loved working with my original WWB organizing colleagues, our differing philosophies created irreconcilable tensions. We were envisioning very different futures for this entity we had all nurtured into existence. This was one of the few times in my life that I made a conscious decision that, even without any supporters, my view was worth fighting for. The next year, during the second UN world conference on women at Copenhagen during 1980, I was elected founding president of WWB for the first of two five-year terms.

I remember that before leaving Copenhagen, I faced my fears about the responsibilities of leading a global banking institution, fears I had not experienced even as one of the first women on Wall Street. Back then I had role models to look up to and superiors who directed me to new challenges. Now I as leader had to accept the responsibility to make decisions that could have major impacts on others and also accept the loneliness that went along with that.

Getting Help

Before I left Copenhagan, the Rockefeller Brothers Fund gave me an office for six months that I shared with an assistant, Susan Eddy. We then moved into two rooms in my friend Carol Hyatt's offices that she generously rented to me for two years. Tom Hunter, a CPA, helped us set up our accounts and bookkeeping records. Ada Molinaro, a retired secretary, joined me and turned out to be a gift from heaven. Lilia Clemente, a former financial officer at the Ford Foundation who had just established Clemente Capital, became our trusted financial adviser. The humor and very humane and pragmatic commitment of John Hammond, the former president of ACCION, a major worldwide micro-lending institution, to development for the poor made the program design truly believable. Along with the initial board of directors, I found real comfort and support from Beatriz Harretche, an older professional role model and friend. These are just a few names among those who made up a committed, loyal group of people with some understanding about what WWB was striving to do. Working over time, we were bound together by trust in each other and the idea that we could make a difference and have a good time doing it.

Since men controlled most of the financial institutions of the world, I knew it was important to find male allies for WWB. On the advice of a friend, I had gone to see J. Burke Knapp, executive vice president of the World Bank. My fears about whether he would be open to our ideas were unnecessary. He immediately saw the potential of WWB and realized we were serious and pragmatic about creating a viable institution. He was so taken by the commitment and experience of the women he had met at the 1979 Amsterdam meeting that he agreed to join our board of trustees. He introduced us to Lester Nurick, the World Bank's general counsel, who later became WWB's general counsel. Two foundation program officers, with whom I worked for several years, later said that they had given us financial support because these two men were behind the idea. This gave me some assurance about the importance of professional credibility and fiscal responsibility that WWB would require.

WWB would not have become a reality had it not been for the support we received from many individual believers in my dream. Bradford Morse, Arthur Brown, and Tim Rothermel at UNDP were initial donors and supporters. Because Brad believed in our determination and the viability of WWB, he recommended his deputy director, Arthur Brown, for the WWB board of trustees. As we approached the end of the fourth year and faced a short-term cash flow crisis, UNDP gave us unrestricted support and saved WWB from closing its doors.

My work on WWB involved all the growing pains of any entrepreneurial start-up and more challenges than I could have imagined. There was never an easy answer. We raised some money to cover operating expenses from the UNDP, the Rockefeller Brothers Fund, the Seven Springs Ranch, and a number of loyal supporters and old friends who bought the dream. Among the latter were Dorothy Lyddon, Jacqueline Charnow, Peg Snyder, and Ann Roberts. Even with their help I often had to face the painful reality of not having enough to pay professional salaries or hire sufficient numbers of people. At the end of WWB's fifth year, one of the hardest lessons I had to learn as an entrepreneur was laying off people because of severe financial restraints.

Financial support received from governments and other sources went into a restricted capital fund. In 1982 the Norwegian government gave an initial U.S. $3 million to the WWB Capital Fund. The Netherlands, Swedish, and Canadian governments followed with an additional U.S. $7 million. The corpus (the principal or capital, as distinguished from the income, as of a fund or estate) of the WWB Fund was designed as a guarantee to help local affiliates negotiate loan programs for low-income women and as a resource for leveraging additional capital funds from central banks and international banks and agencies. Earnings from the fund were used for program development.

Creating Affiliates and Seeking Bank Partners

Once a group of women had organized as a WWB member affiliate and successfully registered as a financial institution in a country, WWB had the option of providing loans to them for direct micro-lending or of working with local banks and affiliates to provide security for new business loans for women who otherwise could not qualify for traditional bank loans. Within four years WWB had requests from over forty local groups of women wanting to become affiliated with WWB. It took another ten years to develop strong training programs and tight systems controls and contracts to help assure that these lending systems were effective and profitable for both the affiliates and the borrowers. In the process women gained knowledge about lending and other financial services and the banks learned that women could be good customers.

In the early days we struggled in search of a potential bank partner. We conducted a survey among banks in developing countries to determine the ratio of female to male recipients of loans. Not surprisingly, banks advised us that they didn't keep that kind of record. Mary Okelo, Barclays Bank's first African woman vice president and bank manager and founder of Kenya Women's Finance Trust, succeeded in signing WWB's first joint loan guarantee agreement, between KWFT and Barclays in 1983. The affiliate helped individual women prepare and defend their loan applications at Barclays. The Bank, at no risk of loss to itself due to a guarantee from WWB and from Barclay's foundation, opened the first ever line of credit for women in Africa. Thanks to Mary Okelo and her colleagues, a seed planted seven years before finally sprouted.

Margarita Guzman was the first courageous voice to establish a WWB affiliate in Latin America, located in Cali, Colombia. It remains one of the most successful and profitable WWB affiliates and the catalyst for creating additional affiliates in five other cities throughout Colombia. Margarita's creative energy and commitment became an inspiration to design forward-looking training and management procedures for WWB's affiliate directors and administrative teams.

Some governments and individuals challenged the idea of establishing an invested capital fund rather than distributing the money outright to developing country projects. To them, WWB simply was not helping the poor in developing countries when the money was not directly used to build homes or provide food, health services, and education. The concept behind the strategy of building a capital fund was creating financial leverage through local banking and other financial institutions. This was a very difficult concept for many to understand, but a $10 million capital fund, if successfully invested and managed, could be leveraged at least eighty times through co-financing and joint guarantee projects. This would allow WWB to reach and connect the smallest business owner—generally a woman—to the formal economy within her community, her country, and on a global basis.

Difficulties and Accomplishments

By the late 1980s, WWB's strategy of letting a thousand flowers bloom, combined with the public's increasing interest in micro-credit, was causing major problems. A very small staff was trying to deal with rapidly growing demands. In hindsight, I realize I had been running WWB under crisis management mode for ten years. We did not spend money that we did not have in hand or was not pledged, but I was not confident that we could guarantee the future. With no long-term professional staff, I made all management decisions. This management and budget crisis struggle eventually clashed with the expectations of our forty-six affiliates around the world. Our small staff was drowning in administrative details and my constant travels added to the chaos. The affiliates were struggling as new enterprises and required communication and attention. None had yet reached a level of knowledge or financial well-being needed to pursue effective management on its own. Yet excitement ran high, even though most of those struggling with start-ups did not completely understand how WWB was managed or the financial leverage reasoning behind it. By 1987 we had raised over $4 million in operating funds and our initial capital fund had grown to $6 million, but we were still educating donors and potential affiliates that WWB was not simply another private-sector banking institution looking for grants to set up projects to extend credit.

During 1987 I began to realize the enormous costs involved in training women to manage and build their own local-global organization. The development world was more committed to micro-credit for the poor than it was to women's empowerment through ownership. To me, credit alone was a limiting concept. My vision was based on women working together to manage their own successful and growing businesses. Unlike today, many donors did not understand micro-credit and there was little commitment among donors to support the creation of long-term management training for building micro-borrowers' capacity for ownership.

We had originally thought that at the end of ten years WWB would be deemed a success if it had helped set up and was working with ten local affiliates around the world. By 1988, its eighth year, WWB had requests from forty-six global affiliate registrants. Out of 56,000 loans amounting to nearly $12 million, there had only been $35,000 in losses to WWB's capital fund, a default rate of 2.9 percent. I had raised $10 million, a remarkable amount for any women's institution at that time, and was confident that the cornerstone had been cemented into place for real change in women's roles in the economies of nations. But I was also beginning to believe that I lacked sufficient energy, experience, and desire to run a corporation of the size and complexity I envisioned for WWB. I had learned years before that an entrepreneur who can create a good business is not the same as a manager who can sustain it. Fifteen years was long enough.

Trusting Changes in Leadership

In 1988 I announced to the trustees my intention to step down as president. A colleague reacted by saying, "You don't just create something and walk away from it!" It is never easy for founders to turn over the reins to the next generation. A right of passage is never fully accepted by all of those involved. The ensuing two years represented a very difficult time for the organization. Often new entrepreneurial ventures, wherever they are in the world, do not succeed in redefining themselves under new management. Transitional stages in any organization are marked with vulnerability, and for new ventures such as WWB, little is known about the process. Trust in the people and belief in the mission are the strengths that carry them through early periods of change. In addition to having limited funds, our board had to deal with great insecurity, restlessness, and confusion among an overworked and stressed staff. Who was going to be my successor? Will she—there was no question that my successor would be from within WWB—be bold and experienced enough to take on the responsibilities? Would WWB hold on to its underlying values? Could WWB count on continued donor support to help it grow to its potential?

Under the leadership of Nancy Barry and the next generation of members, the institution has succeeded in building a flexible and well-managed global structure, has maintained its legal and financial independence, has sustained its members' loyalty and self-reliance as well as its clients' satisfaction. It has adapted well and grown in changing political and economic environments. But most important to me, the fundamental premises upon which it was founded have not changed. I have remained connected to WWB because I believe strongly that roots and generational ties to history help strengthen organizations, families, and individuals. There have been times when I have had personal disagreements with colleagues about plans and decisions in WWB. Over time, however, as in any long-term relationship built on respect, friendship, and love, differences that once existed have faded away.

Thoughts in Retrospect

Beginning in 1982 WWB held biannual global meetings to build understanding, trust, and loyalty among people who were interested in or had

already begun building local affiliations. For the most part, these were courageous women from around the world who shared the vision of furthering
women's economic growth. The four-day meetings were often raucous, with
women sometimes in tears; they often ran well into the night because of failures to understand that money was not immediately available for direct dis-
persal to participants for handing out to the poor. Many did not understand
what I was trying to say about the mechanisms by which we would achieve
our goal. WWB was, in essence, a mechanism through which women could
create economic empowerment for themselves through the formal economy,
and on a deeper level a means to build a global network of trusting relationships that would ultimately lead to an increase in women's status within their
societies.

I regret I was not more successful in explaining my ideas to others, but I
am grateful that I had the courage and stubbornness to keep my commitment to build a solid financial institution for women that fitted into the
realities of the global banking system and to help local affiliates accomplish
what they wanted in real partnership with others. My deep-seated belief
that it takes relationships and trust to succeed, and that real accomplishments are achieved through people, not institutions, carried me through
WWB's start-up phase. Team building and relationships were rarely discussed openly in the corporate world until the birth of WWB and its wheel
philosophy.

When it was suggested I write this chapter, I had to rethink WWB's
formative years and my successes and failures, fears and joys, expectations
and exasperations. For many years I was confused about why so many
women fought against my ideas. Until recently, I did not understand their
lack of knowledge about money flows and market capitalization. I have also
realized that under circumstances where dissenting opinions and disagreements exist, power struggles are an inevitable, even among women who are
working together to achieve the same goal. We all dislike conflict, but if
women have more opportunities to experience it, they will realize, as I did,
that it is all right to shed tears over deep-seated frustration and to engage in
conflict if the goal is to reach a shared vision. The identity of women has
changed with the times, and so has mine. I found my identity in Beirut,
Lebanon, and Mexico City. I have worked for thirty years to help build
partnerships and financial strength for others through WWB, Women's
Asset Management, and recently through my work with young women at
Manhattanville College. At the end of 2003, WWB's capital funds value
was approximately U.S. $35 million with 56 member institutions servicing
15 million borrowers. At Manhattanville, the Global Student Leadership
Institute, which I launched, now has a network of over fifty former students
from 25 countries who are linked to each other via the Internet. One student from Ghana is now in Yale's graduate school doing environmental
studies; another is in graduate school in Johannesburg, South Africa. A

Dominican Republic student, whose mother was one of the first WWB borrowers in that country years ago, is graduating from Washington University in St. Louis with a double major. The process of exercising, studying, and promoting leadership pays off. Working together, millions of women are achieving greater economic independence for themselves and for other women worldwide. They are also helping each other, in the words of environmentalists John and Nancy Todd, "to live more gently on the earth." We have only just begun.

Michaela Walsh's personal papers and those of the Women's World Banking sorted to date have been deposited in the Princeton University library.

Devaki Jain

Devaki Jain's life has been a constant effort to push back the boundaries that surrounded women in India. She was born in 1933 in the city of Mysore into a family of high social standing. Her father was a civil servant; her mother managed the large household. After convent schools, Devaki was allowed, after some debate, to attend college, first in Bangalore, and later in Oxford, England. She then became a lecturer at the University of Delhi.

Devaki was married at age thirty-three, late by Indian standards, to a man of her own choice. According to her, "The fact that he happened to be of another caste and region meant I was breaking a long-held convention of the family, and that was something the family found difficult to accept." In 1969 she resigned from the university to care for her two infant sons.

Working on her book, *Women in India,* set her on a feminist journey in which she sought to sharpen and broaden her understanding of women's issues by being involved in a range of activities: writing, lecturing, networking, building, and leading and supporting women. This journey led her down many an untrodden path, but links with scores of people from various walks of life and in different parts of the world enriched her life and increased her understanding.

A View from the South: A Story of Intersections

In her last book, *My Professional Life and Publications, 1929-1998,* Ester Boserup traces her intellectual history by describing her various encounters, whether at a teaching post or a job at the UN or a field assignment, and lists her articles and books that expound the theories and propositions she arrived at because of that stimulus. Her book is only sixty-two pages long, but it reveals how much we are influenced by the journey of our lives, especially a visual, physical encounter, a direct observation. I was fortunate to be considered a friend by Ester; both of us had worked on *Asian Drama,* by Gunnar Myrdal, between 1958 and 1960, and had shared some of the learning as well as the discomfort of that experience. Ester later contributed a chapter to my first book, *Indian Women,* published in 1975, which attempted to capture the status of Indian women.

The value of the visual is reflected in my own journey with development. Living in India, side by side with not only poverty but also the sight of women bending, carrying, walking, breaking, cutting, doing all the time, provided themes about women's lives that became the areas of my research. The historical period in which I graduated from college also defined my perspective. Indian independence was less than ten years old in 1956, when I took my first job, and there were many post-liberation initiatives and experiments to efface the pains of colonization.

One of my formative experiences was walking from village to village following Vinobha Bhave, a disciple of Mahatma Gandhi, as he asked landowners to gift land to the landless as a moral act. This approach to leveling the inequality in the ownership of land, the most desired and valuable asset, had attracted idealists and the young from all over India and the rest of the world.[1] This walk, and the hope in the human spirit that it evoked in me, were instrumental in my selection for a seminar at Harvard University in 1958 and my admission to St. Anne's College at Oxford. Both were impressed by the nature of my experience, participating in such a groundswell transformative movement.

Subsequent travel to various countries of the Global South made me aware of the potential for unity among its countries and continents. This awareness underlined another aspect of my politics and accounts for many of the initiatives and positions I have taken, including my presence on the South Commission. This commission of twenty-eight eminent economists from the Global South was set up by Julius Nyerere, former president of Tanzania, in 1987, to assess the possibilities of building an "economic South."[2]

When I met Dr. Nyerere, I told him that he was two years behind us, the women of the South. Back in 1984 we had created a South-South network, DAWN, whose focus was on finding our own framework for understanding the location of poor women in our development trajectories and offering approaches for their emancipation. When he gave me the names of the people he had chosen to be on the commission, I exclaimed, "What are you doing with a bunch of tired old men?" (I was fifty-three years old at that time.) That very evening I was invited to join the commission. Two other women also became members: Marie Angelique Savane, who had founded the Association of African Women in Research and Development, and Solita Colles Monsood, an accomplished macro-economist.

Most of the members of the South Commission, however, were influential men who tended to see the world of the South through the columns of the *London Times* or the *New York Times*. I repeatedly protested against their stereotypical images of our societies. I pointed out that the continents of the South were not as separated as media and scholars of the North perceived. Rather, many lines, threads, and habits bound us together. Strong intellectual and political energies were bubbling in our countries, and a process of self-definition was occurring.

This pulse of change was palpable to those living the South.[3] I contend, therefore, that the lived context is a crucial tethering for that amalgam of thought and action that characterize those engaged in transformation, including feminists. Myriad corners and colors shaped and lit my journey. Three perhaps are most significant: first, women in poverty (and therefore, the questions of women and work); second, Gandhi's brilliance in thinking of and working toward a just and compassionate society and economy; and third, my location as one who belongs to a developing and thereby ex-colonial and relatively poor country of the South.[4]

A Woman's Beginnings

None of these coordinates can be directly traced to my upbringing, either at home or in the educational institutions I attended. I was born in 1933 in the city of Mysore. My mother provided a home rich in culture while raising seven children. She was married at eleven years old to a brilliant civil servant who later became the premier of a state in India.[5] She ensured that her three daughters learned to speak English, the language of power at that time, a skill she did not have but tried to acquire as an adult. As the wife of the mayor of the city of Mysore, she went to the convent for private tutorial. My own schools and colleges were rather aseptic places. The nuns steered clear of politics for their own protection.

Higher education for her daughters was not on the agenda, though it was carefully planned (including training abroad) for my four brothers. I was being prepared for marriage after I finished high school, since female puberty in my family meant marriage. No one in my family or in school discussed this discrimination; we lived it. It was not even perceived as unfair. The allocation of roles and futures was all part of the given. Its objective reality had not yet become the vivid and articulated issue it is now. I escaped this destiny using cunning and subterfuge, but my motivation was more an innate stubbornness than any feminist consciousness. Furthermore, even in my case, post-graduate education was not possible, since all the post-graduate courses were in co-ed colleges, which were out of the question for me.

Becoming Conscious of Gender Issues

Nonetheless it was not these facts that pushed me into the domain of women. After college I had become a self-confident young woman who, as a university lecturer in economics from 1963 to 1969, found the company of male colleagues far more interesting than that of women colleagues. By 1974 I had resigned a later post to care for my two infant sons. Until this time I had been a queen bee. Then a friend asked me to work on replacing an old book, called *Women of India*.[6] She wanted the new book in time for International Women's Year in 1975. Since it was to be home-based work I accepted, although I knew almost nothing of the subject. I drew on my various academic friends and asked them to go beyond the strict boundaries of their discipline and consider the status of Indian women. We melded together the book *Indian Women*, which was released by the then-president of India.

The introduction to that 1975 volume marks the start of my journey toward understanding the dynamics of gender. Even at that time, struck as I was by the injustice of gender discrimination, I sensed that women need not become men (a desire I had had as a girl) to set things right. Women needed to fight for their place in this scenario, as women.

It seemed to me that it was a recognition of the distinctive features of womanhood and the identification of its advantages, its special value, and then the use of that identity by women that would strengthen our place in the construction of gender. I was troubled by the words "status" and "liberation" and tried to clarify them. I was also overwhelmed by the data. Women were bearing the greater share of the burden of poverty whether measured in terms of scarce resources, food, clothing, shelter, medical care, education, or social hierarchy. I found women beautiful. I wrote that I would like men to join us, not the other way around.

ISST: Building a Base for Research and Action

In the 1970s an energetic, intellectual, and political environment prevailed in India, with the interweaving movements of coalitions and platforms across diverse, distinct social and political movements. Most of them were dedicated to deepening democracy and eliminating poverty.[7] It was possible to get support for unorthodox ideas from orthodox people. For example, I received an unusual fellowship from the Indian Council for Social Science Research to conduct a field study on women's use of time though I did not have an advanced degree nor was I attached to any recognized institution.[8]

With this fellowship I went on to investigate a phenomenon that was taking place in Ahmedabad, the capital of the state of Gujarat. A large mass of women working as cart pullers, vegetable vendors, rag quilt makers and so on, had been organized into a trade association. A visit to SEWA, the now-famous women's trade union, and the uncovering of the difference between poor men and poor women in their economic domains, generated the idea that women had to organize separately around their economic activity if they were to claim recognition in all spheres: under the law, in social status, and in economic services. Organizing around work as the first pillar of any process of empowerment of poor women became the creed, not only for me, but in the policy-making arenas too.

Thus began my research about what I called the "worksheds" of many women, leading to the book *Women's Quest for Power*.[9] I examined five endeavors built around women's stereotypical work to assess how far the genesis and ideology of the effort and the nature of the leadership influenced the agency of the women workers. All work did not necessarily empower women, nor did all organizations built around work. It took something more, and that seemed to be feminist leadership.

Since I was looking for an organizational base from which I could continue my engagement with these issues, I resurrected an organization called Institute of Social Studies Trust (ISST), pioneered in 1963 by an economist whose main interests were poverty, inequality, and employment. Over time this became the bedrock from which my studies, the sensitization of sister organizations, and the birth of other networks were generated.

In 1974 the concept of time use was not known in India, though the methodology was being used in the North. I intuitively came to it out of disbelief in what I saw, namely women who were working everywhere in the fields and roads but whose work was not being counted in the national economic statistics. Something was wrong with the method of measurement of work. My study of time allocation by men, women, and children in six villages in India provided data in support of a different form of measurement; it also revealed the difference between the nature of men's and women's economic activity, especially among the poor.[10]

Differentiating between men and women among the poor, now known as gender differentiation, became the theme of all the research and advocacy of ISST. This uncovering of women among the poor as a class by themselves was of crucial importance to my journey, as it challenged political ideology from a perspective that was not economic programs.

Role differentiation revealed the kinds of burdens, such as time fetching water or fuel, that women bore which had not even been identified, much less counted as work. In a different study I pointed out not only that women were the majority of the workforce in what the ILO (International Labor Organization) calls emergency employment,[11] but that the seasons when women were not engaged in agriculture were different from those of the men, thus challenging the perceptions of seasonal unemployment. At ISST we then moved on to examine the differing choices made by men and women. We drew on the narration of the Chipko movement, in which the men were willing to sell the existing trees to lumber mills and replant the hill slopes with commercial fruit trees, while the women did a "hug-in," and saved the trees for their fuel and fodder value. Thus, the class issue, and the plea for class before gender was somewhat melted down by the uncovering of these hard disparities and differences between poor men and poor women. We also conducted the most elaborate study of female-headed households to determine the various causes of female headedness.[12]

My first foray into a public lecture from a podium that represented the intellectual establishment was in 1982 at the Nehru Museum and Library in New Delhi, to deliver a Memorial Lecture.[13] This gave me a chance to wave our findings from the rooftops, so to speak, and to challenge social scientists. What was this sociological family that they talked about, with rules and regulations that created a bonded unit? In contrast we found many non-families among the poor, ones in which women battled for survival. What was this counting of workers, and the hierarchy of work, that the statisticians were putting forth that left out women's work?

The intellectual environment at the time was such that these ideas and findings were taken seriously by the mainstream. Women did get identified as a subset of the poor for both statistical and programmatic purposes. Their occupational characteristics, with often a man and woman within a poor family having different sources of income, was taken note of by the Planning Commission. Also, India's sixth Five Year Plan (1976–81) for the first time had a separate section on women's employment, with tables showing the sectors where women were bunched in particular occupations. These data also revealed that women were the least paid workers.[14]

Responding both to the notion of integrating women into development, a message from the UN's 1975 World Conference on Women at Mexico City, as well as the concern for women in poverty, ISST undertook a study of the planning process of the government of the Indian state of Karnataka. This was called integrating, or mainstreaming as it would be called today, women into a state five-year plan.[15] The study brought into focus the question of development transfers to the poor and what their real impact was, and also brought into sharp relief the conditions and the context within which poor women can be enabled to escape their poverty.[16] The study also made the more fundamental observation that development design and development transfer themselves were flawed. The ways of ending women's poverty could not be considered in isolation from the mechanisms used to deliver the services intended for them. They were a political matter that had to be located in a broader critique of the system; the method; and the local macro-economic, political, and social context.

Between 1977 and 1987 the ISST went into overdrive; its output of research, its outreach to grassroots organizations of women, and its organizational strength both financially and in numbers of team workers grew tenfold. We were publishing annotated bibliographies of women and work studies in India, reviewing the statistics on women in agriculture in India, and training statisticians in other countries. We were invited to participate with many international agencies to design studies of women and poverty. We were also enabling the birth of an NGO network with our expertise. This period saw the birth of the Indian Association of Women; Kali for Women, the feminist publishing house; and Mahila Haat, an association of women producers.

Building the Base for Thinking About Development

During the 1970s and 1980s the women's movement in India and abroad was lively and active. The Mexico conference of 1975 was a defining moment for many of us. It linked us to many friends and networks and gave us visibility within the international community, including the UN. The Indian government brought representatives of women's organizations onto its national preparatory committees for world women's conferences in Copenhagen (1980) and Nairobi (1985) and at the Non-Alignment Movement conference in Cairo on women prior to Nairobi.

In 1983 I presented a paper on the impact on poor women of development transfers at a meeting of the women in development (WID) group of the Organization for Economic Cooperation and Development/Development Assistance Committee (OECD/DAC) in Paris. To prepare for this lecture, "Development As If Women Mattered, Can Women Build a New Paradigm?" I requested Karin Himmelstrand, then the WID program officer of the Swedish International Cooperation Development Agency, to send me evaluation reports of all the donor grant projects throughout the continents of the South. Reviewing this literature, I concluded that all was not well with development programs, whether a program was an area development project in Ethiopia or an income-generating project for women in Sri Lanka. Development transfers had pushed poor women into deeper corners, just as they had in India.

At a 1983 seminar in Harvard University convened by Diana Eck called Women, Religion, and Social Change,[17] I explored the possibility of a Gandhian feminist perspective on development. In the book *Speaking of Faith*, co-edited by Diana and myself, we concluded that there was a universality in the attitude of religions toward women, as they all sanction an inferior position for women, but there was also universality in the potential for a common spiritual consciousness.[18] Women can take the best of each religion's essence, establish this consciousness, and be the builders of bridges across religions because of the similarity of women's experience of patriarchy, bigotry, and discrimination.

The year 1983 was a landmark because it became the year of many streams which eventually led, among other things, to the pool from which DAWN sprang the following year. One significant event was a meeting with Katherine McKee, the program officer for women's affairs at the Ford Foundation. She was looking for ideas to fund at the forthcoming UN conference on women to be held in Nairobi, Kenya, in 1985. I shared with her my concern as expressed in my Paris lecture at the OECD/DAC and in my critique of the "catching-up-with-men" approach that was embedded in the UN framework for reporting to the Nairobi conference. I suggested panels and platforms from which women from the developing countries could present their own act, a presentation of views from the South, recalling those moments of distance and discomfort that we from the Third World had felt in the North. Kate's response was encouraging and we decided to begin the process by having a consultation. I insisted it be in the South. Women from all the continents of the world were invited to Bangalore in August 1984.

In three unforgettable days the group transformed the framework given by the UN for Nairobi and, as we realized later, the experience transformed each individual. On the first day we took the UN framework and put up the usual paper charts for jotting down ideas. The day ended in deep frustration. On the second day, Fatima Mernissi of Morocco, tired and angry, said, "Off with all those wall papers. This is not the way to think, against some one else's framework." In a flash we started to identify the various crises in our regions, starting with Africa, where the flash point was hunger, a food crisis. Soon Latin America's debt, South Asia's poverty, and the Pacific Islands' militarism were identified as the major preoccupations. Poor women in these regions were not only totally engaged in the economies of these countries, but were both suffering from and responding creatively to these onslaughts. The framework began to emerge. Next we thought about how it could be captured in panels and in a document for the Nairobi conference.

A process plan for accomplishing these things was prepared. The title for the idea for this project we called DAWN—Development Alternative with Women for a New Era. The DAWN follow-up cell was located at ISST and remained there until September 1985, when the cell rotated to Latin America. (See Antrobus, this volume.) For the next ten months ISST not only began to manage the process, but also raised funds to support consultations regarding the document as well as for the Nairobi panels. Meanwhile, I traveled wherever I was invited to mobilize support, drafting proposals en route. Besides Ford, support was provided by the Population Council and the Norwegian and Finnish governments.

The first round of drafts emerged in Bergen in the spring of 1985, drawn up by small working groups. The drafts contextualized the analysis of poor women's responses to development in their regions but moved on to generalizations; combined, they recognized the women's movement as the crucial vehicle for change and offered an alternative vision for development. The final draft was then worked on by Gita Sen and Caren Grown and published as *Development Alternatives with Women for a New Era: Development, Crises, and Alternative Visions: Third World Women's Perspectives.* This book, which reflects a new development paradigm, has been widely quoted by development agencies and is often used in university courses.

This process and its outcome have taught many lessons and uncovered many ideas. First, it showed that thinking should not be structured. In the traditional societies of the South, thinking together is through open-ended, unstructured conversation. This permits the emergence of the most creative aspects of a group's thinking, whereas structuring would groove their thinking along pre-established channels. Second, it demonstrated that when an idea resonates in other minds and hearts, then the flow of support—moral and financial—happens readily. It takes off, perhaps demonstrating a feminist view that an idea is born in many places at the same time and cannot be individually claimed. The third lesson emerged when feminists in the North showed delight at the initiative of women of the South to claim their political identity and actively supported their effort.

Roadblocks to Transformation

In assessing the advancement of women, many things must be taken into consideration. At the start of the twenty-first century their achievements are being stressed, as part of significant benchmarks and the end of a millennium. Women are writing their histories, claiming to have generated an idea or prompted a program. Women are being honored for bringing about change. Such celebration, however, has also raised difficult questions. Who really uncovered the shroud, coined a phrase, or fostered a movement? Because the written word and its dissemination are dominated by the English-speaking North, the South often is denied the credit it is due for the many discoveries made there, especially in the field of development.

More significant and more troubling are questions about the extent of accomplishments. Statistical evidence documents the unyielding nature of poverty among women along with the unyielding nature of men's control over every domain, whether in society, government, the intellectual world, or the United Nations. The transformation that women are seeking seems to be on hold; our endeavors to highlight the power and value of women's presence in any space have still not yielded significant relief from the overall assault on women, in the form of physical violence at home or at theaters of conflict.[19] It may not simply be a matter of men being reluctant to change; some have said that we have failed because of our own virtues. We like to be free, different; we stress individuality and emphasize cultural and other forms of group diversity among ourselves. Has this meant that we cannot be that tidal wave which crashes with a united force, smashing received ideas and practices?

At international conferences and within global agencies, other processes are taking place. Since these theaters of activity are located in the North— New York, Washington, or Geneva—those who are close to these cities remain close to power. In these theaters, there seems to be a growing trend to replace the concept of "development" with that of "rights." With sleight of pen and mind, Amartya Sen has called development "freedom," and the UNDP's Human Development Report has enshrined this change in its 2000 Reports, which describes development as freedom from basic horrors like hunger and illiteracy.[20] Because most of those working for social justice are now engaging laws, the courts, and the judiciary rather than the state, the rights framework looks more attractive and is easier to glide into than the development approach. But after all the litigation, the issues nonetheless come back to economics and development, as resources are also required for that freedom. The rights framework easily becomes a transnational actor, a characteristic that, while it has many positive values for women, also has some troubling edges in the realm of affirming national sovereignty in an increasingly globalized and polarized world. Significant changes are taking place in international financing arrangements and ideologies regarding what constitutes economic success, apart from global governance, with significant shifts in the role of the UN itself in the global arena. Many of these trends are not to the advantage of the South.

As feminists we need to reflect on these phenomena. Feminists are known for challenging inherited theories of knowledge and practice. Whether it be through theology, psychology, social anthropology, or history, we are continually exposing the error in the information base, in the understanding and reconstructing of these sciences. Now we need to define a way forward that enables us to make the quantum leap into the mindset of the "Other" as well as to participate with eyes wide open in the international politics of economics.

Feminists working in development across the North-South divide have formed wise alliances against economic, social, and cultural injustices, but North-dominated political economy plans still dominate. Closer alliances and struggles within national bounds, which press for the deepening of democracy and the strengthening of national sovereignty, are called for. Globally, we feminists must foster regionalism and work for the creation of institutional frameworks for decentralizing economic and political power.

Peggy Antrobus

Peggy Antrobus is from the Caribbean and holds degrees in economics, social work, and education. Since the 1960s she has worked with government and NGO programs in the field of development and social change. She is a feminist activist in the women's movement and has a special interest in issues of women's leadership. In the 1980s she was a founding member of the Caribbean Association for Feminist Research and Action (CAFRA) and of the network of Third World women promoting Development Alternatives with Women for a New Era (DAWN), of which she was general coordinator from 1991 to 1996.

Over the years she has written and published extensively on a wide range of topics related to women's roles in and perspectives on international development. Her doctoral work focused on the impact of government policies on women and the ways in which these policies reflect global trends. Her current work focuses on women's leadership. At the invitation of Zed Books of London, she is currently engaged in the risky task of writing a book on the global women's movement.

A Caribbean Journey: Defending Feminist Politics

It all started with Lucille Mair. She was a leader in the second wave of the women's movement in the Caribbean in more ways than one. As an historian, she helped retrieve the history of our foremothers, the women whose struggles secured and sustained a people uprooted from ancestral homes to form new families and communities in circumstances of unimaginable hardship and inhumanity. She inspired us with images of nameless rebel women who used every means to secure their people's well-being.[1]

From her youth Lucille was a person of deep political conviction. She was among those who helped shape the vision of Michael Manley's Third Way in Jamaica in 1972 and became that nation's first adviser on women's affairs; she headed the newly established Agency for Public Information in 1974, and from there went on to hold even more important positions in the field of diplomacy. In 1980 she made Caribbean women proud as the secretary-general of the UN Second World Conference on Women at Copenhagen.

Heading the Jamaican Women's Bureau

In 1974 Lucille thought me a suitable replacement for her in the advisory position on women's affairs. I had a degree in economics, professional training as a social worker, and experience in community development. But I think that to Lucille my best qualification was my ability to define a post and advance a program. In her eyes I was a good and dedicated manager and she believed that this offset my lack of a feminist background and experience in the field of women's affairs. Perhaps she even thought the lack of these attributes advantageous. I had no preconceptions of what was required, no personal ambitions beyond doing a good job, no political agenda of my own, and no labels to raise suspicions or create hostility. I was someone who could figure out what was needed to move toward the goals forged by those with vision. I could listen and learn and turn ideas into action.

The women in Manley's People's National Party (PNP) did not share Lucille's views as to my suitability. They said: "Who is this woman? What does she know about Jamaican women? She is not even Jamaican! She doesn't belong to the party!" The reaction of the bureaucracy was different. The head of the Ministry of Community Development, to which the advisory post was attached, made it clear the first time we met that he considered the whole project women's affairs unnecessary. He went to his bookshelf, produced a copy of the laws of Jamaica, and showed me the one that stated that there should be no discrimination on the basis of race or sex. What more could these women want? He must have been greatly relieved that I lacked the credentials of an activist. I was not someone who would rock the boat. With my apolitical and fairly conservative background he didn't believe that I would challenge anyone. He didn't know about the transformational power of feminism or about my openness to new ideas.

On the eve of International Women's Year in November 1974, I was appointed to a part-time post in the Ministry of Community Development. The job's scope was wide open. There were no guidelines and the precedents were not appropriate. I managed to persuade the bureaucrats to release me from the burden of being an "adviser" and to designate me director of a women's desk. Then I decided to start by leaving my desk and going into communities across Jamaica to learn about Jamaican women from the women themselves.

Since I had no staff or funds I could turn this to advantage by drawing on the field staff of the Ministries of Health, Education, Community Development, and Agriculture, the women whose work it was to be out in the parishes providing public services. This kind of activity was something in which I had experience, having set up the Community Development Department in St. Vincent nearly ten years earlier. Had I been a lawyer, a researcher, or an activist, I might have chosen a different strategy for launching the program.

In addition, I reached out to the women's organizations—the Soroptimists, Business and Professional Women's Clubs, the Jamaica Federation of Women, and the YWCA—that had been formulating recommendations on laws and projects so that I could be informed about what was needed. Finally, I sought help from faculty at the Mona Campus of the University of the West Indies (UWI) to do the research required for the earliest situational analyses of women in Jamaica.

Political will was critical. My most strategic support came from the women in the PNP. Putting aside disappointment at getting a non-Jamaican, non-party woman in the post they had struggled for, they worked closely with me in a strategy of three interlocking components: the bureaucracy, women within the ruling political party, and autonomous women's organizations (in my experience, the most effective combination for generating action). They respected my role within the bureaucracy, strengthened it by effectively demanding that the desk be upgraded to a women's bureau, and transferred it to the Office of the Prime Minister where it could and did receive his strong support, under the tutelage and watchful eye of his wife and other wives of ministers, collectively called Cabinet Wives. We each understood the limitations of our different spheres of influence and built on the relative strengths of these separate locations.

The success of Jamaica's national machinery for the integration of women in development was, in its first years, more than anything else due to the commitment, vigilance, and support it received from the leadership of the women in the PNP Women's Auxiliary. These women were feminists, meaning they understood women's subordinate position in society, and were committed to challenge and change it in solidarity with other women. They saw this as an essential part of the meaning of democratic socialism and they understood that the women within the party would have to organize themselves to work for gender equality within this agenda. They transformed their own organization from a women's auxiliary into a women's movement, a change that was more than a semantic one. They claimed autonomy within the party, building strategic alliances with women in the other parties to fight for the inclusion of domestic workers in minimum wage legislation and for maternity leave. They insisted on supporting women as candidates over the objections of men within the party. They held ministers accountable by calling them to report on their performance at their conferences.

At a personal level, my work with the Jamaican Women's Bureau was transformative. Starting out with no feminist consciousness, I developed one from my experiences with working-class Jamaican women. From these women I learned about the contradictions of class privilege and women's autonomy, the ways in which privilege can work as a barrier to freedom of expression and association. From women not normally accorded respect within a colonial class structure, I learned to respect myself as a woman.

The Women and Development Unit (WAND)

I left Jamaica in July 1977, having learned more about women, about development, and about power and politics than I had learned in three years reading for a degree in political economics at a British university. Accompanying my husband to Barbados, where he had a new post, I decided to try to leave behind the struggle and return to the more acceptable role as full-time housewife and mother. It lasted for a year. I found that leaving Jamaica was easier than leaving the movement.

Just before my departure I had worked with the staff tutor in social work in the outreach program of UWI to organize a regional seminar titled Integration of Women in Caribbean Development. The idea for a regional meeting was born of my concern that the interests of Caribbean women were not served by being linked to the larger region of Latin America, as was the custom at the UN. At regional meetings organized by the UN Economic Commission for Latin America—at that time the Caribbean was not even mentioned—I found the other Caribbean participants were often as ignorant of the issues on the agenda as I had been when I first started this work. Making matters worse was the contrast between the experience of Latin American and Caribbean women in terms of education, the family, and participation in the labor force.[2]

The seminar named me a member of the steering committee appointed to follow up on its recommendations and I was able to develop a proposal for a regional women's development program, raise funds for it, and negotiate for it to be located within the outreach programs of UWI. The Women and Development Unit (WAND) was launched in 1978. Its objectives were broadly defined so as to allow its program to be shaped by its constituency. WAND was not just another project within UWI, but an attempt to define a different relationship between the university and the communities it was established to serve. WAND was to be a link between academia and activism.

WAND's values were primarily a deep commitment to the women of the region, and especially to those marginalized by poverty and a lack of resources, trust in regionalism and regional approaches to social change, faith in the ability of Caribbean people to find creative solutions to our development problems from within the region, and belief in UWI's capacity to take leadership in this quest. WAND's programs focused on five strategies: communications and awareness building, capacity building through technical assistance and training, the use of pilot projects to explore alternative approaches to development, and networking and advocacy.

The Unit evolved over time. In the case study of WAND in her book *Transforming Development*, Peg Snyder, the first head of the United Nations Development Fund for Women (UNIFEM), then known as the Voluntary Fund for the UN Decade for Women, has written: "The history of the partnership between WAND and UNIFEM is in many ways a story of the evolution of the women and development movement itself over its first one and a half decades." She refers to its shift "in just a few years from integrating women in development" to "empowering women for social change."[3] But here I want to underline the fact that the history of the shift is also a story of the evolution of my own feminist consciousness, combined with a three-tiered annual evaluation exercise in which decisions regarding WAND's work and future direction were made. These evaluations were taken on the basis of an analysis of global trends, an assessment of regional developments, socioeconomic and institutional, and a critique of our activities.

This combination of an internal process of "conscientization" with the practice of engaging the whole staff in reflection and analysis of the external environment in relation to what we were attempting served to ensure that WAND's work was always relevant to what was happening in the wider society. Three stages can be discerned in the evolution of WAND's work from the time of its inception in August 1978 to August 1995, when I retired.

Three Stages of Evolution

The first stage ran from 1978 to 1981. Its focus can be characterized as one of putting women on the agenda and of exploration of the territory, casting the net wide to understand where we stood as a regional program for women and what was needed throughout the region, in terms or institutional arrangements and awareness, to enhance the participation of women in regional development. That stage ended with the establishment of the Women's Desk in the Caribbean Community, which took over WAND's functions in relation to awareness and capacity building within government programs and national machinery for the advancement of women. The Caribbean Association for Feminist Research and Action built on WAND's early work with women's organizations, and the launching of Women and Development Studies groups on the three campuses of UWI and at the University of Guyana. The Women and Development Studies program would do within the university what WAND was neither equipped nor inclined to do: the painstaking but necessary academic work. WAND was a catalyst for all these programs.

In the second stage, from 1982 to 1985, the focus can be characterized as the search for alternatives. This was prompted by the realization, based on my assessment prepared for the Copenhagen Conference in 1980, that despite progress on many of the recommendations of the Plan of Action from Mexico City, the situation of women was actually worsening world-wide. While we had not yet done the analysis that would have explained why this was so, it was clear that we would need to explore alternative development strategies.

Our pilot projects were implemented in this second phase. They involved community development in St. Vincent, St. Lucia, and Dominica, where we worked with community-based organizations and nongovernmental organizations (NGOs); focusing on nontraditional skills in Grenada, and food preservation in Barbados; and used radio, in a program called *The People of Tomorrow*, to stimulate and support young people in search of employment.

Another important experimental project at this time was Planning for Women in Rural Development, a research project that was carried out in collaboration with the Population Council of New York in Jamaica, St. Lucia, and Dominica, to explore a different approach to policy-related research and planning. In this project WAND worked with representatives of rural women, NGOs, and national ministries of agriculture and community development and planning units to define the questions that needed to be addressed if rural development projects were to benefit women.

In the mid-1980s, WAND implemented a Training of Trainers program to transfer methodologies and skills learned in the community development projects to a wider group of people working in rural and community development throughout the eastern Caribbean. The methodologies have become part of the range of skills incorporated into the practice of people working in the field of rural and community development throughout the region.

The third stage, starting in 1985, was the most fundamental shift from a primarily technical and professional to a more political and feminist approach. It was a search for a new development paradigm, prompted by my involvement with the network of Third World women researchers and activists called DAWN because we were proposing development alternatives with women for a new era.

With the emergence of DAWN feminists at the NGO Forum at Nairobi in 1985, Third World women found a voice that was to challenge and change the discourse on women and development. By locating women's experience of development in the colonial and neo-colonial context and the macro-economic policies that reflected this colonial relationship, we introduced an analytical framework that was to change the terms of the debate on women's issues worldwide. The DAWN network's analysis of the interlocking, systemic crises of debt, deteriorating social services, environmental degradation, food security, religious fundamentalism, and militarism and political conservatism grew out of the experience of poor women living in the countries of the economic South. It provided the global women's movement the tools for advancing a different perspective on all development issues, from environment to human rights, from population to poverty.

I was a founding member of DAWN and its general coordinator from 1990 to 1996. During those years DAWN's secretariat was located at WAND. This association enabled Caribbean women to make the link between the work we had been doing at sectoral and community levels with an understanding of the macro-economic framework within which countries of the region were beginning to operate, the framework of structural adjustment.[4]

Extending WID

The interesting point is that while we may have been unaware of the wider significance of what we were doing, WAND was defining an approach that was to challenge and transform the field of women in development. According to Nora Cebotarev, professor of sociology at the University of Guelph in Canada, WAND's approach had elements of WID, in terms of asking for amended legislation and equal opportunity for women, but it has a broader political framework. Women's problems are not seen as solely created by a lack of equal opportunity, but are also the result of the colonial and neo-colonial system of exploitation from the North. Thus, in WAND, work with women is not only concerned with meeting their practical needs, but there are also attempts to create a political consciousness about international dependency relations and the resulting socio-economic exploitation that affect both women and men.[5]

In this approach many of the same activities have been undertaken as in the prior one, resulting in benefits similar to those of WID with the additional advantages of creating a much more critical political consciousness in women's groups and of conducting research that showed not only the structural impediments experienced by individual women, but also the difficulties encountered by entire dependent countries. WAND's approach attempts to empower women, but its primary purpose is to disclose and fight the vestiges of colonialism and the Western view of development—in this approach, as in the previous one, there was no explicit acknowledgment of gender as an important consideration. However, some embryonic initiatives included men in the predominantly women-oriented work.[6]

Above, I quoted Cebotarev's words in full, for sometimes others perceive our intentions and actions more clearly than we ourselves do. When we chose to name WAND Women and Development rather than Women in Development, we never realized that we would be creating a new approach. We simply wanted to underline the relationship between women and development. However, I was fully conscious of the need to explore a different approach from that which followed in the conventional WID approach through advocacy for equal opportunities and resources for women; passage of anti-discrimination legislation; establishment of national machinery for the integration of women in development; and launching of projects in the areas of income generation, literacy, and research on women.

The context in which the idea of women in development (WID) was formulated is important for an understanding of the approach. The 1970s, the Second Development Decade was a time of hope and optimism. Drawing on the lessons of the First Development Decade of the 1960s, the limitations of market-led growth were recognized. The assumption that the wealth created by economic growth would trickle down to the poorest in society proved false. Attention turned to the role of the state, and particularly to ways the international community might address structural imbalances between the industrialized countries of the North and the developing countries of the South. Issues of equity and participation were at the center of the discourse on development. It was the decade of North-South dialogue and the call for a New International Economic Order. It is significant that the Decade for Women fell partially within the 1970s.

By 1980 the context had changed to one in which the emphasis was no longer on equity but on efficiency, and the focus shifted from the role of the state to that of the market. The 1980s have been characterized by Latin Americans as "the Lost Decade," during which many of the gains achieved by women in the areas of education, health, and welfare, were reversed in the framework of structural adjustment programs advocated by the International Monetary Fund and the World Bank in response to the debt crisis. It was clear to many that we could no longer assume that women would benefit from integration into a process that was fundamentally exploitative. The shift from women in development to women and development was in part a response to this changed context.

Between 1984 and 1995 WAND explored an approach that extended WID. We questioned the mainstream concept of development and introduced a broader framework of analysis that acknowledged the structural and political barriers to women's participation as well as the extent to which economic development, far from excluding women, actually benefits when women's time, labor, and sexuality are exploited. Our approach emphasized women's strategic gender interests and their empowerment to promote and protect gains made within the framework of WID.

Finally, we included men in many of our programs. And although we did not use the word "gender" in our work, we certainly confronted gender issues by drawing attention to the asymmetric relations between men and women and the implications for development policy and practice of women's multiple roles and their primary role in social reproduction.

Feminist Politics and Its Challenges

What does all of this mean for the women's movement and for the field of women and development in this region today? While writing this essay I was also updating an article I had written for the *Oxford Companion on the Politics of the World*. As I reflected on both these pieces it seemed to me that we need to be much clearer concerning the distinctions between the women's movement as a social movement; the feminist movement as a particular kind of politics within the wider movement; women's organizations as part of the spectrum of NGOs; and the programmatic fields of women in development (WID), women and development (WAND), and gender and development (GAD). We have tended to refer to these interchangeably, which has served both to confuse and obscure the problems we now confront when attempting to focus on women's issues in the Caribbean.

Because of its negative connotations we have avoided using the word "feminist," referring instead to the women's movement or more often to women's organizations. "Feminist" is a difficult word for many Third World women and for women of color. I had never heard the word when I first became involved in this field. I recall the 1976 meeting in Bangkok called Feminist Ideology and Structures in the First Half of the Decade. It was an extraordinary, groundbreaking meeting in many ways, a turning point in the lives of many women, including me. Sponsored by the Asia and Pacific Center for Women and Development, a UN agency, it was probably the first and last time a UN meeting was labeled feminist.

The meeting in Bangkok, however, was the turning point in my political development, so that while I had tried to avoid the use of the word "feminist" before attending the meeting, I left determined to use it as often as possible—while always being careful to define it, of course. The appeal of the word to me lay in its acknowledgment of the political nature of most issues. Listening to Charlotte Bunch's account of the origins of her feminist consciousness in the U.S. civil rights movement, where she discovered her own oppression as a woman even as she worked against racial oppression, I saw for the first time the parallels between the power relations based on class, race, ethnicity, and gender on the one hand, and in international relations between rich and poor countries on the other.

In the experience recounted here I have tried to show how a particular kind of politics, feminist politics, informed the establishment and shaped the programs within institutions such as the UN, governments, and universities. It was this politics that breathed life and passion into what would ordinarily be just another conference, another bureaucratic initiative, or another university project. Failure to acknowledge this is to condemn our efforts to failure. For it is only a clear recognition of the energy of feminist politics in our work as administrators, teachers, researchers, practitioners, and organizers that will save it from becoming meaningless exercises and save some of us from colluding in the undermining of our vision.

There currently exist efforts to de-politicize the field and the women's movement by eliminating the feminist political agenda. I see evidence of this in the co-optation of feminist language (as in "empowerment"), feminist concepts (as with "gender"), and feminist visions (as with "transformational leadership"). I also see it in various bureaucratic devices such as gender mainstreaming, gender analysis, and the substitution of the word "gender" for "women" in so many programs. Much of what was conceived in feminist politics has become, or is fast becoming, something else.

The mainstreaming of women's projects was meant to be a strategy for linking them into the processes of development planning and delivery systems so that women gained access to mainstream development resources. The feminists who proposed the use of the concept of gender did so in order to gain a deeper understanding of the ways the social relations of gender—both those that determined the division of labor between men and women and those that created the unequal relations of power between them—contributed to women's marginalization in the development process. Finally, the introduction of gender management systems was supposed to be a way of incorporating gender sensitivity into governance in the name of good governance, equity, and efficiency.

Without commitment to gender equity, however, the use of the concept of gender can lead to the removal of the focus on women altogether. Indeed, it appears that gender is being increasingly used to give more attention to men's needs. The emphasis on bureaucratic approaches to women and gender in/and development, along with a denial of the political and feminist roots of the WID initiative and the feminist politics that has advanced the WID agenda, is serving to de-politicize women as a constituency in development.

It might also be viewed as parallel to the rise in religious fundamentalism on the political front. The struggles in Copenhagen in 1980 and Beijing in 1995, and more recently in the Review of the International Conference on Population and Development (Cairo + 5), to undermine the new framework of health, rights, and empowerment secured in Cairo at the 1994 population conference, demonstrate the price of success on these fronts. In addition, in the Caribbean countries and elsewhere there are signs of a backlash as expressed through increasing articulation of "male marginalization" and "men in crisis" theses.[7] While there may be some comfort in the thought that the backlash is evidence of the effectiveness of the challenge of the women's movement to the status quo, we must be careful not to miss the wider implications of the discrediting of feminism.

Throughout this essay I have been talking about a particular type of leadership and a particular type of politics. It starts with an understanding of the way injustice is embedded in the social relations of gender and grounded in a politics informed by that analysis. It ends with a passionate commitment to work for gender justice as a way of addressing all other issues. This kind of leadership is to be found everywhere: in a university classroom or residence hall, the bureaucracy, political parties and trade unions, social movements, women's organizations and other NGOs, and community-based organizations. Throughout our society there are men as well as women who manifest it. They are in all our institutions, including legislatures, churches, schools, and families.

Today more than ever, in the context of a global economic system designed in the interest of multinational corporations and unapologetic in its promise of unlimited wealth for those with the resources to use technological advances to their advantage, there is a need for leadership informed by a politics grounded in a consciousness of the ways in which women's subordinate position in society serves as the basis of an economic system that is fundamentally exploitative of people. We need a politics that understands the link between women's oppression and the oppression of other marginalized groups and sectors. We need a politics committed, on the basis of this consciousness, to challenging these structures of oppression and the institutions that promote them. We need a politics that seeks to work through the mobilization of women to demand policies that would put the interests of people first.

Women can lead the challenge to globalization, as we did in challenging policies of structural adjustment. As the DAWN platform for Beijing puts it, "women stand at the crossroads between production and reproduction, between economic activity and the care of human beings, and therefore between economic growth and human development. They are the workers in both spheres, those most responsible, and therefore with most at stake, those who suffer the most when the two work at cross-purposes, and most sensitive to the need for better integration between the two."[8]

The time has come to rethink our strategies and priorities if women are not to be used to bolster and promote policies that run counter to our practical and strategic gender interests. In fact, the time has come to reclaim and acknowledge the feminist politics that has been our source of strength and energy.

PART III

In and Out of Government

Vivian Lowery Derryck

Vivian Lowery Derryck is senior vice president and director of public-private partnerships at the Academy for Educational Development, a U.S.-based private voluntary organization. From 1998 to 2000 she served as assistant administrator for Africa in the United States Agency for International Development (USAID), administering an annual budget of more than $843 million. Prior to her USAID service, she was the senior advisor of the Africa Leadership Forum, an organization concerned with promoting democratic development. From 1989 to 1996 she served as president of the African-American Institute in New York, where she had also worked immediately after graduate school.

Under Presidents Jimmy Carter and Ronald Reagan, she served as a deputy assistant secretary of state and then moved to the National Council of Negro Women, where she was executive vice president and director of its international division. In 1984–88 she was vice president of the National Democratic Institute for International Affairs, executive director of the Washington International Center, and a vice president of Meridian House International.

She has taught at New York City Technical College, developed African curricular materials at the Education Development Center in Boston, and spent 1973–77 teaching at the University of Liberia and working with the Liberian Ministry of Education. A graduate of Chatham College and Columbia University, Ms. Derryck is a member of the Council on Foreign Relations and the Bretton Woods Committee. The recipient of several awards, including the Guggenheim Humanitarian Award and the Martin Luther King Public Service Award, she has an honorary doctorate from Chatham College.

Searching for Equality: WID Needed at Home and Abroad

"Women hold up half the sky." Proverbs like this have always helped to keep me centered, and being centered was very important to a shy, black, only child growing up in Cleveland, Ohio, in the 1950s. I found refuge in books. I wanted to learn about people like me and about foreign lands. The only trouble was that in the 1950s, very few authors were writing about women and virtually no one was writing about black women. I searched library shelves but came up empty-handed nine times out of ten. I vowed that "when I grew up" I was going to work to be sure that blacks and women were featured as prominent entries in major reference books and encyclopedias. Well, I haven't realized that vow, but for more than thirty-five years I've worked consistently on women's equity and social justice in the U.S. and abroad. From NGO leadership positions such as president of the African-American Institute and vice president of the National Democratic Institute, the National Council of Negro Women and the Academy for Educational Development (AED), to senior government positions at the Department of State and as U.S. Senate-confirmed Assistant Admin-istrator for Africa at the U.S. Agency for International Development, I hope that I've been a constant voice for women's equality and racial justice.

Women and Race

For me, women and race were inevitable preoccupations in a middle-class household where discussions of race dominated the dinner table and professional women were confidently opinionated. My grandmother and great-grandmother were teachers; my mother had a B.A. degree in social work. I lived in a world of housewives, teachers, and social workers, the latter two being the two professions open to black women then. But outside their social network, these highly competent black women were invisible. I saw the dual burden of race and gender weighing on these magnificent women, and I chafed that they didn't openly confront the inequities. I couldn't understand why women, black and white, weren't more assertive in public. (I didn't know about distinctions between public and private power at age eight.) Why weren't women making decisions?

The only way to answer that question was to learn all I could about women and to become a decision maker myself. I read every biography of women I could get my hands on and used every opportunity for school talks (daily five-minute presentations by a student to classmates) to talk about a woman. One day a classmate, Kay Richardson, and I were in the school library, doing research for our upcoming talks. Bored with taking notes, we began fantasizing about what we wanted to be when we grew up. This was fairly soon after Queen Elizabeth II's coronation and I declared that I wanted to be a queen. "You can't be a queen. There are no black queens," Kay laughed.

"Oh, yes I can. I can be queen of Ethiopia!" I shot back.

I think that exchange, almost fifty years ago, got me hooked on Africa. I didn't know whether Haile Selassie shared his throne with a queen, but that really wasn't the point. I suspect that I was signaling a yearning to move beyond the safe world of black middle-class Cleveland. It was a comfortable world, but a world in which it was clear that black women carried the dual burden of race and gender. Any astute little girl could see that. This little girl also knew that if she was interested in international affairs, she had to leave Ohio.

And leave I did. But I carried the commitment to women and racial equality with me. I've been driven by two goals: increased education for minorities and women as the key to upward mobility and social equality, and a fierce desire to improve women's economic and political equality in the United States and the developing world.

"For wisdom is better than rubies." That quote from the Bible in Proverbs 1 has always sustained me.

Perhaps because the teachers in my family influenced me, I believe that education is central to women's empowerment. In the developing world, education holds the key to women's economic and political integration. Education for women means higher labor force participation rates; lower crude birth rates; healthier, longer lives; and fuller economic integration.

I wasn't aware of the statistics on women when I went to Côte d'Ivoire (Ivory Coast) in the mid-1960s as a participant in Operation Crossroads Africa. Founded by a visionary black pastor, Reverend James O. Robinson, Crossroads was the precursor to the Peace Corps, organizing exchange programs in which African and American young people worked together on development projects during U.S. summers. My college roommate persuaded me to meet Reverend Robinson when he visited Pittsburgh and our college campus (Chatham) to recruit students for the program. I had won a fellowship for summer study abroad and as I toyed with the choice of Crossroads or studying the grand cathedrals of Europe, my major professor advised, "Go to Africa. It's changing fast and those cathedrals will always be there."

Therein hangs the tale of my next thirty-six years. That summer of 1965 in Côte d'Ivoire changed my life. I witnessed unrelenting poverty and social and economic discrimination that rural women had to battle every day. In the village of Ferkessedougou, women chopped wood, hauled water, pounded foufou, and bent over feeble cooking fires. Without a viable mechanism for increased opportunities, I could foresee generations of this bare existence for rural women. The way out, the way to break the cycle was through education. But as the colonizers well knew, education could be subversive; once you can read, you can read anything. Education is the ultimate gift, a gift truly better than rubies.

After that memorable summer I returned to college, reinvigorated, motivated to become a development professional. I felt that I had a duty—a responsibility of black American privilege—to ally with these women to work to alleviate poverty and promote education. I graduated from college, started a master's program at Columbia, got married, had a son, and moved to Liberia, where I taught at the University of Liberia after giving birth to a daughter at a local hospital. At the university I managed to integrate a women's component into my classes and identified local women leaders in an initiative to add Liberian content to the country's secondary schools' social studies curricula. In 1975 I worked with Liberian women world conference colleagues on preparation for Mexico City, vocally bemoaning that I couldn't be a part of their representation at the conference but heartened by the Liberian delegation's emphasis on education.

In 1977 two senior officials from the new Carter administration visited Liberia and recruited my then-husband to work for Action, the combined Peace Corps and VISTA voluntary service agency. After four years in Africa, it felt heady to return home and to meet Irene Tinker, Perdita Huston, and Arvonne Fraser, icons in the growing field of women in development (WID). In Arvonne, I found a fellow traveler just as impassioned as I was about the centrality of education. In a United States Agency for International Development (USAID) study funded by her office, I differentiated between formal education for girls, nonformal programs for female adults, and informal programs for those women hardest to reach. The study corroborated the benefits of female education for economic growth, identified major constraints, and advocated increased investment in education for girls.

In the almost 25 intervening years, multiple studies have confirmed the benefits of educating girls. The World Bank has become a champion of girls' education, the Academy for Educational Development has marked girls' education as one of its signature accomplishments, and lip service is paid to the need to educate girls by virtually all the donors to development. Perhaps policy makers have made the investment because studies have demonstrated that the best development investment is an investment in girls' education, but more likely we see the investment has been made because of the advocacy of women's groups and development economists' new understanding of its importance.

Thirty-five years after my Côte d'Ivoire epiphany regarding education, the picture for women's education is still dismal. There has been progress, but in sub-Saharan Africa advances occur at a snail's pace. The reluctance to invest in female education is astounding. Problems of retention, equal access to places in secondary education, and the poor quality of African tertiary education still bedevil education systems and women's advocates.

I still worry about illiterate women eighteen years and older. Who will speak for these women? Viewed in many countries as politically expendable, they have no allies and no advocates. I continue to ask why is it so difficult to get male policy makers in African countries to accept the economic and social value of an investment in adult women. Twenty years ago, the answer to that question led to a disturbing picture of government. Behemoth governments are hard to move, especially if there is no interest group or constituency to highlight inequities and demand changes. Since there were no champions for these women and, unskilled in the techniques of advocacy, they knew no options beyond their villages, their issues and education options languished. They needed a constituency. I needed one, too, if I hoped to push the issue.

I found a gold mine for the education issue among colleagues in the international women's movement. By 1979 I had expanded my advocacy on women's education and was able to move into work on women's political participation, It had taken me more than a dozen years to be able to focus on women and political participation, my specialty in graduate school. I dreamed of new alliances and political awareness through the UN Decade for Women and the Mid-Decade Conference at Copenhagen.

Women's Work Sustains Men's Power: Lessons at the Copenhagen Conference

"Women's work sustains men's power" is a phrase I like that was introduced by the Australian delegation to the 1980 Platform for Action adopted at the world women's conference held at Copenhagen. The UN Decade for Women was a watershed for women's empowerment. Playing a pivotal role through its convening power, the UN brought together in three landmark conferences during the Decade over 20,000 women who ranged from WID supporters in both industrialized nations and less-developed countries to royalty (the Mid-Decade Conference in Copenhagen, Denmark, was opened by Queen Beatrix in 1980) to political activists such as Bella Abzug and Palestinian freedom fighter Leila Khalid.

The Decade was even more remarkable when one considers it was declared in the midst of the Cold War. By 1980 and the Mid-Decade Conference, the USSR had invaded Afghanistan, U.S. diplomats were captive in Iran, and African liberation wars raged in South Africa, Angola, and Namibia. In the United States, UN-bashing reached its height in 1980. Yet American feminists were still on a high from International Women's Year in 1975, the subsequent Houston Conference in 1977 and the resulting publication, *The Spirit of Houston*, plus the Plan of Action adopted in Mexico City at the International Women's Year Conference.

But the Mid-Decade Conference was still a UN meeting, subject to all the political maneuverings that occurred during any UN conference during the Cold War. It was one in a series of conferences in which four matters inevitably dominated debate. These were a Third World–proposed New International Economic Order that would give a larger amount of the world's wealth to the poor majority; the New International Information Order to restrain media criticism of government policies; criticisms of Israel and its actions in the occupied territories; and denunciations of the apartheid-riddled states of Southern Africa. The USSR and its supporters sought to insert the phrase "Zionism is racism" into all UN documents related to Israel and to usurp the moral high ground on apartheid by inserting phrases that would force the United States to vote against any racial equality resolutions tabled at UN meetings.

These ploys manifested themselves at the Copenhagen conference through three contentious documents. The first, "The Effects of Israeli Occupation on Palestinian Women Inside and Outside the Occupied Territories," was ripe for insertion of the "Zionism is racism" phrase. The two others, "The Role of Women in the Struggle for Liberation in Zimbabwe, Namibia, and South Africa" and "The Effects of Apartheid on the Status of Women in South Africa and Namibia," were intended to paint the United States and its allies as pro-apartheid.

I was appointed executive director of the U.S. secretariat to prepare for the Copenhagen conference. Since the conference merited a White House appointment, I worked closely with Sarah Weddington, special assistant to President Carter for women's affairs. Sarah was and is a household name, famous for successfully arguing *Roe v. Wade*, the abortion case, before the U.S. Supreme Court. As the secretariat director, I was charged with coordinating U.S. responses to the political agenda as well as the UN's data collection requests. I also managed the extremely delicate task of sorting through and recommending to the White House proposed candidates for the thirty-nine-person delegation that the United States planned to send to the conference. The UN allowed each country only five delegates, so we had thirty-four "advisers." Our delegates were the U.S. permanent representative to the UN, Ambassador Donald McHenry; Sarah Weddington, who alternated with him as chair of the delegation; the head of the Women's Bureau and later the Clinton administration's secretary of labor, Alexis Herman; the then-deputy assistant secretary of state, Sarah Goddard Power; USAID's WID director, Arvonne Fraser; and myself.

Our strategy was to keep the conference from degenerating into the acrimony of previous meetings. At preparatory committee meetings in New York and in regional meetings in Caracas, Lusaka, and Brussels, we tried to develop relationships with other delegates. As is traditional, we divided the world regionally and each member of the delegation was responsible for a country or a region. I, of course, was responsible for Africa. We were a proactive delegation, working with women from Côte d'Ivoire and other African countries enabled us to craft a racial equality resolution that didn't include the phrase "Zionism is racism." But political operatives of the Eastern bloc maneuvered to have the odious phrase inserted, and hard as we worked, with African support, we lost.

I was devastated, convinced that this "tainted" resolution was a personal failing. In retrospect I realize that the insertion was inevitable for several reasons. At the time, "Zionism is racism" was commonly inserted into every document at UN conferences. Many delegates had just arrived from a meeting of the Islamic Conference, with its anti-American rhetoric. Moreover, women delegates often didn't have the political savvy, knowledge of their own political systems, or the political will to fight the professional diplomats.

Our delegates and advisers had the advantage of knowledge about the UN system and substantive expertise. Two delegation advisers, Margaret Galey and Margaret Goodman, were congressional staffers skilled in the Byzantine workings of the UN. U.S. permanent representative Donald McHenry spent considerable time with me and others, always urging us to focus on substance and only fall back on procedural tactics as a last resort. Yet for all of our knowledge, I believe we thought subconsciously that working together on a noble idea was enough to transcend policy. Were we wrong? We were very wrong, as I began to realize when I tried to broker a deal in which the United States would abstain on a motion condemning apartheid. I called the Department of State and spoke with the assistant secretary for international organization affairs. He told me that the United States couldn't change policy midstream to accommodate one conference. The potential deal disintegrated.

The "Zionism is racism" phrase in the document meant the U.S. had to vote "no" on the conference's entire Program of Action, the blueprint for the way forward in the second half of the Decade for Women. In a last ditch effort, I met privately with the secretary-general of the conference, an elegant career diplomat from Jamaica, Ambassador Lucille Mair. While she heard me out politely, she was unwilling to help remove the offending language.

The ultimate blow came at 3:00 A.M. on the last night of the conference as I cast one of four "no" votes. As our Canadian colleague sobbed her "no" vote—she was under instructions to follow the U.S. lead—I bitterly noted that when it came to endgame negotiations and the final vote, male political operatives from outside the Western European and Others Group took the chair, mouthed platitudes about their countries' deep-seated respect for women, and gloated over the adoption of a flawed document.

Despite our infamous "no" vote, the United States experienced some successes. Women's groups and individuals forged enduring alliances. The Voluntary Fund of the UN Decade for Women was sustained and today thrives as UNIFEM, the United Nations Development Fund for Women. The Convention on the Elimination of All Forms of Discrimination Against Women was signed and soon came into force. (Although the U.S. still hasn't approved this Convention, it is an important force worldwide.) We also learned some lessons as a delegation and hopefully as a country. We learned that politics often trumps principle in the UN and that no matter how strong the commitment to a goal, a world conference or any international forum, including a women's conference, is fair game for radical ideas calibrated to irritate the great powers.

After Copenhagen, I was acutely aware of the limitations of a superpower. Now as the U.S. dominates the globe as the only superpower, I continue to reflect on the resentment of some developing countries and some of our allies. The superpower needs to tread gently.

I also discovered the extraordinary power of Congress to express its displeasure. It demonstrated its anger with the "Zionism as racism" outcome by eliminating funding for the next fiscal year for INSTRAW, the International Research and Training Institute for the Advancement of Women and for the Voluntary Fund. The Fund implemented projects offering literacy training, income-generating skills, and health services—practical programs that could change women's lives. Loss of U.S. funding meant that some programs had to be curtailed. It took years for the Fund to recover.

Perhaps the most important lesson that I learned is the value of having a single idea, keeping it simple, and selling it. The Australian delegation came to the preparatory committee meetings and the conference determined to insert a single clause into the Program of Action, namely "Women's work sustains men's power." Consistent and relentless, the Australians negotiated, prodded and convinced enough other delegations to accept the clause. Ultimately they were successful.

The Power of NGOs: As Winston Churchill said, "Never give up. Never give up."

The 1980s and early 1990s were a difficult time to focus on women's education and women's political development in the Third World. Advocating for female education and WID and trying to find space for political development in the sustainable development world kept me busy. I was fortunate to join the newly established National Democratic Institute (NDI), the Democratic Party's international affairs voice. There, a small band of us pioneered U.S. involvement with political parties and civic education around the world as means of promoting civil societies. NDI offered an incredible opportunity to hone advocacy skills, encourage the integration of women, and build a network of vital women interested in women's political participation.

One of our earliest programs was the Eleanor Roosevelt Symposium on Women in Politics held in San Francisco in 1985. Billed as a precursor to the Nairobi Conference of 1985 at the end of the Decade for Women, this gathering was a "who's who" of global women in politics. The president of the Philippines, Corazon Aquino, the prime minister of Dominica, Eugenia Charles, college professor and later U.S. Secretary of State Madeleine Albright, U.S. representative Barbara Mikulski, and former vice presidential candidate Geraldine Ferraro painted pictures of heady possibilities for women and left us giddy with optimism about what women could accomplish. Geraldine Ferraro in particular was the guiding light, bringing enthusiasm, practical experience, and fundraising power to our efforts.

As part of its mission NDI also focused on democracy building in the developing world. In a landmark NDI conference, NDI president and future USAID administrator Brian Atwood, Madeleine Albright, U.S. Senator Paul Simon, future UN Secretary General Boutros Boutros-Ghali, U.S. Representative Julian Dixon, and Democratic Party Chairman Chuck Manatt all journeyed to Senegal to dialogue with African leaders on democratic development in Africa.

None of the African delegations included women, so Madeleine and I were the only two females involved substantively. But by our very presence we made a statement. I'm still close to some of the Senegalese, including senior government officials, and I still prod and applaud them on women's issues. While they look at me with bemusement and sigh, "Ah, Vivian and her women," they also recount proudly their success in integrating women into senior political and economic circles.

NDI provided a wonderful experimental lab in which to work on women's political empowerment. During the mid-1980s, in a political milieu that wasn't always sympathetic to WID issues, NDI was an oasis, the vanguard promoting political inclusion of women. The lack of attention to my issues of women's education, political development, and increased foreign assistance to Africa reinforced the need for alliances. During those years I learned the importance of obtaining support from unexpected quarters and the particular benefits of working with men in alliances. In fact, that's how I met Bob Berg, a well-respected international development strategist regarded by many as an icon in the field.

Bob had been a vocal advocate for WID issues since the early 1970s, but I met him in the 1980s, when we served together on the board of the Association for Women in Development (AWID). I remember an early conference in which he sat on a female genital mutilation panel because he thought the issue needed male support. I was impressed. Years later, both divorced, we married in 1989. Friends queried whether it was a marriage or a merger. The relationship has been both. We've learned that common interests and shared advocacy on subjects we both care about deeply strengthens the relationship. Our work in international development has also helped our children develop good relations with their respective step-parents, as we engage them on everything from career advice to feminist politics to fiancé visas.

Children are an incredible blessing. I am often asked how I juggled two children and an international development career. As a divorced mother, I had strong support from women friends, my mother, and a great church network. Friends would juggle car pools to accommodate my schedule. My mother would travel from Cleveland to stay when I had to travel. But when I returned at 11:30 P.M. from the disastrous 1987 Haitian elections, bone weary and emotionally drained, having seen corpses and body parts and having narrowly averted being shot at, my mother met me at the front door, waving a sheaf of messages from alarmed friends who'd seen the violence on CNN and pointing to my twelve-year-old daughter who had fallen asleep on the sofa waiting up for me. No greeting from my mother, just a fierce hug and the edict, "Find yourself another job." I did. Without that sitter support when I had to travel, I really couldn't be effective at NDI. I spent a year and a half at Meridian International Center before moving to New York to assume the presidency of the African-American Institute (AAI).

The African-American Institute introduced me to a new realm of possible allies on women's issues. Bankers, business men and women, philanthropists, and well-known educators were among its board members. Board chairman Maurice Tempelsman proved an important ally in advancing women's issues within AAI's programs. I got to know Nigerian president Olusegun Obasanjo when he received AAI's annual award in 1989. We chatted before the awards dinner about inequities in women's treatment and the lack of political options for African women. During his acceptance remarks, he referenced our conversation and called upon the assembled opinion makers to work fully for the integration of women.

I had a similar experience with Boutros Boutros-Ghali. In 1991, immediately prior to the Gulf War, AAI held its annual conference in Cairo. U.S. Representative Bill Gray and Boutros-Ghali, the Egyptian minister of state for foreign affairs, were the co-chairs. I worked closely with Boutros on the program. At the press conference, which featured the two co-chairs and me, reporters kept asking for Vivian Lowery Derryck.

"Where is he," they demanded.

Bemused, Boutros patiently and carefully pointed to me, giving them a lesson in emerging social equality.

USAID

From the Department of State to NDI to AAI, I learned that as a woman I often was not heard or understood the first time I made a point about an issue. Perhaps my perspective may not have been in keeping with the audience's priorities. Maybe my voice was not authoritative enough, I thought. Nevertheless, gradually I learned the need, however difficult it may be, for tenacity in making a point again and again until I got a hearing.

I tried to take that tenacity to USAID in 1998. As the assistant administrator for Africa, I was finally the decision maker I had dreamed of becoming as a young girl in Cleveland. My rock-ribbed belief in the primacy of education and women's political participation had been constant since my first experience in an Ivorian village as a wide-eyed college sophomore. I had taken satisfaction in the affirmation of education's importance through World Bank studies and donor attention and commitment to girls' education. Gradually, with a congressional assist through the Child Survival and Disease Account of USAID, the importance of increased female literacy had been recognized in senior policy-making development circles.

With direct responsibility for over $900 million in assistance to Africa, I hoped to increase attention to education and to include a major WID focus in my three priorities of conflict resolution, poverty alleviation through increased attention to agriculture, and human capacity development (education). However, even before I was sworn in, I knew that HIV/AIDS had to be the first priority, for the disease was wiping out decades of development advances and snuffing out lives in their most productive years. And again women were differentially impacted.

I wanted to remain focused on those four areas and assure that women were part of the mainstream. However, early on I bumped into arcane regulations and a resulting rigidity that give government a bad name. Take conflict resolution as an example. Africa is riddled with hot wars, as more than a dozen conflicts currently roil the continent. Women bear the brunt of the fallout from the fighting, so one of my goals was to highlight women's roles in conflict resolution. African women are highly active in the field. Women united to support interim Liberian president Ruth Perry and became key actors in the 1996 resolution of the Liberian conflict. By sheer force of will, Sierra Leonean women organized and administered the country's successful 1996 presidential and legislative elections and Femmes Afrique Solidarité, a Geneva-based African women's organization, has supported women's peace missions to Burundi, Rwanda, and the Democratic Republic of Congo (formerly Zaire), among other places.

Here was an opportunity to direct resources to bolster an important constituency, but the bureaucracy strangled my best efforts. I applied all the lessons learned about advocacy, tenacity, and coalition building but still could not prevail. In other areas I was more successful. In HIV/AIDS, for instance, colleagues and I were able to redirect several million dollars of bureau resources and assume a leadership role in the famed Washington turf battles.

The New Millenium: Dangers and Opportunities

"Until lions have historians, tales of the hunt will always be told by the hunter," goes a Camerounian proverb that is very apt for women. Two dominant trends have reconfigured the world at the turn of the new millennium: the explosive growth of civil society and globalization. The fall of the Berlin Wall opened new opportunities for civil society, while technology spurred globalization. Together, the two enabled women to organize and communicate freely.

Globalization is hard to define, but it is relentless, drastic, and unforgiving. If we're not careful, it will also promote inequalities.[1] Two possible inequalities concern me. First, globalization allows more written communication, so literacy is a prerequisite, since the overwhelming majority of the world's illiterates are women and it's terribly difficult for illiterates to get on the globalization bandwagon. The second potential inequality that concerns me is a gender-race digital divide. I don't worry about black women's involvement in civil society, but I do worry about our involvement in technology-based communications. Anecdotal evidence suggests that we're not as technologically savvy as our majority sisters. Even as activists, we don't tend to be prolific writers, although we understand the need to increase written contributions of black women to the literature in all fields.

After my stint at USAID concluded with the end of the Clinton administration, I returned to the Academy for Educational Development (AED), where I look at global trends and focus on developing public-private partnerships. It is gratifying to be an integral part of an organization that is deeply committed to girls' education and women's equality. As I reflect with AED colleagues who are involved in domestic as well as international activities, I'm grateful to the women's movement and its embrace and alliance with women in development initiatives. For me, WID gives form to professional and intellectual pursuits and provides my organizing principle for activism.

Through WID and the women's movement that spawned it, I've developed lifelong friendships and a rich support system that both nudged and nurtured me. Grand dames of the movement such as Dorothy Height, president emerita of the National Council of Negro Women, and C. Delores Tucker, president of the National Congress of Black Women Inc., taught me the value of tenacity of purpose and loyalty. They steadied me when I needed a soothing hand, pushed me when necessary and vigorously supported my candidacies for major private and government positions. Above all, through friends and mentors like Arvonne Fraser, I've learned the importance of giving back. So now I consciously seek young people to ensure that we have a rising generation committed to WID.

From my vantage point, the future of WID looks very positive. Internationally, the Nairobi and Beijing conferences spawned a global awareness of the international women's movement with a focus on sustainable development. In the United States strong, vibrant organizations like AWID and others, such as the African Studies Association, support women's caucuses and encourage their autonomy.

What we women don't have is economic clout.[2] Key financial decision makers are not women. So my next push—in addition to political integration, involvement in resolving conflict situations, and battling HIV/AIDS—is not only for expanded traditional formal education but also for economic literacy. My vision of the twenty-first century includes a high percentage of women from developing countries matriculating at the best business schools in Europe and the United States, women who are dedicated to returning to their respective countries to reform financial systems, to make their private sectors accountable, and to assume managing directorships of major private companies. My vision can be realized if our network is solid, if our coalition holds, if we address problems of race forthrightly, and if we appreciate the potential of globalization. After all, women still hold up half of the sky.

Arvonne S. Fraser

Arvonne S. Fraser was coordinator of the Women in Development Office at the U.S. Agency for International Development (USAID WID) from 1977 to 1981. During 1993–94 she was U.S. representative to the UN Commission on the Status of Women with the rank of ambassador. She was also a member of the U.S. delegations to the first two UN world conferences on women and to the UN World Conference on Human Rights in 1993.

She is currently senior fellow emerita of the Hubert H. Humphrey Institute of Public Affairs, University of Minnesota, where from 1981 to 1993 she organized and directed the International Women's Rights Action Watch (IWRAW) and co-founded the Institute's Center on Women and Public Policy. During the 1970s she served as president of Women's Equity Action League (WEAL) and helped found numerous national and Minnesota women's organizations. She is currently a public member of the Minnesota Board of Law Examiners, president of the Friends of the Minneapolis Public Library, and proud grandmother of seven grandchildren.

Active in liberal politics since graduating from the University of Minnesota, Fraser was a Democratic Farmer Labor Party officer in the 1950s and an unsuccessful candidate for lieutenant governor of Minnesota in 1986. With her husband she is the co-recipient of the Louis B. Sohn Human Rights Award of the Washington chapter of the United Nations Association and in 1995 she received the Prominent Women in International Law award of the Women's Interest Group of the American Society of International Law.

Seizing Opportunities: USAID, WID, and CEDAW

Growing up on a Minnesota farm during the 1930s, I never dreamed I would become an international feminist focusing on women's human rights, much less a U.S. representative to the United Nations. The United Nations didn't even exist until I was a student at the University of Minnesota. Reared on hope, hard work, and my parents' strong belief in education, I was sent off to "the Cities," as Minneapolis and St. Paul were called, to find my way during World War II. Like many women of my generation, I worked odd jobs during college—even in a foundry—and later supported my lawyer husband as he built his career. We then contributed more than our share—six children—to what became known as the baby boom. Having married another man earlier, during college, I had to admit my mistake publicly when divorce wasn't so common. After that, admitting mistakes was easy.

Smarter in my early career choice, after graduating from the university I became secretary-receptionist in Hubert H. Humphrey's first campaign for the U.S. Senate in 1948. (Learn to type, my mother had ordered—good advice for the computer age.) There I discovered that politics and government were my calling, a heritage from my father. He believed, to put it in today's terms, that democratic governance was the means for solving problems individuals couldn't solve for themselves. Another part of my heritage was an interest in people and treating them fairly, what we now call an appreciation of diversity and respect for human rights. This heritage had been reinforced and intellectualized by stimulating university professors. Humphrey was passionate about civil rights, meaning ending discrimination against American blacks, and about the promise of the then-new United Nations.

A Feminist Volunteer

During the 1950s I managed political campaigns from my kitchen, neglecting housework but not the children, and was a state Democratic Farmer Labor Party officer and community activist until my husband was elected to Congress in 1962. After I discovered that wives were supposed to gladly give up their careers, pack up the children, and follow their husbands to Washington, the burgeoning feminist movement got an eager convert.

Rootless and depressed because I'd had to give up my career—

albeit an unpaid one—I hired a maid-sitter on the premise that she was cheaper and more useful than a psychiatrist, and went to work part-time in my husband's office—still unpaid. After reading Betty Friedan's *Feminine Mystique* and learning about the new women's liberation movement, I organized a consciousness-raising group of friends and peers that we called the Nameless Sisterhood after a reporter asked who our husbands were. Recruited as legislative director for the Women's Equity Action League (WEAL), I became its national president in 1972. WEAL concentrated on breaking economic and educational barriers for women, helped open the Rhodes Scholars and other prestigious fellowships to women, and successfully supported legislation and court cases to end discrimination against women.

My husband became a member of the House Foreign Affairs Committee, but my initial interests were in social security, education, and employment issues. As the wife of a congressman, a politician in my own right, and a mother and a feminist, I got a fair amount of attention for my activities when the U.S. media was portraying younger feminists as bra burners who hated men. I thought of feminism in its dictionary meaning: the struggle for equality between men and women. Admittedly, I was an elite woman, a type scorned by more radical women's liberationists. As the new feminist movement gained power and media attention, radical feminists made me and my colleagues look respectable and thereby contributed to our effectiveness. Behind the scenes, we "legalists"—as those who worked for law and policy change were called—and the more radical liberationists joined forces with traditional women's organizations and civil rights groups in pushing the white male establishment for change. This was a good lesson for me in the effectiveness of coalitions and the importance of networking.

One day in 1973 Irene Tinker, another Washington activist, and Mildred Marcy, former head of the League of Women Voters' Overseas Education Fund, called on me to push my husband to hold hearings on the situation of women in developing countries. Mildred had drafted the Percy Amendment and her husband, a Senate staff member, helped get it introduced. Adopted that year, the amendment instructed the United States Agency for International Development (USAID) to integrate women into their development programs with the aim of improving women's status and assisting the total development effort. (For additional discussion of the Percy Amendment see Irene Tinker's essay in this volume.) Then, in 1974, I was appointed to the U.S. delegation to the UN Commission on the Status of Women meeting in New York as it was preparing for the First World Conference on Women held the following year in Mexico City. Although many Americans find the UN slow and confusing, I found it compelling as it encompassed a new kind of politics—feminist politics—on the international level.

Aziza Hussein of Egypt, later president of International Planned Parenthood Federation, taught me how to write resolutions in UN format. Our resolution encouraged women to organize in their respective countries to improve their status and deal with the problems of development. Despite strenuous opposition from the Soviet Union, it was adopted. Working to pass it, I discovered that many governments did not allow any nongovernmental organization (NGO) to operate without government approval, an incomprehensible idea to an American who took it for granted that if she saw a problem, she organized a group to solve it.

By 1975 and the Mexico City conference, I knew my days of full-time volunteerism were ending. I needed to start earning money to help pay for our children's college costs and retirement, but the conference and the 1976 presidential election took immediate priority. The token Democrat on the U.S. delegation to Mexico City, I also became the token grassroots member one morning when anti-American demonstrators attempted to break up our delegation meeting, charging that we were all elite women bent on telling the rest of the world what to do. As the daughter of farmers, I was called on to speak to the demonstrators and assembled onlookers, playing my own farm connections to the hilt. What could be more grassroots than a farmer?

Despite many other tense moments, an aggressive Plan of Action was adopted at the Mexico City conference, illustrating that women worldwide had common concerns transcending political differences. I was so excited about the Plan that I decided to publish and distribute a condensed version of it under WEAL auspices. I knew the long UN version would never get wide distribution and thought the world's women—including the too inward-looking Americans—needed to know more about its inspiring agenda, centering on education, employment, women's legal rights, and the promotion of women's organizations. Joan Dunlop, later a founder of the International Women's Health Coalition, convinced her then-employer, John D. Rockefeller, to provide the funds for the project.

USAID: The Office of Women in Development

I was still distributing the Plan in the summer of 1976 when I was recruited as the upper midwestern regional director for Jimmy Carter's presidential campaign. After he was elected I joined the White House Office of Presidential Personnel, recruiting and screening female candidates for appointive office. My international career took firm shape one April morning in 1977 when the newly appointed head of USAID, former governor John Gilligan of Ohio, called and asked if I would consider becoming head of the Office of Women in Development. He said he needed someone to give substance and visibility to the Percy Amendment and thought both my U.S. and UN experience would be good background for implementing the amendment effectively.

Is this appointee simply a political payoff or can she make something happen? That's the question in civil servants' minds when administrations change. My success depended on engaging civil servants in the women in development effort and finding committed people to help me. Among the civil servants I inherited were two gems: Mary Herbert, the office secretary, and Fay Thompson, a program officer. They knew the agency rules and procedures and, as Fay said, "where all the bodies are buried," meaning they understood the informal hierarchy within the agency's bureaucracy. Knowing that informal hierarchy, the unofficial leaders who wield power and influence in any organization, is essential. As black women, Mary and Fay also understood race and sex discrimination. I gained two allies when we immediately challenged the agency's white male culture by my insistence on having a typewriter at my desk and a chair that fit me. In precomputer days no female executive was supposed to admit she could type; executive chairs were made for six-foot men and furniture arrangements emphasized power, not efficiency. Our success in this little episode went around the agency's grapevine fast.

The agency venerated Ph.D.s and overseas experience, qualifications I lacked. Recruiting Elsa Chaney, an academic fluent in Spanish and experienced in working in Latin America, gave the office credibility, but I also tapped Elsa because she was a feminist with political experience. Together, Elsa and I adopted a multi-pronged strategy. We commissioned, collected, and distributed research and data on women's participation in the economies of what was then called the developing world; we enlisted the talents of committed technical experts to help design and implement women-oriented projects for the agency; and we supported indigenous and development-oriented women's organizations. We also took advantage of opportunities for networking with and educating not only the USAID bureaucracy, but other international organizations and the media as well.

Assuming a Broad WID Mandate

We understood that the movement to increase women's participation in the development process had many facets and that there was little consensus about exactly what women in development or WID, as it came to be called, meant. To some it meant simply taking account of women in economic development projects; to others it meant finding ways and means to increase women's income and decrease the effects of poverty. Still others, including Elsa and I, looked at this movement as a means to help improve the status of women in developing countries. We knew every activist would pick her particular issue or issues, whether education, family planning, credit for women, appropriate technology, or legal rights. All this led to our interpreting our mandate very broadly. We shared the view that almost anything that improved people's lives in the long term qualified as development, but we also knew that most USAID employees worked under the assumptions that economic development was primary, that modern infrastructure was the means to that end, and that women were the dependents of men. A big part of our job was to challenge those assumptions. We had to find—or grab—every opportunity to do that.

Among the many studies we commissioned was Mayra Buvinic and Nadia Youssef's *Women Headed Households: The Ignored Factor in Development Planning*, written under a contract with the International Center for Research on Women. Their research showed that one-third of developing country households were female headed, data we later used as background for inserting language in UN documents directing that attention be paid to such households and in counteracting the woman-as-dependent mind-set.

The budget for our office was miniscule compared to the whole agency's. We had only $300,000 the first year, but money is not the only measure of power. We denied—with humor usually—most of the various bureaus' requests to fund women's components of projects, arguing that the Percy Amendment required integrating women; that the various bureaus were supposed to use their own budgets to make women beneficiaries of donor assistance as well as men. I divided our budget according to the priorities Elsa and I had set, allotting a good portion to the support of women's organizations. Powerless women contribute little to a nation's development; women working together in formal and informal groups have a greater measure of power and effectiveness than individual women. In groups, women as well as men learn from each other and develop problem-solving skills; also, through group work, leadership emerges.

I also shared with my husband the view that development assistance should not be solely focused on economic results. He had authored Title IX of the Foreign Assistance Act, which stated that a goal of development assistance should be institution building and the promotion of what today is called civil society. This was a very long-term view, but it seemed to us and like-minded colleagues that people in the developing world should be thought of not only as beneficiaries but as partners in world development and nation building.

With Fay's help I soon learned that contracts under $10,000 could be let with little bureaucratic paperwork. I also knew from my own experience with women's organizations that $10,000 could be a great boon to women's groups, including U.S. women's groups doing women in development research, and therefore began to write numerous contracts, with the help of the cantankerous gentleman in the contracts office who, at first grudgingly and later with some joy and respect, taught us exactly how to write an acceptable and more quickly approved contract. One of our early contracts was for the publication of Fran Hosken's world directory of women's organizations. We distributed this widely simply to prove that women were organized and therefore were something of a political force.

Early in my tenure as head of the WID Office, when Vice President Walter Mondale, a friend and fellow Minnesotan, could not keep a speaking engagement before Title XII agriculturists, I was asked by the White House to be his representative. Title XII of the Foreign Assistance Act gave land grant universities special consideration in USAID's agricultural programs. This was a golden opportunity to explain what the Percy Amendment meant and how these universities could help implement it. Subsequently, we organized an effective women's research and technical assistance network within these land grant universities.

Copenhagen Conference

Another opportunity presented itself when Lloyd Jonnes, USAID's representative to the Development Assistance Committee of the Office for Economic Cooperation and Development (OECD/DAC) in Paris, came to see me. This committee facilitated collaboration between donor nations, and by this time European donor nations along with Canada and Australia had also established WID offices. Jonnes thought a women in development subcommittee of the DAC should be formed and proposed a meeting in the Paris headquarters.

I was delighted with Jonnes's proposal but didn't tell him I wasn't hopeful about integrating women into the large infrastructure projects most donor nations were then supporting. I thought working with WID officers of other donor nations to support the UN Decade for Women (1976–85), established by the UN after the Mexico City conference, was a better path to follow. If we could make the Copenhagen Conference in 1980 a success, we would not only put the women in development concept firmly on the international policy and program agenda but the NGO Forum that was traditional with every world conference on women would be a tremendous networking opportunity.

When the DAC/WID group—as it came to be known—met formally in Paris, I became its first chair because forming the group was a U.S. initiative. In addition to exchanging information and developing international guidelines for development projects, our group held informal meetings focusing on preparations for the 1980 conference and forum. The group accepted my view that the conference and forum were an opportunity for women leaders and representatives of women's organizations from developing and industrialized countries to meet, network by exchanging ideas and experiences; and learn how to work and influence the UN and their own national systems. We also agreed that the 1980 conference document had to give direction regarding the goals and objectives of the women in development movement.

This consensus generated an almost competitive atmosphere among donor countries. The Nordic countries provided generous funding for both the UN conference and the forum and also produced excellent materials for free distribution at both events. At USAID we obtained, with help of colleagues such as Vivian Derryck in the Department of State, a grant to support conference preparations as well as a commitment from our overseas missions to select and fund participants from developing countries. Our office contracted with the Equity Policy Center, the International Center for Research on Women, the Overseas Education Fund, and the National Council of Negro Women to organize forum workshops and fund the participation of developing country leaders at the conference. Many donors also supported the International Women's Tribune Center in organizing forum activities.

Most reports about the 1980 conference focus on its politicization and overlook the more important story. Copenhagen was not only the place where developing country leaders agreed that women's organizations were a force for change; it was also the place where governments began to understand that women in development was not a fad and that women were becoming a political constituency that demanded attention. Over fifty countries stepped forward during the conference's opening ceremonies to sign the Convention on the Elimination of All Forms of Discrimination Against Women (CEDAW), which within two years became a women's human rights treaty. Our DAC/WID members were all on their countries' delegations to the Copenhagen conference and the preparatory meetings preceding it. Working with UN allies, we inserted language in almost every section of the Program of Action—the document emanating from the conference—that explained, amplified, or instructed governments about the goals of the women in development movement. We also inserted language about the importance of women's organizations in assisting development efforts. In various paragraphs it was stated that NGOs could aid governments by investigating the problems of different groups of women, by promoting attitudinal change and public acceptance of family planning, and by explaining government policies as well as international standards and UN programs for improving women's situation. Inserting this and much more language in the document couldn't have been done without our DAC/WID network, especially Geertje Thomas (now Geertje Lycklama à Nijeholt) of the Netherlands, Karin Himmelstrand of Sweden, Ulla Lehman Nielson of Denmark, and Bjorg Leite of Norway.

By the time the Reagan administration came to power in 1981, we had put the USAID Women in Development Office and the DAC/WID group on firm footing. With the support of congressional staff such as Margaret Goodman and Margaret Galey, we helped strengthen the Percy Amendment and educate more members of Congress about women and development. We had also inserted strong language in UN documents, made intellectual inroads, and changed policies in international institutions. It was time to go home.

Humphrey Institute of Public Affairs

In 1981 Dean Harlan Cleveland offered me a senior fellow position in the new Hubert H. Humphrey Institute of Public Affairs Institute at the University of Minnesota, created to honor the man I began working for in 1948, who had been not only a distinguished U.S. senator but also vice president. "Reflective practitioners" is what Cleveland called the senior fellows he recruited. We had to raise our own project funds but this was an opportunity to continue my international interests in the NGO and academic worlds. Again, feminist and political networking paid off. I badly needed moral support because just as I was leaving Washington for Minneapolis, one of our daughters committed suicide. In work I have always found solace.

Jill Sheffield of the Carnegie Corporation in New York knew of my interest in women's legal rights and in the 1985 UN World Conference on Women. I had been intrigued by the women's legal literacy programs that I had discovered while at USAID. Silu Singh of Nepal, the first woman lawyer in that country, had established a fascinating legal rights project that USAID and other donors, including the Ford Foundation, supported. Silu not only taught women their rights, she represented them in court. Her program was an excellent, early model and I had encouraged our overseas missions to support such programs, knowing that rural and illiterate women, especially, did not know their legal rights or how to claim them. As a farm girl, I knew that being able to own and inherit land, buy and sell goods without a male's consent, and travel independently were absolute necessities.

And I had friends who shared this view, including Frances "Sissy" Farenthold, a Texas lawyer and political leader and former president of the National Women's Political Caucus in Washington. Back in Texas, Sissy represented Genevieve Vaughn, a European–American feminist who was interested in supporting women's causes internationally. Along with Catharine Cram, a local feminist philanthropist, these women became financial godmothers for my Women, Public Policy, and Development project at the Humphrey Institute and later human rights work.

Nairobi Conference

Jill Sheffield and I were determined to build on Copenhagen and help make the Nairobi conference an even bigger success. With neither the UN nor the Kenya government very interested in the conference, success meant mobilizing the international women's community, finding financial backing for the NGO Forum, and getting the maximum number of involved participants to the conference. Dame Nita Barrow of Barbados, a former head of the World YWCA, had been appointed Forum Convenor and Eddah Gachukiah, a University of Nairobi professor and former member of parliament, was chair of the Kenyan NGO Organizing Committee. With the Carnegie Corporation's backing and building on our previous international contacts, Jill and I organized a series of ad hoc working group meetings to introduce Nita and Eddah to potential funders and help coordinate planning activities between international NGO leaders. Staff of the Wingspread conference center in Wisconsin and Rockefeller's Bellagio conference center in Italy generously hosted international planning meetings for us.

In the summer of 1984 Eddah invited me as a consultant to the Kenyan NGO Planning Committee meetings at Egerton, an agricultural college in the Rift Valley in Kenya. As we arrived, women of all ages, some in traditional dress, were pouring out of buses, vans, and cars to attend the two-day planning meeting. One young, seven-month pregnant woman from near the Sudan had ridden ten hours on various buses to join women farmers, parliamentarians, college professors, and leaders of women's organizations at the meeting, some of whom had been in Kenya's independence movement. I realized then that the women in development movement was an integral part of a burgeoning international women's movement.

"What would you like to see accomplished for women by the year 2000?" was the question put to the working groups at Egerton. The participants urged women to organize and be more active in decision making and called for an end to polygamy, improved schools, increased support for cooperatives, and revolving credit funds. Their report also asserted women's right to family planning and urged women to seek legal intervention in wife and child battering cases. Submitted to the Kenyan government, the report caused a furor in government halls and in the media because it was thought to be too blatantly feminist, flaunting African customary law. The political sagacity of Eddah and other leaders quieted the opposition and preparations for the world conference continued.

At the same time, my deep interest in women's legal rights led me back to the Convention on the Elimination of All Forms of Discrimination Against Women, the women's human rights document signed at Copenhagen. By late 1981 it had been ratified by enough countries to make it a treaty. Yet few women activists were using it or even knowledgeable about it. I knew it would be a powerful women in development tool if it were better known and utilized, since its seventeen substantive articles covered all aspects of women's lives from family planning to education, employment, health, law, and full participation in society. Jill put me in touch with Stephen Isaacs, director of the Development Law and Policy program at Columbia University in New York, and Rebecca Cook, a lawyer at the International Planned Parenthood Foundation in London. She knew they were also interested in development and women's legal rights.

I met Rebecca in London. Walking around Regents Park and in my hotel room, we designed a series of workshops on the convention for the Nairobi conference and a plan for what eventually became the International

Women's Rights Action Watch (IWRAW). Dorienne Wilson-Smilie, director of the British Commonwealth Secretariat women's division and now known as Dorienne Rowan-Campbell, offered help. Dorienne and I had first met in Jamaica in 1974 at a Caribbean conference preparing for Mexico City. We had worked together with the Secretariat's Legal Division on a publication describing women's rights laws in thirty-five Commonwealth countries.[1]

With Commonwealth and Carnegie support, we recruited Norma Forde, a Barbados family law expert, and Jane Connors, an Australian law professor teaching in England, for our Nairobi workshops. At the workshops Silvia Pimentel, a Brazilian law professor, using appealing gestures when her English failed her, emphasized how important and useful the treaty could be, not just to lawyers but to grassroots women. Isabel Plata explained how women at Profamilia, a Colombian family planning organization, wasted doctors' time complaining about their domestic problems. What they needed was legal, not medical, assistance.[2]

Another day a Kenyan farm woman, carrying pounds of legal documents, pleaded for help in gaining the title to her land under Kenyan divorce law. And members of the UN expert committee responsible for reviewing and ratifying country reports said they needed NGO support in monitoring national implementation of CEDAW. Before the end of the conference, scholars and activists from our workshops helped us launch the International Women's Rights Action Watch, or IWRAW (pronounced "Eeeraw"), with my project at the Humphrey Institute and Columbia's Development Law and Policy Program as co-secretariats.

We began publishing and distributing condensed versions of the treaty in English, French, and Spanish and issuing a quarterly newsletter, *Women's Watch*, to report on specific abrogations of women's human rights and successes in treaty implementation. With the Commonwealth Secretariat we published a manual on how to prepare the required periodic government reports from ratifying countries and encouraged NGOs to use the manual to assess discriminatory laws and policies in their countries. We also submitted "shadow" country reports to the monitoring committee, realizing its members could not be experts on women's rights in every ratifying country. Often we were unable to reveal the sources of our information for fear of subjecting our informants to retaliation. Supporting two court cases in Africa involving inheritance rights and the nationality of children was a concrete example of how CEDAW could be used not only to change national policy but also to help individual women with very personal legal problems.[3] (For additional discussion of CEDAW see Aziza Hussein's and Leticia Ramos Shahani's essays in this volume.)

Vienna Conference on Human Rights

Between 1986, when IWRAW was formed, and 1993, when a world conference on human rights was held in Vienna, the issue of violence against women gained international attention. At Nairobi, informal meetings in the Peace Tent, supported by Genevieve Vaughn and the Women's International League for Peace and Freedom, revealed that millions of women were coalescing at local levels around this very old but newly public issue. Worldwide organizing increased and the issue drew media attention.

At Vienna in 1993 virtually every government felt compelled to talk about the issue, not only because it was receiving attention but because women's and other human rights NGOs mounted a large and effective forum at the conference hall. As a result, a strong section on women's human rights was included in the conference document. Eventually, this emphasis on women's human rights changed the whole field of human rights from an emphasis on civil and political rights—and abrogations of those rights by authoritarian regimes—to a broader agenda, including the economic and social rights included in the Universal Declaration of Human Rights. In Vienna and later at the Beijing Conference in 1995, it was amply demonstrated that women mobilizing at local and national levels were contributing to the growing international movement for democratic governance and the creation of civil societies. In short, a critical mass of women had become change agents who influenced international policy.

Looking back, the prediction made in 1975 in the Plan of Action adopted at Mexico City that "in our times, women's role will increasingly emerge as a powerful revolutionary social force." That prediction has been fulfilled. A peaceful revolution is underway. Women everywhere continue to organize not only to demand law and policy change but also to provide information, services and know-how to other women. One of the most satisfying pieces of mail I ever received was from Brazil, where an IWRAW colleague, Shireen Huq of Bangladesh, wrote saying she was visiting the women's police stations in Brazil along with our colleague, Silvia Pimentel. This was a marvelous example of new South-South exchanges, she said, attributing it to our international networking. And now not a week goes by in which I do not read in the *New York Times,* my daily newspaper, a story or two about women making demands and progress in countries all over the world. As members of the DAWN group said in Nairobi, "in terms of women, the whole world is developing."

Arvonne S. Fraser's personal papers, except for WID materials, are at the Minnesota Historical Society. WEAL archives are at the Schlesinger Library at Radcliffe.

Geertje Lycklama
à Nijeholt

Geertje Lycklama à Nijeholt has a Ph.D. in sociology and studied at the Free University in Amsterdam. She lived in Pakistan from 1962 to 1970 and then moved to the United States, where she worked as a researcher on the migration of farm labor at Cornell University from 1970 to 1973. After her return to the Netherlands she became the first policy adviser on women in development issues to the minister for development cooperation in 1977, where she designed policies in the area of women and development and represented the Netherlands in various international forums dealing with women in development. At the same time she held a professorship at the Agricultural University of Wageningen, focusing on social movements, in particular the women's movement. She moved to the Institute of Social Studies (ISS), The Hague, in 1983, where she became the head of the Women and Development Programme and a full professor in Women and Development Studies. After serving the program from 1983 to 1990, she was rector of the ISS for five years, retiring from that organization in 1999.

From 1995–2003 she was a member of the Senate of the States-General (the upper house of the Dutch Parliament) and chaired the Labour Party group in the Senate. Her academic work—teaching, research, and writing—deals with policy issues related to women in development. Within this broad area she focuses on strategies for change and processes of institutionalization. She has published works on labor migration, in particular labor migration of women.

Toward Empowerment: Influencing the Netherlands Aid Programs

The outbreak of World War II and the German occupation had, and to some extent still has, a great impact on people's lives in the Netherlands. Two years before the war broke out I was born in a small rural village in the province of Friesland in the northern part of the country. The war drastically changed the peace and quiet of the rather isolated village. The villagers were among those faced with patrolling German soldiers, air raids, and an emerging resistance movement. Reared in a Calvinistic tradition of responsibility and societal involvement, my parents joined the resistance movement. This meant hiding people in danger of being arrested and organizing food for the Amsterdam area during the "hunger winter" of 1944. It also meant listening secretly to messages from England announcing in code nightly weapons droppings. Thus, traditionally inward-looking village life changed into active and direct involvement in a worldwide battle for freedom and human rights. World maps were brought into our home to follow the progress made by the Allied forces. An international outlook entered our family life forever.

For us as children the charming aspects of village life remained; only seldom did we sense that life for our parents had become much more dangerous and tense. It had also become more exciting and adventurous, as they told us after the war. I was very proud that when the war was over, I was given the renovated bicycle of one of the woman couriers of the underground movement. A few years later, encouraged by my parents, particularly my mother, I entered a secondary school that prepared students for university education. This was unusual for a village girl, let alone the eldest. Only once did my mother share with me that she had much wanted to become a schoolteacher when she was young, but that her father—a very nice and charming grandfather to us—decided otherwise. In his view it was better for her to take courses in home economics after she finished primary school. I am quite sure that then and there she decided she was going to educate her daughters.

At the Free University in Amsterdam in the 1950s I studied sociology, a logical choice for somebody brought up in a family with strong social and political commitments. It was then that the issue of development emerged and was hotly debated at the university, fueled by the violent cutting of colonial ties with Indonesia, in particular with what is now Papua New Guinea. The university organized a large conference titled The Far-Away Neighbor. I attended the conference with my future husband. We were deeply impressed by the magnitude of the problem and the responsibility that we, as citizens of a rather well-to-do country, carried. We felt personally challenged by a speaker who had just returned from Pakistan. It

was good to hear the beautiful statements about solidarity and commitment to development being made, he said, and challenged students in the
audience to apply for higher education vacancies in what was then West
Pakistan. One vacancy was for an economist in a college in Sialkot. My
partner and I looked at each other—he would soon finish his studies in
economics—and that is how we arrived in Sialkot in December 1963.

In preparing for our stay in Pakistan we took weekend courses in Islam;
the history of the Indian subcontinent; the local language, Urdu; food and
health in the tropics; and so on. We were well prepared. Yet it was a shock
to face the appalling poverty, abuse of human rights, and harsh feudal relations still dominant in many parts of the country. For me the segregation of
the sexes provided new opportunities. Being able to speak a fair amount of
Urdu opened up doors. I had intensive contacts with women in the town's
slums, wives of campus employees, my husband's colleagues, and, sometimes, wives of the local elite. This variety of contacts along with some
research on the living conditions of the poor made me very much aware of
the unfairness in the relations of sex and class in Pakistan society and the
power and powerlessness this involved.

After six years in Pakistan it became increasingly difficult for foreigners
to work in higher education. In 1970 we left and faced reintegrating into
our own or another Western country. On the advice of American friends in
Pakistan, we decided to go to the United States for my husband to obtain a
Ph.D. A three-year fellowship from Cornell University made it possible to
make the move with two small kids. I got a job as a research specialist in the
rural sociology department working on employment insurance for agricultural labor on the East Coast of the United States. Part of the data that I
collected allowed me to write my Ph.D. thesis on the migration of agricultural labor in the Netherlands after we returned there in 1973.

Completing my doctoral dissertation in 1976, I began working for the
Emancipation Council in the Netherlands, which advised the government
on developing a coherent policy for women's emancipation. My experience
in Pakistan and some acquaintance with the women's movement in the
United States made me keen to find out what was going on in my own
country.

Women and Development at Foreign Affairs

The 1950s debates on development led in the Netherlands to the creation
of the post of minister for development cooperation within the Ministry of
Foreign Affairs in 1965. In 1973 this post was taken up by Jan Pronk, a
Social Democrat. Politically alert and with a strong commitment to development and poverty alleviation, he understood the importance of women
for development. In preparation for the first world conference on women in
1975 at Mexico City, he commissioned Leiden University to prepare a

report on women in developing countries. The team of female anthropologists doing this was also to advise the Netherlands delegation to the women's conference. An important outcome of these preparations and the world conference was the creation of a special post for dealing with women's issues within the Ministry of Foreign Affairs. The post was to be filled by two women working part-time, one from inside the ministry, one an outside expert. My experience in Pakistan, at Cornell, and with the Emancipation Council turned out to be ideal preparation for the outside expert part of the job. In mid-August 1977 I entered a freshly painted (to be read as a sign of warm welcome by our male colleagues) attic room of the Policy Planning Section of the Directorate-General for International Cooperation in the Foreign Affairs Ministry. As coordinator of international women's affairs, I was to work in an advisory and policy planning capacity for the top leadership of the department and to ensure that measures were taken to improve the position of women in all aspects of the nation's foreign policy, including development cooperation and internal management.

Where to start? After the warm welcome in the ministry and sensing the high expectations of the women's movement and the Third World movement, this was the question. It soon became clear that although the coordinator was adviser to both the minister for development cooperation and the minister of foreign affairs, the main emphasis was on development cooperation. In spite of the ministers' support, we discovered in no time that women and development was not a burning issue for the bureaucracy. In retrospect, two strategically important steps can be distinguished in carrying out our assignment: the designing of a policy with implementation measures and the choice of allies. We struggled with many other issues, but these two were the most important.

Policy Design and Implementation

At the Mexico City women's conference in 1975, Minister Pronk had made strong statements about the emancipation of women in the context of development. An important first task of our office was to translate the minister's views and promises as expressed to Parliament into concrete policy documents in the yearly Explanatory Memoranda relating to the Development Cooperation section of the Foreign Affairs budget. We realized that formulating clear policy documents was important not only for the minister in presenting policies to Parliament and getting them approved, but also to get the support of the Dutch people and make clear to ministry colleagues what was expected of them.

At that time—the late 1970s—only a small number of people in the Ministry for Development Cooperation thought it important to give special attention to women in development cooperation. Their first response was that they were certainly willing to take care of women's interests in development but did not know how to do it. In response a second step was taken: the preparation of a checklist of measures to ensure women's participation in program and project activities. Since handing out a checklist is not enough, we held small, explanatory meetings with country and program desk officers. To counteract the criticism that we were exporting Western feminism to developing countries, we obtained, through our NGO contacts, a checklist from India that we modified for use in the ministry.

As a third step we formulated an overview of policies in a paper sent to Parliament in 1980. Based on existing literature and direct discussions with women in developing countries, the paper emphasized the following policy principles:

1. Women should have more influence on and take part in development planning and implementation at local, national, and international levels;

2. Development policy must aim at increasing women's economic independence;

3. Development policy aimed at improving the position of women must be an integral part of development policy as a whole, which in turn, taking into account and building upon the existing culture, will be designed to improve the living conditions of women and at the same time ensure that the traditional western sex role patterns are not taken as a model for relations between men and women in developing countries.

4. Support must be given to women's groups and organizations that are striving to change their traditional dependent situation;

5. Channels of information and communication between women in developing countries must be established so that women learn from each other's experiences.[1]

For many years these principles guided the Dutch policy for women and development. In preparing the policy document the following sentence was the one most fiercely debated within the ministry: "In most countries of the world we observe an institutionalized inequality in status and power between women and men." For most male colleagues this was going too far. In their view a family was a harmonious institution without power struggles where husband and wife together and united worked for the well-being of their children.

In this and other battles the support of the political leader, namely the minister, was of crucial importance. In December 1977 the government changed and Minister Pronk was replaced by Jan de Koning, a Christian Democrat. Minister de Koning was equally supportive of our work. We were fortunate that I knew him from the Free University. We had worked closely together for some time as he had been the supervisor for my master's thesis. I took care, of course, that this was known in the ministry, and the possibility of direct access to the minister (which I never needed to use) greatly helped us in obtaining the needed support of colleagues and higher-ranking ministry officers.

In 1983 the first major assessment of the implementation of our women and development policies was carried out by Ria Brouwers. The major thrust of Brouwers's analysis was that the situation had improved quantitatively. A comparison of project activities in 1975 and 1982 showed that while in the earlier year practically no attention was paid to women's needs and interests, the number of projects paying heed to them had increased considerably by the later year.[2] However, in spite of the checklist, lack of standardization turned out to be a major weakness in policy implementation. Brouwers's research showed that the objectives for women's emancipation in development were well defined. But the study also stated: "What is lacking, however, is operationalization into an activity plan for all the executive units. Also the infrastructure is insufficient and as a consequence the realization of the objectives depends to a large extent on the goodwill of individual civil servants. Sometimes this works out well, but in most cases it does not."[3] The study ended with a set of important recommendations, many of which were implemented after I left the ministry in 1983.

Choosing Allies in the Ministry

For effective functioning the full support of ministry leadership was of crucial importance. However, the support of colleagues inside the policy unit and of those working in the executing sections of development cooperation should not be underestimated. In addition, since in the Netherlands development is seen as a political issue, it is regularly debated heatedly inside as well as outside Parliament. The support of those participating in public debates and of NGOs carrying out development work was equally important. Last but not least, close cooperation with colleagues in the Organization of Economic Cooperation and Development (OECD), the United Nations, and the European Union (EU) was important for strengthening our position. All this strategically important work of securing support was carried out by two women working part-time; consequently, choices needed to be made and priorities set.

We decided that in view of the time available, we would bet on those colleagues who showed openness towards women and development issues and not waste time on those showing little inclination to take these issues seriously. Despite the backing of a number of supportive and helpful colleagues, both male and female, implementation of women and development policies progressed only slowly, partly because from 1979 to 1981 a major reorganization of the bilateral assistance division took place. This was a period of staff uncertainty in which there was little receptiveness towards new policy issues, and in particular not to the kind that looked like they would require a lot of work.

Allies in Civil Society and Parliament

As in other European political systems, a dense and highly institutionalized network of interest groups clusters around the major ministries and government departments. In the Netherlands these networks usually consist of civil servants, parliamentary specialists, and representatives of interest groups, together known as "iron triangles." The iron triangle in agriculture, for example, was famous for its strong hold on policy. One way or another we needed to experiment with building some kind of iron triangle.

We started in 1978 when a small group of women came together to discuss a master's thesis on the impact of the Netherlands' development aid on women in Sri Lanka. The group represented staff of Leiden University, development specialists from nongovernmental development agencies, and representatives from the Ministry of Foreign Affairs/Development Cooperation, including the coordinator of international women's affairs. The meeting turned out to be very useful. Participants shared a concern for the negative effects—such as a decrease in women's economic independence shown by the research—of Dutch development projects on Sri Lankan women. We also realized that this was not a unique case.

To change this, the group decided to meet on a regular basis for consultation, advice, and concerted action. Members would learn from each other's knowledge and experience and through mutual support would feel stronger in their often-isolated positions in their respective organizations. So as to have an impact on policy, the network limited its membership to professional women working in development organizations. Furthermore, since all women involved were working in development institutions, it was decided to form a loose network; this made it possible for all to participate in a private capacity, enabling each of us to avoid being a representative of one's organization.

This was particularly important for members working in government and nongovernmental development agencies, since otherwise they would get involved in the hierarchical reporting-back system of their organizations. It was decided also that meetings should take place during working hours and not in the private time of evenings and weekends. It took the members' organizations quite some time to accept this. Again and again, questions were raised concerning the organizational structure of the group, including questions from conservative members of Parliament to the minister for development cooperation. In the late 1970s a nonhierarchical network was still quite an unusual phenomenon. However, the answer that the network form of organization is based on feminist principles and is common in the national and international women's movement usually stopped further questions.

One of the important achievements of the network was the checklist mentioned earlier. As a next step the network, which took the name

Vrouwenberaad Nederlandse Ontwikkelingsinstanties (Women's Consultative group of Dutch Development Organizations), prepared a questionnaire for all Netherlands development organizations. The purpose of the questionnaire was to gain a better insight into how the various organizations were shaping their policies with respect to women in development, regarding not only content, but also personnel and financial resources. Discussions about the results of the questionnaire were held by teams of network members with the management of these organizations.

In the discussions, the importance of women in development was emphasized and an inventory made of the needs of the organizations for assistance in the formulation and implementation of policies. As a result, network members contributed to seminars, workshops, refresher courses, and so on in each other's organizations. As most of the members were the often rather isolated women and development officer in their organization, such concerted efforts strengthened their position. Discussion of the questionnaire results introduced competition to some degree, since some of the organizations were ahead of others and none wanted to be perceived as backward and conservative. Because the Netherlands is a small country and everybody in the field knows each other, this strategy of exposure was quite effective.

Another concern of the network was development thinking in the country as reflected in major policy papers presented by the government to Parliament and in policy papers prepared by the private development organizations. To express their concerns, network members would write official comments on such a paper or express their views in a newspaper article. In the case of a government paper, they could present their views in a hearing organized by Parliament. Network members other than those of the organization concerned would sign the statement, write the article, or present the network's views in a hearing. Another achievement was in the renewal of the contract between the government and the four major private development organizations. Through a well-documented memorandum, the network managed to turn a vague sentence of good intentions into a concretely spelled-out commitment.

In the process of lobbying for inclusion of women's perspective in development policy making, contacts were established with individual members of Parliament and the parliamentary commissions for development cooperation and emancipation. The same was done with the members of the National Advisory Council for Development Cooperation (a few women in the network were members of this council) and the National Emancipation Council. In addition, network members remained in touch with many of the feminist and other activist groups in Dutch society concerned with development issues.

A few activities were carried out in direct cooperation with women in developing countries. The most important was the establishment of a clearinghouse for requests for support from women's groups and organizations in developing countries that were not easily accepted by development agencies because they did not fit established criteria. These requests concerned support for a house for battered women, a printing press for a feminist group, a feminist journal, and so on. With network support such requests were directed to the organization best fitted to respond positively.

Looking back, I sometimes wonder how we managed. While our meetings were during working hours, much of the work was often done at the kitchen table in our homes by teams of two or three network members. In particular, my kitchen was regularly witness to such hard-working teams from 1981 to 1985, when I chaired the network.

Although the network evolved from a small group discussing a research paper into a pressure group that was paid serious attention, changes in policy making came only very slowly. In an assessment by members of network achievements in 1983, five years after it had started, they indicated that the network had been very important to them personally. We all were positive about the cooperation, learning, and exchange of ideas and materials. The network form of organization was seen as appropriate and it was felt that as a pressure group trying to impact government policy formulation it had been quite successful. Less positive was the assessment of progress made in the nongovernmental development organizations. Although in some cases the efforts of the network had created more openness towards women's issues among colleagues, in organizational terms (procedures, staff training, number of female staff and board members), little had changed in spite of promising policy statements.

With the arrival in late 1982 of Eegje School, a female minister for development cooperation on the political scene, new opportunities presented themselves. Although she had no experience with development cooperation, she was familiar with women's issues because of her previous job as chair of the National Emancipation Council. In close consultation with the network, the new minister decided to use the opportunity provided by the UN Third World Conference for Women at Nairobi in 1985 to make an assessment of the Netherlands' development cooperation efforts concerning women during the preceding ten years. The network was asked to organize a two-day seminar to this end. Backed by the power and financial resources of the minister, a thoroughly prepared seminar was organized in April 1985, attended by close to 150 people. To make it impossible for policy makers to dismiss any findings as not relevant to their organization, case studies of their own projects of the government and of nongovernmental development organizations were prepared for discussions in small groups. In addition, Third World women who were familiar with these cases in their countries attended the seminar, providing first-hand information.

Through this exercise a series of very concrete recommendations was formulated and accepted. The seminar was the first direct, large-scale dialogue between women committed to improving the living conditions of women in developing countries and policy makers of development organizations. Many men were present, but women formed the majority; furthermore, the organizers were women and men were invited to participate on the terms set by women. The seminar was a great success and provided a turning point in women and development policy making. Soon after, two of the large nongovernmental development agencies created internal focal points to develop and monitor a reorientation of all their policies. The subsequent demand for information, advice, evaluation, and participation on committees and advisory councils was beyond the carrying capacity of the network. An executive secretariat was badly needed. This, however, had consequences for organizational structure. Receiving funds and employing people requires an organization that is incorporated. After long discussions, the Vrouwenberaad finally decided to give up its network structure and become a nonprofit foundation.

International Allies

With the creation after 1977 of new women and development posts in many countries—advisers, officers, coordinators—international contacts between these new functionaries became of great strategic importance. An example is the Development Assistance Committee of the Organization for Economic Cooperation and Development (OECD/ DAC). DAC member countries at that time were responsible for about three-quarters of official development assistance that flowed to developing countries. The DAC monitored and evaluated the performance of each donor country regularly through the DAC exam. On the initiative of Arvonne Fraser at USAID, a number of us came together, including Bjorg Leite of Norway, Ulla Lehman Nielson of Denmark, Karin Himmelstrand of Sweden, and myself. We decided to meet once a year with speakers, well-prepared documents, and so forth. In 1981 we formalized ourselves as the Correspondence Group on Women in Development (DAC/WID).

We saw the DAC exam as an important instrument to help integrate women into the development policies of the member states. To that end we worked toward the inclusion of questions related to women in the exam. In addition we argued for the use of sex-segregated data in the statistics used by DAC. Subsequently, to put more pressure on the member states, the DAC/WID group formulated a document titled "Guiding Principles to Aid Agencies for Supporting the Role of Women in Development." It was a considerable success when the document was officially adopted at the DAC High Level Meeting in November 1983. Through these principles, member states committed themselves to formulate a mandate, policy, and plans of action for women in development; establish a structure for the systematic implementation of policy; and elaborate policy in all phases of the project cycle.

I recall the January 1983 meeting of the DAC/WID group as particularly stimulating. Devaki Jain presented a very thought-provoking paper titled "Development As If Women Mattered, or Can Women Build a New Paradigm?" Her Third World perspective was enriching and stimulating for the debates on the need for a paradigm shift in development thinking that I was involved with in the Netherlands. On the basis of this DAC/WID discussion, I was later invited to participate in the project called Development Alternatives with Women for a New Era (DAWN). An initiative of Third World women, DAWN had a great impact on the NGO Forum at Nairobi in 1985 and contributed to a strong regionally based international women's movement with a very critical perspective on development.

Compared to the success of women and development donor coordination within OECD/DAC, progress within the EU was very slow. By instituting in the 1970s three guidelines on equal pay, equal employment opportunities, and equal rights to social security benefits, the EU made an important contribution to the formulation of women's rights policies in the member states. These measures, however, were not reflected in the EU aid policies. The European Development Fund spent large sums on development cooperation in the fifty-nine African, Caribbean, and Pacific states, including the forty-two African signatories to the Lomé Convention, but not even in the African countries was the contribution of women to development taken into account.

Changing this situation was not high on our list of priorities, because in the Netherlands and in other Northern member states, the EU program for development cooperation was not very much appreciated. Only in 1981 did the EU Council for Development Cooperation decide to have a meeting on the issue of women and development. This resulted in a report that was accepted in 1982 by the Committee of Permanent Representatives and reconfirmed in 1985, with no action in between. In the end, after I had left the ministry, the Dutch government decided to finance, on a temporary basis, a women and development officer in the EU Directorate General for Development Cooperation.

However, we did find important allies within the United Nations and international NGOs. The difference here was that those allies were looking at us full of expectations, hoping we would find the financial resources they so badly needed. Sometimes battles were lost and we could not deliver, but trust and friendship always remained. It turned out that the 1980 policy document—with its principles of giving support to women's groups and organizations and of facilitating channels of information and communication—was very important. These principles made it possible to support many UN and NGO initiatives undertaken by women within organizations. Prime examples that stand out in my mind are: Isis, headed by Jane Cottingham, Marilee Karl, and Ximena Charnes; Anne Walker and the International Women's Tribune Center; Peg Snyder and the Voluntary Fund (later UNIFEM); Noeleen Heyzer of the Asian and Pacific

Development Centre; Women's World Banking and Michaela Walsh; Zubeda Ahmad at the International Labor Organization (ILO); and Ruth Finney at the Food and Agriculture Organization (FAO). We all worked very hard, were deeply committed, but also, as I remember it, we had a lot of fun together.

Back to Academia

While I was working part-time at the Ministry of Foreign Affairs, the Agricultural University at Wageningen established a privately funded special Chair on Social Movements, in particular the women's movement. I was invited to apply and started teaching in January 1979. Although the chair was of limited duration, it was the first recognition of women's studies at the professorial level in a Dutch university; the emphasis, furthermore, was on women and development. The job was a recognition of my work in women and development and nicely complemented my job as coordinator of international women's affairs at the Foreign Affairs Ministry.

Over time, in particular through the many contacts with women from developing countries, I became convinced that helping women in developing countries to take development into their own hands should have priority over sending experts from the West. For that reason I reacted positively when female staff members from the Institute of Social Studies (ISS) in The Hague asked me to apply for a full-time professorial post for which they had recently received funding. After strong international competition in 1983, I became the first professor of women and development studies at the ISS, an international graduate school of policy-oriented, social science teaching; interdisciplinary research; and advisory work. This was an opportunity to build (not without many battles) a strong women and development specialization within the field of development studies. On a yearly basis some twenty to twenty-five developing country women received master's degrees in this specialization. In retrospect, I believe this was my most important contribution to strengthening the women's movement worldwide.

In order to get to The Hague and the ISS, these young women had already fought many battles. It was quite common to have women from sixteen to eighteen different countries, ranging from China to Chile, in one class. They were all strong women who—through their master's degree studies and, most important, through learning from each other—returned to their home countries equipped with new theoretical and practical insights and determined to change the oppressive conditions of women in their countries. Among themselves they called this "the program that changes your life." Over the years we received many compliments from development workers and diplomats who told us that everywhere they went, they were meeting these strong women from our program. The women were hardworking development experts who put their mark on development in their countries, in particular by empowering women.

Entering Politics

After serving the Women and Development program for seven years, I was appointed Rector of ISS for the period 1990–95. Then, in 1995 when the Labor Party chairman asked me whether I would become a candidate for the Senate, I said yes and was elected. In the Dutch system the Senate is called the "chamber of reflection." It is a prestigious position to be in at the end of one's professional career. With respect to development cooperation it gives space for direct debates with the minister. The minister for development cooperation during my last term as senator was Evelien Herfkens. She actively worked to empower women in the processes of development. Development cooperation with respect to women is a different world today than it was in 1977, when I entered the freshly painted room in the attic of the Ministry of Foreign Affairs. The difference is illustrated by the Utstein group. In 1999 the Norwegian minister for development cooperation invited her three female colleagues from Germany, the Netherlands, and the United Kingdom for a meeting in a medieval cloister in Utstein, Norway. All four ministers were then members of the Development Committee of the World Bank and close in their political ideas and views on development. They decided to operate as a team and regularly discuss their strategies for making the international development bureaucracy more responsive to the poor, and in particular to women. Initially, they were met with laughter. Four women ministers holding a press conference is not a familiar sight in the world of development. But it worked. The laughter has stopped. Presently, in International Monetary Fund and World Bank circles and in the European Union, these ministers are listened to and have become influential in decision making on development policies.

Geertje Lycklama à Nijeholt's materials are archived in the library of the institute of Social Studies in the Hague.

Jane S. Jaquette

Jane Jaquette is the Bertha Harton Orr Professor in the Liberal Arts and professor of politics at Occidental College. She did her undergraduate degree in political science at Swarthmore College and received her Ph.D. from Cornell University, with a dissertation on the politics of development in Peru. She began teaching at Occidental College in 1969 and, shifting her focus to women's issues, edited the first "second wave" anthology on women and politics in 1974. In 1979 she joined the staff of the Women in Development Office at the United States Agency for International Development (USAID WID) as a policy analyst, returning to Occidental in 1981.

She has published numerous articles on women and development, international feminism, and women and democratization, including *The Women's Movement in Latin America* (1989 and 1994) and *Women and Democracy: Latin America and Central and Eastern Europe* (1998, co-edited with Sharon L. Wolchik). She has served as president of the Association for Women in Development (AWID) (1990–92) and the Latin American Studies Association (1995–97) and is a member of the Council on Foreign Relations and the Pacific Council on International Policy.

Crossing the Line: From Academia to the WID Office at USAID

During 1978 I began thinking I really needed a change. A professor at Occidental College, I had just recovered from having two children two years apart and felt I had lost my professional momentum. During this period I ran into Elsa Chaney—an old friend, second wave feminist pioneer, and fellow Latin Americanist—at a professional meeting. She asked if I'd be interested in a job at the Women in Development (WID) Office at the United States Agency for International Development (USAID), an office that had been established by Congress under the Percy Amendment. Elsa was deputy director and clearly was excited about her job. She told me I could work for USAID/WID under the Intergovernmental Personnel Act (IPA) program, which funded exchanges between universities and U.S. government agencies. Therefore, I could risk Potomac Fever without having to give up my tenure. She arranged for me to talk to Arvonne Fraser, who had taken the job of director after heading Jimmy Carter's midwestern campaign for the presidency. A few minutes with Arvonne and I was hooked. I packed up my children, my skeptical husband, and our dog and set out for Washington, D.C.

I knew something about women and I knew something about development. But I wasn't sure whether what I knew would be of use in my new job. A friend in the State Department told me I would be working for a low-on-the-totem-pole office in a demoralized agency and that I would soon get tired of being marginalized. I didn't. I loved every minute of it.

My first assignment was to write the WID section of "Development Strategies" for USAID's annual report to Congress. I had just walked in off the street, had no idea what the WID Office strategy was, and no idea why anyone would trust me to articulate it in such a public forum. It turned out to be a great mapping exercise, a quick way to learn what the office was doing and where it fit into the bureaucratic scheme of things.

To write the section, I had to interview key people in the office and in the agency, get to know WID's resources and activities, and learn our "line." I made good contacts and learned that several people in the agency were secretly sympathetic to WID. I also learned that many were cynical or simply opposed; they viewed the WID Office as just another political hurdle that Congress had thrown in the way of their getting their job done. I could also sense some turf wars. Some who had been involved in WID before Arvonne was appointed felt she had taken over; others thought the WID Office was superfluous, that the agency was already doing enough for women through population and maternal and child health programs.

I also learned what the WID Office did not do. Under the Percy Amendment, it was authorized to contribute to policy, monitor projects, contract the research needed to carry out those functions, and train staff in Washington and in the field. But WID had virtually no operating budget of its own. Unlike the United Nations Development Fund for Women within the United Nations Development Program, it did not carry out its own projects in the field. All WID projects, whether women-specific or mainstreamed, had to be funded by others (although Arvonne did get the office up to a $3 million budget in the course of her tenure). This meant that our main job was selling WID to the rest of USAID.

The WID Office had some important advantages. It had congressional authorization; was located at the top of USAID, in the Policy and Planning Bureau; and had a politically visible and charismatic administrator. But the latter was also a disadvantage; Arvonne's political clout was resented. The agency preferred to deal with its own and to hide its political agendas under the patina of expertise. To be credible, we had to become experts in a hitherto nonexistent field.

The Percy Amendment did not spell out how USAID would carry out its new mandate—that was for us to figure out. A book written by a Danish economist, Ester Boserup, turned out to be a godsend. *Woman's Role in Economic Development* not only defined the issue but provided powerful pragmatic arguments for integrating women—not into development, as Boserup's point was that women were already involved in economic production, but into development planning, where they clearly were not integrated. The case for women was not obvious. Many academics and practitioners saw women as bulwarks of traditional values and therefore hostile to change. Women were not considered as producers, only as reproducers; their unpaid work was not seen as "real" work.

The Boserup Rationale for WID

Convincing the development community to invest time and resources in women was not the straightforward proposition it seems today. Few men or women were interested in women in development, and most offered standard defenses to the suspiciously feminist-sounding arguments for women's equality. Women were simply not involved in economic production, we were told, and many feared that men in developing countries would resent efforts to reach their women or interpret USAID's efforts as cultural imperialism. When we had opportunities to promote the WID cause, I often found myself sparring with a male expert, usually a decade or so older than I, who had a degree in agriculture or engineering, usually from a good midwestern university. He "knew" that men were the farmers and that women worked only seasonally and then only in auxiliary roles. Or, as an expert on water pumps or forestry, he knew that women were irrelevant to these projects (except perhaps as ultimate consumers or as individuals unaware of the environmental damage they were doing). Women were part of the problem, not part of the solution. He also knew that in the United States success meant getting women out of the fields by having men earn enough to take care of their families. Women's equality might be an issue for wealthy countries (though it was clear that many of these men didn't think it should be), but it was a distraction from trying to improve the economies of countries like Ecuador or Mali.

Wielding Boserup (and simplifying her analysis), we countered that, as recently as the mid-nineteenth century, agriculture in Africa (both agriculture and Africa were USAID priorities) had been a female farming system, with women and men playing complementary roles in agricultural production. In Africa, women still accounted for a majority of food production (another USAID priority). There, as elsewhere, women were farming, but their work was invisible to development project workers and census takers. The British and French colonial bureaucrats brought with them their European sex role expectations, giving men the newer technologies, seeds, and fertilizer, along with credit, to grow cash crops for export, while women grew food on increasingly marginal land.

Boserup proved very useful for promoting WID in a male-dominated, economistic, and results-oriented bureaucracy dominated by economists. She challenged the assumption that women's equality increased with modernization, and countered the objection that improving women's access to resources would violate local norms. Because she argued that women in Africa had been marginalized not by economic forces but by the conscious policies of bureaucrats, we could argue that what a colonial bureaucracy had done badly, an enlightened bureaucracy could reverse. I quickly learned how to use these arguments by watching my skillful WID Office colleagues, especially co-IPAer Kathy Staudt. As more sex-differentiated data began to come in from USAID's work in the field, it was easier to convince people that projects that didn't take women into account would be likely to fall short of their goals or have unintended consequences. We quickly began to widen the lens and do gender analyses in other sectors, where we could often count on support from people who had parallel agendas that could benefit from more attention to women. These included environmentalists worried about deforestation and unsustainable farming to the new cohort of anthropologists that USAID had begun hiring in the 1970s to implement its new focus on poverty.

The Population Issue

Reducing poverty was not only a goal in itself but was directly linked to the U.S. goal of slowing population growth. This goal had broad political support. It was important to USAID, which had virtually no domestic constituency and many critics eager to cut its budget. But the USAID's approach to slowing population growth emphasized getting women to accept birth control, not improving their access to resources. Many felt that the best way to help women was to improve maternal and child health, which was also a convenient way of disseminating birth control information and technologies. As WID fought for a place at the table, it had to compete with the much better funded Population Office for scarce resources and attention (and deal with feminist backlash against USAID's coercive population control efforts). In contrast to most population programs, the WID Office emphasized women's economic status and their need for more power in the family, which could come from independent earnings. As WID began to emphasize efficiency rather than simply argue for women's equality, it made more progress, although the effect was to argue that women should have access to resources because they could produce, not because they had a right to such access or because women and children are the vast majority of the world's poor.

Obstacles to WID Efforts

Once we had brought attention to the problem, the question was how to advance the idea of women and development effectively. I had assumed the agency was sitting on a gold mine of project information that could be used to specify best practices, but I found that the evaluation process was cumbersome and that evaluations rarely reported sex-differentiated data. When I asked why evaluations in general were so rarely used to improve USAID projects, I was told they were often buried in the agency's files because a negative report could damage the careers of those involved.

This meant that in 1979–80 we were still in the target-of-opportunity stage. WID was built into USAID's programming through the country assessment and project review processes. In theory, the approval stage seems like a good time to see whether and how women are included, and Kathy Staudt defends this approach in her chapter in this volume. I conclude that she was better at it than I, since I found the reviews frustratingly unproductive. They took the form of meetings, often with thirty to forty people present, representing the regional bureaus, staff from the missions (as USAID calls its field offices), top administrators, and representatives of the offices that had been mandated by Congress—such as WID, but also Human Rights, Population, Environment, Energy, and others—to see if the project had sufficiently addressed each of those issues. The document under review was always a major tome. There were no small projects; as Judith Tendler's well-known study of USAID observed long ago, the business of donor agencies is to move money. Doing small projects was too expensive, another factor that made it difficult to integrate women

I had the best of intentions, but I soon realized I could do very little for WID under these conditions. I always had two cups of coffee before I went in but I simply could not stay awake. Aside from the traumas of my personal life (I was by then going through a divorce), I believe there were structural reasons for my difficulty with the process. The country and project plans were already well defined by the time we entered the room. Language had been negotiated earlier, leaving little scope for change, and there was little patience in the group for dealing with what were considered marginal issues. It wasn't all pro forma. Washington and the country's mission did not always see eye to eye, which provided some controversy, although both were united against offices like ours which were trying to get our concerns into the final document. My job was to read the project document or country proposal, look to see if women were included, and if not, to find ways of including them. At some point I was expected to raise my hand and say "Women" while almost everyone in the room and at the table looked at the ceiling until I finished.

Of course, I had to say a bit more, but there wasn't room to say much. Project boilerplate sometimes included references to women, but it was far from clear that mentioning women would have any real impact on the allocation of resources within a project or a country plan. Our interventions were seen as one more check-off, along with environment, human rights, and population, among others, and they all had more clout. I remember one important exception. It came when Arvonne herself went into a meeting to argue for higglers' rights in a planned central market construction project in Kingston, Jamaica. The room was tense with expectation and full to overflowing. Arvonne had recruited some allies to back her up and some of the office staff went too.

In my memory, Arvonne's challenge was dramatic. I see microphones and flash bulbs and reporters trailing after her when she finished her speech (though I am sure they were not really there). She did have an impact on the project. But in spite of all that effort, I know she was frustrated by the final result. Few projects lent themselves to a direct challenge on WID grounds, and in any case we couldn't send Arvonne and the troops in every time. In my experience as a lowly staff person, the room simply waited until you finished speaking, then went on as if you weren't there. If there was a response, it was the kind that made you permanently skeptical of mainstreaming. The blanket defense was that all projects affect women, so all projects have some gender content even if no specific effort is made to actually reach women. The classic example is the argument that road projects should be seen as meeting WID goals because "women walk on roads."

In 1980 Congress tried to bolster WID a bit by requiring USAID to spend at least $10 million on WID projects. Outsiders (and some within USAID) assumed that we now had real money, and some actually made tracks to our door to see if we could cooperate on new projects. But of course that was not the case. The legislation required the missions to report the percentage of their budget that could be construed as helping women. In a then–$3 billion to $4 billion budget, $10 million was barely a drop in the bucket, quite likely less than USAID was already spending on women, so the figure itself was no spur to change. But the reporting requirement did prompt some of the missions to design new projects and gave local WID Officers (who often had several other assignments as well) more voice in the missions' activities.

The monitoring requirement brought to the fore a long-simmering debate within USAID over whether population and maternal and child health projects could be counted in the WID column. The WID Office firmly resisted counting them on the grounds that women did not gain any economic resources or skills from such projects and that they were essentialist in their reinforcement of the image of women as mothers. But maternal and child health involved many women experts within USAID, making the debate an unpleasant women-against-women battle. We soon concluded that performance reviews, which gave all personnel who were responsible for WID successes some real credit (in terms of promotion and salaries) would be the most effective way to integrate WID into the agency. This was easier said than done. Instead, the WID Office was encouraged to serve as a gender training unit, which put the emphasis on procedures rather than outcomes and lowered the political and intellectual profile of the office. This turned out to be a workable approach for the Reagan years, when many of us who had worked in the Carter administration were surprised to see that WID survived at all.

Institutionalizing the WID presence within USAID was an important gain and the WID Office continues to operate today, despite pressures for mainstreaming from inside and outside the agency and despite a major restructuring. In the Clinton administration, the WID Office became part of the Global Issues Bureau and continued to play a constructive role. In retrospect, though, I think the two specific initiatives I was involved with that had the most impact were implemented outside of USAID.

The Census Project

The first was the Census Project. Elsa Chaney had worked hard on it, but when I was assigned to it, no one seemed to know exactly what it was. Despite several hurdles, the Census Project eventually produced a first-rate product. Its intent was simple: to do a series of regional studies comparing women and men on as many indices as we could justify over three census decades, in order to be able to compare countries and regions and get a sense of trends in women's status. To accomplish this, the WID Office contracted with the international division of the U.S. Census Bureau, following a common practice in USAID of working with other agencies, such as the Department of Agriculture, to plan and staff USAID initiatives. I was to be the voice of the WID Office in the planning process while Ellen Jamison played the key role at the Census Bureau.

Designing the project was not simple. Censuses can only track a limited number of basic demographic variables, and these must be narrowly defined so that censuses can be used to compare data over time. The bureau carries out more specialized household surveys on a sample basis, but they are expensive and may not yield cross-national comparisons. The WID Office was in a position to "buy" data analysis from the Census Bureau, and it could argue for future changes in the way data was gathered. But it was in no position to collect new data or to get data in the form most useful for what we most wanted to know. Labor force participation data for women was notoriously poor, and there was virtually nothing on women's political participation. Demographic information on births, deaths, marriages, number of children per family, and so forth was often analyzed in ways that reinforced the traditional images of women's roles. One benefit of the project was the greater attention given to the serious undercounting of women's labor force participation, where women's (and children's) work as family labor and in the informal sector had been largely overlooked by census takers and often underestimated by women themselves. Another was the attention to male-female differences in literacy and education. The availability of this data helped make education for girls an international priority at UN meetings and in World Bank projects.

I became very enthusiastic about the Census Project because I saw it as providing a global fix on the comparative status of women across and within regions and because of its potential usefulness to policy makers, advocates, and practitioners. In 1981 I chaired a conference on macro-data sets at the Population Council in New York, funded by the WID Office and with participants from the Census Bureau, the UN, and NGOs interested in developing sex-differentiated data sets. There was a serious disagreement between those who thought we should not produce data sets unless we could improve the reliability of the data, and those who felt that it was important to begin with what we had, so that the obviously bad data would create pressures for improvement.

The WID–Census Bureau reports finally came out, and Elsa Chaney wrote the Latin American regional analysis. Under the leadership of Joanne Vanek and others, the UN went on to develop innovative new indexes of women's status. There have been widespread efforts to improve labor force data and even include women's unpaid work in national accounts. In the past, creating such data sets was Big Science, available only to a few and likely to be used by governments and to support the status quo. However, this is no longer the case. There was resistance in the office to supporting the project on the grounds that women might be proven less productive than men (which, if true, would undermine the efficiency argument now gaining ground in USAID). The feminist skepticism of WID was not likely to be remedied by a project employing "male" science. But I still argue that data is important to feminists. Amartya Sen, the 1998 Nobel Prize winner in economics, could not have raised the alarm over 100 million missing women in South Asia without demographic data, which can often be the critical factor in the successful advocacy of policy change.

The Copenhagen NGO Forum

The WID Office also spent its funds on a project that I would define as political rather than bureaucratic, namely its support for the UN Mid-Decade Conference on Women. Originally scheduled to be held in Iran in the summer of 1980, the conference was moved to Copenhagen in the wake of the 1979 Iranian revolution. I had attended the first conference that precipitated the UN Decade for Women (1976–85), the International Women's Year meeting in Mexico City in 1975. Making a Super-8 film there with Occidental College colleague Pat McMurray, I found North American feminists surprised to discover that not everyone shared their view that patriarchy was the major cause of women's oppression, and that Third World women held views closer to Marx than Friedan.

I was one of the four official delegates to the regional mid-decade preparatory conference held in Venezuela in November 1979. Barbara Good headed the delegation and Vivian Derryck and a woman from the Labor Department joined me in representing the United States. We four sat near the large Cuban delegation, with whom we were to have no contact. The meeting was run by Mercedes Pulido de Briceno, who went on to a star career promoting women's equality in the UN Secretariat but was then the head of Venezuela's Ministry of the Family. I remember the president of Venezuela giving his keynote speech on how environmental genetics could be used to breed more intelligent citizens, hardly an appropriate topic for a regional gathering to promote women's equality.

In Venezuela I learned how UN conference documents are finalized at the last minute. We were to discuss and then approve a regional draft version of the Program of Action. We spent most of the allotted time listening to the delegates give reports on the status of women in each country, but despite a vocal Latin American gallery of observers, I remember little debate on the floor. As with USAID's project reviews, the regional program had largely been hammered out in earlier meetings. When the bracketed paragraphs (indicating lack of consensus at the preparatory committee) finally came up for a vote it was late on the last day, and only by working until dawn were we able to agree to compromise language. "We" were the few who stayed up all night to fight it out.

On women's issues the U.S. delegates had few complaints; the document placed a strong emphasis on women's economic participation. The real battles were not about women but about international politics. As U.S. delegates, we had to represent the official U.S. position, which meant vetoing any language that condemned Israel or Zionism or recognized the Palestine

Liberation Organization. Although Henry Kissinger had abandoned full-scale U.S. resistance to language attacking Western capitalism and calling for a New International Economic Order (NIEO), we were to fight that as well. We did succeed in keeping references to Zionism and the PLO out of the regional document, although the U.S. delegation in Copenhagen was not so fortunate.

Now, however, it's hard to remember what the NIEO was, much less why it was so important, or how Middle East politics had isolated Israel and the United States in the General Assembly.

During the spring of 1980, with the Copenhagen conference rapidly approaching, the WID Office joined other donors to bring hundreds of women from developing countries to Copenhagen to the parallel NGO Forum scheduled for midsummer. The WID Office funded many forum participants from developing country NGOs and helped design the open structure of the forum itself, with planned workshops and a mechanism to allow for spontaneous civil society organizing. I didn't get to Copenhagen, but I had one of the memorable moments of my life when those of us staffing the delegation in Washington got a call to check with a feminist prostitutes' organization called Coyote before deciding what position the United States would take on condemning trafficking in women (which ultimately was to condemn the practice but not punish women who earned their living as sex workers). I had met the leader of Coyote before on an academic panel, and one of my students had worked for Coyote as an intern, but I never expected to be consulting her in an official capacity.

In retrospect, I believe the support WID and similar offices gave for women's participation in the conference and the forum was critical to the progress of the decade. The Decade for Women was still an experiment, and the General Assembly was dominated by male-defined issues. Men led many of the delegations to Mexico City and Copenhagen, a pattern that had changed by the Third World Conference in Women at Nairobi in 1985. What we now think of as the international women's movement had barely gotten off the ground. The foundations for a worldwide movement could not have been laid without broad participation and a genuine effort to draw in international grassroots women's goals, goals backed by innovative WID Office funding and promoted by the office's encouragement to other donor agencies and foundations to do the same.

We are now past Beijing + 5 and counting, but those of us who went through the early stages of the contemporary wave of women's international mobilization know it was fragile and tentative. The issues have changed now, and cultural rather than ideological differences are more likely to divide us. But women's cross-national connections are strong and continue to expand. Early money is like yeast.

Final Thoughts

My experiences at USAID continue to shape my thinking on issues that are now hotly contested: women-specific versus mainstreaming approaches to women and development, autonomy versus co-optation, the difficult relationship between women's studies and women and development, and the best balance between working inside and outside the state.

As I reflect on these matters I am confident that, despite the tensions, it is possible to bridge the gap between women's studies and women and development and between academia and bureaucracy. Without question, academic research and critiques improved WID arguments and (though this is harder to prove) WID practices. However, there are recurring signs of alienation. I helped found the Association for Women in Development (AWID), and served as its president in 1990–92, but today I no longer belong to the association and feel it has reduced its academic commitment in favor of policy makers and practitioners. Many academics seem convinced that working for governments is prima facie evidence of co-optation, and one intent of this piece is to show what it's like inside and to make the case that more academics should make the leap. Feminism may have a case against bureaucracy, but it cannot expect change without adopting strategies that work from within as well as from without. And as women gain more representation in legislatures and other policymaking bodies, they will require more activist and intellectually well-grounded bureaucratic support to turn ideas into facts on the ground and to generate new approaches.

There has always been a tension between my academic and my bureaucratic selves, but it has been almost entirely creative. I can understand why staying on the outside is both intellectually and morally appealing. But I cannot imagine how I would have learned as much about government, diplomacy, women's movements, or bureaucracies—for good and ill—had I not gone to work for USAID. There are challenges and excitement, but also inevitable frustrations that accompany any attempt to turn theory into action, particularly when large bureaucracies are involved. Redirecting the goals and resources of existing institutions cannot begin with a clean slate, but must always start with structures of power that have been put together for other purposes. Change can only happen when others can be convinced to give a little in terms of their power—and even their ideals—to accommodate and then support a new vision. At USAID, as in other spheres of life, I value those moments when this delicate pas de deux takes place.

Elsa M. Chaney

Elsa M. Chaney was a retired political scientist turned anthropologist. She received her Ph.D. from the University of Wisconsin in 1970 and taught both at Fordham University and the University of Iowa, where she directed a women in development program. She was active in the Green Party of Iowa City and in the Section on Gender and Feminist Studies of the Latin American Studies Association.

After graduating from high school in 1946, she attended a small junior college in Kansas where she was deeply challenged scholastically by Ursuline nuns and where students from Latin America inspired her initial interest in the region. After nine years in the Grail, an activist Catholic lay movement that was profoundly feminist without the label, well before the second wave of feminism took hold in the United States, she worked as press assistant for two U.S. senators.

She served as deputy coordinator of the Women in Development Office at the United States Agency for International Development in the late 1970s. She then did independent contracting and research on women in development issues, won a Rockefeller residency fellowship to do research on rural women and feminist issues in the women's studies program at the University of Iowa, and served as volunteer adviser to the Latin American and Caribbean Confederation of Household Workers.

(Editors' note: Elsa Chaney, ill with cancer, traveled to Brazil in April 2000 for one final stint of work with the domestic workers' organization she had been assisting for years. Returning to the United States in early May, she completed her chapter for this book and died July 16, 2000.)

Full Circle: From Academia to Government and Back

During the depression years my mother, younger sisters, and I followed our father as he found work in California, Arizona, and Kansas. We were "reverse Okies" in our rusty old truck, heading away from California, which had turned out to be no promised land. Between high school and college I spent a year on the Parsons *Kansas Daily Sun* staff as society editor in the morning, relief switchboard operator at lunchtime, and proofreader in the afternoon. Then a good thing happened. I was awarded a scholarship to a small junior college where I was deeply challenged by Ursuline nuns and where students from Latin America inspired my first interest in the region to which I would dedicate my professional life.

My first overseas exposure came through membership in the Grail, a Catholic organization preparing women for the lay apostolate. The idea of joining other women to develop and use our talents and bring a spirit of service to others was appealing. In 1948, at the age of twenty, I left Kansas City and set out by Greyhound bus for the main center of the movement, Grailville, near Cincinnati, Ohio.

The Grail had its roots in the Netherlands. When I joined, the movement was already working in several countries and would become increasingly international, with branches in Asia and Africa. Grailville's program was greatly influenced by the National Catholic Rural Life Movement. Physical as well as mental labor was honored. We plowed and sowed, composted, harvested and canned, baked whole grain bread, wove beautiful cloth, sewed simple outfits, and ate nutritious meals from our gardens long before these things became fashionable.

Most of my Grail years were spent in the Writing Guild, producing publications and propaganda for the movement, but my ambition was to join Grail activities in Latin America. In 1959 another member and I traveled to Colombia and Peru to seek placements for women trained at the Grail's Overseas Institute in Brooklyn. In Lima I was invited by the Juventud Obrera Católica (Young Catholic Workers), a Belgian movement, to a meeting of household workers preparing to launch their own organizations to improve their wretched working conditions. Years later I would encounter domestic worker leaders in many Latin American countries who had been "conscientized" by the Juventud Obrera Católica, and I would be assisting domestic worker organizations myself.

After graduating from Fordham University with a major in journalism, I left the Grail and headed for Washington, D.C., to work as a press assistant, first for U.S. Senator Eugene McCarthy of Minnesota and later for U.S. Senator William Proxmire of Wisconsin. Although women were allowed to join the Senate press secretaries club, none of the three or four women members held the title of press secretary. We were classified as secretaries or clerks and paid at that level. One day an amazing announcement crossed my desk: the new Land Tenure Center at the University of Wisconsin in Madison was offering forty full fellowships.

Suspecting that even then the center might welcome one or two women, I applied, thinking a Ph.D. would be my ticket to a position of real responsibility in government. Accepted but an oddity, I was the oldest student at age thirty-four, majoring in comparative politics of developing nations. In 1967 I set out for Peru and Chile on a Fulbright dissertation grant, interviewing women politicians in both local and national government. The study became *Supermadre: Women in Politics in Latin America*, the first work on women in Latin America based on survey research.

My growing interest in women's issues was greatly stimulated by membership in the New York Women's Anthropology Caucus which brought together women who would make key contributions to what came to be called women's studies, including June Nash, Helen Safa, Constance Sutton, and Eleanor (Happy) Leacock. I joined with June and Helen to propose to the Social Science Research Council that it bring together Latin American and North American researchers who were beginning to study women.

In the spring of 1974 some fifty women scholars gathered in Buenos Aires for a seminar, Feminine Perspectives in Social Science Research, and that summer Helen Safa and I ran a two-month seminar on the same theme in Cuernavaca, Mexico. Among the 285 applicants were many of our friends, but we decided to include only younger women without their Ph.D.s to push forward the nascent field of Latin American women's studies.

Squashed together in a dismal hotel with constant rain, many of the participants expected that Helen and I would neatly lay out the foundations of this new field and that participants would leave with dissertation projects in hand. The truth was that we were still struggling and had no secrets. In subsequent years we forged strong working relationships across national boundaries with many of these women as the understanding grew that we would build this new field together. Among the participants were Carmen Diana Deere, a future president of the Latin American Studies Association; my current colleague in the household worker research project, Mary Goldsmith; and Ruth Sautu of Argentina who dedicated her recent book to Helen, June, and myself as "those who put into motion studies about women in Latin America."

My focus on women in development began that same summer of 1974 when I learned about the Percy Amendment, a new congressional mandate requiring that international assistance programs of the U.S. government include women in their programming. I filed this information away but didn't forget it.

The Women in Development Office at USAID

After several years of teaching at Fordham and Wisconsin, I needed a change. In 1977 I heard that the new coordinator of the Women in Development (WID) Office at the United States Agency for International Development (USAID), Arvonne Fraser, was recruiting, and I applied. One does not easily shed experiences of the 1960s. At the University of Wisconsin I had not only protested against the Vietnam War but had been active in Citizens United with the Peoples of Laos, Cambodia, and Vietnam, and had met in Paris and Montreal with Madam Binh, the North Vietnamese secretary of state, and with persons in the shadow government of South Vietnam.

When I first walked into the State Department building, I said to myself, "Well, here I am in the heart of the beast." Was I "selling out?" I argued with friends about being "inside" (you'll be swallowed up, compromised, they said) or staying "outside" to continue the radical critique of the whole development enterprise. But Arvonne won me over when she said, "This office is about subversion." Not that she intended to overthrow the U.S. government, only that there were millions of dollars floating around and she intended, she said, to get a lot of them for women.

She offered me the position as her deputy and I accepted with joy and trepidation. The first step was to secure a high enough civil service grade so that I could function effectively in the agency. Arvonne and I called on her friend at the Civil Service Commission who laid out the key words that must appear in my application, such as "directed," "initiated," and "innovated." Without the magic words I would not qualify as deputy. This was my bureaucratic baptism.

I arrived at the start of the Carter presidency. The beginning of a new administration is a good time for joining a government agency. It affords a window of time in which real changes can be made. Once authority is established—if it is—there are about two years to work. During the last year everybody is focused on the next elections, and nothing new gets initiated.

Making the WID Concept Respectable

Arvonne had already made the decision that our strategy would be to address what we could handle—what seemed important—and ignore the rest. In the early days we confronted daily the agency's perception of women in what at that time were called Less Developed Countries, or LDCs. With few exceptions, women were viewed only as "targets" in the agency's population, and mother-child health programs and the word "women" rarely appeared in documents unless prefaced by the phrase "pregnant or lactating." Nonmothers, girls, and older women were invisible.

Though most of the world's women still lived in peasant or quasi-peasant economies where they farmed alongside their men or often alone, the agency directed its agricultural projects exclusively to men. The failure to see what most developing country women actually were doing was epitomized by a USAID officer who said to us one day, "I don't know what in hell you mean by women in development. The happiest day of my life was when my mother no longer had to go out to work in the fields."

We decided to attack such notions head-on and give the concept of women's participation in the development process intellectual respectability. Our first excursion was to colleges in Massachusetts, where political scientist Susan Bourque of Smith set up meetings for us. This trip helped us launch three seminars for scholars doing research on women in Asia, Africa, and Latin America. Then we began funding new research, publishing the results, and created a resource center in our office. We distributed resource materials widely throughout the agency and its field missions; to USAID contractors, namely the universities, NGOs, and development consultancy groups that carried out many of USAID's projects; and to others interested in or working on development.

We did a lot of luncheon meetings, both in the agency and outside, to promote the new women in development idea. Gradually we built an in-house support group, although many agency women wanted nothing to do with us, fearing damage to their careers if they collaborated with feminists. (Over the years, this attitude changed and several later WID directors moved on to higher positions in the agency or in the Foreign Service.) I also participated in the WID lunch group that Jim Bass, an economist at the Inter-American Development Bank, ran for several years. WID officers were being appointed in the Peace Corps, the World Bank (Gloria Scott was a strong, early ally), and other international agencies. From the Inter-American Foundation, Sally Yudelman fostered women's projects and collaborated with us. We often consulted with Judith Bruce at the Population Council in New York and with the Tribune Center there. Another valuable ally was the International Center for Research on Women, founded by Irene Tinker and at that time the only nongovernmental organization doing policy-oriented research on women.

We were all struggling to define our new venture. Most of us were feminists, but we could not march under that banner. The choice was between the equity and economic arguments. The former stated it was right that women share, to have a stake in development. The latter stated that economic progress required including women. We made a strategic decision to emphasize the latter, to demonstrate not only that the inclusion of women would improve results, but that many projects would fail if women were left aside.

Emphases in development constantly changed, and we were assisted by the ideas embodied in the latest development approach, BHN, or Basic Human Needs, which asserted the right of all to nutritious food, clean water, decent shelter, and education. This fit well with our preferred emphasis; that women already were contributing to the development of their countries in myriad ways. Our task was to make visible, to support, and enhance what women had been doing for centuries.

A key difficulty stemmed from the way the all-important agency paper moved, the intricate hurdles from project identification and design to funding and implementation. Negotiations with host government officials, consultations with experts, endless meetings, and many drafts and redrafts of documents often added up to several years of work. By law, all projects had to include women. Most often project proposals arrived at our office at a very late stage. Sometimes there was no mention of women at all. At other times, the "Oh gosh! We forgot the WID statement!" was rectified by the cut and paste ruse that involved cutting the WID statement from another project paper and pasting it into the new one. The men did not believe they could learn much from us. I remember how excited Arvonne and I were when we were asked to address a meeting of the BIFAD, the prestigious Board for International Food and Agricultural Development. We spent a great deal of time honing our allotted fifteen-minute presentations. But just as Arvonne started to speak, the BIFAD director slipped out of the room, his telephone messages in hand. Time to catch up on his calls since nothing important was going on.

Creating a WID Database

One of my first tasks was to help create a WID database. We were spurred on by the 1977 Foreign Assistance Act that instructed USAID to employ socio-economic criteria to measure development. International data collected by the World Bank, the International Labor Office, or even the UN were either inappropriate or not disaggregated by sex. I proposed a contract to the Center for International Research, Bureau of the Census. With Lois Godicksen of USAID's Social and Economic Data Services and Ellen Jamison of the Census Bureau, we designed and redesigned twenty-five initial tables on women in education, the labor force, and other key variables for the USAID countries—all the budget allowed. Later, the database was expanded to include all countries. When there was no data for certain variables that also was valuable; it told us that something needed to be done.

In 1977–78 we sponsored three experts' meetings on social indicators, plus a two-day seminar at the Belmont Conference Center near Washington. At these we brought together labor economists who had been designing and testing time-budget and similar methodologies to measure women's economic roles and social scientists studying women's contributions to the household and the larger economy. A result of these meetings was that we collaborated with the Census Bureau in publishing four *Women of the World* handbooks, based on a much enlarged WID database made possible by additional funding. These were published with my volume on "Women in Latin America and the Caribbean" included.

My happiest days in the office were shared with academic activists

Kathleen Staudt and Jane Jaquette, recruited under an exchange program between government agencies and universities. Kathy was (and is) a wonder. It took me at least two months to begin to function efficiently in the bureaucracy. Kathy was fully operational in a week. She used her year in the WID office to hone keen insights on bureaucracy and left with 4,000 pages of notes, written at night when the long workday was over, on which she based several of her later books and articles.

I coincided with my Latin Americanist colleague, Jane Jaquette, for only a few months, and was impressed particularly by her political savvy. She and Arvonne were true political professionals, and Jane made a lot of friends for the office. She carried on both the outreach to scholars and the WID data project. Years later, when Jane was president of the Latin American Studies Association, she arranged a panel based on my work in Latin America. She cried when she got to describing our years at AID, and couldn't finish. Truly, there was something magical about being young, enthusiastic, and to pioneer in a new field.

When Paula Goddard was hired to replace me, Arvonne used her political skills to arrange for us to be, in bureaucratic lingo, "double encumbered," that is, to work together in the same position for six months. Keenly intelligent, Paula also was a bureaucratic natural, knowing just which levers to push—and relishing her skill in navigating the agency.

In Jamaica and the Dominican Republic

During the ten years between leaving USAID in 1979and landing in Iowa, I worked as an independent contractor. The rules for contract consulting are simple: do good work and deliver assignments on time. I was able to alternate work on projects with research, affiliating with Irene Tinker's new Equity Policy Center. I spent two wonderful years in Jamaica, where I had two projects back-to-back. One was a study of how outmigration affected the women left behind in Jamaica and St. Lucia; the second was at the Caribbean Food and Nutrition Institute, where I studied the effects of migration on smallholder agriculture, food, and nutrition.

I returned five times to Plan Sierra in the Dominican Republic on various assignments. Twice Martha Lewis and I organized seminars there that brought Dominican and U.S. scholars together to talk about women's participation in agriculture and forestry. In her essay Martha describes our work in the II Integrated Rural Development Project in Jamaica—my first experience as an independent contractor. Women's components of donor-funded projects were an attempt to pry loose some resources for women in large development projects; we were years away from any serious attempts at mainstreaming women. With a Jamaican colleague, Scarlett Gillings, I returned in 1986 to Christiana, where I had worked with Martha's crew eight years earlier. Scarlett had done her graduate thesis at the Institute of

Development Studies in The Hague, on our women's component in Jamaica and was interested to see what had happened to the project in the intervening years.

Our journey confirmed my own ambivalence about the whole development enterprise as it was (and still is) conceived and carried out by donor countries. Bedeviled by politics and corruption, the project had been closed down by USAID two years before its time. As Scarlett and I gazed in disbelief at the rotting hulks of trucks and farm machinery, the neglected buildings, the files scattered over office floors, we meditated on the futility of so many development efforts. Our women's component had possessed no fancy tractors or other equipment. We had hired a local ironworker to cast the gardening tools, paid for by a small grant from the WID Office. Yet an independent final assessment of this multimillion dollar project noted that the women's component had been its best feature.

Learning from Rural Projects

How ironic to remember the report I had found in 1977, tucked away in the library of Jamaica's Ministry of Agriculture, documenting a Netherlands project much like this one, carried out twenty years earlier in the same watersheds. It was also a soil conservation effort based on terracing the steep hillsides where poor Jamaicans have farmed since slavery days. Never cited in any of the later rural development project papers, its lessons therefore unlearned, this project also had failed and for the same reasons: the local farmers were not convinced the terraces were useful. They "took up space where we could plant crops," the farmers said.

It was clear that the farmers—male and female—had never been encouraged by the outside experts to regard the project as their own. The projects created jobs and paid farmers to terrace their own land. Scarlett and I found many who, angry at the project's closing, had let their terraces fall. "The terraces belong to the project, let them come back and fix them," was a common response of many farmers. Others had actually ripped the terraces out. Yet Scarlett and I were pleased to discover that many women were still planting their Martha Lewis gardens.

My work in rural areas of Jamaica, the Dominican Republic, and other countries convinced me that agriculture probably represents the best opportunity for rural women to contribute most effectively to their families, communities, and nations. Where women have access to land, their comparative advantage is producing food for their families and selling the surplus. Where they do not have rights in land, it is crucial that this situation be rectified. Despite the fact that in many countries the farmers are women, many land reform programs and agricultural projects still leave women out.

As increasing numbers of men throughout the world seek off-farm employment, often in other countries, women's traditional resource bases have eroded while their economic responsibilities toward their children and the old increase. As HIV/AIDS or migration have removed both parents in recent years, often grandmothers are raising the children. In Christiana, I remember driving into a yard where an old farm woman, almost blind and 102 years of age, was trying to care for two little girls. Her granddaughter had left them, saying she was "goin' to foreign" (Jamaican for migrating).

Incorporating poor rural women into the formal labor market is not a feasible goal, so efforts must also build on women's well-established custom to engage in informal, nonagricultural activities to produce secondary income. However, care should be taken that income-generating projects do not divert women from their agricultural base. I have seen too many projects founder when women were encouraged to process, weave, sew, carve, and manufacture items unsuitable for either local markets or the tourist trade. As Maryanne Dulansey, a pioneer in women and development work, often used to ask, "How many baskets does the world need?"

Thirty years have passed since the U.S. Congress first directed that its foreign assistance programs should give particular attention to integrating women into development. During that time, a consensus has emerged among women in developing countries (now called women of the South) that they must articulate their own aspirations, define their own goals, and devise their own strategies for reaching those goals. In fact, women of the South truly took over the women in development enterprise at the Nairobi world conference on women in 1985.

Our education in the North has at times been painful. We had to learn to listen to those whom we wanted to assist and to understand how they wished us to work with them, not for them. Out of the continuing discourse, carried out in countless conferences and seminars as well as through women of the North and South working together, agreement has been reached on many basic concepts.

Migration and the Feminization of Farming

Early in the life of the Women in Development Office, Arvonne suggested I choose an issue of my own and "see how far you can take it." I decided to work on the impact of international migration on development. Large numbers of rural men and women not only go to the capitals and provincial towns of their own countries, they also move across national boundaries. Migration occurs not only because of discouraging conditions in agriculture, but also because schools, medical clinics, and commercial and recreational facilities are much more available in towns and cities. Many farm youth the world over are rejecting farming as a way of life, with the result that in many world areas the farmers are getting older.

The movement from rural areas is accelerating. Yet those who leave the countryside are not easily absorbed into the under-industrialized economies of the towns and cities. They find intermittent jobs in the informal labor market, with wages far below the lawful minimum and benefits nonexistent. Increasing numbers of women are being trafficked for marriage, domestic service, and prostitution.

Outmigration creates disorganization not only in cities and towns, but also in the countryside. It leads directly to another scenario associated with hunger and malnutrition: the deterioration of the small farm sector, where the food of the poor has traditionally been produced. Smallholder agriculture is beset with severe soil erosion, an uncertain supply of inputs and credit, a lack of price incentives, and marketing problems. Not only are new lands not coming into production; total acreage under production is, in some world areas, decreasing. Estimates in the Dominican Republic and Jamaica, for example, are that about one-third of the arable land in the smallholder sector is not being cultivated. The result is lower production of the foods that poor people eat in both the urban and rural areas, namely yams, green bananas, cassava, potatoes, and legumes.

The deterioration of the small farm sector is intimately linked to another scenario: the feminization of farming. This phenomenon is not confined to the poor countries of the South; recent studies in such widely disparate places as Spain and Japan point to similar trends. In most regions women have always played their part in both commercial and subsistence agriculture. Rather than having a diminishing role in agriculture, as some have suggested, studies show that women are becoming more involved as men leave. Sometimes the women carry on with little or no drop in production, but in many cases women are stretched. In addition to their agricultural work, they haul wood and water; bear and care for children; and process, preserve, and prepare food. Moreover, they often do not have access to credit, agricultural extension, and inputs. Unless women are supported in overcoming these difficulties, they, too, will migrate to the city, and the interlocked scenarios of higher migration and decline of small farm agriculture will begin all over again.

A Domestic Workers' Confederation

In 1989 I was on a consulting assignment with the Women's Service in Agriculture and Rural Development program at the Food and Agriculture Organization in Rome when word came that I had won a Rockefeller residency to do research on rural women and feminist issues in the women's studies program at the University of Iowa. After the residency, I was asked to stay on to direct the university's women in development program and teach in the anthropology department. I had come full circle: the WID program at Iowa had been inaugurated ten years earlier with a grant from our WID Office at USAID.

I also came full circle in terms of my interest in domestic workers. Engaged for the past five years in a remarkable, exciting project, I've made eleven trips to Latin America. Two colleagues, Mary Garcia Castro, a Brazilian sociologist, and Mary Rosaria Goldsmith, a North American–Mexican anthropologist, and I form a technical team to assist household worker (domestic servant) associations and labor unions in seven Latin American countries on studies of their own reality. Our aim is to take the mystery out of survey research. One of us helps initiate the project, training the household workers themselves as coordinators and interviewers and assisting them in planning the fieldwork. On their own, they carry out the interviews and code the results. Then I help clean their data and run tables so they can write their reports. Additionally, I work as volunteer adviser to the Latin American and Caribbean Confederation of Household Workers, the sponsor of the studies.

The seeds of the confederation were planted by a panel on household workers that Mary Castro and I put together for the 1983 congress of the Latin American Studies Association. We invited two household worker leaders to comment on the four scholarly presentations, the only studies on household workers we could locate at that time. At the congress, we academics asked the workers what we might do to assist them. They had two requests: to link them with other domestic worker organizations in Latin America and to help them plan a *gran encuentro* (large encounter) of workers from other countries. "We've heard that household workers are organizing," they said, "but we don't know how to get in touch with them. We don't have the chance to travel the way you do."

The *encuentro* that resulted in the founding of the confederation finally took place in Bogotá, Colombia, in 1988 after four years of fundraising. There now are twenty-three national affiliates, ranging from the newest organization in Costa Rica with about fifty members, to the Federaçao de Trabalhadores Domésticos do Brasil with forty-nine local affiliates. That might sound impressive, but domestic workers represent between fifteen and twenty percent of the counted female labor force in Latin America, and at most only five percent are organized.

The confederation links these organizations through seminars and congresses and publishes a newsletter. And household workers now travel in their own right, They have gone to the Fourth World Conference on Women in Beijing, funded by the United Nations Development Fund for Women, to seminars on trafficking in women in Brussels and on women and migration in Geneva, and to many other international events. Teaching and writing books has been satisfying, but putting research into practice has been the most rewarding work I have ever done.

Jacqueline Pitanguy

Jacqueline Pitanguy is a sociologist and political scientist who is founder and director of Citizenship, Studies, Information and Action (CEPIA), a research and advocacy organization in Brazil that works with a gender perspective in the areas of health, violence, and access to justice. CEPIA is also the secretariat of the Civil Society Forum in the Americas, a network of NGOs from a number of Latin American countries aiming to strengthen civil society by building common strategies among organizations with different agendas. She is a former professor at the Pontificia Universidade Católica of Rio de Janeiro and at Rutgers University. From 1986 to 1989 she was president of the National Council for Women's Rights, a position in the cabinet of the Brazilian government.

She is also a co-founder and board member of the Commission on Citizenship and Reproduction and a board member of the Inter-American Dialogue of UNESCO's Institute for Education, and the Society for International Development. Currently president of the board of the Global Fund for Women, she is also a member of the International Human Rights Council, headed by former U.S. president Jimmy Carter, and the International Advisory Group of the MacArthur Foundation.

She has published extensively and has been awarded the Medal of Rio Branco by the Brazilian Ministry of Foreign Affairs for her work on behalf women's rights. The mother of one daughter and two sons, she resides with her family in Rio de Janeiro.

A Brazilian Feminist and a New Constitution

There is a gap between our daily life, filled with repetitive gestures, and our remembrances. Fortunately, memories are selective; they skip routines and emphasize moments and impacts. I remember, in every detail, the day of the inauguration of our new democratic Constitution for Brazil. It was October 1988 and I know what I was wearing and where I was sitting at the National Congress. If I close my eyes I can even feel again the deep sense of accomplishment that filled my heart. I was celebrating the rights of women that were written into that Constitution. I was proud of the role that the National Council for Women's Rights (NCWR), which I headed, had played during the constitutional process, which lasted three years, and happy with my part in that process. It felt then like the culmination of a long feminist journey.

I believe that journey started in the early 1970s, when I came back to Brazil from Chile. I am part of a generation of Latin Americans that lived their high school years and began their college studies under the military dictatorship of the 1960s imposed in 1964, a generation that moved from one to another country in the Southern Cone of the continent in a kind of political diaspora. There is gain and loss in this diaspora. The major gain, besides being alive, is to feel that you have played a role, that you were not a passive spectator of history. I was in Chile as a student of sociology when Salvador Allende was elected president. I lived through the euphoria of believing in the possibility of a democratic socialist regime in South America and through the despair of the end of this dream. At that time, however, women's rights were not part of my political agenda.

My feminist journey began when I came back to Brazil and I was working as a researcher in the Department of Sociology at the Catholic University of Rio de Janeiro. In my research I came across the deep inequalities of women's participation in the labor force. I was analyzing census data, and can still remember the impact of that statistical evidence and the urge to better understand and do something about discrimination against women in Brazil. I felt very lonely at that moment. My peers were deeply involved with the struggle for the democratization of the country and gender inequality was not an issue. One of the key memories of the beginning of this journey goes back to the moment I found a group of women who were asking the same questions. With them in 1974 I started Grupo Ceres, one of the first feminist groups in the country. That is when domestic and sexual violence, sexuality and reproductive rights, and gender discrimination in legislation, the labor market, education, and political life became central issues in my view of a just and democratic society. Brazil was still under dictatorship, but a transition process had started by the end of the 1970s and early 1980s. The interesting thing about this process is that, by then, women's movements had become visible political actors and the democratic agenda had become more complex, encompassing issues of gender, race, ethnicity, and the environment in addition to social, civil, and political rights.

As a result of the many years of dictatorship in Brazil, there was a great divide between the state and civil society, with the latter diametrically opposed to the state regarding human rights. While struggling for the end of the military regime, many women's rights activists had plans to end this divide. We felt the state owed us something for all the years of authoritarian rule and that we were entitled to use the power of the state in order to propose and implement public policies and legislation that would promote gender equality and social justice.

A major moment in the transitional process toward democracy was the election in 1985 of the first civilian president since the 1964 military coup. By then I was a mother of three, a girl and two boys, living with my husband, Carlos Manuel, a Chilean economist, in Rio de Janeiro. I had some visibility as a feminist activist, was working as a researcher at the National Council of Science and Technology while in a Ph.D. program at São Paulo University, which meant commuting. I had also co-authored three books that dealt with the condition of women from different angles: women in the labor market, sexuality and social identity, and feminism as a political movement.

Life was hectic, and I was moved by the inebriating feeling of being part of a movement in which we shared dreams, plans, and fears. The year 1985 was a key one in my life as a civil rights and women's rights activist. While celebrating the fact that we finally had a civilian president in Brazil, I was part of a group of women who were articulate and strong enough to demand the creation of a national organization that would have the authority, administrative autonomy, and budgetary allocations necessary to counsel the president on women's issues and to propose and implement federal public policies and legislation.

The National Council for Women's Rights

The campaign to create the NCWR (National Council for Women's Rights) was waged in the context of Brazil's re-democratization and the occupation of federal executive power by sectors of society that had been held at bay for more than two decades. The council was created in August 1985 by a congressional law. From that moment until 1989 my life was deeply connected with the NCWR, which took me along a new path in my feminist journey.

My memories as the president of this new governmental institution are filled with feelings of deep joy over our victories and of anguish over difficult moments. In the years I was there, we had few defeats. I moved to Brasilia, the capital of the country, while my family stayed in Rio de Janeiro. Since my post was a cabinet position we couldn't tell how long I would hold my post; it didn't seem right to my husband and myself for him to leave his work or to move the children, who were doing well in school. As it turned out, I stayed in the capital four years. Despite the constant movement that has always characterized my life, I am very much a family person, so this period was one of loneliness. It is significant that I did not decorate my apartment in Brasilia and had only the things strictly necessary for sleeping and working. Looking backward from a psychological perspective, I believe that this ascetic way of living had some ingredients of the guilt that women characteristically have when we are not meeting the social expectations of our traditional role.

I was, however, working with a large and diverse group of women, both within the NCWR and from organizations of civil society, who were also deeply committed to our mission and dedicated to a common cause. Our board, where I served before becoming president, was composed of women from different political spectrums as well as from labor unions, the arts, and the university. It was a diverse group and sometimes the members' differences would erupt in board meetings. However, by the time we faced the outside world—in which, ironic as it might seem, we included other sectors of the government—we had reached consensus. We supported each other because we knew that our time was not measured by a regular clock; our minutes were measured by a political watch. Would we have enough time to guarantee women's rights in the constitutional process that was taking place? Would we have enough time and political strength to influence legislation and public policies on reproductive health, domestic and sexual violence, and the social and labor rights of working women, including rural and domestic workers? Would we be able to change family laws that still placed men as the head of the family? Could we influence the education of boys and girls so they would reject sexual stereotypes? Would we have enough time to denounce racism and the situation of black women, enlarge maternal rights, and struggle for free day care facilities for children?

As most of us working at the National Council came from civil society organizations, we were not familiar with the rituals of state power. We were newcomers in the sphere of federal power, and were trying to work inside a state machinery that had served the authoritarian regime for two decades. It was a big challenge for the staff, because we were in a process of learning by doing but were not allowed to make mistakes. The NCWR had no political history or tradition to support failures, no important economic interests to back it up, and our agenda was uncomfortable for many and dangerous for others, including the conservative and powerful sectors of the Catholic Church. Yet we not only survived for more than four years but became visible, strong, and respected and were contributors to significant advancements in the condition of women in Brazilian society.

Going back over my memories of those years, it is hard for me to separate out one specific moment or episode as being more significant than another because our gains in the Constitution and in public policies were part of a process of mutual reinforcement that led to the improvement of women's citizenship rights in many different areas. It is also important to say that I share with many other women the memories of these heroic years, since our victories were the result of a collective effort.

Structure and Strategy

From the moment the NCWR was conceived in early 1985 by a group of feminists, we proposed a structure that, being governmental, would have a strong interaction with civil society through the NCWR board, whose members were not part of the government. The president of Brazil would appoint the president of the NCWR, nominated by and chosen from among board members.

In terms of operational organization, the NCWR started with three divisions: technical, social communications, and finance and administration. Later we added a fourth division, research and reference data. We had a staff of approximately one hundred persons. The technical department included commissions dealing with subjects such as reproductive health, violence, black women, legislation, women and labor, including rural women, childcare support (nurseries and kindergartens), and education and culture. These divisions developed their own programs while also working in coordination with other federal and state governmental units in order to maximize our influence and outreach.

The main challenges came from the fact that we were dealing with deeply rooted gender power relations that were sustained by laws, customs, and values. It was a difficult matter to question the status of men as head of the family as defined in civil law or the requirement of a marriage certificate for the state to recognize a stable union as a family. Proposing that the regulation of fertility be recognized as a citizen's right and that the state had a duty to provide information on sexual and reproductive health and access to contraception represented a controversial political platform at that time. We needed not only to have our proposals well-grounded on solid data and juridical arguments but also to spend a lot of time in political negotiation inside the government.

Being part of the government, reproductive health was always a crucial but delicate area for us to work within. Throughout my four years we faced the Catholic Church's direct opposition to our proposals on sexual and reproductive health. Large sectors of the Evangelical Church were also opposed, along with other conservative forces. They were all represented in the National Congress and had a strong influence within the executive branch of government. We understood that we had to build alliances with health professionals and to dialogue with those elements in the government that were not particularly susceptible to the church's power. One of our first efforts to build support was to organize the First National Conference on Women's Health, attended by more than one thousand people and representing health professionals, women's health advocates, social movements, and governmental health departments.

The guidelines for our health division, which included access to contraception and abortion and the implementation of a comprehensive women's health program, were derived from this meeting. Coming out of such a representative meeting, our program was not only more democratic but also more powerful as an instrument of negotiation. We made clear to the executive and the legislative arms of government that the NCWR's agenda was expressive of the demands of a much larger and more diverse constituency than just NCWR itself.

This strategy was adopted whenever possible, especially when dealing with controversial issues. We brought together women from the three main federations of labor unions, which were usually competitors, in a large meeting where they worked together, reaching consensus on a common agenda and expressing their demands and propositions regarding the Constitution, as well as for social security and labor legislation. Among other questions, there was agreement that maternal leave should be extended to four months, that men should have the right to a paternal leave, and that the majority of other dispositions in the labor code that protected women were in fact obstacles to them and should be abolished. The women from the labor federations also issued recommendations for their own trade unions to ensure gender equality.

Besides strategizing with working women from the modern urban trade unions, the NCWR paid special attention to rural women, campaigning to ensure that they would have the right to own land, irrespective of their marital status. We also worked closely with domestic workers, who still represent one of the most neglected and least organized sectors of the Brazilian labor force.

The NCWR faced different degrees of difficulties in implementing its agenda, according to the issue that we were dealing with. It was easier to advance without significant conflicts with other governmental organs or with conservative sectors from society in the area of domestic violence than in matters regarding reproductive health. Over the previous ten years the feminist movement had brought this issue of domestic violence to public light, demanding the recognition of it as a crime. By 1986 society at large already saw this as a legitimate claim. The goal of the NCWR was to expand the number of DEAMs (special police stations to attend women victims of sexual and domestic violence) and improve their quality. We set out to gather national data on this issue and then take on the great challenge of facing the judiciary with the flawed logic behind the sentences handed out for crimes against women, particularly those involving domestic violence, rape, and murder, the so-called passionate crimes or, in the case of slayings, the honor killings.

Constitutional Campaign

I will not go on recounting the many programs and activities developed by us at the NCWR except to say that in one way or another, they all supported and converged in our constitutional campaign. The year 1986 was important for the democratization of our country. The new, democratically elected National Congress had the task of drawing up and voting on a new constitution as a substitute for the charter of the military regime. From its creation in 1985 the NCWR undertook a public campaign called Constituição Para Valer tem que ter Direitos da Mulher (A Constitution, to Be Worthy, Has to Guarantee Women's Rights). This campaign lasted three years and is an episode that I want to highlight in these memoirs.

The campaign can be divided into two stages. In the first stage, which preceded the elections for Congress, our goals were to raise public awareness about women's rights, enlarge women's representation in Congress, and to create a general pro-women's rights attitude among all candidates. We reached these goals. Women's representation in the National Congress, even if still low in absolute terms (twenty-six representatives), had never been so high (over six percent) in relation to men's, and there was a generally positive atmosphere toward women's rights. During the first year we distributed posters all over the country, set up billboards in all state capitals, displayed TV ads, and aired radio spots demanding that women be represented at the Congress and that the Congress be aware of our rights. Women's movements in the various states organized in coordination with the NCWR, seminars, public events, and marches all over the country. During the campaign we also collected all sorts of propositions, demands, and suggestions regarding women's rights. We were supported throughout the constitutional process by a remarkable group of women lawyers, who—working pro bono—helped us in analyzing these suggestions from a legal point of view.

The second stage lasted until the end of the constitutional process. It can actually be divided into two processes, although they overlapped. The first resulted in the organization of our platform of propositions for the various chapters of the Constitution. This was an extended process that involved reaching consensus and then formulating the consensus into constitutional provisions. Soon after the new National Congress was elected, the NCWR held a historic meeting at the congress that brought thousands of organized women from all over the country. The goal of the meeting was to draft and approve a document called Letter of Brazilian Women to the Constituents, containing our agreed-upon demands in the areas of family law, labor and social rights, health and reproductive rights, racism, violence, education, and access to power, among others. This letter, later handed in a ceremony to the president of the Constitutional Congress, marks the moment that ended the first process.

The second moment lasted until that afternoon in November 1988 when the Constitution was finally promulgated. For almost three years we had advocated to guarantee our rights in the Constitution, working in coalition with women's groups, professors at the universities, trade unionists, rural workers, gay groups, black and indigenous women's movements, professional associations including physicians and lawyers, and state and municipal councils on women's rights. We had coordinated an advocacy and lobbying effort that was known as Lobby do Batom (Lipstick Lobby). We had a small and very effective group working in the NCWR only on this constitutional process, but our various other activities, developed in different areas, converged and mutually reinforced this effort. We worked closely with a group of congresswomen who formed a coalition from different parties, as well as with progressive male representatives. Throughout the constitutional process we presented more than one hundred proposals and amendments leading to the fact that eighty percent of our demands were included in the Constitution.

This represented a victory not only in terms of what was written in the text of the Constitution, but also in terms of what was not included. An example of the mobilization to keep certain proposals out was the struggle in alliance with civil society groups to keep the issue of abortion out of the Constitution. At the NCWR we made a strategic evaluation of our negotiating power over a provision decriminalizing abortion and agreed that we would lose. The conservative forces were working hard to place "the protection of life from the moment of conception" into the Constitution. They were stronger than we were. All over the country this issue was raised in Sunday Mass and Catholics were called upon to support it. We were facing the danger of a major backlash, since existing legislation allowed a pregnancy to be terminated in case of rape or when the mother's life was at risk. In accord with feminist groups and women's rights activists we agreed upon a joint strategy. These groups would present a proposal, coming from civil society—which was allowed, as long as it had over 150,000 thousand signatures—simply proposing the decriminalization of abortion. This would be the counterpart of the proposal to protect the life of the unborn. The NCWR would then take an in-between position, simply saying that abortion was not a constitutional matter. We thought that we would have the chance to win. And we did. In the chapter of the Constitution on the family, the head of the family, ascribed to the man, was gone, along with all the discrimination that it carried.

As for what was included, reproductive rights were affirmed when the Constitution recognized the right of women to choose freely the number of children they would have and permitted access to contraception. Social rights were extended to rural women and domestic workers and social security rights, such as four months maternal leave, were given to all working women. Women in prison had their right to breast feed assured and the state recognized that it had the duty to attend to situations of intra-familial violence.

It was thus a moment of great joy, that day in November 1988. I did not know then that there would be a bitter taste to such an astonishing victory. The history of Latin America illustrates the conservative elite's capacity to organize and determine the direction of the state. These forces were already regrouping. For the next year, NCWR suffered all sorts of pressures from within the government, including budgetary cuts of seventy percent, coming particularly from the Ministry of Justice with the support of the president. Our achievements were uncomfortable for the federal government. From that point onward, it was clear that the NCWR did not reflect the hegemonic tendency within the new configuration of state power. The crisis of the NCWR occurred within the framework of changes and rearrangements of political forces within the state.

The legitimacy the NCWR already enjoyed, the support that we received across the country—from women's movements, trade unions, and other organizations in civil society, as well as from some progressive representatives in the National Congress—enabled us to remain in power until 1989, when I, the members of the board, and most staff resigned. We knew that to remain would mean to be co-opted by the conservative forces. A deeper reflection about this moment would lead to a more theoretical discussion on the possibilities of alternative projects, from within government. I won't go into that discussion here.

I want to retain the sense of accomplishment of this movement of which I still feel I am part of. Our accomplishments have been important not only for Brazilian women, in terms of legislation and of the creation of instruments to develop public policies, such as Councils for Women's Rights and DEAMs, but also to women in other Latin American countries.

While at the National Council for Women's Rights, I traveled several times to Argentina, Chile, and Uruguay—countries that were also undergoing processes of democratization—to share our experiences in bringing gender issues to the democratic agenda. I was also a member of the Brazilian delegation to the UN Commission of Women, which met in Vienna and then in New York. Besides going through the lengthy and formal discussions during official UN meetings, I got acquainted with members of the UN committee monitoring implementation of the Convention on the Elimination of All Forms of Discrimination Against Women. I also met many interesting women's rights advocates in the corridors of the UN who were holding lively discussions during coffee breaks. I understood the importance of sharing, at an international level, our national experiences and the need to build transnational coalitions.

New Developments and Activities in the 1990s

The international exposure that I had during the 1980s has been intensified in the 1990s when some major trends can be identified. Women's groups that were loosely organized became more institutionalized through nongovernmental organizations (NGOs). While the role of Brazil's National Council for Women's Rights and some other state-level councils declined, NGOs and networks of civil society organizations continued to play an important role in our national arena. There was a proliferation of transnational coalitions and networks developing campaigns, building common strategies, and participating in international forums. The technological revolution in communications facilitated international interchanges between networks, which played a key role at the UN conferences held during the 1990s. Women became powerful actors in this arena, having played a particularly important role in the UN Human Rights Conference held in Vienna in 1993 and at the Cairo Population and Development Conference in 1994. Important paradigmatic shifts took place at those gatherings, such as the consideration of domestic violence as a human rights violation and the change from a demographic-driven population approach to one based on the recognition of reproductive rights. All of which were consolidated at the Fourth World Conference on Women at Beijing in 1995.

All through the 1990s I have been involved in this transnational dynamic. I feel that I am part of an international movement that is capable of building consensual agendas and strategies that cross cultures and countries. I also feel that, at the same time, we can only be truly international if we belong nationally, if we are deeply committed and involved with what goes on in our own country. The linkages between the local and the international are clear: the international commitments assumed by the Brazilian government have always been a powerful instrument to undergird and sustain our national demands. On the other hand, we can only advance internationally at the internal or national level if these international commitments are consolidated in national laws and programs.

Since 1990 I have been with Citizenship, Studies, Information and Action (CEPIA), a nongovernmental organization founded in 1990. Since its creation I have been developing its goals and strategies with Leila Linhares Barsted, a feminist lawyer with whom I also shared the experience of Grupo Ceres. We have a skilled and committed staff and, although facing the NGO nightmare of constant fundraising and the uncertainties of the Brazilian scenario we celebrated our tenth anniversary with great joy.

Working from a gender perspective and within a human rights framework, CEPIA focuses on issues of health, sexual and reproductive rights, violence and access to justice, and poverty. Advocacy is also an important part of CEPIA's agenda and we propose and evaluate public policies working both locally, at Rio de Janeiro's state level, and nationally.

The growing effects of the globalization process cut across diverse issues and require common transectorial agendas. This led us, along with the Center for Health and Social Policy, a U.S.-based organization, to take the initiative in 1997 to bring together representatives from NGOs working with different agendas—health, environment, gender, development, and human rights—to create the Civil Society Forum of the Americas, of which I am currently the executive director.

I am more and more convinced that we have to build agendas that cut across different sectors and that it is urgent to deepen the dialogue with other civil society organizations in order to make gender equality a central issue of any democratic debate, not only an issue for women's activists. There is still a long way to go in that direction.

From my perspective of two and a half decades of struggle for gender equality and women's rights, I have seen backlashes against women's rights in Brazil and elsewhere. When they occur, the story of *Alice in Wonderland* comes to my mind. There is a moment when Alice runs and runs and stays in the same place. Our walk is not linear. Frequently we run in order to stay in the same place, to protect what we have already achieved. But the ground is not the same; we have made great progress, especially in changing laws and constitutions. In this new century, we face the crucial challenge of diminishing the gap between laws and the cultural reality many women still live with.

PART IV

Influencing
Development Policy

Marilyn W. Hoskins

Marilyn Hoskins is an anthropologist working on local governance and community development with equity. She focuses especially on the interface between local women and men and the tree and forest resources upon which they depend.

Between living and working in Southeast Asia and Africa, she returned to the United States to hold the Chair for International Development at Virginia Tech, where she established and managed the Participatory Development Program. In 1984 she joined the Policy and Planning Division of the Forestry Department of the Food and Agriculture Organization (FAO) in Rome as senior community forestry officer and chief of the Community Forestry Unit, where she developed and coordinated the Forests, Trees, and People Program. She was the first social scientist in the Forestry Department.

In 1996 she returned to the United States, where she writes and lectures, participates in international forums, and continues work with FAO, the United States Agency for International Development, and the World Bank. She is a member of the social ecology group of the U.S. Forest Service and works with forestry and community groups in the United States and abroad. A recipient of the Distinguished Service to Rural Life award from the Rural Sociological Society, she also has honorary doctoral degrees from the State University of New York and Syracuse University for her work in sustainable natural resource management and in improving the quality of life among the poorest people of the world. She was a scholar in residence at the Workshop for Political Theory and Policy Analysis at Indiana University for 2002–03.

Pioneering Women's Forestry Issues at FAO

I was born during the depression at a time when girls were expected to go to school, marry, and have a family. Although my mother wanted to be sure I grew up strong and confident, the whole family expected me to become a full-time wife and mother. I would probably have happily finished my days doing exactly that had I not met a number of challenges and opportunities, traveled, encountered new learning situations, and met supportive women and men. Certainly, I never thought that I would join the Forestry Department in the Food and Agriculture Organization (FAO) of the United Nations as a social scientist directing the UN's community forestry program.

I finished university and graduate school in Columbus, Ohio. I married and had children when, in 1962, my husband became the regional legal adviser for the United States Agency for International Development (USAID) posted to Vietnam. The idea of moving there fascinated me. I read all I could, learned French, packed my children (ages two and four), and we were off. In the 1960s wives of men of diplomatic status in USAID (or the State Department and the military) were not permitted to work; they were supposed to entertain and do diplomatic tasks of a wifely sort. After much searching I finally found a real, although volunteer, job with the United Nations Educational, Scientific and Cultural Organization, as research adviser to young urban university trainees for future positions in UNESCO training centers in rural areas.

I loved this job because it brought me into homes in the countryside where I learned from people about their lives. I learned that we, as outsiders, brought with us many inaccurate assumptions and often failed to observe complications related to generations and gender in designing development programs. Schools trained boys in agricultural methods, and agricultural extension programs reached only men, even though women did much of the agricultural work. Women, who controlled the money, were never acknowledged as decision makers and agriculturists or given the opportunity to evaluate new agricultural information. Our program tried to design information to reach the gender and age of those who needed it.

Coming home from Asia on a visit in the mid-1960s, I joined a panel organized by Irene Tinker that discussed the differential impacts of projects on women and men. I was shocked that so few people in development circles seemed to acknowledge the importance of understanding the tasks of men and women in project design and evaluation. For the first time I realized the need for working with others in remolding development efforts so they would help rather than disadvantage women. I was determined to become more involved.

In 1965 we were evacuated from Vietnam to Thailand where I designed programs for women with Thai women social workers. But I realized that I needed more skills and tools to gain the credibility.

Working in Upper Volta and Virginia

Taking the opportunity to get a master's degree in anthropology during our several-year interval in the United States proved important to my future, because early in 1973 we moved to Ouagadougou, Upper Volta (now called Burkina Faso), in West Africa. We arrived near the end of an exceptionally serious drought, during which crops had failed and herders had lost their animals. Developing systems to help local people reestablish access to productive resources was essential and challenging.

Rules barring spouses of Foreign Service personnel from working had changed by the 1970s, but there were still problems. My husband headed the USAID mission in Upper Volta. As a wife I could work as long as what I did had no relationship to his agency or the organizations it worked with, which included all development groups. For months I studied local culture and worked as a volunteer, teaching English to researchers in an African regional research institute. Finally, I was able to create a job for myself. I joined and became head of the Department of Culture, Tradition and Environment. This institute did research for African governments and non-governmental groups in the Sahel region. When the institute did research for the local USAID mission I made myself scarce. Perhaps because the salary was so small—$100 a month—no one objected.

My job took me to rural communities were I learned firsthand about daily life. The distribution of responsibilities and tasks was quite different than in Asia. The African women I met were not in charge of the family money and the division of agricultural work between men and women was much more pronounced. Within the institute I participated in African teams doing feasibility studies and project design and wrote a number of publications for the ministries of environment, education, and development. As I gained experience I briefed consultants from various countries and personnel working for USAID. Upper Volta had a very large donor program and it was an excellent place to meet, talk, and work with some of the most—and least—experienced development workers.

The regional USAID office funded a project I designed and managed in 1975–76, a series of workshops with women in which they discussed how developments in diverse sectors affected them and the direction they wanted these sectors to take. The series included workshops on health, law, enterprise, education, and agriculture. No one had mentioned the potential for a forestry workshop. However, in the agriculture workshop women started the liveliest discussion of the series on the importance of trees and forests and the devastation brought by current forestry projects.

Conventional forestry in Europe had been an elite training for sons of wealthy landholders to manage family estates for timber, game, and beauty. Foresters learned to manage trees and had military training to protect the land from intruders. In colonial times the forest services in West Africa managed land classified for forests to benefit the state. Forestry projects took over some land not planted in grain—and sometimes land that was—to expand the colonies' forest resources, causing much local resentment. To complicate matters, African foresters were often not paid much and gained some of their livelihood from selling permits and administering fines.

Women at the workshop were unanimous that forestry activities and projects still caused, instead of solved, problems for rural people. Participants spoke emotionally of the hardships faced by families when pieces of land that may have looked empty to outsiders were co-opted by the government for forestry, often in the name of improving their rural livelihoods. Women told how essential many different species of trees were to their family well-being and described traditional uses of the trees and ecologically sound management practices.

On the semi-arid land of Upper Volta, the fields are traditionally used for several years and then allowed to recuperate through being left fallow, so that farming is alternated with growing trees and shrub cover. During each fallow year the land produced important wild products essential to women's quality of life, the health and nutrition of the family, and women's income. Objectives written into many donor project documents were to help rural women have more access to fuelwood. But in practice local land users lost any access to wood from the land for either use or sale; the land and all output historically used by local families now belonged to the government. Wood, poles, or timber were sold by the forest service in the towns. Rural life and the traditional agricultural system were compromised. While men focus mostly on using the land as future grain fields, women are equally concerned about usufruct rights.

In Upper Volta, as in many African countries, women traditionally have a number of family tasks. They work on specific jobs with men to produce grain, but men control the grain supply and the fields on which it grows. Women are almost totally in charge of all other food. They garden in plots near the village and collect many types of nuts, fruits, and leaves, all of which constitute vitamin and mineral content for the starchy grain diet. They collect and process herbs for traditional medicines.

Men might have several wives; every wife must earn enough money for her children's school fees and clothing for herself and the children, as well as for gifts when they visit their home villages. Women do a number of things to earn money. They cook and sell food and condiments in the market; collect reeds; and make hats, mats, stools, and baskets. They collect pods for tannin, leaves for dye, and herbs to use and sell. Even potters depend on tree and forest outputs for the wood necessary to fire the pots. Some women also raise small animals that graze on the leaves of the newly growing trees and shrubs in the nearby fallow. When the land they use for these activities is taken away, the women lose family status and freedom. Studies we did showed that when forestry projects take land to plant trees, they usually start with the land close to the villages, where women have their gardens.

Studies showed that when these resources were not available to women their social life was handicapped, as they no longer could take the required gifts when visiting their home village. Children often dropped out of school as women's moneymaking activities declined. Family nutrition was endangered when a range of vegetables and plants was not available. Also, fallow areas were a type of social security, because various grass seeds and small plants that grew there were used when lack of or poorly timed rains caused the annual crops in this drought-prone land to fail. When these "hunger foods," or foods of last resort, were not available, many husbands had no choice but to leave the family in search of work, creating all of the well-known problems of women-headed households.

The women of West Africa knew a great deal about the qualities and management of a range of tree and shrub species important to family survival. They explained that tree and forest products or lands classified by the government as forestland are involved in almost anything women do to earn money, especially since the men control the grain. Men also control women's access to land and women are given no garden land when grain land is scarce. Since these African women also help produce the grain, they understand that all farming requires trees for erosion control, water management, soil fertility, and microclimate production.

Women showed me projects considered successful by development standards (because they increased available biomass) but which in fact left women with more work and less resources to fulfill their family needs. In Asia I had learned that men and women had different and often complementary responsibilities toward the family; in Africa I learned that trees were essential to women and the fulfillment of their tasks, which are necessary to their families' well-being.

In 1977 I returned to the United States on my own with a young daughter, expecting to get contracts from consulting groups I had worked with abroad. I had a full résumé and had written and published extensively in both Asia and Africa. However, when interviews came to the point of my earning history, my credibility fell to the floor. My highest salary had been $100 per month. I took small consultancies from people willing to take a chance on me until I could build an earning record.

Arvonne Fraser, head of the Women in Development Office in USAID, asked me to write a paper on women's issues in forestry. It was the first document that showed how intimately women were involved in tree and forest use and management. After that I found consultancies with major development agencies such as the Food and Agriculture Organization and the

World Bank, beginning a field later called community forestry because it focused primarily on local needs and control over forestlands rather than on forester-managed reserves and industrial timber.

In 1980 I accepted a one-year chair—it turned into four—at Virginia Polytechnic Institute and State University to help faculty become more active and effective in international development activities. The university was participating in a forestry project in Nepal and I went there to design the socio-economic component, including gender issues. I worked to integrate women into forestry both as foresters and as beneficiaries of forestry activities. In this position it was possible to make small but important changes. For example, plans for a new training institute had no campus housing for women, which was essential for women's participation. When I pointed this out, the dean took a pencil and designated a house for women. The problem, seen early enough, was easily solved.

At the university I read material not available overseas. I obtained grants for the faculty and continued to take part in contracts overseas. I also collaborated in developing management seminars for international women leaders with Mary Rojas, then director of the international women's program for the university and later president of the Association for Women in Development. In this capacity I ran sessions at the NGO Forum at the world conference on women in Copenhagen during 1980, focusing on women and their access to forestland and other natural resources. I also helped organize the NGO Forum at the New and Renewable Sources of Energy Conference in 1981 at Nairobi. There I led a session on women and forestry, a new topic for many of the participants. I added to my own understanding of women's roles in forestry through research in the Virginia mountains with Peggy Shifflett, a fine rural sociologist specializing in women's issues in Appalachia.

FAO's Forestry Department

Both before and during the time I was at the university, I was a consultant for the Forestry Department of the UN Food and Agriculture Organization in Rome. My first consultancy came after Natalie Hahn, of the FAO Women and Development office, asked if I would stop by its headquarters in Rome the next time I was traveling. She felt there were not enough women working for FAO and set up interviews for me. One was with the Forestry Department, where foresters were trying to design a new project and hoping for Swedish support. Their new approach was called forestry for local community development. The aim was to change some of the foresters from managers of trees to advisers supporting rural people who needed trees for their well-being. The Swedish delegation said that conventional foresters would need input from social scientists and community development specialists. A woman member on the Swedish team pointed out that in Sweden as elsewhere, women were much involved with forests and therefore essential in the design phase. Because of pressure from this donor, the FAO foresters were looking for a social scientist who had rural development experience in Africa, who spoke French, and who had an interest in forestry—and perhaps who was even a woman. I was selected in 1977.

It would be misleading to make it appear that the whole consultancy was went smoothly. The Forestry Department had seldom worked with either women or social scientists. Most of its staff was uninterested, thinking I was there simply as a palliative for the Swedes. When I arrived for the first briefing the forester who was team leader had a big desk, while I was assigned a very small table in the corner. Rather than complain, I decided to sit at that table as though it were a big desk. The FAO foresters seldom looked at me. It was not until the debriefing that they saw I had information on local institutions, tenure and access rights, and local uses of trees. Coming from applied anthropology, I presented concrete ideas for a participatory program. From that time on it was much easier for me to connect with these foresters. Discussions with the Swedes were successful and I continued consulting.

One time, on the way through Rome to Sierra Leone, I was asked to apply for the position of chief of the FAO Women in Development Service. I was pleased to be offered such a prestigious position, but realized during the interviews and discussions that there were strong conflicts over what such an office should do. Some recognized that women were actively involved in farming, business enterprises, and other activities beyond conventional home economics activities. Others, including many of the higher (male) officials, felt that it was an imposition of Western imperialism to give women training related to anything outside household duties. The fact that women produced large amounts of food in many societies, including the United States, was largely unacknowledged and in some societies was considered an embarrassment. I realized that the position, while political and controversial, would be challenging and interesting.

One week in Sierra Leone I stayed in a village tracing the activities and discussions of various people, especially as they related to their production system and to trees and forests. I stayed at the home of a policeman, the informal community leader. Every evening people gathered around his home to discuss issues and ask advice. One man came every evening but only on the last day did we have a conversation. He said, "We are so glad you have come. Maybe you can help our women. They are very ignorant." I responded that the women seemed very competent at fishing and farming. Yes, he said, but could I teach them something useful? Pausing, he looked up with a bright smile and said, "Teach them to embroider flowers on our pillowcases."

I thought about this for days. The man was unaware I had spent a day with his wife. She woke at 4:00 A.M. and worked until well after dinner. She fished, gardened, helped in the grain fields, brought water and fuelwood, built and tended the fire, cooked, smoked fish, made and mended fishing nets from forest reeds, and cleaned and cared for the children and the home. She had no time to start a new activity. I decided to turn down the women in development position because I could do more to improve women's lives by focusing on access to productive resources through community forestry. Community forestry sounds benign, but it focuses on local control and power as well as tenure and access rights, communal management, and conflict management, which are not at all benign.

In 1984 I left the university to join the staff of FAO's Forestry Department in Rome. The post was newly created and I had a great deal of flexibility, as no one in the department knew what a social scientist could really do. On the first day I was requested to comment on how a project was dealing with regard to a questionnaire on fuelwood. I noted that since it was given only to heads of households it would certainly miss women's viewpoints and made suggestions for changes. I was shocked the next morning when I received copy of a memo going to the project director saying that the technical staff required that these changes be made. Little by little I learned to write comments in a direct style rather than the typically feminine style of "perhaps you could" and "it might be better if." I learned to be direct in requesting realistic changes that were necessary to improve the impact of our projects on local people and thereby gained the confidence of many field staff personnel.

Gaining Acceptance

However, getting started was not always easy. It was not always clear whether problems arose because I was a social scientist in the midst of foresters, because I was a woman among mostly males, or both. I had to convince the others that my contribution was sound, and in trying to do so found women could be as difficult as men. For example, the only other professional woman in the department was a very skilled geneticist. After reading a project document for Nepal that was going to various divisions for comments, I wrote that in Nepal it was important to give controlled access to women for certain forest products even before forest inventories were completed. The woman geneticist was angered because she thought I was not serious about forest inventories. She wrote a long, scathing memo asking what foresters could possibly say to me, a nonforester, to make me understand the importance of forest inventories. Perhaps I could understand their importance if, she said, I considered the difficulty of baking a cake without a recipe.

I had to think about how to respond to this insulting note from a woman with whom I would be working. I wrote a very careful and objective response, stating that I understood the importance of forest inventories, but that the understory plants in question would not even be included in a forest inventory. Further, foresters did not know anything about the allowable cut or the management regimes for those plants nor did they have any control over the contractors that were harvesting them. I suggested allowing women to harvest these products using a conservative plan and monitoring the effects, thereby benefiting local women and giving foresters a basis for future control. I never got another insulting memo.

I needed to have a good sense of humor while the men were getting used to the fact that I was a member of their department. I thought it was important to work with young people and had numerous interns. Many, though certainly not all, of the young professionals interested in this field were women. One day an Australian forester came into my office, looked around, and asked if he could call it "the women's room." I laughed and answered that was fine as long as I could call all the other offices in the department "men's rooms." Another asked where I got all these "cute young things." I answered that I had not known that getting a master's degree in forestry and working in field posts was supposed to make young professionals ugly. Meetings outside FAO were even more difficult as I was often the only woman. The theme of communal management and women's access and responsibilities in forestry was new and uncomfortable for many. The idea that local people could manage pieces of forest was threatening to people's image of themselves as professionals; it felt demeaning to accept local knowledge, especially from women.

The Community Forest Unit

The community forestry unit, which I headed, was in the division of policy and planning, whose work involved providing input into policy papers and representing forestry in many other FAO divisions including women in development, nutrition, population, food security, and the nongovernmental organization office. Within the Forestry Department I designed and evaluated the socio-economic aspects of forestry projects, starting with only a couple of projects but later growing to well over one hundred. Meetings were held on conservation and development and policy discussions with government visitors. Tasks also included project design and evaluation and designing and carrying out training programs, workshops, and seminars. But the most time and energy went into managing the global community forestry program, because it represented a revolution in the forestry field.

The program itself was not just about women, but as half of any population is women, it was important to make their relationship to forests and trees visible. We produced several documents and case studies from many parts of the world which showed foresters and others that women were interested in, knowledgeable about, and dependent upon tree and forest products. Few foresters had seen local tree-related interests of men or women as being different from forestry goals, although they usually were. As soon as it became well accepted that women had specific forestry issues, we focused on gender analysis, emphasizing the complementary nature of women's and men's tasks and the need for tree and forest outputs in family survival strategy. In contrast to a focus on the inequity of women's work or simply on women and their problems, this approach emphasized women's relation to trees and forests within the context of their contribution to the family. This undermined the belief that the topic of women and forestry was alien to local culture, making it less threatening and more effective.

Another program focused on forestry, food security, and nutrition. Research was necessary to demonstrate precisely how tree leaves, fruits, and nuts, as well as small animals from the forests, are a major element in the daily food supply, and even more important when other food is scarce. We did workshops, published articles, and wrote policy papers. We developed guidelines on how to work with communities in identifying nutritional and food security issues. We wanted foresters to be aware that projects could decrease food security for the vulnerable, but that adding nutritive plants into the nursery could help address nutritional problems such as lack of Vitamin A. We even developed school materials and a comic book called *I Am So Hungry I Could Eat a Tree.*

To change policies as well as projects where there was concern about the future of forest control and management, it was necessary to demonstrate that many rural communities were worried about the future of the forests and had created local institutions to establish rules about their use and conservation. These local management systems were often especially relevant to women. Our program needed concrete information on how people were managing forests and when and under what conditions communal management can be successful. Most of the available data focused only on measures of trees and biomass, but for reforming policies and management, sexually disaggregated information was needed on local use, rules of management, history, and socio-economy. FAO joined with Elinor Ostrom of Indiana University to develop a new international research network with a database incorporating biophysical, social, economic, and institutional factors. Centers with trained local researchers now exist in a network in Africa, Asia, and Latin America. The data contributed to indigenous people obtaining forestland rights in Latin America, a government incorporating demographic information in long-term forest management planning in Africa, and it also serves as a basis for dispute resolution in Asia.

Our office in FAO decentralized the community forestry program in a network called Forests, Trees and People. Projects were no longer planned and implemented by outsiders but were managed in the developing countries, where local issues and knowledge would have greater play and local women and men would have a better chance to be heard. Vastly different activities were identified in different countries. The Bolivia program, for example, developed university courses on women and forestry specifically for Latin American foresters, while in Costa Rica emphasis was put on developing approaches for local participatory evaluation of forestry activities.

In 1996 I left FAO and the program that had been a major part of my life to return to the United States and start a new life yet again. I chose Washington, D.C., where I could see many of my friends from other countries and the states, and where opportunities exist to be involved in equity and natural resource issues. I had learned that many of the problems identified in less industrial countries, stemming from top-down planning, lack of respect for local knowledge, and an imbalance of power, also exist in the industrialized world. A recent workshop showed Swedish communities losing control over their productive resources because of government policies on tree harvesting and forest access similar to those reported in India, Bolivia, Scotland, Thailand, Canada, Liberia, and the United States. I am trying to bring insights from international development back to disadvantaged communities in Washington, D.C., and to work in other U.S. programs as well as on international development issues.

Overall, I am extremely satisfied with the development of my life. Despite the problems of the times, such as wives not being paid for work, I had a chance to stay with my children longer and still develop a professional life. As I see many of my young professional friends with spouses working in separate locations, I think that current freedoms have their problems as well.

Lessons Learned

In my professional work, I learned a number of important lessons. First, it is important to see how things are related and to work with an integrated picture that includes the cracks between disciplines. No single focus can address a complex problem. It is important to move from a focus solely on women to the family and community while keeping the woman visible. Anthropology was a very good background for this and for learning from women and men about the issues of importance to them.

Second, participation is more than a buzzword. When women were included in the planning of forestry activities, the species selection and timing of work was different and more successful. In doing Asian case studies of gender and forestry, we included forestry policy makers as advisers. Those who participated may have been sympathetic to begin with; in Bolivia the team using the integrated database method was made up of indigenous people, university researchers, and foresters. Because this range of people was part of the process, the information was more accurate, the report could be used by the community to support adjudication of their land claims, and the foresters were supportive of developing a local forestry management plan. When we decentralized the community forestry program, the national facilitators and the local and community organizations with which they worked developed a feeling of ownership. The activities they developed were responsive to the needs of local women and men and were creative and effective beyond what I could have imagined

Third, it was enriching for me to have experienced a variety of situations. I had opportunities to work on a sustained basis in the field; consult widely in numerous countries, gaining a broader understanding of the possible range of issues; and withdraw to an academic surrounding to read and write and talk with theorists. When I joined an international organization, I supported the development of ideas, tools, and approaches and their application and dissemination and helped create space for discussion and networking. Now I am trying to bring those ideas back to the United States.

Fourth, mentoring is very valuable. In all of my experiences I had the support of excellent colleagues and directors and I have tried to support young colleagues. Finally, when starting anything new, it is important to identify your own bottom line and be persistent in holding it. Humor helps, along with a clear focus on what you want to achieve. It is often important to sit, as I did on my first FAO consultancy, at any table as though it were a big desk.

Most of Marilyn W. Hoskins's early data on community forestry remains at FAO in Rome.

Dorienne
Rowan-Campbell

Dorienne Rowan-Campbell was born in Jamaica and her tertiary education has been in the United Kingdom (the Middle Temple) and Canada (Carleton University, English and history). Her education continues in India at Sumhedas, an organization working on the human context in development and organizations, societies and cultural values.

In her pathbreaking work, Dorienne Rowan-Campbell began the process of institutionalizing the Department on the Portrayal of Women at the Canadian Broadcasting Company, was the first director of the Women and Development Program of the Commonwealth Secretariat, and helped start the Gender and Development Centre of the University of the West Indies. She is now pioneering the growing of organic Jamaica Blue Mountain Coffee with her own marque, Rowan's Royale. She has worked at the Jamaica Broadcasting Corporation, the Canadian Broadcasting Company, the Mexican News Agency, and TV Ontario, where she co-hosted a development series called "One World."

Living between Jamaica and Canada, she brings bifocal vision from these cultures to her work as a development consultant, particularly to management of change, gender equity, and environment. She donates time to work with communities and NGOs in Jamaica. One son and two stepsons have gifted her with three grandchildren. She has been married for the last years to a childhood friend.

Creating a Commonwealth Sisterhood

When I think back, my move from Canada to the Commonwealth Secretariat (Comsec) in London in 1980 was a kind of homecoming, because although I was Jamaican, it knit together location, academic interests, and avocation. London, where I began my undergraduate studies, is one of my favorite cities. My focus in undergraduate work had been Commonwealth studies. Also, my job at the secretariat was to work officially on critical women's development issues that I so passionately espoused all my life. Although that very first clear autumn morning in 1980 it did not feel like a homecoming when, direct from Heathrow airport having left my husband and son in Ottawa, I entered the flat that was to be mine for the next three years.

This is not to say that the Commonwealth Secretariat itself was welcoming; anything but. I initially met polite suspicion, as much from women as from men. I was not only the first female among fourteen directors but also the youngest, and director in an area no one imagined of much import. Initially I found that, apart from its establishment, few had given much serious thought to what the Women and Development Program (WDP) might be and become. This would be useful in the development of our program.

Setting up a New Program

The Commonwealth is a voluntary association of fifty-four independent states with shared experience as British colonies. Comsec is one of the younger international organizations. Born at the instance of Commonwealth governments, which required an international civil service to give effect to their mandates, it was established in London in 1965. A policy-focused organization, it addresses priorities defined by governments at periodic Ministers and biennial Heads of Government meetings. Priorities are addressed through the provision of policy advice, short-term experts in country, expert groups, meetings, workshops, and publications.

The Comsec nerve center is Marlborough House, an imposing palace in central London very close to Buckingham Palace. When I arrived at the Secretariat, the major offices were all located in Marlborough House. Lofty as my title was—director of women and development and adviser to the secretary-general—it was apparent that my advice was not envisaged as being required on a regular basis. I was relegated to offices on St. James Street, a few blocks away, and shared a floor with the Commonwealth Youth Program. Initially I was very concerned that being out of sight might mean being out of mind.

Despite some vagueness about what exactly this new unit would do, Comsec took some critical first steps. The Mid-Decade World Conference on Women was held at Copenhagen in August 1980. Prior to officially taking my position in September, I was asked to represent the organization at the conference, and was accompanied by the assistant director for information, Patsy Robertson, a fellow Jamaican. Copenhagen provided a strategic opportunity. I was able to meet with all Commonwealth delegations, get a sense of their priorities, and develop a wish list for the Women and Development Program. If the staff of the secretariat had little sense of what the WDP might be or might achieve, women of the Commonwealth had some very clear ideas. Thus armed, my first task was to analyze the organization and see how these clear ideas might fit with the Comsec mandate.

My previous employment with the Canadian Broadcasting Corporation from 1971 to 1980 proved an excellent training ground. At the time it was the largest broadcaster in the world, with radio and television services across Canada in French, English, native Inuit, and Indian languages, and international service as well. As assistant in the Corporate Film Department in Ottawa, I had coordinated a TV project on global innovation, working with production crews to share what was new, challenging, and worthy of note in the world of television and explore with them its relevance to their own productions and audiences. I moved on to initiate a unit dedicated to enhancing the portrayal of women in radio and television programming. These tasks provided a crash course in how to effectively insinuate a discrete concern into the wider organizational fabric. The policy emphasis in this work skewed my approach at Comsec to a focus on policy rather than projects.

In many ways Comsec was an old-style, traditional civil service, yet it managed to accommodate flexibility and tolerate innovation. This was possibly less the result of its management structure than the lack of it. Much operated by gentlemen's agreement. Not being a gentleman, I was free to challenge the rules. I took annual work plans and budgets very seriously. Apparently, the practice was that everyone proposed his or, in my case, her plan, everyone got cut, and everyone agreed. Unaware, I argued the need for coherent funding to start up the WDP program and provided an impact analysis of proposed cuts. As a result, we ended up getting what many viewed as more than our fair share. Traditional decision-making techniques had been surprised by alternative approaches.

Introducing a new element into a corporate structure often provides opportunities that give an unfair advantage to anyone prepared to be innovative or subversive. I was both. We achieved what we did in part because the organization did not perceive the changes being instituted as important or even possible. The others had not recognized that one could not advocate heightened awareness of and attention to women's and gender issues in member countries without the internal dynamic of the organization changing to reflect this orientation.

New Directions of the WDP

WDP's creation of a more sensitive, aware, and equal work environment for both men and women was welcomed by much of the Comsec staff. This groundswell helped push changes in Comsec itself, not an easy task in a Britain, which at that time had little sense of what was politically correct regarding gender relations in the workplace. The structure of Comsec, whose familial relationships allowed for personal connections in member countries, was ideal for developing a new and different type of women's program. Its isolation from the central office actually proved a forcing ground for the program. We worked with little oversight from our deputy secretary-general, a Bangladeshi with a penchant for silk scarves and bomber jackets who treated us with courteous disinterest. Because Comsec had never been involved in women and development issues before, there were no parameters and only a vague direction. We had a clean slate. This allowed me to take the staff positions allocated and, maintaining the outward form, change their functions. By the time my deputy, New Zealander Mary Sinclair, the senior documentalist, took office, we were both clear that she would be doing little library work.

A first task, daunting and lonely, was to produce, and have approved, a plan of action for the program. It was built around established Commonwealth priorities, soundings from member countries in Copenhagen, my emerging sense of Comsec as an organization, WDP's limited capacity, and some of my own strongly held prejudices.

The Commonwealth has a tremendous reach. At that time its tentacles surfaced through meetings of ministers for agriculture, education, health, youth, industry, and science as well as annual meetings of the International Labour Office and the World Bank. Our task was to influence the agenda of these meetings and through them the agendas of individual countries. We utilized the various means of influencing the Commonwealth agenda and, ultimately, policy: expert groups, workshops, reports, commissioned studies, and publications. We had to make an impact on policies that touched the lives of women—that is, all policies. It was also clear that the approach would have to be gradual, if unrelenting, and that the three staff WDP had been allocated could not do it alone. Our first task was a search for allies. We needed a team.

I had a dream about taking the physical space we had been given and using it to create emotional space, ideological space, and epistemological space where words gave meaning to something different and dynamic. I wanted to create a nonjudgmental space where ideas could be discussed, challenged, dissected, and acted upon—a safe, welcoming space for women in the secretariat itself and for the many women who would visit from their home countries and institutions as well as for men who cared to join us.

It was the unofficial Commonwealth that joined us first, professional and nongovernmental organizations which fall under the umbrella of the Commonwealth Foundation. The Commonwealth Parliamentary Association and the Nurses Association were the first two nongovernmental agencies to welcome and support our office. The fourth estate played a great role in our support team. My Canadian broadcasting background connected me to the electronic media. BBC regularly invited me to talk on their world service programs about our work; Sandra Brown from Thames Broadcasting gave us ongoing support.

Help from UK and Commonwealth Women

The United Kingdom of the 1980s was a wonderful place to be, as much of the emerging thinking on women, gender, and development was centered there and was moving praxis forward. Maxine Molyneux, Kate Young, Caroline Moser, Ruth Pearson, and Diane Elson were all challenging and expanding concepts about women. They were an inspiration to work with, reinforcing our mutual goals. We supported Kate Young in developing the Women, Men, and Development course at the Institute of Development Studies at the University of Sussex and Caroline Moser in her Gender Planning course at the Development Planning Unit at London University. Their institutions mounted courses for Commonwealth women, the Commonwealth Foundation provided scholarships, and I lectured at them. Those women in turn became part of our expert team. Slowly, partnerships within Comsec also emerged. Stimulating times were had working on management issues with the staff of the Management Development Division and on violence with the Legal Division. Economic Affairs remained skeptical to the last but finally worked as a partner building the framework for a study on structural adjustment.

Women had fewer opportunities to travel and visit Comsec than did their male peers. London, however, is a good transit point for many areas of the Commonwealth. My apartment rapidly became a hotel for women passing through to meetings in other countries as we encouraged them to add a day or two to their itineraries. This allowed them to see firsthand what we were trying to do, make their own contributions, and take new messages back home. I have joyful memories of wonderful lunches and long, intense evenings where UK women met with visitors from far-flung reaches of the Commonwealth. They arrived as colleagues and left as friends, perhaps one of the most wonderful legacies of my time at Comsec.

As our program work developed, the team enlarged to include ministers for women's affairs. On one occasion a request for funding for work on violence against women was cut from the budget. Fortunately, Ann Hercus, then minister of justice and of women's affairs, was visiting from New Zealand. When she heard of our plight she went to bat with the deputy secretary-general responsible for planning. The funds were quietly restored and we never had a problem supporting our work on violence again.

The concept of teamwork extended to the program itself. It meant greater autonomy for all staff but also greater responsibility. Everyone had to understand our goals and activities and be able to represent them to a stream of visitors. Committed to building capacity in our countries, we did the same at WDP through intra-divisional training sessions in which we all participated.

Expanding our Programs

Isolation from the Marlborough House offices helped us grow; disinterest allowed us to carve out our own territory. Moni Malhoutra became our new deputy secretary-general at just the right moment. Incisive, farsighted, demanding, and sometimes impossible, he challenged us, went out on a limb to give us room to experiment, and became a member, if an exacting one, of the team. He accepted what we had achieved, pushed us to go further, required excellence, and helped us find our wings. In a system change we became part of the Human Resource Development Group, a rearrangement of divisions that was much to our advantage, since WDP worked best through collaboration.

WDP grew. By 1984 we had three professional staff, two secretaries, an administrative assistant, and an excellent representation of the Commonwealth countries: New Zealand, Malaysia, Sri Lanka, Zambia, Zimbabwe, Canada, and Jamaica. We all worked far too long hours, but it was worthwhile, as we established a Comsec Plan of Action, endorsed by Heads of Government in 1987, that helped shape international development dialogue on women and gender issues.

Women's Bureaus

Under the mandate of Mexico City in 1975, governments had set up women's bureaus to be the focal point for representation of women's concerns. However, they were not performing. I felt they required support to improve their interactions within governments rather than the current training that focused on fundraising, project preparation, management, and community leadership. Bureau heads needed to appreciate their policy-influencing role, sharpen their negotiation and analytic skills, and devise strategic arguments that would compel policy makers to listen to their messages. A skills workshop became the first step in capacity development.

The Commonwealth has a preponderance of small and island states; they were, and remain, a priority for action. What better place to introduce the skills workshop than the small island states in my own Caribbean? Comsec works through regional organizations such as the Caribbean Community (CARICOM), the Caribbean regional organization.[1] In June 1981 a week-long workshop was held in Grenada. That September a workshop for the Pacific region was held in Western Samoa in collaboration with University of the South Pacific and, in October, in the Seychelles for Cyprus, Malta, and Indian Ocean states. These workshops examined the mandates and functions of bureaus and developed, with the help of local trainers, the skills participants felt they needed.

While the workshops were underway, we commissioned case studies of Caribbean bureaus. Next we brought together bureau heads and their permanent secretaries. It had become clear that secretariats had little idea of what was expected of the bureaus or what their potential might be, and so had given them scant support. The insights from this workshop and the case studies were published as *Ladies in Limbo: The Fate of Women's Bureaux.* This book proved so useful that the Netherlands government funded a print run large enough to provide a copy for each official participant at the Third World Conference on Women at Nairobi in 1985.

Commissioned studies became the vehicle for developing and widening the experience of women analyzing and writing about their countries. The emphasis was on young women, who thus gained a foot in the consultancy arena. Experts are created, not born. Believing that prophets are honored in other countries, we took experts from Tanzania and sent them to work with Kenya, from Jamaica to work with Dominica, and so on. After their foreign exposure these experts became better recognized and accepted in their own regions and countries. Many now work as international consultants. Following the Nairobi conference, we responded to its Forward-Looking Strategies and the mandate of our ministers by offering a policy development extension service, providing a team to visit countries and assist in developing women and gender-specific national policies. Many national polices resulted from this service.

Civil Servant Courses

In 1980 there were not many courses on women and development accessible to Commonwealth women in their own countries. The Eastern Southern African Management Institute under Misrak Elias was creating space for women. We also found a World Bank report on the lack of an efficient and trained civil service that supported our decision to run a course for senior women mangers in African civil services. With a committed tutor, Pauline Glucclick, from the British Civil Service College, and in partnership with Sue Burke of the Management Development Division of the Economic Commission for Africa, we developed and tested a course and then adapted it for an African context. In 1983, with funding from Canada's development agency, we ran the first course for thirty managers, preceded by a training of trainers for the institute staff who took the program over.

A link was then made with Indira Parik of the Indian Institute of

Management in Amadebhad and with similar programs in Sierra Leone through the Pan African Institute for Development and in the Caribbean through CARICOM. The courses allowed senior women to meet, to compare and contrast problems and solutions, and to learn how to operate within systems and change them. As an antidote to the vaunted Queen Bee syndrome, the importance of mentoring and assisting other women was stressed.

Violence Against Women

The violence against women issue was dealt with in a sanitized manner at Copenhagen in 1980. Addressed under the peace section of the agenda, the final text contained pious rhetoric rather than action statements. I had been exposed to domestic violence in a first, early marriage and was determined to make my institution respond in a more positive manner. Our first act was to undertake a comparative analysis of the legal framework for addressing rape and domestic violence in the Commonwealth. Armed with this information and with the view that this violence was not a women's but a societal problem, we held a series of expert meetings with lawyers, police, magistrates, and persons working with abused women and abusive men; together we devised a number of action points. These included training for magistrates, curricula for Commonwealth law schools, and training for police officers.

We even managed to fund a village pilot project in India that used puppets to break the silence about domestic violence. Indeed, we developed a comprehensive methodology for policy process and action. Most importantly, we got these issues on the agenda of law ministers and government heads. To pull all this together we produced a *Manual for Commonwealth Action*. The UN, impressed with what we had achieved, hired our main consultant, Australian Jane Connors, to work with them and began to build on what we had started in order to move the issue of violence away from rhetoric and onto the UN action agenda.

Women's Employment

Policy makers conceived of women's lives as driven by welfare rather than economic concerns and located women's bureaus in welfare-oriented ministries. This had to change. We documented some of the nontraditional work women do in Marilyn Carr's *Blacksmith, Baker, Roofing Sheet*. In 1983 we produced an analysis of the policy implications of women's informal economic activities for labor ministers, followed by workshops bringing together the poorest Commonwealth countries. Each country sent five participants from government agencies dealing with employment creation and an NGO effective in this field. In this way we tried to break down the isolation of women's bureaus, stimulate alliances, and shift agenda from income gencration to employment creation. Key partners in this activity were Gloria Scott of the World Bank and Marilyn Carr of the International Intermediate Technology Group.

The Commonwealth needed tools to persuade policy makers that investing in women's employment made economic sense. We provided a cost-benefit methodology in *Investment Appraisal of Supportive Measures to Working Women*. At the request of ministers for women's affairs at the Nairobi conference of 1985, we began work on the impact of structural adjustment on women. This culminated in 1987 when the Heads of Government mandated an expert group on structural adjustment, which gave birth to our publication, *Engendering Adjustment*.

Preparing for the Nairobi Conference

I was convinced of the truth of the axiom our secretary-general, Sir Sridath Ramphal, was fond of stating: "The Commonwealth cannot negotiate for the world but it can help the world to negotiate." Our preparatory work for Nairobi verified my faith. You cannot inform an agenda if you do not know a meeting is taking place and have not been asked to give your input. So WDP needed to find means of getting out information in a timely manner about what was going on in the international arena. When it became clear that a list of meetings was insufficient, we provided a set of notes, with references that set out the issues, possible actions, and women's or gender perspectives for all UN and related meetings during 1984 and 1985, whether the meeting was on transnational companies or disarmament or the New International Economic Order. This approach was meant to help Commonwealth women get their perspectives into the mainstream of development debate. We called the publication we put out *Working Into the System: A Calendar for the Integration of Women's Issues into International Development Dialogue*. Ingrid Palmer worked with us on this effort and continued with us in preparing Commonwealth women for Nairobi.

We held a meeting of senior officials for women' affairs in October 1984 and agreed on strategies for maintaining consensus during the contentious preparatory meetings for Nairobi. In addition, we held an orientation workshop led by two Commonwealth doyens, Gloria Scott of the World Bank and Lucille Mair of the UN, to prepare participants for UN conferences. A third doyen, Dame Nita Barrow, convener of the NGO Forum, also lent her assistance. Such an approach was necessary because I had noticed at the Copenhagen conference of 1980 that many women who represented their countries were inadequately prepared. They did not fully understand UN procedures and thus could not participate as effectively as they might.

Comsec served as a partner to Kenya as it prepared for the conference. We were given an office in the conference center, secretarial assistance, and transportation to provide support for small states and a focal point for

Commonwealth participants. I was often invited to sit in on Kenya's delegation meetings and helped them work with Commonwealth delegations to try to reach consensus. In the end it was the Commonwealth that broke the deadlock and allowed the Nairobi conference to move ahead on women's issues and not shrivel over rigid geopolitical stances on apartheid and Zionism. Mama Kankassa, leader of the Zambian delegation, spoke to her president, who sanctioned a move away from the agreed position of the Organization of African Unity. Other African countries followed. The conference document, Forward-Looking Strategies, was agreed to by consensus.

How We Succeeded

In retrospect, it is clear that the achievements of the Women and Development Program were based on partnership; our survival and accomplishments are a tribute to the vision and commitment of countless women worldwide who together made the program work. The orientation of the program was based on my sense of what being feminist meant: a fight for a more equal world for both men and women, for partnership, for justice. It was not exclusive, it was not separatist, it was not radical. Many of our strongest allies were male. One was a bureau head who shared our passion for equity and justice. We invited male colleagues into our world and work and courted the whole secretariat with parties on International Women's Day and outings when the occasion arose. One night over fifty of us, men and women, went to Leicester Square to see the movie *9 to 5,* which dealt with female retribution against an abusive boss. We had dinner after at ManFuKung, a vast Chinese restaurant next door. This got the message out that feminism was not incompatible with fun.

We built alliances through the staff association by our efforts to bring positive changes for all staff. Our early isolation meant that staff who felt they had problems could easily come and report to us and that we would then try to see their concerns addressed. Secretaries and mail carriers became our great friends, bringing us news and organization gossip as well as mail. Soon we had eyes and ears all over the secretariat and knew in advance of meetings planned from which we might be excluded. We knew what was happening before many others did, a clear organizational advantage.

The work was fulfilling but exhausting. So much of it involved absorbing and deflecting hostility and negative energy and transforming it into positive actions. It was not easy. Working on the cusp of change is lonely, but growing up in Jamaica I had learned one important survival skill: "you take bad sinting mek laugh." That laughter at myself and circumstance would often see me through. The mission to succeed consumed me, and succeed we did, but it was success at a cost. If I was happy at work, the commuting life between London and my husband and son in Ottawa was lonely. His year in London, and his accompanying me during his vacation time to places like Zimbabwe where I was working, did not fill the gap for time missed in my son's teenage years. Although my husband joined me for the last three years of my stay in London, the stress told on us and for the second time my marriage ended in divorce.

How My Background Supported Me

The sense of homecoming I found in Comsec forced me to examine my direction in life. I came to Comsec representing Canada. Jamaica also claimed me. But I began to see that, in reality, I was an outsider in both cultures. I was valued but not fully integrated. Historically and emotionally this child of the colonies was more comfortable in and understanding of British society than that of North America. The sense of homecoming was intensified because the multicultural and multiracial character of Comsec provided camouflage. In Canada I was always visible. Whatever I did was somehow colored by being "other." I was not just a voice for whatever issue I espoused; there was the subtle and burdensome expectation that I represented a minority position. Such assumptions often distracted from the central message. In the Canadian Broadcasting Company I was exceptional; there were not many black senior staff. It was good to be ordinary for a change.

My many selves came together in a wonderful reconciliation of my heritage. Jamaica is a very mixed society. I, with white, African slave, and East Indian blood, embody the motto, "out of many one people." When I worked in India I was accepted as Indian, in East Africa they were certain I was from Zanzibar, in West Africa from the north, in the Pacific I looked familiar enough. By the time people discovered I wasn't who I seemed, I had been welcomed. The Commonwealth is referred to as family. It was my family. I was treated as daughter, sister, aunt, sometimes mother, and always with love.

I began to realize that my success in Comsec owed a great deal to my ancestry. My grandmother, aunt, mother, and a host of great aunts provided strong role models. My mother reminded me ad nauseam that I had potential and must live up to it. My father, a lawyer, encouraged any venture I wanted to undertake, never making a difference between what I or my brother could do. My maternal grandfather provided my first exposure to reading literary criticism at age seven. My paternal grandfather fed my passion for history. None of them gave me the impression that being female could, in any way, determine what I would become.

I went to a girl's boarding school, the third generation to do so. Hampton expected excellence, commitment, and a social conscience of its students. It prodded you to think for yourself. In the sixth forms (the final two years) we were combined with the sixth of nearby Munro, a boys' school where my father and grandfather had been to school. The boys were anxious to carry our books, until we beat them in the first tests. Then normality took over and developed into a lifetime of partnership and friendship. Still, things were unequal. Girls were somehow expected to make concessions that males didn't. Social standards differed. My feminism was born there and by an early reading of Simone de Beauvoir's *The Second Sex,* which defined the barriers I sensed and fought against and encouraged me to not accept the status quo.

Life in boarding school brought an understanding of structure, of how far institutional parameters could be manipulated and spaces created between existing rules and regulations and the true, lived life of the school. I see now that I understood early how to use institutional camouflage, adopting appropriate language and behaviors while working at changing the institution from within, challenging peers and teachers to see alternative ways of doing, seeing, and being. Instinctively, I used that experience at Comsec.

All those formative influences cried out for acknowledgement. Canada gave me remarkable support through Status of Women Canada and through the Canadian International Development Agency. I felt I had served Canada well. Canada is my country of choice. Jamaica, my birthright, is the country where my soul sleeps at night. Now, it was time to try to give back some of myself to the country that truly made me what I am. It was time to leave Comsec, time to go, time to try to find home.

Elise Fiber Smith

Elise Fiber Smith is a respected leader in the field of gender and international development assistance. She has originated and implemented programs in Africa, Latin America, Asia, and the former Soviet Union for over twenty-five years. In the 1990s she initiated and is the president of Women's EDGE, the coalition for Women's Economic Development and Global Equality, which advocates for a gender perspective on issues of international aid and trade. She also founded and directed the Global Women's Leadership Program at Winrock International.

In the 1980s she was executive director of the Overseas Education Fund International (OEF). She was one of the first woman CEOs among the private voluntary organizations accredited by the United States Agency for International Development (USAID) and is a founder of the American Council for Voluntary International Action, or INTERACTION, which has over 160 member associations working in international development and refugee relief.

Currently she serves as a member of the Advisory Committee on Voluntary Foreign Aid (ACVFA), which provides guidance to the administrator of USAID and the State Department's U.S. Advisory Committee on International Economic Policy (ACIEP).

She is a graduate of the University of Michigan and Case Western Reserve University and was a Rotary International Ambassadorial Scholar. Jac Smit, her companion since 1984, shares with her his expertise on regional development and urban agriculture. One of her great delights is spending time with her two sons, Greg and Guy, and their families.

Women Empowering Women Through NGOs

"Never doubt that a small, committed, dedicated group of people can change the world. Indeed, it is the only thing that ever can."
—Margaret Mead

As a student at the University of Michigan in the 1950s, I learned the value of nongovernmental organizations. I was a member and leader of student groups that took on the university administration over discrimination in housing for African American and international students and in the use of university buildings by left-of-center groups. That is where I learned that organized groups, with good leaders, can effect change or at least make their voices heard. At the same time, my roommate and I also made long lists of all the things in the world that needed improvement and discussed which ones we wanted to work on after graduation. Later I discovered there was much more to do than we had thought. The first time was when I worked with U.S. female-headed families that had inadequate health care, food, and housing. Then, during my ten years in Latin America as a spouse, mother, and professional woman, I once again experienced the shock of exposure to extreme poverty.

After graduating from the University of Michigan, I won a Rotary Foundation fellowship to study political science from a European perspective at the University of Strasbourg in France. This was a great honor for a woman back then. World War II had ended only nine years before. Distrust and hostility between countries still existed as Europe was undergoing reconstruction of its destroyed and damaged cities. I didn't realize then that much of what was being done in Europe—building infrastructure, concentrating on economic development—would become the model when foreign donors began providing development assistance to developing countries.

With a *Michigan Daily* press card, I talked my way into the official press corps to observe the recently formed Council of Europe. Besides viewing problems through a European lens, I acquired a knowledge of diverse cultures and languages and gained an understanding of the great ideal of creating a European Union. By the time I returned to the United States, I was convinced that building understanding across national boundaries through exchanges and other cross-cultural programs was critical. That was when I traveled all over Michigan speaking to Rotary Clubs about my experience, emphasizing the importance of scholarships and study abroad.

A Latin American Awakening

Living in five Latin American countries—Mexico, Ecuador, Venezuela, Peru, and Colombia—during the 1960s and 1970s with my foreign service husband and two young sons convinced me that working with women on poverty alleviation was essential. I remember the shock of arriving in Guayaquil, Ecuador, a very poor port city that was also the commercial banking center of Ecuador. Mile after mile of slums encircled the downtown and stretched out to the barrios on the fringe of the city. When my Spanish became proficient enough to communicate with community development workers, government officials, and grassroots villagers, I felt compelled to get involved. In community organizations I learned more about children without health care, families without enough food, high infant mortality rates, and illiteracy among children and adults who had little or no opportunity for education. I discovered that many women had few if any skills to earn income and no access to credit or other resources to start small businesses.

At Centros Communales in Guayaquil, where a group of community centers struggled to respond to community needs, I also saw the scarcity of trained community development workers. The gap between rich and poor was greater than I could have imagined. I understood why liberation theology evolved within the Catholic Church. I also discovered that women were the most unequal and poorest. My understanding of the very difficult role of Latin American women grew as I met and worked with women at all levels of society in community centers, innovative preschool programs, universities, and women's organizations. In some Latin American countries, forty percent of all households were single parent and female headed. Educated women also felt constraints. In many Latin American nations, women couldn't leave the country without the husband's permission, couldn't control property, and had no access to credit. Inheritance laws did not protect widows and discrimination existed in the job market.

As a spouse of a foreign service officer, I also discovered what it is like to be a second-class citizen. Wives were expected, without complaint, to volunteer time to embassy functions and use our homes for entertaining whenever embassy officials requested. We were not to engage in controversy or be involved with any political cause that seemed left of center. In one Latin American country, when I tried to facilitate meetings between Marxist leaders and government officials with my church group, a highly placed embassy official told my husband to inform me that the embassy did not approve of my activities and that I should discontinue them. I continued associating with whomever I wanted, albeit more quietly.

In a slum area of Lima, Peru, I was a member of a community development group. Working with poor Indian women and their children who had recently arrived in Lima from their mountain villages, I learned about the power of nonformal education. We initiated a culturally adapted Head Start program. In this program Indian women learned new skills as they prepared their children for success in school, participated in income-generation activities, and learned how to survive in an unfamiliar urban environment. Teaching at the Catholic University in Lima and at the University El Rosario in Bogotá, Colombia, I observed that many of my female students lacked self-esteem. Working with them on defining their common problems and ways to cope with barriers to career choices increased their self-confidence. This experience convinced me that participatory and experiential learning methods are strong tools for empowering women.

The Overseas Education Fund: Leadership to Empower Women

Back in the United States, in 1974 when my spouse was reassigned to Washington, D.C., I worked with international students and then got involved in the Overseas Education Fund (OEF), which had been founded by the League of Women Voters in 1947 shortly after the United Nations was formed. OEF's original work as a nongovernmental organization involved responding to requests for citizenship education from foreign communities rebuilding after World War II. The U.S. State Department sought OEF's help in Germany, Italy. and elsewhere. OEF also monitored the work of the then-new UN Commission on the Status of Women and served as an informal information distribution and communications link for commission members and other interested women's groups between the sessions of the commission. When the UN Development Decade was instituted in the 1960s, OEF turned its attention to the problems of women in developing countries.

During the 1960s and 1970s, OEF's goal was helping to assure the full participation of women in the social, economic, and political life of their countries. In the early 1970s it recognized the need to refocus the social welfare orientation of many women's groups and voluntary organizations toward a self-help community development approach. The emphasis was on techniques for including low-income beneficiaries of development assistance in the planning and decision-making of development projects, reversing the traditional paternalistic approach of working with low-income communities.

Before becoming OEF's executive director, I did an evaluation in 1978 of the organization's work in Central and Latin America. I reviewed the organizational capacity of the voluntary organizations and the effectiveness of their development projects with low-income people, especially income-generation projects. Overall, voluntary organizations had the capacity to carry out integrated community development programs. However, many organizations needed strengthened management capability if they were to carry out complex development projects. The groups also needed to upgrade their professional capacity in program implementation, including needs assessment and evaluation. Volunteer trainers needed more preparation to work successfully with low-income women in income-generation programs. Yet economic programs were not enough. Women needed assistance and support in overcoming barriers imposed by society and, too often, by their families.

In my recommendations to OEF, I emphasized that programs designed for low-income women needed to be holistic. Nonformal adult education methodologies had to integrate income-generation activities with training to build self-confidence, self-esteem, and leadership skills. OEF also needed more field-testing and pilot projects to improve the methodologies of their approach to development.

When Willie Campbell became OEF president in 1978, I was appointed executive director. Now I had an opportunity to carry out my ideas. Willie and I shared a common vision of increasing OEF's potential to help improve the economic status of women and the quality of life for poor women in developing countries. We convinced the board to change its policies and concentrate on providing technical support to poor women and grassroots women's groups. Although OEF was historically a board-run organization, in this new era I was expected to hire more professional staff, increase overseas programs, expand our technical expertise, and strengthen the funding base. Willie and I also believed it was important to lobby policy makers on Capitol Hill and in the foreign affairs agencies on behalf of women's needs in development assistance.

Based on our own experiences, Willie and I shared the view of the Women in Development Office at USAID that helping women in developing countries to organize and supporting existing organizations was key to women's effective participation in development. It had been my experience at the University of Michigan and in Latin America that sharing ideas and learning from others in organizations achieved successful results. The more leadership responsibilities that women assumed, the more new skills they learned. This increased the capacity of individuals and organizations to take risks, to try new things.

We were also convinced of the importance of nonformal education and training—that is, learning outside a formal classroom through experiential and participatory techniques which recognize that adults bring knowledge and experience to the learning process. The teacher, or leader, commonly called the trainer, brings certain expertise, but the adult participants are the experts concerning the relevance of the knowledge to their situation and how best to apply the learning. In the early 1970s the University of Massachusetts led the way in developing the field of nonformal, participatory adult education, especially at the village level in developing countries. Many of the techniques used arose out of the early training and experience of Peace Corps volunteers in the 1960s. My experience in Latin America had convinced me of the need for more nonformal adult education. Because developing country governments have such weak formal education systems, they supported nonformal participatory adult education and training sponsored by nongovernmental organizations.

I hired Suzanne Kindervatter, an acknowledged WID leader in the international development community and an expert in nonformal education, who developed a trainer's manual to empower semi-literate and illiterate poor women. After field-testing, a groundbreaking training manual called *Women Working Together* was produced by OEF in 1983. It focused on increasing women's confidence and ability to work in groups to achieve their goals. It is still one of the most popular training manuals in use by development practitioners around the world.

Making Catsup in El Salvador

A bottle of catsup from the El Castano Tomato Processing Plant in a village in the province of Sonsonate, El Salvador, sits in my office. Looking at it always reminds me of what a small group of impoverished women in a rural area accomplished with technical assistance and training from OEF and other partners. Soon after I became OEF executive director, I went to El Salvador and met with a small group of women in an outdoor courtyard near the El Castano farming community. Delmy Burgos, OEF's El Salvador coordinator, had set up the meeting. The women had already agreed that earning income was their most important need. They thought catsup and canned tomatoes would be good products because so many tomatoes rotted in the field while canned tomatoes and catsup products were imported. A feasibility study validated the market for the proposed products.

The women's very practical dream was to have a tomato-processing factory near their village, but they needed land on which to build the factory. OEF staff and the leaders of the village cooperative—all women—met with municipal officials to see if they would give or lease the women land for the factory. For over a year they kept trying to convince the officials that they had the capability to build a factory and process tomatoes. During this year OEF and the local cooperative continued to train the women in organizing and management skills while the local university provided training in canning and processing. Finally, the municipality agreed to give the cooperative a ninety-nine-year lease for a parcel of land on which to build the factory.

The next challenge was funding, which meant getting a building loan from the InterAmerican Development Bank's (IDB) Special Projects Fund. The loan request was rejected because bank officials did not believe the women's cooperative was capable of handling such a loan. We disagreed and appealed to U.S. senator Nancy Kassebaum, a supporter of OEF and of women in developing countries, to use her influence. She helped us set up a meeting with the president of the IDB to make our case. We argued that the women already had demonstrated their competence in running the cooperative and that, with OEF technical help, the co-op would be able to manage the loan. I again traveled to El Salvador, this time to a meeting organized by the cooperative with local IDB staff. Success came only after a year of advocacy. I firmly believe that if it had been a male cooperative asking for such a loan, the group would have received it without such a long hassle.

The plant has now been in operation for over fifteen years, with a second generation of women working in the factory. Men now belong to the co-op as well. The business is profitable and the citizens of El Castano are proud of the women who began this endeavor. Income for many families has been increased by employment in the plant and from the profits generated by it for the farmers selling tomatoes.

Building on the El Castano project, OEF launched a new initiative called Economic Empowerment for Low Income Women. Again, Suzanne Kindervatter, with support from Marcy Kelly and others, took the lead in developing training programs for women in small business skills. Most private voluntary organizations doing development work believed poor illiterate women couldn't learn how to do a feasibility study or a marketing plan. Using nonformal educational techniques, we developed a training program and manuals that proved they could. For example, a group of village women, with only one literate member, can go to the local market and assess what products are most in demand and which get the best prices. With the literate member, they can then develop and carry out a marketing plan for the products they find most viable to produce. Based on OEF's experience working with women's groups, two training manuals, field-tested in several countries, were developed for a new OEF Women Entrepreneur Series, *Carrying Out a Feasibility Study* and *Developing a Market Plan*.

Law As an Instrument for Development

In the early 1980s, legal programs for women were not considered a useful part of the development agenda by the male-dominated development establishment. However, if women were to be truly empowered economically, socially, and politically, Willie Campbell, OEF board members Fay Williams and Nancy Rubin, and I all believed that laws must be fair and nondiscriminatory. We knew the demand for legal programs existed, as a number of overseas women's groups working on legal issues locally and nationally had contacted OEF and the Women's Legal Defense Fund in Washington, D.C., for assistance. We decided to take up the challenge by initiating a new Women and Law program. Margaret Schuler was hired to develop and implement the program. Though not a lawyer, Marge was an expert in human resource and organizational development and had excellent organizing and facilitation skills.

Marge traveled throughout what was then called the developing world, meeting with women's groups working on legal issues, helping them to identify their specific needs and develop responses to them. Based on her work and travels, OEF obtained a grant from USAID's Latin America Bureau to develop a Central American Regional Women and Law program. At our first meeting, hosted by women from democratic Costa Rica, women came from Honduras, which had a military government, and Nicaragua, with a Marxist government. We were unsure whether women from three such different political systems could work together, but the meeting dynamics were electric. There were no major ideological debates; the women all agreed that their countries had discriminatory laws and that, in many cases, women did not know their country's laws or how to use the legal system. At the end of three days the Central American Regional Women and the Law Network was born.

Over time, when other groups were ready to set up regional networks in Latin America, Asia, and later Africa, Marge realized that a book documenting women's experiences from different national perspectives and legal systems was needed. Experts from various countries wrote individual case studies, detailing how their country's laws discriminated against women and the strategies they used to overcome such discrimination. Based on the case studies, the opening chapter of the book, *Empowerment and the Law*, set out a framework for assessing the law and its relation to women's status and circumstances and for designing action strategies.

A global women and law network eventually formed with regional coordinating centers on three continents led by women's law groups in Zimbabwe, Malaysia, and Peru. They devised and implemented new mechanisms to make the existing laws work for women, developed awareness among women about their legal rights and customary laws, and created new training methodologies in legal literacy and advocacy.[1] At the Third World Conference on Women at Nairobi in 1985, OEF—under Marge's leadership and with all of the regional partners and networks participating—cosponsored a major three-day forum on women and the law. The purpose was to assess progress in developing countries in using the law and legal systems to eliminate discrimination against women and to analyze what worked and what didn't. The Nairobi conference was a major breakthrough, with new leadership emerging from women of the South.[2]

Organizing to Promote Development

When I joined OEF there were few female heads among the USAID-accredited private voluntary organizations (PVOs) doing development work overseas. There was also increasing reluctance on the part of the U.S. Congress to adequately support development assistance. Again, on the theory that in organization there is strength, I helped form two new umbrella associations: Private Agencies in International Development in 1980 and INTERACTION in 1984, which is now a 160-member association of PVOs working in international development and refugee relief.

In 1989 Winrock International's charismatic president, Robert Havener, convinced me to come to Winrock to develop an African Women Leaders in Agriculture and the Environment (AWLAE) initiative. Winrock International, a nonprofit organization, is a heritage of the philanthropy of Winthrop Rockefeller and other Rockefeller family members. It works worldwide to help the poor and disadvantaged by increasing economic opportunity, sustaining natural resources, and protecting the environment. Bob Havener knew the important part female farmers played in food production—growing from sixty to eighty percent of the food Africans ate— and was convinced of the importance of women's leadership for Africa's future. He believed more potential women leaders needed graduate degrees in agriculture so they could become decision makers in Africa's agriculture sector.

In the beginning, my work at Winrock was considered controversial, if not revolutionary, by older professional staff—primarily male—who came out of U.S. agricultural school backgrounds. With few exceptions, they had little understanding of the importance of African women in achieving sustainable development. Bob Havener and I both knew that women farmers had little access to extension, credit, seeds, fertilizers, labor-saving technologies, or land ownership, and that male agricultural extension workers had little interest in working with women. My companion, Jac Smit, who has shared my life since 1984, was another exception, sharing his extensive knowledge of overseas development and urban agriculture with me. He supported what Bob Havener and I knew so well, that working with African women and sympathetic men to develop a strategy to remove the obstacles that women farmers faced would be a major contribution to Africa's future.

But how would I develop the AWLAE initiative? Bringing together Africans to design the strategy was an imperative. We organized regional workshops in Kenya and Côte d'Ivoire (Ivory Coast), with over fourteen countries represented. Participants were acknowledged leaders in the fields of agriculture and the environment from all over Africa. I used my OEF contacts, including Eddah Gachukia, a respected educator and senior member of UNICEF staff in Africa at the time, to identify and select the workshop coordinator and the participants. The latter presented papers on the constraints women faced in the agricultural sector and suggested strategies for future action that evolved into a three-pronged strategy for the AWLAE program.

The first objective was to secure graduate and undergraduate scholarships for potential leaders, while also providing leadership training and professional development for the few women already in agricultural institutions. The second involved creating opportunities for the advancement of women in agricultural institutions and providing gender analysis and sensitivity training to policy makers and managers in key institutions. The third objective was to facilitate the development of networks, national action committees, voluntary professional associations, and other non-governmental groups to support and help implement this agenda. Women leaders such as Charity Kabutha from Kenya and Reine Boni from Côte D'Ivoire directed implementation of this strategy.

The AWLAE program now operates in fourteen countries. Since 1992 pioneering African women have participated in a yearlong Leadership for Change training program developed by Maggie Range and other African trainers. Out of this training the women launched sixteen professional associations to sustain their work. In the 1990s eighty women from thirteen countries received scholarships for study in U.S., African, and European universities. Funding for another 113 scholarships was secured for new programs in Ethiopia and Angola. Returning scholars developed professional associations of women agriculturists and natural resource experts in Ghana, Benin, and Nigeria.

AWLAE members in Uganda, working with rural women, are examining the shortfall of resources going to women farmers in four provinces of Uganda and advocating for equity in the allocation of resources. Over 1,500 members of the Tanzanian Association of Women in Agriculture have advocated successfully with the ministries of agriculture and the environment to address the advancement of women within those ministries. In Kenya the minister of agriculture, acknowledging the role of AWLAE, established a formal gender unit within the ministry. In Côte d'Ivoire, the Center for Ivoirien Social and Economic Research offered half of its 1996 fellowships to women. Other groups worked to change the way that statistics are gathered on rural women and to make the curricula at agricultural universities more sensitive to women.

In 1992 Winrock began a second major initiative called the Global Women's Leadership program when development assistance was extended to Eastern Europe at the end of the Cold War. During the transition era from Soviet domination, women had been particularly negatively affected. They were often the first to lose their jobs, health services for women declined, government child care no longer existed, and women were invisible in the new power structures. My job in the program was to assess the changing situation of women and the newly emerging independent women's organizations and identify possibilities for collaboration with U.S. organizations.

Russian and Ukrainian women wanted a consortium of equals through peer-to-peer relationships with U.S. women's groups to obtain information and training in leadership, law, advocacy, and fund-raising. They also wanted access to credit and to entrepreneurial training so they could start small businesses. They did not want charity but rather increased capacity to manage their organizations using their own strategies. They had never had an independent women's movement but were highly educated compared to women in many other countries. Yet like women everywhere, they suffered from serious discrimination in their patriarchal societies. We set up a consortium involving women's groups in the former Soviet Union and U.S. women's groups advocating at USAID and before Congress to provide more resources to support the emerging women's movement in these countries. The consortium gave women's groups in the former Soviet states more visibility, voice, and power and helped in soliciting more resources for the emerging women's movements. Elena Ershova of Russia became a leader in the founding of the consortium and Martina Vandenburg provided critical and superior leadership in the endeavor. Returning to the United States, I advocated that women's participation was critical to the development of more democratic societies, free market economies, and most importantly, the long-term stability of the two countries.

There are now over 250 NGOs in the NIS-U.S. (New Independent States and the United States) Consortium. In Russia and Ukraine more than 5,000 women have been trained in women's leadership, organizational management, advocacy, and business skills. The Ukraine Consortium alone created 1,000 jobs for women. The Russian Consortium collaborates on social and economic policies with committees at the Russian Duma. It has also carried out advocacy campaigns on women's employment rights. Seven new national women's organizations have become members of the consortium: Moldova, Belarus, Armenia, Georgia, Azerbaijan, Kazakhstan, and Uzbekistan.

Organizing Women's EDGE

When I moved from director of the Global Women's Leadership program at Winrock to senior policy adviser on gender there in 1998, I had time to take on a new initiative to fulfill a dream: the building of a major coalition to support women and development internationally. I had long believed our informal coalitions were never able to achieve sufficient clout and power. Meeting with the policy chairs of the Association of Women in Development (AWID), Jean Weidemann and Kristin Timothy, I found them eager to involve AWID's 900 U.S. members in advocacy. I also found a very talented woman, Ritu Sharma, to become the executive director and a co-founder of a new group we called Women's EDGE, a coalition for women's economic development and global equality. Meeting with women leaders from U.S. nongovernmental organizations working overseas, we agreed that indeed there was a special niche the coalition could fill on issues of economic development, globalization (trade and investment), and gender. None of the new networks and coalitions formed since the Fourth UN

World Conference on Women in 1995 represented a cross-sectoral coalition to advocate before the U.S. Congress and executive branch on gender concerns that should be reflected in U.S. aid and trade policies.

EDGE has grown from the initial ten founding members to seventy organizations with an e-mail network of over 8,000 individuals. With a staff of seven and a very active board, EDGE works with the office of the U.S. trade representative and other entities to raise awareness of gender issues in U.S. trade negotiations. We also work with the President's Interagency Council on Women task force on globalization issues. Recently, EDGE helped convene the first ever meeting of U.S. trade negotiators and women's groups to discuss gender and trade issues. Our proposal to brief trade negotiators on gender concerns in trade policy was accepted. Most importantly, we have been focusing on the Free Trade Area of the Americas agreement being negotiated, working with Latin American and U.S. groups to bring gender concerns to the table. We are also now working on developing a framework for carrying out a social impact assessment of U.S. trade policies before they are finalized to ensure that gender concerns are addressed. The work of the World Trade Organization is being carefully monitored regarding fair trade for women.

During the Association of Women in Development's Eighth International Forum in 2000, EDGE took 150 women from the United States and around the world to Capitol Hill in Washington. Groups called on more than thirty-five congressional offices to present their views on development and trade from a gender perspective. A major legislative campaign, the GAINS for Women and Girls Act of 2001, is aimed at strengthening U.S. investments in women and girls in developing countries and newly independent states. EDGE has also initiated a new constituency-building program in five midwestern states, a collaborative effort with Partners of the Americas. The goal is to form a network of citizen advocates outside Washington to lobby policy makers on aid, trade, and gender issues. EDGE also actively supports the Advisory Committee on Voluntary Foreign Aid's (ACVFA) Assessment of the USAID Gender Plan of Action. The Advisory Committee is a public commission that provides guidance to the administrator of USAID.

This is an exciting time for women working on global issues. The explosive growth of women's groups worldwide has opened up uncounted avenues for women to shape policy and influence events. Using information technology, women can organize new campaigns and initiatives at national and international levels on a far greater scale than ever before. We can't foresee the total impact of this revolution—the international women's movement—but women continue to forge the changes needed to shape a future in which women and men will have equal rights and opportunities across the world.

Finally, there is no way to list the many women and men who have supported, inspired and collaborated with me over the years. From the University of Michigan, where I learned to strategize and build coalitions to the forming of Women's EDGE, I never could have accomplished my goals without the colleagues and believers who toiled with me.

The OEF archives, including some of Elise Fiber Smith's papers, are in the MacKellin Library Archives Collection at the University of Maryland.

Martha Wells Lewis

A native of Wisconsin, Martha Lewis earned a bachelor's degree in economics from the University of Wisconsin at Madison. She began her career working in farm organizations and on political campaigns and has served as an officer of her family's farm corporation.

Martha Wells Lewis served on the staff of Partners of the Americas, a non-governmental economic development organization and the largest volunteer force working in the Western Hemisphere in socio-economic development. Before retiring from Partners in 1996, she served as director of the Partners' Women in Development (WID) Program, managed Partners' Family Life Education Program, and served as senior adviser to a program funded by the United States Agency for International Development (USAID) to achieve full political and social participation of women in civil society. She directed staff services for Partners' U.S.-Caribbean partnerships and represented Partners at the UN Fourth World Conference on Women at Beijing in 1995.

Lewis has served as a consultant on women's issues and food production for USAID, the Peace Corps, and the Cooperative League of the USA. Her professional work has taken her to the Dominican Republic, Jamaica, India, Scandinavia, Argentina, New Zealand, Australia, and Somalia. In 1994 she received the Association for Women in Development's Award for Achievement. She is the mother of four and grandmother of four.

Gardening for Development

The change in my life during the ten years between 1975 and 1985 was dramatic. In 1975 I was fifty-three, children grown and gone, a support system and office wife for my husband's projects, a volunteer activist for my own causes, picking up a short-term research job here and there and wistfully wishing I had a real job or the money to get an advanced degree. In 1985 at age sixty-three, I was a full-time professional director of the women in development (WID) program for an international private voluntary organization; an officer of the Association for Women in Development (AWID); and part of a vital, stimulating group of women scholars, researchers, practitioners, and policy makers working in international development.

The beginnings of this late but rewarding career probably lay back in what I had learned long ago from a frontier grandmother, a midwestern childhood, and my early married life. I had no idea these life skills and experiences would be transferable to the workaday world, or that because of them, I could bring to the field of development an observant and knowing eye. I was trained by my first experiences in homemaking after the war and by following agricultural policy issues with my husband in his work. Married for three years, mother of one, expectant mother of another, I found I had useful skills and the capability to cope in a situation for which I was not aware of having been prepared.

World War II was over and housing was scarce when my soldier husband came home. The only house we could find that was close to his work organizing marginal farmers for the Farmers' Union was a cabin on the Yellow River in northern Wisconsin without electricity, telephone, heat, or even water as the well had gone dry. I bathed myself and the child in the river and hauled pails of river water up a steep bank to wash diapers. Bob came home on Friday nights, bringing me drinking water, food, ice, and newspapers. He left again early Monday morning to be gone all week driving the back roads of the north to sign up members in the Farmers' Union.

What kept me going in this isolated place were the wonderful stories I had heard from my grandmother. Born during the Civil War on a frontier farm in Wisconsin, where survival took skill, know-how, and enormous effort, she knew underdevelopment firsthand and what it took to get beyond it. Widowed young with three children, she managed to raise and educate her children, but had to give up her farm to work as a cook for wealthy Chicago families. She was realistic about how hard one had to work to live but confident of what women could do.

I had an eighteen-month-old baby and another on the way that summer on the Yellow River, and while I had no neighbors or doctors within reasonable reach, in summer the living was relatively easy. With a battery radio I followed courses at the University of Madison, learning agriculture from the farm program, housekeeping from the homemakers' program, and psychology and Greek drama from classes broadcast by the College of Letters and Science. Worried about nutrition for my unborn, the toddler, and myself, I started a vegetable garden. Solving my own problems gave me a feeling of confidence.

Living as an impressionable child in the 1930s during the Great Depression, I had seen the devastation caused by wrongheaded economic policies and the importance of democratic political action in changing directions. Later, through volunteer work, I built a rich and wide network of friends who, with the new women's consciousness of the 1970s, were exploding out of child raising and domestic life into professions and work of all kinds. This change began in the disillusioning years during the Vietnam War when my friends and I were questioning everything, including our political loyalties and our work in Washington, D.C., for better schools and political enfranchisement, which seemed pointless as our communities were burning. We also looked at our lives and our marriages. I was assessing myself and my life to see what I still believed in, what I would do with the rest of my days, and especially what resources I had to do anything other than what I had been doing.

My work had made my husband Bob's involvement in farm policy and politics possible, yet according to government and university economists my work had no economic value. I was a dependent. Through Bob's work I met and talked with farm wives all over the United States. Farm women were directly engaged in the heavy work and decision making on the farm, yet there was little accounting of this productive work in custom or in law. When Bob was a delegate to the International Federation of Agricultural Producers, I accompanied him to the meetings and found the same situation prevailed in other countries—farm wives' work was invisible and remuneration was intangible.

All this was good preparation for international development work, but I didn't know that until I learned of Ester Boserup's work on women and agricultural production in Africa and its invisibility to agricultural development planners. The parallels stunned me. She described the staggering cultural blindness on the part of project planners in dispensing credit, technical assistance, training, and participation opportunities to men in agricultural development projects but not to women. African women's traditional roles, according to Boserup, were being diminished or destroyed. They were excluded from the benefits of development. They resisted the new passive, noninvolved, and non-wage support roles assigned them by foreign planners by refusing to cooperate or collaborate in their own marginalization, resistance being the only power they had. It was all too familiar.

After our move to Washington, D.C., in 1952 when Bob was hired to write for the National Farmers' Union, I became an avid and productive gardener in my city backyard as well as on our Wisconsin farm. The gardening was more than just another household duty, however, and it led me to study nutrition and various horticultural theories. No one in the neighborhood had a vegetable garden when I started mine, and I had to figure out how to handle a new climate and soil type. I soon discovered publications on the French Intensive Biodynamic Gardening System and other systems that made life interesting. I also began to think about the economic value of the gardening, sewing and house construction I had done and realized that income conserved is as important as income earned and should be factored into the economic opportunity costs of a wage-earning job. In women's groups in Washington, I found a forum for my interest in the economic value of housewives' and farmwives' work, although this was not high on the list of important issues of urban professional women.

A Bibliography on Gardening and Nutrition

In 1977, when my friend and colleague Arvonne Fraser was appointed director of the Women in Development Office at USAID, I talked with her about women and food production and vegetable gardening as a rational family food production and nutrition improvement strategy. As a daughter of farmers herself, she understood its importance and gave me a contract to put together an annotated bibliography on vegetable gardening and family nutrition. I look back on that project as the graduate study I had wanted. I searched the rich collections in the Agricultural Library and Library of Congress in Washington, D.C., interviewed U.S. Department of Agriculture Extension personnel, surveyed the history and materials of state extension services' vegetable gardening programs, and collected old World War II victory gardening materials along with some from the depression era of the 1930s. Accompanying Bob on a trip to India, I visited vegetable gardening projects sponsored by CARE, an international agency for hunger relief. These were primarily school gardens whose major purpose was growing vegetables for school lunches; there was no strategy for transferring the gardening technology or nutrition information to families. Coming home through Rome, I stopped off at the Food and Agricultural Organization of the United Nations to look at reports on its gardening projects. Those I talked to at FAO seemed open to my idea of promoting small, intensive family production fortified with nutrition education. They may have seen that this strategy was easily incorporated into integrated rural development projects, as agricultural development projects had come to be called. I could find no publications or reports on family gardening projects and reports on school gardens did not glow about the success of nutrition education or improved family nutrition.

Interest in the bibliography grew after it was published in 1978 and distributed widely by the Women in Development Office. A woman working for the Tuskegee Institute in development projects told me she always took it with her when she worked in Africa. It came out when the development world was looking at more integrated approaches to rural development, so a rational approach to nutrition improvement that appealed to workers in the field seemed to influence policy as well as program people. More recently there has been growing interest in urban agriculture—which essentially is community gardening—a good and old idea with a new and grand title.

Suddenly I was a specialist, or at least had a proficiency. I had no degree in horticulture or nutrition, but I did have a lifetime of experience and some insight in social and economic history. The concept of the centrality of women in all aspects of food, whether production, processing, preservation, selection or preparation was by now widely held.

In 1978 the University of Arizona held a conference in Tucson on women and food. I was invited to be on the planning committee, where I was able to identify women active in American farm organizations to participate along with university and government people. It was exciting to be among research nutritionists, agricultural economists, seed-saving anthropologists, home economists, and professional development planners who were interested in what I was talking about. I felt like a professional among colleagues and got to know and work with Kate Cloud, the organizer of the conference and an important agent in the new WID movement.

A Project in Jamaica

In 1980 an opportunity to meld theory and application presented itself when the USAID mission in Jamaica asked the WID Office to help develop a women's component for a soil erosion control and rural development project. In Jamaica farmers could not get loans if they did not have clear title to the land they tilled. This made for a serious disincentive to agricultural development and promoted low returns and thus rural to urban migration. Many of the farmers in the hills were older women; since no one wanted to farm if they had any other choice.

Elsa Chaney, USAID's former deputy director of women in development, went to Jamaica to assess needs of local women. She reported back that the majority of requests were for nutrition education and vegetable gardening instruction, and she recruited me as a consultant. We made a good team. Elsa knew the research and the way to meet bureaucratic paper demands. I had practical know-how and on-the-ground observation skills. I could also talk farming with the agriculture development planners and even teach them a thing or two about world market prices and comparative advantages. The project staff was both Jamaican and American. Having worked with farm people for years, I got along well with them as well as the old women farmers. I learned from these old women about traditional foods and gardening practices and how they had dried fruits to conserve their surpluses. Houses were small and storage space minimal, so drying made sense because it reduced the bulkage of the stored goods.

The young Jamaican extension agents in the project often didn't know the important traditions of these women or didn't respect them, thinking that new and imported foods were the better way. Jamaica's foreign currency reserves were being drained by food imports, quite unnecessarily in a land with no winter, good soil, and adequate rainfall. Therefore, I designed a model garden using intensive gardening techniques with a system for continuous planting and harvesting. All the vegetables in the model were familiar in the region except for kale, which was more nutritious than the leafy green amaranth, called calaloo, in common use. Harvesting the outer leaves of kale encouraged more growth, making it a good selection for limited space. The older women told me they had heard of it many years ago. Proof of success came about a year later when kale was served to me at a hotel, and I learned that the cook had bought it in the market near our project. The Kingston newspaper, *The Gleaner,* also published an article on the benefits of kale, reporting that I was now considered "Mrs. Kale" for having introduced it. The older women also taught me that the raised-bed technique I had introduced could be improved by making a little valley on the top of narrow raised beds to capture moisture while allowing the heavy rains common in that part of Jamaica to drain away in the deeper side trenches.

Helen Strow, a U.S. home economist with a long history of working in development, was collaborating with Jamaican home economists. She analyzed the local diet and identified the nutritional elements that were lacking. I selected vegetables that would supply these elements, could be harvested over long periods, and could be transplanted into the garden as seedlings grown in old pots and pans under the trees in the yard.

In our project, twenty young Jamaican women from the region, all unemployed high school graduates, were selected to be the local extension agents. I trained them in intensive vegetable gardening techniques and selection of specific vegetables for improved nutrition, while U.S. home economists taught them nonformal teaching techniques and basic family nutrition. After the course, they fanned out and covered the project territory, also teaching young mothers about infant nutrition and the reasons for spacing babies. Sometimes they met with their assigned community in churches; other times all the families along a road would meet for a demonstration session on vegetable gardening and basic nutrition. Older men and women joined in these sessions. In the final evaluation of the entire multi-million-dollar project, the evaluators reported that the only aspect that had any lasting value was our $60,000 women's component.

Building on Success

Back in the U.S., Elsa charted out a plan to promote the idea of initiating other food and agricultural projects. The Jamaica project was written up in an article in *Agenda,* a USAID publication, and we gave talks about it to development organizations. I was also asked to help design a woman's project for the Somali Women's political party. It was quite amazing to see people look upon as innovative the simple concept of combining vegetable gardening with nutrition information.

The Dominican Republic

The agricultural development officer of the USAID mission in the Dominican Republic saw our work in Jamaica and became interested. He thought the concept might be applicable in a project in the mountains of the Dominican Republic supported by that country's government. In 1980 Elsa and I were sent by USAID to look at possibilities there.

The project, Plan Sierra, was trying to reduce soil erosion, but planned to do it by having the farmers, or campesinos, substitute coffee trees and other cash tree crops for traditional slash and burn food crop agriculture. That meant, of course, that there would be less food produced for family consumption in the project area. We urged the director and his staff to add a family food production component in their project design. Trained as an agricultural economist, the director, Blas Santos, believed that increased income from the new cash crops would raise a family's income enough for them to purchase food from intensive irrigated production in the valleys. I made the case for family food production by adopting his argument that small developing countries are always at a disadvantage in trading with large developed countries. I stated that, similarly, rural people are at a disadvantage when selling and buying in urban markets. Blas was converted, and four years later invited me to return to see the 5,000 "Martha Lewis vegetable gardens" in the project. He wisely did not hire Elsa and me to design a project for him. Instead, Blas sent members of his staff to Jamaica to look at our project. They then designed their own, a Dominican version.

Partners of the Americas

By 1981 the women in development concept no longer produced derisive laughter and jokes among agriculturists. It had caught the attention of private voluntary organizations. Alan Rubin, president of Partners of the Americas, had been looking for an opportunity to demonstrate Partners' commitment to women's programs. When I told him about our Jamaica project, he saw it as a natural for Partner volunteers to observe how the concept of women in development was applied. The Caribbean Basin Initiative, sold to the American people by the Reagan administration as a barrier against Communist take over in the entire Caribbean region had money to back up the policy. Rubin thought Partners could demonstrate its people-to-people linking of volunteers from the U.S with Central American and Caribbean people working together in community development projects. Partners of the Americas is the largest program of private voluntary technical assistance in the western hemisphere, linking U.S. citizens from forty-five states with counterparts in thirty-one Latin America and the Caribbean countries.

The Partners' program and way of working were new to me. Rubin asked me to help find financial support and hold a workshop using our Jamaica project as an example. Although I had never done anything like this before, I knew my Jamaica project well and had contacts in the Jamaican Ministry of Agriculture and the Kingston USAID mission. The Kingston mission gave us permission to hold the workshop there, approved travel of the attendees, and helped with press coverage. The ministry provided transportation to the project from the airport in Kingston for our participants, helped us get speakers from the University of the West Indies and the government, let us use its training facility and project trucks for field trips, and made staff of the project available for instruction.

The Women in Development Office at USAID was in transition between the Carter and Reagan administrations and the Partners' workshop was nicely timed to give positive exposure to a WID project. Sarah Tinsley, the new WID director at USAID, was also new to the field of development. She decided to attend the workshop to see a USAID/WID project for herself and to meet volunteer women from the United States and Caribbean and Central American countries.

For our workshop Partners brought together sixty-four women from the U.S. and the Latin American or Caribbean side of the partnerships. We trained them to work as Partner teams in identifying needs and in planning, designing, and developing projects. They learned how to use linkages with institutions and networks in their communities to support and give technical assistance to their projects. They rehearsed how to work with their committees back home to develop WID subcommittees. Many of the participants from both the South and the North had never been to an international workshop before, and their enthusiasm was high.

The logistics were challenging. All participants from Central American countries and Colombia had to fly to Miami to get an American carrier to Jamaica to comply with U.S. Government requirements. That meant getting a visa just to change planes. The participants arrived in Kingston where the Jamaica Partners met the planes and got them loaded on busses supplied by the Jamaican Ministry of Agriculture. The buses took them to the workshop site in Christiana, two hours away up in the mountains. Housing such large group in this highland village wasn't easy. I rented all the rooms in the one guesthouse in the village, took over the IRDP's entire training center and then visited every homemaker I knew in Christiana to rent spare rooms. I hired a cook, the watchmen and other help and even bought a goat for making the traditional goat curry. Providing simultaneous translation was hard in the hilly terrain where the electricity was at best whimsical. I brought translation equipment, borrowed from the State Department, down with me from Washington and the sheets for the training center beds.

The Americans loved living in the West Indian homes, and the villagers and the project staff enjoyed having an international meeting there. It was a joyous week. The project provided trucks with guides for our field trips, the agriculture ministry provided speakers on the economic and agricultural situation, Jamaican media covered the workshop, and the local Partner members came up from Kingston for many sessions. Faculty from the Mona campus of the University of the West Indies gave presentations. I had never managed such a complicated operation before, nor have I since. Every Partners workshop I organized after that was easy.

A total of seventeen U.S., Latin American, and U.S.-Caribbean teams were formed through this event. Women in these teams went on to become leaders in their Partner committees and in the international organization. This helped change the gender makeup of chapter presidencies and the international board of directors within a few years. With its broad base of members across the hemisphere, Partners' WID program spread understanding of and support for women in development among people who were neither development practitioners, researchers, nor women's issues activists but rather were community volunteers from a variety of professions.

Food and Domestic Violence Program

Sarah Tinsley and her deputy director, Paula Goddard, were pleased with what they had seen and heard of the workshop, so I was emboldened to approach their office for a grant to do follow-up work. Partners was awarded a three-year grant to establish what we called the Women: Partners in Development Program. In 1982, at age sixty, I was hired to direct the program. It was my first full-time professional job since I had worked as a material weight analyst in the building of the B-29 bomber for Fisher Body Corporation in 1943, almost forty years earlier.

During the early years of our Partners WID Program, we concentrated on family food production and leadership development, holding workshops on small business management, backyard food and fish production, solar dehydration, and leadership. On the basis of the USAID grant, we obtained a grant from the Hewlett Foundation to develop family planning and maternal health projects. Anne Firth Murray, the program officer at Hewlett, believed WID projects could be successful vehicles for family planning education and expected Partners could demonstrate that point. In one project, the North Carolina-Cochabamba (Bolivia) Partners used the Hewlett grant to equip a clinic for women in a jail where no health services or medical attention was provided to prisoners. A Partner volunteer physician worked at the clinic and nurses and family planning workers from North Carolina visited and helped train its staff.

We in Partners went on to address domestic violence at a time when it was still considered by many a subject too sensitive to handle across cultures. Caribbean women had talked with me about child sexual abuse and I had observed it myself in Jamaica and was enraged by the passivity of the community in ignoring it. I heard about incest being treated the same way. Many of our Caribbean Partners were social workers, health professionals, and teachers who saw these disturbing events. Accustomed to working with their New York partner committees—where they visited frequently and with which they felt a connection—they did not see taking on such issues as interference coming from the North. I was encouraged to hold a regionwide seminar on domestic violence and sexual abuse in 1987.

I am confident that being an older woman is useful when working with people on sensitive issues such as these. We heard reservations from some of the New York male leadership, but the women were foursquare. As they were going to be the ones to develop the programs and internships, arrange housing, and transport participants, their attitude was what mattered. Elsewhere, too, men were the ones who said such matters were too culturally sensitive to bring up. The first time I broached the idea to the president of Partners, he also shied away; but when I checked it out with Dame Nita Barrow of Barbados over breakfast at an AWID conference, she urged me to go ahead. She had been head of the NGO Forum at the Nairobi world conference on women, and was, at the time we spoke, the ambassador from Barbados to the United Nations. She introduced the subject in her address the very morning I spoke to her, calling for women to help each other across national boundaries. On this problem outside help could make a difference.

Armed with her encouragement, I stopped off at the USAID mission in Barbados the next time I passed through and got approval for funds to train Caribbean health workers in recognizing and handling domestic violence. We used funds from the Hewlett Foundation grant and with excellent support from the New York committees, we held a monthlong seminar in New York State for social workers, nurses, and educators from eight Caribbean countries. All aspects of the pathology of domestic violence and sexual abuse were covered. The participants visited programs at police departments, social service agencies, courts, and shelters. We arranged short internships in these programs for the participants so they could continue to connect to the program where they interned for information and advice after returning back home. For example, the head nurse of Grenada lived for a week in a shelter in Binghamton, New York, and worked as intake person there. The president of the Albany-Barbados partners at this time, Rosalind

Preudhomme, held a high position in the New York State Governor's Commission on Youth. She knew all the social service agencies in the state and she used her knowledge and connections to put together a remarkable final week in Albany for the group. She also arranged to have the entire week's program taped for television and some of these tapes were played throughout the state for weeks, provoking a large number of call-ins.

This 1987 seminar was the first directly addressing domestic violence in an international setting. Follow-up exchanges were supported to observe agencies and methods and to train police officers, teachers, and social workers. It did much to change Eastern Caribbean ways of addressing domestic violence. The issue came out of the closet in a dramatic way after our seminar, and there has been tremendous change in social attitudes and community practices in the entire region.

In the fall of 1995, following the Fourth World Conference on Women at Beijing, we held a follow-up meeting in Trinidad for Caribbean-New York partners to organize support for and follow through on the conference's Platform for Action. A survey of participants showed that action on domestic violence was the highest priority of all Caribbean participants; they developed plans for political action to mobilize group pressure on governments to enforce existing laws and on legislators to pass laws where needed. I consider this the most important work I did in women in development because of the way it unified women across cultures, class, race, nationality, and all the other categories that divide us. I also believe that until women are free of oppression of that kind, they can never fully develop themselves.

My Reflection

This very personal report is given to demonstrate the development of a person through, with, and by the development of a movement. It is also intended to describe the unique culture women create when they teach each other and work together to realize their vision of a better way to manage a family, a community, and a world. An example of this unique culture was the Association for Women in Development. Its board met at Partners' offices in Washington for many years with the blessing of Bill Reese, Partners' president. He was one of the best practitioners of the idea of women in development, practicing what he preached by hiring many women, instituting a compassionate family leave policy, and supporting the women's network in every way he could. Because I opened my house in Washington to members coming for AWID meetings without per diem, for twelve years I was enriched by quarterly house parties with the brightest, most energetic, thoughtful, committed, and remarkable women as guests. Sometimes there were enough beds for everyone; sometimes not. Then all couches were filled and the floor looked like a middle school sleepover. This convivial atmosphere allowed for post-mortems and advance planning, for easy and open give-and-take, building trust, and generating ideas. During these weekends, we all learned about the new ideas evolving in women's studies on campuses, the new writers and important research published, and successes and failures in projects in the developing world. Surrounded by women intensely engaged in their careers and their families, I was stimulated, engaged and renewed. Serving on the board of AWID as secretary and then treasurer for about ten years took time and energy, but we were confident we were building an organization needed both by the beneficiaries and the agents of development. It is still needed today to keep the issue of women in development in front of national and international policy makers.

PART V

Education and Development

Cornelia Butler Flora

Cornelia Flora is Charles F. Curtiss Distinguished Professor of Agriculture and Sociology at Iowa State University and director of the North Central Regional Center for Rural Development. One of four U.S. regional centers, the NCRCRD combines research and outreach for rural development in the twelve north central U.S. states. Her past positions include Endowed Chair in Agricultural Systems at the University of Minnesota, head of the Sociology Department at Virginia Polytechnic Institute and State University, University Distinguished Professor at Kansas State University, and a program adviser for the Ford Foundation.

Past president of the Rural Sociological Society and president-elect of the Community Development Society and the Agriculture, Food and Human Values Society, she recently published *Interactions Between Agroecosystems and Rural Communities: Legacy and Change, Rural Policies for the 1990s,* and *Sustainable Agriculture in Temperate Zones,* as well as over 180 books, chapters, and articles. She participated in developing a PBS video course on rural America and the PBS series, *Americas.*

She obtained her B.A. from the University of California at Berkeley (1965) and her M.S. (1966) and Ph.D. (1970) are from Cornell University, which awarded her the Outstanding Alumni Award, College of Agriculture and Life Science, 1994. She is currently on the boards of directors of the Heartland Institute for Community Leadership, Board on Agriculture of the National Research Council of the National Academy of Science, Northwest Area Foundation, and Winrock International. She is a fellow of the American Association for the Advancement of Science.

The Ford Foundation and the Power of International Sisterhood

Growing up on a navy research and development base in the middle of the Mojave Desert gave me a pretty straight view of male and female spheres during the 1950s. Men were scientists and engineers. Women were librarians, secretaries, and mommies. My father was a physicist, working in solid-state propellants. My mother was a technical librarian. But because she was also a mommy, she took her reproductive responsibilities very seriously. She was our Girl Scout leader from fifth grade through high school. My father included us in activities of the Rock Hounds (a group that combed the desert looking for various rocks and geological formations) and Toastmasters. We learned never to cross a picket line. We all cleaned house on Saturday mornings, then did the grocery shopping on Saturday afternoons, when we had to go off the navy base because we were civilians, not military (although we had equivalent civilian rank and lived in a duplex with a similarly ranked military family). Everyone had productive, reproductive, and community maintenance work, including my sister and me. Our productive work was to do well in school so we could go on to college and thus support ourselves. Our family was a little bit different.

But not that different. If I had been a boy, I would have become a physicist or an engineer. But because I was a girl, I became a sociologist. I decided that humans were even more interesting than molecules, and that surely we had similar laws of nature that determined what we did. I was determined to discover them and use them to make the world a better place. The atomic bomb blast shown during the playing of the Star Spangled Banner, which preceded every movie at the base theater, convinced me it was necessary.

Early Activism

During my time at the University of California at Berkeley as an undergraduate during the early 1960s, the teach-ins on campus made it obvious to me that being in Vietnam was a great mistake. I was outraged by how the media turned an action for racial and worker justice into the Free Speech Movement, stressing language more than goals. There were women leaders in both movements on campus, and I wondered at their nerve in confronting men in heated conversation in coffee shops and street corners. My work as a cook for mule packers who took campers, fishers, and hunters into the wilderness area at Mammoth Lakes during summers while I was an undergraduate reinforced a gendered division of labor, although I added saddling horses to my cooking duties.

When I got to Cornell as a graduate student in rural sociology during the fall of 1965, I was heavily involved in Latin American support work and anti-war activities. The United States had landed its troops in Santo Domingo and our military advisers were more in evidence in Vietnam. I married a fellow activist and fellow student, Jan Flora. It never occurred to me in 1967 to keep my maiden name. Jan led a national war resistance movement that culminated in burning draft cards in Sheep's Meadow in New York's Central Park. He got arrested at a demonstration at the Pentagon, and his glasses were broken. I changed the venue of my dissertation research from Chile, in the Southern Cone of Latin America, to Colombia so I would be nearer to him when he went to jail.

But Jan didn't go to jail. The grand jury did not indict him, in part because he had to change his glasses after being arrested, which made positive identification from the photographs impossible. We both received Social Science Research Council dissertation grants and went off to Colombia in Latin America to do our research. He was willing to do his research in Cauca Valley because that was where my research was already underway.

I was interested in social movements and in 1966 discovered that Pentecostals had more support in the poor neighborhoods of Bogotá than did the radical student groups with which I hung out. So Pentecostalism—its sources, structure, and impact—became the topic of my dissertation. Women in the Colombian Pentecostal Church of Colombia who served as evangelists accompanied me on some of my research trips, but the pastors and priests I interviewed were all males. I interviewed community leaders in all the communities in the intervillage systems in the Cauca Valley and then conducted a survey of members of the Pentecostal church in a rural trade center, while also taking a comparison sample of non-Pentecostals. In the process of working within such a male-dominated culture, I almost left women out—surely they would have nothing particularly important to add.

By the time we got back to Cornell, the anti-war movement was in full stride and the black power movement and the women's movement had become intellectual centers on campus. I participated in one of the first women's studies courses in the country in 1969 while analyzing my Colombia data. The combined influence of my experiences in Colombia and Cornell changed my life and my work.[1] In my dissertation I included women and their experiences as a key component of the Pentecostal movement.[2] That part of my research on Pentecostalism in which I focused on the changing nature of what constitutes male's roles as well as what constitutes women's roles continues to be used by scholars who are analyzing the gendered nature of this growing movement.

Jobs and Family

With our raised feminist consciousnesses, we determined to get a job where we could be equals and to privilege my job over Jan's. It seemed logical, as

Jan's basic commitment to social justice made it easy to understand the power of patriarchy in the marketplace. We took jobs at Kansas State University in 1971, doing teaching and research.

Jobs in hand and dissertations finished, we determined it was time to start a family. We postponed starting our jobs until the baby was born, deciding to do postdoctoral research in Colombia and have the baby there. The Vietnam War was still in full force—the United States had just bombed Cambodia—so we wanted to give the child a choice of citizenship. I began work as director of the Population Research Laboratory at Kansas State University in July 1970 so I would have health insurance to cover the baby after she was born.

While in Cali, Colombia, before and after Gabriela Catalina's birth, I took advantage of an offer by feminist sociologist Pauline Bart to contribute to a special feminist issue of *Journal of Marriage and the Family*.[3] At that time Pauline had to negotiate hard to get the topic of women into a journal on family. I began research on the presentation of women in popular magazine fiction in the United States and Latin America. That research—which I decided I could do while recovering from childbirth by reading the stories while Gabriela nursed and coding while she slept—linked me in with Ann Pescatello, who was putting together *Female and Male in Latin America*, the first edited book which addressed gender in Latin America.[4] Those of us who contributed to the book participated in the first panel on gender at the Latin American Studies Association meeting in 1971. We shocked many who attended—and formed lifelong working friendships. Elsa Chaney was an essential member of that group. In her nurturing, inclusive way she kept me networked into women and development circles beyond Latin Americanists. It was through her that I met Arvonne Fraser when she started the Women in Development Office in the United States Agency for International Development (USAID).

In the early 1970s, our daughter Gabriela accompanied us in our anti-war and G.I. counseling activities and to the meetings at Kansas State University, where we set up the Kansas State University Commission on the Status of Women and planned the establishment of the Women's Studies Program. From the time her sister, Natasha Pilar, was born in September 1974, she came to class with me.[5] Jan and I team-taught Introduction to Sociology to classes of 350 and we took turns holding her while the other lectured. I breast-fed her until we went to China in January 1975.

Natasha accompanied me to any number of feminist gatherings at professional meetings, in the community and in Washington, D.C., with development agencies. She attended the Kansas meeting of International Women's Year (IWY) as well as the national meeting, carrying her tote bag which proclaimed, "I'm a mini-feminist." Through International Women's Year we began to understand the organized opposition to the Equal Rights

Amendment and to many other progressive efforts to enhance the position of women in the United States. The John Birch Society and the Eagle Forum, in concert with fundamentalist Christian churches, brought busloads of women to these meetings, where—after checking with their male pastor at each vote—they systematically opposed each progressive resolution. At the Kansas IWY meeting, Gloria Steinem confronted the group with its dependence on a male's opinion, although it did not change the pattern.

In Kansas, agrarianism was the emerging social movement, and both Jan and I began a series of research projects on the sociology of agriculture and rural communities. My interest was focused on women in agriculture and in rural communities where, during the 1970s, women were increasingly moving to the foreground in the community work they had always done.

Entering the Foundation World

As a result of my research on rural women and my friendship with social anthropologist Susan Almy, a program officer for the Rockefeller Foundation, I was included in a Rockefeller-funded conference on the social aspects of agricultural development, which was also attended by representatives from the Ford Foundation. As a result of those contacts, in 1978 I received an invitation to apply to be program adviser for agriculture and rural development for the Andean region and Southern Cone of Latin America. Jan and I decided to make a joint application.

The appropriate people in the Ford Foundation decided we could do the job. At the time we were hired, my feminism and feminist scholarship was of relatively little interest. What mattered was our knowledge of Latin America, agriculture, and rural development. After unsuccessfully trying agronomists and agricultural economists in that position, the foundation determined that agriculture and rural development actually dealt with social issues, which required the insights and expertise of sociologists like us. Next, they had to decide *just how* to employ us. Another couple had been hired in the Mexico City office for the same position. They determined that the husband would be the program adviser and that the wife would work as a consultant. We told them we wanted to be equal so that either of us could talk to a grantee as a "real" program adviser. Although the people in the foundation's personnel department didn't know how to do it, we insisted, and they creatively solved the "problem." Our orientation at foundation headquarters in New York included a chance to share perspectives on women and development with Adrienne Germaine. She encouraged me to continue to examine the negative impacts of the current development model on women and to try to build programs that included women, realizing that the model would be different if women were included as both the objects and subjects of development. Our family of four headed off to Bogotá. We arrived there on September 18, 1978.

The Macro Setting

In 1978 prices for all commodities rose as the dollar reached an historic low. This meant that the Ford Foundation had fewer dollars, which in any case were worthless, to spend overseas. Expatriate staff being an expensive piece of international work, field offices in the Andean region and the Southern Cone (Santiago, Chile; Lima, Peru; and Bogotá, Colombia) were consolidated into the Bogotá office. In addition to agriculture and rural development, our portfolios and area of coverage were expanded to include social science, education, human rights, and health and nutrition. The increase in breadth allowed an opportunity to integrate women into all program areas and to start women's programs. Because of my intense interest in the area, which I shared with Adrienne Germaine, then with the International Division based in New York, I took on the responsibility to set up women's programs in the Caribbean and Central America, with some work in Brazil and Mexico. It was an incredible opportunity to help exceptional women get access to resources to both implement and legitimate their work for bettering the lives of women, particularly poor women, in the hemisphere.

The Foundation Setting

The goal of a philanthropic foundation is to support the great public good. That means they can make decisions based on things other than profitability and net worth, which are the measures of success for a multinational corporation, or balance of trade, debt repayment, and gross national product, which are measures critical to national and multilateral banks. Further, because foundations are nongovernmental, they do not need to be justified in terms of the national interest or specific foreign policy goals, which are required of national development entities such as the USAID. For foundations, bettering the human condition is a requirement of the U.S. tax code, their articles of incorporation, and usually, their boards of directors.

Fascinated by the process of inserting women into the male world of international development, I conducted a study of Ford Foundation documents in 1981 to understand more about the context in which I had worked.[6] In that study, the degree to which women and men were committed to improving the status of women worldwide and to changing the organization in real ways, including allocation of funds in times of cutbacks, was impressive.

New York City was an important center for the U.S. feminist movement in the 1970s, and many of the women who worked at the Ford Foundation were feminists. They participated in feminist groups outside the foundation and formed feminist discussion groups within it. Although separate from governmental groups, they worked with those groups directly and indirectly through the policy-relevant, nongovernmental and community-based organizations they funded through a variety of domestic programs.

Foundation boards generally comprise distinguished individuals who have a broad view and a wide range of contacts. The structure of the board of trustees of any corporation, organization, and foundation reflects in part the connections of the chief executive officer. Indeed, the board of trustees names the foundation president. When we joined the foundation staff, McGeorge Bundy was the president. A former dean at Harvard University when it was all male, and a high-ranking adviser in the administrations of John F. Kennedy and Lyndon Johnson, he was a liberal highly concerned with international issues. A colleague from those administrations, Robert McNamara, was on the board of trustees. A former president of the Ford Motor Company, he was also president of the World Bank. The networks of the board of trustees were as important as those of the staff in setting the climate in a number of critical development agencies.

The board of trustees made the final decisions on budget allocation and program direction. Program officers determined worthy programs that met the goal of the foundation namely, to contribute to the solution of problems of national or international importance. Working with potential grantees, program officers developed projects and programs that allowed groups and individuals to work toward their goals and those of the foundation. In clear and persuasive prose, the program officers presented the case to the country representative, the Area Program (Latin American and the Caribbean; Africa; Asia and the Pacific) staff, the International Division, and the president, who would then forward the request for funding to the board of trustees.

The Percy Amendment to the Foreign Assistance Act, which authorized funding for programs dealing specifically with women in development, had passed—with no funding—in December 1973, partly in support of International Women's Year of 1975. In response, women on the foundation staff, including Elinor Barber—who chaired the International Division's Committee on Women's Programs in collaboration with other feminists—were involved in the International Women's Year efforts. They outlined four potential areas where the foundation could make a useful contribution: data collection, support of women in formulating an agenda for government action, day care, and sponsorship of conferences prior to the Mexico City Conference.

David Bell, foundation vice president for the International Division, made a strong statement through the Committee on Women's Programs that the issue of women in development was a legitimate one. But in the Ford Foundation field offices around the world, most program officers were men. They found it difficult to find "sound scholars" or "legitimate institutions" to address that issue. Indeed, their correspondence to the New York office insisted that feminism was cultural imperialism and that the foundation should avoid it. For example, they noted that if the custom of the country was to exclude women from higher education, it would be too intrusive for the foundation to insist that women's dormitories be established and that scholarships be given to women as a condition of a grant. Another example was their belief that sexuality and women's right to control their bodies were things that were of concern only to U.S. feminists. Yet many of these same program officers felt no compunction about demanding that human rights and monetary policy be changed, no matter how inconvenient those in power might see such changes to be.

The interlocking directorates among male leaders of international development agencies—including the World Bank, the United Nations Development Program, USAID, the Population Council, and the Ford Foundation—were influenced by the reasoned communications they received from their feminist staff members, who were also interlocked through informal networks, including those where female leaders were outspoken about the importance of women in development. These feminist networks within male-led organizations were the necessary prelude to the establishment of such women-led institutions as Women's World Banking, established in 1979. These internal and external networks reduced the transaction costs in bringing about changes in perspective—and investment—in the headquarters of these organizations.

Field staffs of all these organizations, including the Ford Foundation, were isolated from the U.S. feminist movement and were more likely to be male than the headquarters professionals. Internal foundation correspondence shows they were more resistant than their male colleagues in New York and Washington, D.C. It was clear that women needed to be sent to the field.

Moving Feminists to the Field

Mary Ann Schmick provided early support to the Brazil field office of the Ford Foundation as a consultant. I was the first program officer on the ground in Latin America and the Caribbean who wanted to build a women in development portfolio as a primary program emphasis.

It took more than New York's blessings and a highly motivated field presence to build a solid program. Many of the most important feminist groups in Latin America were established and maintained by women who had been active in parties on the Left. They were very suspicious of all U.S. institutions and assumed that the Ford Foundation was an arm of the U.S. State Department, CIA, or Department of Defense. It took time to build relationships and then build good programs.

Women researchers in male private research institutions in Ecuador, Peru, Chile, and Argentina were the first grantees, bringing women's issues into the intellectual mix. In the late 1970s and early 1980s, military governments dominated Latin America and social science scholarship took place only in private institutions that were dependent on outside funding for support. For researchers in these institutions in 1978, studies of women provided the first chance they had to do field research since the establishment of the highly repressive military regimes. The subject of women seemed so trivial that the military governments did not feel it worth stopping the studies or repressing the women who participated, either as researchers or researched. However, the knowledge of potential repression—and friends who were among the "disappeared"—made taking on any field research somewhat dangerous. Those women who chose to do it knew of the risks, but also knew of the need to document and analyze what was going on. Ruth Santu, Beatriz Schmukler, and Elizabeth Jelin were some of the Argentinean researchers who took those risks. Other feminist scholars, such as Mary García Castro, left countries under harsh military regimes and began to do research in Colombia and Mexico, which still had civilian governments during the time I began to put together the women in development research proposal for the Latin America and Caribbean Region.

It was harder to develop projects with key activists and scholars in Peru and the Dominican Republic. The research I had done on *fotonovelas* proved an entrée as feminist groups sought new media to reach out to working-class groups. So did our connections with Latin American solidarity groups in the United States. But it took a lot of conversations and a lot of listening—mainly listening. In 1979 I was invited to attend a meeting in Chile put together by the feminist coordination group and to work with the group to develop fundable programs that addressed the related problems of international dependency and patriarchy.

In a foundation concerned with policies at the macro-level and studies that supported those policies through the use of quantitative data, it was hard to defend the action research done by feminist groups. The political climate precluded large samples. Surveys asking the kinds of questions addressed by the feminist researchers, which linked economic and political repression to the realities of women's lives, were impossible.

Feminist action research, although not fitting into the foundation's preferences, provided not only good qualitative data on the impact of neo-liberal policies, but formed the basis of new cross-class analyses between middle-class urban women and working-class and peasant women in a number of Latin American countries. However, even in progressive circles, considering women's particular gender needs was viewed as suspect. In the Dominican Republic, as in other places, leftist men activists confronted feminist action researchers as puppets of imperialism who were deflecting class struggle. I was present at several meetings where Magali Piñeda brilliantly defended her feminist perspective, exemplified by the Center for Research for Feminist Action, which we were able to support through Ford Foundation funding.

In Peru, feminist groups like Flora Tristan (founded in 1979 and named for the French feminist precursor and writer who visited Peru in 1835), Manuela Ramos (founded in 1978 and named after no specific person to indicate the common Peruvian woman), and Action for the Liberation of Peruvian Women (the first Peruvian second wave feminist organization founded in 1972) formed the Feminine Organizations Coordinating Committee during my tenure as program officer. We were able to work with each group to develop research, action, and policy that impacted the lives of women, including women of indigenous origin on the coast and in the Sierra.[7]

Application of the Lessons Learned

The cumulative results of feminist scholarship and action carry over into our own research and development activities in both Latin America and the United States. At the beginning of a USAID-funded project on sustainable agriculture and natural resource management in Ecuador, old guard extension collaborators in Ecuador sabotaged our efforts with Susan Poats to introduce gender issues into the initial analysis of the Sustainable Agriculture and Natural Resource Management Collaborative Research Support Program in a buffer area around a bio-reserve. However, our current Ecuadorian collaborators, male and female, in nongovernmental organizations—which include Heifer Project International, Terra Nova, and the Institute of Ecuadorian Studies—assume that research and action that does not include gender as a guiding principle of analysis and action is not sound and not worth doing. That stance is based in part on studies by such Ecuadorian scholars as Lucia Salamea, Lucia Carrión, and Maria Cuvi. These were funded under the combined women in development and agriculture and rural development Ford Foundation program that Jan and I established in the region.

I now apply much of what I learned to the domestic programs we develop at the North Central Regional Center for Rural Development (I have been the director since 1994), which includes the twelve midwestern states of the United States in research and action programs. The Northwest Area Foundation, on whose board of directors I serve, is transforming itself from a grant-making foundation to an implementing foundation, working with specific communities that combine need and opportunity to reduce poverty, increase social capital, and enhance the ecosystem. Attention to gender issues is crucial in this work. And as a new member of the board of directors of Winrock International, I will use my knowledge of gender analysis and feminist program development to help the board move into the domestic policy arena and work more effectively for sustainable development in the United States and internationally. My volunteer work with the Iowa American Friends Service Committee Immigrants Rights Project provides another venue for insisting that women's issues and organizing activities be a focus of attention.

We were privileged to be a part of a social movement—the women's movement—in both its national and international struggles. The movement continues. The importance of informal connections—social capital in feminist communities of interest—continues to be critical for building toward a feminist future. The impact on us as a family, as well as the continued activities of the connections formed in Latin America and between Latin American and North American scholars and activists, can hopefully continue to contribute to the process of changing the world. As we continue our current research in Latin America and the Caribbean, it is thrilling to find the feminists we supported through foundation grants in positions of influence and even power in emerging democracies throughout the hemisphere. Their knowledge about women's conditions, and their concern about improving those conditions, led to the integration of women into the new Ecuadorian Constitution by explicitly including women in each section of the document, (Maria Cuvi), as well as their placement into policy-making positions at the Economic Commission for Latin America and the Caribbean based in Chile (Cecilia Lopez of Colombia) and the InterAmerican Development Bank (Nohra Rey de Maralanda of Colombia). Others, such as Magdalena Léon in Colombia and Maruja Barrig and Virginia Vargas in Peru continue their research, organizing, and writing about women despite civil disruption. Their solid research and their links to action and policy improves women's lives in a very real way.

Kathleen Cloud

Kathleen Cloud is director of the Gender and Agribusiness Project (GAP) at the University of Illinois. Born in rural Michigan and educated in convent boarding schools, she holds a bachelor's degree in philosophy from Nazareth College (1953), a master's degree in educational psychology from the University of Arizona (1970), and a Ph.D. in public policy from Harvard University (1986). The mother of three children, Christopher, Catherine and Daniel, for seven years she was a full-time mother in New York City.

After a difficult divorce and an early career in the education of culturally diverse young children, her professional focus gradually shifted to issues of gender and development. During her years at the University of Arizona and at Harvard, she directed a number of projects on women's roles in world food systems, and has written extensively in this area. From 1986 to 1998 she was an associate professor at the University of Illinois and director of the Office of Women and International Development. She has consulted extensively with both international agencies and national governments in Asia and Africa.

Hard Minds and Soft Hearts: A University Memoir

Between the two World Wars, the French philosopher Jacques Maritain wrote that much of the trouble in the world occurred because most people with hard minds have hard hearts and most people with soft hearts have soft heads. What the world needed, he said, was more people with hard minds and soft hearts. My memoir documents the efforts of a group of women in American universities to live by that ideal, to use our well-trained heads to move forward the cause of justice and equity for our sisters throughout the world.

Through an accident of history, our American universities assumed substantial responsibility for agricultural development in the Third World just as the women's movement in the United States was gathering force in the early 1970s. Women had begun to understand that the personal was not only political, it was also economic. The civil rights movement had taught us that patriarchy as well as racism was embodied in institutional arrangements and that institutional arrangements could be changed. This historic moment provided us with a unique opportunity to directly affect the lives of poor women in developing countries by using our heads and the political power of our institutional roles to improve the access of poor rural women to development resources.

We started where we were, and did what we knew how to do: research, networking, training, lobbying, finding ways to let the voices of our southern sisters be heard. Always, we were trying to build strategies that would move institutions and individuals to action. The process was far from perfect, but it was exhilarating, and to a surprising extent, successful. There were mistakes and disappointments along the way, and sometimes painful conflicts, but I am proud of what we did, and how we did it.

In 1975 I was the single mother of three adolescents, working at the University of Arizona in a national poverty program. I was also actively engaged in the creation of the women's studies program, chairing the faculty committee that convinced the university to establish it. Finally, I had a long-standing but dormant interest in development through my membership in the Grail, an international Catholic women's movement, where I had developed deep friendships with three African women.

I worked with Head Start and Follow Through, national programs to improve the early education of poor children. The Arizona Center for Educational Research and Development was part of an enormous and outstandingly successful program, involving fifteen universities and one hundred school districts for a ten-year period. The center was responsible for twenty-three school districts ranging from Alaska to Mississippi to

Newark. We had two charges: to change radically what went on in the classrooms and to empower parents by involving them in the governance of the schools. The lessons I learned on the creation and management of this institutional change proved invaluable in my work on women and development.

All these strands—women, development, and institutional change— began to come together in 1974, when Arizona received funding from the United States Agency for International Development (USAID) to work in French-speaking West African countries devastated by prolonged drought. This new program resulted, in part, from lobbying by universities for larger development resources to address world hunger. Their success was reflected in the 1973 amendments to the Foreign Assistance Act which provided New Directions to USAID that focused on meeting basic needs of people in developing countries. Under Title XII of the amendments, use of the technical assistance capabilities of U.S. land grant universities was mandated, especially in agriculture. A Board for International Food and Agricultural Development (BIFAD) was created to collaborate with USAID in managing this effort and strengthening grants were provided to participating universities. The Percy Amendment, mandating attention to women both as agents and beneficiaries of development, was passed by Congress the same year. Thus, U.S. universities moved toward major involvement in agricultural development just as attention to women's roles was required by Congress.

In the summer of 1974 I went to Harvard University for a summer workshop on early childhood. There I met Ibrihama Fall, a Senegalese working for the United Nations Children's Fund (UNICEF) in West Africa, where several years of repeated drought had devastated farmers and herders alike. Most development efforts focused on restoring the production systems, but UNICEF was interested in the situation of the women and children. Ibrihama was trying to understand the potential effects of prolonged malnutrition on children's mental and physical development. He was also asking, "What are the likely effects of malnutrition on pregnant and nursing mothers? Does the drought have different effects on women than on men?"

Arguing for WID

When I returned to Arizona, I began to search for answers with colleagues in women's studies, the medical college, and the Arid Lands Center. In the process I found Ester Boserup's *Women's Role in Economic Development*, which had a great deal to say about African women's agricultural roles and the problems caused by ignoring these roles. I also found a seminar series designed to give our technical people a better grasp of the ecosystems and social systems they would be dealing with in the Sahel. One of the few women present, I kept asking, "But what about women?" Male colleagues had few answers, but to their credit, they were interested in the question and took it seriously.

There was a growing number of women in Title XII institutions who had read Boserup and learned of the potential for perverse effects of development on women's status. We felt that we were responsible for the behavior of our own institutions to assure that they would not unknowingly do harm to women in other societies. To undercut the perception that we were American women trying to push our feminist agenda on Third World women, we used two arguments: those of policy and of efficiency. We pointed out that we were simply asking our institutions to implement existing policies; the Percy Amendment mandated their attention to the issue and several UN resolutions on rural women signaled the agreement of developing countries. With the collaboration of the Women in Development Office at USAID (USAID/WID) we also made it clear that the agency was monitoring contractor compliance with the Percy Amendment. This was something of an overstatement, but it often worked.

Data Collection

To make the efficiency argument successfully, we had to convince the overwhelmingly male technical people that women had important agricultural functions, including the production, processing, storage, and marketing of food. In the university, data is a very powerful tool. We needed solid empirical evidence that what women did mattered to the success of university projects. So collecting, organizing, and presenting information on women's agricultural roles was a necessary first step.

Given Arizona's lack of knowledge about the work of Sahelian women, the obvious first step was to ask the women themselves about their roles and needs. In 1976, together with Myra Dinnerstein, a women's studies colleague trained as an African historian, I asked for and received strengthening grant money to go to Senegal, Mali, Niger, and Burkina Faso and speak with the women there. Everywhere, both professional and village women were eager to speak to us. They were articulate in describing not only their lives, but the systems that encompassed their lives. Many male officials were also helpful.

Village women were very clear and concrete in describing their needs. They wanted resources to help them in the production of vegetables, goats, sheep, and chickens; assistance in acquiring better means of food preservation; better access to water; carts for transporting loads; and anything else that would relieve the tremendous burden of their work. But most of all, they wanted ways to generate cash income.

Upon our return I was funded by USAID's Sahelian office to write a comprehensive paper drawing on our interviews, titled "Sex Roles in Sahelian Food Systems," as well as on an extensive annotated bibliography on food systems commissioned by that office.[1] David Shearer, the office director, was firmly committed to the issue and had the paper translated into French. It was widely used for several years in briefing technical people as well as for academic purposes.

Over time the available research on the work of rural women expanded to include substantial data in many different agricultural systems. This early growth in knowledge was due in part to the USAID WID Office's commitment to finding, funding, and disseminating such research, and in part to the university women who dug data out of existing research in many different disciplines. Increasing amounts of data were also generated by university projects.

Creating a Network of Influence

But data alone was not enough. Ten years of experience with poverty programs had taught me that in addition to clear policy and rational arguments backed up by good information, real change depends upon the commitment of people with the power to influence and drive it. Some of these people must be within the institution and others outside, applying pressure. Once USAID and the host country had decided on the general outline of a particular project, what happened to women depended on how the project was designed and executed; who got hired; and which farmers got seeds, credit, and extension. Since these tasks were largely the responsibility of the university contractor, both data and the power to insist on its use were crucial at this stage. We had to get knowledgeable women advocates into the room when projects were being planned and implemented. Although increasing numbers of men became allies, the issue was much more central for women and their presence was necessary to assure explicit attention to women.

This posed an institutional problem. Historically, women faculty in colleges of agriculture were concentrated in home economics. Although increasing numbers of younger women were coming into production agriculture areas of study, few had the seniority that would automatically entitle them to participate fully. We needed to reset the norms so that both younger women and senior home economists would be seen as capable participants with special knowledge of women's issues. We also needed to ensure that social scientists from other parts of the university could be included in the agricultural projects.

Understanding this, I began an activity designed to assemble not only data, but also a network of people committed to change. Together with John Fisher, a University of Arizona agricultural economist and former USAID mission director, I proposed and USAID WID funded an international conference, Women in World Food Systems, in January 1978. It was attended by 250 women and men from twenty-three countries representing universities, developing countries' ministries, the U.S. government, and the

United Nations. To assure the presence of multiple perspectives, we funded the participation of ten Consortium for International Development (CID) women graduate students from developing countries to co-chair the daily small group discussion sessions. This emerging network provided political power in pressing for stronger policy implementation both at the campus level and within USAID.

The next step was a three-week workshop in August 1978 at USAID in Washington, D.C., for women representing thirty-two Title XII universities to insure they understood both the substantive issues and USAID's mode of operation. Women nominated by their institutions were predominantly senior faculty in home economics, but there was also substantial representation of social scientists as well as younger agriculturalists.

USAID bureau chiefs and department heads were asked to meet with the group and explain how they were integrating attention to women into their activities. We asked each woman to identify herself by name and the name of her university before she asked a question. Colorado State asked about programs on women's political rights. Michigan State asked about research on beans and cowpeas and Arizona about goats, all traditional women's crops in much of the world. Kentucky wanted to explore how attention to nutrition was included in agriculture projects. Florida A and M queried the role of the historically black schools in development assistance. The experience of facing a large group of women who represented politically powerful state universities and who asked pointed questions was more powerful than we had anticipated in convincing USAID personnel that there was a national constituency for the issue. Many of the men seemed quite shaken by the experience.

Turning to their own institutions, participants also generated a set of recommendations for implementation of the Percy amendment within Title XII.[2] The recommendations spelled out ways of achieving four objectives:

1. To strengthen and expand the involvement of American women in Title XII activities.

2. To increase the involvement of host country women in the planning, implementation, and evaluation of Title XII development and research activities.

3. Through research and dissemination, to increase the knowledge and understanding of the significant contributions of women in developing countries to food and agricultural production and processing and utilization, as well as nutrition and rural development.

4. To assist the USAID/BIFAD structure to respond more effectively to the New Directions legislation in its entirety.

These activities further tightened the links among university women and gave them invaluable help in penetrating their universities' development activities. With the knowledge gained in the workshop, the women were often included on drafting committees because, as several said, "they knew what AID wanted." On many campuses a WID group was formed that sought funding from their campus strengthening grant for a simple office and paid staff time to collect and organize information on women in the areas where that university worked or hoped to work.

Over the next year, a series of small grants enabled me to monitor what was happening on a campus-by-campus basis and feed the information back to the network, to BIFAD, and to USAID. In 1979 I proposed and USAID WID funded the Women and Food Information Network to collect and disseminate information and publish a quarterly newsletter. The network also served a liaison function between BIFAD and the WID Office. Over the next five years I attended monthly BIFAD board meetings, prepared numerous reports and briefing papers, participated in campus and regional workshops, and spoke on women and food systems before professional associations including crop breeders, animal scientists, and water management personnel. In 1980 we held a second Title XII meeting with WID representatives from forty-two universities; it included a presentation of state of the art research for BIFAD, which was very well received.

We were also reaching out to strengthen our international dialogue. In 1980 I participated in the rural women's network at the Copenhagen conference, connecting with women working on these issues all over the world. In the summers I traveled to Asia and Africa to exchange information and strategies with research centers, government ministries, and nongovernmental organizations (NGOs). Although the network began by serving as a support function for the Title XII universities, over the six years of its existence it expanded to more than 2,000 members in forty-nine countries and developed exchange arrangements with centers all over the world.

During this period my other responsibility was that of WID coordinator for the Consortium for International Development (CID), an association of eleven western land grant universities. To staff and manage projects more effectively, most universities had joined regional groups: the Southeastern Consortium for International Development, the Midwestern Universities Consortium on International Assistance, and CID in the arid regions of the West. Women used the institutional arrangements of these consortia to exchange information and strategies with varying degrees of success. Some universities moved forward swiftly, others were stubbornly resistant. Midwestern universities seemed the most conservative, while universities in the West and South were often more open to change.

Within CID, campus WID groups were busy collecting and disseminating information on women's work and holding seminars and workshops as well as writing. Several universities collaborated in organizing information on women in Egypt and Yemen while Arizona produced briefing papers on women in Niger and Burkina Faso, all countries where CID had projects. In all cases, consistent efforts were directed to consulting with host country women, utilizing host country research, and drawing upon the knowledge of students from developing countries

Payoffs

Pressure for institutional change was also beginning to pay off in projects managed by our universities. After hosting a regional WID conference where the upcoming Tanzanian Farming Systems Project was analyzed in some detail, Colorado State substantially revised its management plan to include more direct attention to women. Three university WID groups collaborated in convincing the Yemen Horticultural Project to include a half-time WID person on the implementation team and later to include a WID position in the Yemen Poultry Project. Two large providers of technical assistance to USAID missions worldwide made a serious attempt to ensure that their personnel would be prepared to address women's issues. The Water Management Synthesis II Project, managed by Utah State and Colorado State, funded my travel to India and Sri Lanka to look at innovative projects and institutions and to prepare a briefing paper outlining the major issues in women's access to irrigation water, with suggestions for workable ways of addressing them. Idaho State, which managed the Natural Resources Management Project, ran a WID workshop for potential participants.

We were also more successful than we had expected in working with BIFAD. Both the chairman of the board, Cliff Wharton (president of the State Universities of New York), and the executive director, Woods Thomas (international dean at Purdue University), were knowledgeable and committed on the issue, and their leadership gave us invaluable credibility in moving the issue forward. This excerpt from a letter I wrote to university women in the early days of the network gives a flavor of BIFAD support:

> This fall Dr. Sterling Wortman, vice president of the Rockefeller Foundation, appeared before the board to discuss his book, *To Feed This World,* an overview of the world food crisis which argues that the crisis can be solved, and that the means to feed the world are now emerging. Hard headed, practical arguments are made for assistance to the small family farm. There is no mention, however, of the roles of women; the assumption of the male farmer persists.
>
> At the end of this two-hour presentation, President Thomas of New Mexico State said, "There is one last question I would like to ask. I realize that this book has been in preparation of several years.
>
> Knowing what you know now, how would you change it today to more accurately reflect the role of women in farming?" He then launched into a statement in praise of farm women. Somehow, friends,

when the president of a western land grant college challenges the vice president of the Rockefeller Foundation on the role of women in agricultural development, I think we're in possession of an idea whose time has come.

Creating AWID

Unfortunately, Title XII institutions lost traction after Ronald Reagan's election in 1980 as development policies shifted from a basic needs approach to an emphasis on the value of the private sector. Hunger and poverty issues received less attention. The emphasis on privatization also led to a change in institutional arrangements; design and management of development projects shifted to private contracting firms, and the universities' participation in development gradually declined during the 1980s.

As strengthening grants were cut and then eliminated, most campus WID groups lost their funding, although happily, Arizona's WID program survived and CID continued to fund a WID position well into the 1990s. The Women and Food Network funding ended in 1984 as a new USAID policy decreed the end of all free information dissemination. By then, the research establishing the importance of women's participation in agricultural systems had entered the mainstream. Basic knowledge was no longer the problem; application of the knowledge in day-to-day operations had become, and remains, the focus of effort. Loss of the university role in project implementation meant loss of an arrangement that permitted women to exert pressure on their institutions to "do the right thing" on a project-by-project basis. It was a serious loss, particularly since it came just as the universities' efforts were beginning to pay off in the form of better project designs and implementation.

Creating the Association for Women and Development

Fortunately, university women did not passively accept their disenfranchisement. During the early 1980s we realized that we needed a place of our own that was not dependent on donor funding, so we created the Association for Women in Development (AWID). Because we envisioned it as a professional association, we immediately reached out to colleagues in development agencies and NGOs, hosting an organizational meeting at the Wingspread Foundation in Wisconsin in 1982. Much of the early logistical support came from the universities through the National Association of State Universities and Land Grant Colleges, which not only gave us office space and meeting rooms, but also printed and distributed early newsletters.

The first AWID conference was a great success. We have had seven more since then, with a vibrant international membership growing to some 1,200 members. I served on the board from 1981 to 1998, as the first convener, then secretary, and finally membership chair. For all these years, Martha

Lewis's home was a central node of the networks, and the conversations on Martha's back porch one of the great joys of my life. (For additional discussion of AWID see Jane B. Knowles's essay in this volume.)

Gender Training

During the late 1970s I was still working part-time at the Arizona Center for Educational Research and Development while using a series of small grants to do the WID work. With three children in college on scholarships, I took a major risk to create a new life for myself and enrolled at Harvard. I not only learned a great deal, but established friendships with colleagues that have lasted over two decades. In Peter Timmer's class on world food systems there were two other mid-career students who had the same concerns about women as I did: Kristin Timothy from the UN Secretariat and Natalie Hahn from the Food and Agriculture Organization. We kept asking, "But what about women?" Peter was remarkably patient and gradually became a supporter of the issue. On the last day of class we put a sign on the blackboard announcing the time and place for a meeting to organize a Harvard group on women and development. Thirty-five women showed up for a breakfast meeting. Over the next year we created a student group, sponsored by the Harvard Institute for International Development (HIID), that still exists. It sponsors monthly seminars and a yearly conference on specific gender issues. Unfortunately, the group had much less ability to influence the large projects at HIID. There were few women faculty to apply pressure, and most male faculty were actively disinterested in the issue. There seemed to be an underlying attitude that as economists, they already knew all they needed to know.

Nevertheless, the case method of gender training was developed there. It began in September 1981 with a phone call from Gloria Scott, the WID director of the World Bank, to Jim Austin at the Business School. Robert McNamara, World Bank president, had promised his wife that before he stepped down, he would commission a workshop for top bank officials on women in development. Would Jim teach it? The bank's training office had said they didn't know how and had recommended Jim as a good case teacher who might have ideas on how it could be done. Jim talked it over with three of us—Cathy Overholt, who was his wife; Mary Anderson; and myself—and proposed that he would teach us the case method if we taught him about women and development. We jumped at the chance and over the next two years this team did a series of workshops for the bank. Each involved group discussion of a series of case studies of recent bank projects, utilizing an analytic framework that included male-female roles and resources and responsibilities as these related to the success (efficiency) of each project. The Harvard Business School teaching method emphasizes clarifying the facts first and then discussing how problems in the situation might be solved. In this approach there are no prescribed right answers and different groups find very different solutions. Because the process utilizes the technical and managerial skills of the participants, it tends to draw them into the process rather than generating resistance. Over time this "ask, don't tell" strategy has proved very useful in addressing gender issues.

In 1982 our gender training team expanded our activities, submitting an unsolicited proposal through HIID to do a series of USAID project cases and training sessions. Paula Goddard and Sarah Tinsley at USAID WID fought very hard to gain acceptance for the project within the Reagan administration. When it was approved, we commissioned eight cases and three technical papers that laid out the major knowledge of gender issues in agriculture, small enterprise, and technical transfer. By now we were sufficiently confident to insist that good project design demanded more than simply including women; it demanded systematic gender analysis. So we rewrote our analytic framework to make this explicit. After series of successful workshops, in 1985 the USAID cases and papers were published as *Gender Roles in Development Projects*.[3]

These have been widely used for training by the Canadian development agency, the UN Development Program, and the Asian Management Institute, among others, and have proved a model for many other groups in the development of their own teaching materials. Members of the Harvard team did a number of very productive "do it yourself" workshops for developing country personnel in a variety of settings. I remember in particular a Ford Foundation–funded workshop I did in New Delhi in 1989 for a group of young and energetic trainers who were just beginning to use this approach. Since then they have successfully spread the method to many Indian institutions.

During the 1980s Judith Bruce at the Population Council commissioned a series of outstandingly successful farming systems cases that were used with the international agricultural research centers.[4] Hilary Feldstein, another Harvard friend, managed this process with Susan Poats, and did much of the training. In 1991, with Population Council support, Hilary also organized a gender training conference at the Michelsten Institute in Norway to assess what was happening in the field. As part of my work on the planning committee, I surveyed eighty participants from all over the world and was pleased to find that case method was one of the principal techniques in use.[5]

Graduate Education on Women in Development

In 1985 I joined the University of Illinois faculty as part-time director of its WID office. With the help of a very active interdisciplinary committee, I created and directed a graduate minor called Gender Roles and International Development. Since 1987 more than sixty women and men from thirty-five countries have completed the minor while taking their master's or doctoral degrees in disciplines ranging from agriculture and education to business and economics. Most of them have been mid-career professionals from developing countries who have returned home to work in government ministries, donor programs, universities, and nongovernmental organizations.

The WID office also collaborated with MS University of Baroda, India, in exchanges of faculty and students. Together we ran two international workshops on policy-relevant research methods that culminated in *Capturing Complexity*, a handbook on household research which has been very widely circulated.[6] First with an office newsletter and now with increasing electronic capabilities, we are striving to keep our colleagues and students connected with one another in an information exchange that profits us all.

The program has also been responsible for sharing information with the campus at large and for outreach to the state. For several years in collaboration with the women's studies program, we sponsored statewide policy conferences on issues such as women's education. In 1995 we held a large conference focusing on the UN Fourth World Conference on Women at Beijing and its Platform for Action. After a national search, a new director was appointed in 1998 and the program was fully institutionalized with state support for its operation. At that point I returned to my department to write about what I had learned.

Lessons Learned

I had learned a great deal, much of it quite subtle, but one simple lesson still shines through. It is possible to make a difference. Action can produce change, but it requires intelligence and commitment, as well as luck. My strategies were simple: make a believable argument, make allies, take chances, and be assertive, but also understand who you are talking to and what their interests are.

The question of what arguments are best in assuring women's well-being has evolved since 1975. In the early days equity was our rationale; women were victims of development and guilt was the reason for institutions to change their behavior. For those of us in the agricultural schools it became clear very quickly that the American men we worked with were not willing to support interventions in the relationships between men and women in another culture that were justified only by considerations of "Western morality." To them it smacked of cultural imperialism. What they were willing to do, and trained to do, was to create agricultural systems that would work more effectively.

So we framed our arguments in terms of efficiency, insisting that project personnel understand who was doing the work and who needed the resources. During the Reagan years the efficiency arguments served the issue well, but it is important to understand that our underlying concern was always for equality. This point has unfortunately been misunderstood by some our English colleagues, who took the policy argument as the sum total of our concern.

In any policy environment the rationale you use depends on whom you're talking to and how you can best enter their discourse effectively. This point is clear in the use of the empowerment arguments by nongovernmental organizations. Because their work is explicitly addressed to issues of social justice, grassroots organizing of women speaks directly to their core reason for existence. Fortunately, the evolution of the arguments for women's human rights in the past few years provides moral bedrock that is supportive of all efforts to improve women's situation. As a result, concerns about cultural imperialism have become less powerful.

In the early days the American women's movement filled us all with hope and energy and so reaching out to the rest of the world's women seemed natural. The group of women committed primarily to international work was relatively small, but we were connected by active networks, nationally and internationally. Because our commitment ran well ahead of our knowledge, we learned as we went. Most of us were not paid to work on women's issues; we did it in addition to our regular jobs, sometimes with active discouragement from our bosses. Because there wasn't much literature, we read it all.

Now there are many people paid to work exclusively on women's issues and the knowledge base is much fuller. Specialists have replaced generalists and greater resources are available for addressing gender issues. There are many women's movements willing and able to apply political pressure to governments. The potential for groups splitting or conflicting with each other grows as the field grows. For twenty-five years the UN world conferences on women have provided a venue for working through our differences to arrive at deep international consensus, as reflected in the Beijing Platform of Action in 1995. It is for the succeeding generations to preserve and expand upon this remarkable achievement.

Jane B. Knowles

Born in Boston and educated at Syracuse University and the University of Pennsylvania, Jane B. Knowles has lived in Madison, Wisconsin, for more than thirty-five years. Her career at the University of Wisconsin began with the editing of scholarly publications, first for the university's press and later for the Land Tenure Center, a major international program within the College of Agricultural and Life Sciences. Her work at the center began to drift into administration, which prompted her to spend the summer of 1976 in a seminar designed to train university administrators. That led to her work as assistant and associate director of administration for the Midwestern Universities Consortium for International Assistance MUCIA) and later in similar roles in both the Land Tenure Center and the Office of International Agricultural Programs at the University of Wisconsin, Madison. Her career at the University of Wisconsin ended with several years of administrative work in the College of Agricultural and Life Sciences, which diminished her role in international projects. She retired from the university in 1997.

Knowles is the wife of Richard Knowles, a world-renowned Shakespearean scholar who is professor of English and Dickson-Bascom Professor of Humanities at the University of Wisconsin. They are the parents of Jonathan Edward, a professional chef, and Katherine Mary, an investment counselor.

Notes from the Middle Border: WID on Campus

My first connection with the situation of women in developing countries occurred by default. As the only woman during the 1970s working at a professional level in the international programs of the University of Wisconsin's College of Agricultural and Life Sciences (UW-CALS) and the Midwest Universities Consortium for International Activities (MUCIA), all documents with any form of the word woman in their title were automatically routed to me. Presumably, I had some innate knowledge of what to do with them. I tried to read the documents with an open, if relatively uninformed, mind. I took notes on facts and issues that interested me—always women's productive roles in agricultural systems—and then sent the documents on to the University of Wisconsin's Land Tenure Center (LTC) Library, one of the few scholarly libraries in the country that collected, catalogued, and circulated such ephemera. It didn't take long to understand that I needed some sort of intellectual framework within which to fit these documents. So I discovered scholars like Ester Boserup, Irene Tinker, and Mayra Buvinic, who had been thinking seriously for years, within the framework of their intellectual disciplines, about the issues raised by the documents I was receiving simply because of my gender.

What made the new information and insights of these scholars about women in developing countries different and exciting was the fact that so many of us in the university community were discovering them at the same time. There came into being a group of aroused and informed American women who wanted to change the way in which the world—and especially our part of it—was working, for fear we were actually doing harm to women in developing countries.

At that point in my own life, given the dearth of female colleagues at Wisconsin with whom I could share these new discoveries, MUCIA opened a major opportunity, the real start of my work in women in development (WID). The director of the United States Agency for International Development's Women in Development Office (USAID WID), drawing on her knowledge of the intellectual ferment in progress at the University of Minnesota, called a meeting of women from the MUCIA universities at Minneapolis–St. Paul to discuss possible directions for action. Before I went to the meeting, the then-executive director of MUCIA authorized me to offer the consortium's services as a vehicle for action.[1]

A group of about fifteen women met for two days. Very few of the women knew exactly how they had gotten there. Someone just told them to go. The singular exception was Patricia Barnes-McConnell of Michigan State, who had the luxury of a dean of international studies, Ralph

Smuckler, who was a strong supporter of WID from the very earliest days. By the time we left Minneapolis–St. Paul we had agreed on how to proceed. With the permission of the MUCIA board of directors, we submitted to USAID WID a request for a capacity-building grant in WID at the consortium's member institutions.

The MUCIA WID Network

The proposal we submitted, and for which we received funding around mid-1978 from USAID WID, focused on our collective decision to work within our own institutions, building on existing collegial relationships.[2] Our initial goal was to demonstrate our ability to work on WID issues as they arose in development projects. The USAID grant allowed us the luxury of funding a small part of the salary of an individual on each campus (MUCIA allowed me to contribute my time) to take the lead in a range of institution-building activities. There was a set of such activities common to all institutions (albeit managed locally with the inevitable institutional differences), such as the development of rosters of male and female faculty and staff with international credentials and knowledge of WID issues; training workshops to acquaint faculty unused to the complex relations between donor agencies and land grant institutions with the mechanics of proposal writing, implementation and evaluation; regional seminars on various campuses to share experiences, successful and not; and use of existing knowledge and research to document women's roles in developing countries.

The group decided to combine its growing administrative strengths with a typical university data-collection effort to influence a single joint activity, the then-planned but not yet designed USAID-funded consortium project to improve agricultural extension efforts in the island nations of the eastern Caribbean. We worked in three ways to influence project design and implementation: contributing language on supporting women's agricultural activities to the project's design document; preparing a major research study on the role of women in the agriculture of the region; and enlisting the help of important Caribbean women like Peggy Antrobus in our efforts. Antrobus had colleagues on every island where the project was to operate and she kept them informed of project activities that might be of benefit to women.

In hindsight the process sounds much more organized than it actually was. The language on the special role of women in the agriculture of the region that was in the original version of the project design paper mysteriously disappeared in the second iteration of that paper. At the insistence of some members of the original design team, especially Earl Kellogg of the University of Illinois, a somewhat modified version of the language crept back into the third and final iteration. The MUCIA board of directors, unhappy over what it perceived to be interference in the project design by a group of its own faculty and staff, barred the WID group from any role in the selection of long-term staff for the project. The board was also troubled by rumors it heard of quarrels within the WID group. Finally, the directors dismantled the WID apparatus within the consortium, declining permission to apply for renewal of the USAID support grant or for any other grant. By then I was no longer an employee of the consortium, whose headquarters had moved to another campus.

We were not forced to return unspent funds in the original grant and so, with USAID's permission, used them to support additional field research on women's roles in developing countries and explorations of possible training activities outside our own institutions. Each research project was linked to a planned or ongoing development project on the campus of the faculty or staff member proposing the research. The results of the research confirmed our basic sense that we were on the right track. Prospects for training projects were less hopeful, but both data collection and training activities are the intellectual lifeblood of universities and hence were likely to gain the approval and support of colleagues.

By the end of 1982 the MUCIA WID group was essentially a thing of the past. In one sense it had been frustrating, a bit like creating the female chorus in a Gilbert and Sullivan extravaganza: costumed, singing in tune, dancing well, but stuck waiting for rescue by the British navy, a group of bobbies, or some kindly pirates. In a sense it was also a failure, since there was no real demand for the expertise we had created. In part our timing was bad. We were trying to change the mental sets of a generation of male professionals that had been acculturated to the male-female roles formed during a period when American women were relentlessly domesticated. Many members of that generation were not even capable of seeing the historical reality of the structure of U.S. agriculture, which had always relied on the productive roles of women within the farming sector, and so were all the more incapable of recognizing roles played by women in different agricultural systems. To a degree, the structure within which we were working was no better. Donor agencies in these years did not call for or reward attention to women (often even when it would make the difference between success and failure in a very expensive project) and that provided an excuse for our male colleagues to avoid change.

In another sense, the activity had been a success. We had succeeded in creating a community of organized and trained women and men on the seven MUCIA campuses, a fact that had important long-term implications. We turned both inward to create new opportunities on our individual campuses and outward to look in new directions.

Learning in Botswana and Kenya

The start of the 1980s was a time of great intellectual and administrative ferment on all our campuses. Title XII of the U.S. Foreign Assistance Act was putting money, some of it earmarked for WID activities, into the land grant universities. The Association for Women in Development (AWID) was coming into being. Some of us were collaborating with our colleagues in women's studies on joint efforts relating to women. Perhaps most important, more and more of us were getting opportunities to travel to developing countries to get a first-hand look at what we were talking about.

In the early 1980s, for example, I had the privilege of an extended trip to Africa. My traveling companions were two Land Tenure Center colleagues: Marion Brown, then director of the center, whose international experience was in Latin America, and John Bruce, director of the center's relatively new African program and soon to be the center's director. The purpose was to give Brown and me an idea of the realities of project life in Africa. The trip began in Botswana, because the center was implementing a project there focusing on training extension agents, many of them women, in techniques to discourage overgrazing in very dry country. The project was under the direction of Dr. Louise Fortmann, then of Cornell, now of the University of California at Berkeley, who was particularly sensitive to the situation of women left to manage farming operations while their husbands worked in South Africa.

Botswana was a wonderful introduction to Africa, its villages scattered in random patterns like pebbles thrown on the ground, its rural silences a palpable thing within which to live and move. It was in Botswana that I met the enemy only to discover that it was us: female professionals from a midwestern land grant university, home economists trying to convince Botswana women to use efficient charcoal burning stoves to eliminate the grueling daily search for wood in a heavily deforested country, all of us ignoring the facts. Women's nightly fires provided both the only light in the most profound darkness imaginable and the heat required to brew the local beer that was their major source of income to buy household items such as charcoal. We women from the United States and the women of Botswana were Ezekiel's wheels, one inside the other, both driven by good motives, spinning around ignoring the other because of their different connections to reality.

Our last major stop in Africa was Kenya, where I traveled with the Ford Foundation's WID officer, Suzanne Smith Saulniers, a Wisconsin Ph.D. and old personal friend. Dr. Saulniers took all three of us to look at examples of the situation of women in Kenya. We saw a tea production cooperative where women did all the picking of tea leaves, which was surprisingly heavy work, involving a lot of bending and stooping to seek out ripe leaves while wearing a large pannier attached by two shoulder straps. Men received all the profits distributed by the cooperative at the end of a year. Who else should get them, the co-op manager asked? We also went to a rural village recently served by a water pumping station that saved women and older girls four hours a day, hours previously devoted to carrying water for animals and people up hillsides so incredibly steep they would have killed a goat. The women wanted to fill the extra time by making school uniforms on sewing machines they hoped the Ford Foundation would provide. There was also a bee-keeping project in the dry country midway between Nairobi and Mombasa, run by Irish nuns with the help of a young male extension agent dripping contempt for the women project planners and workers.

These kinds of experiences were enormously important to the intellectual development (and the backbones) we needed to cope with what in retrospect I consider to be one of the most active and demanding periods of WID work in the United States and at the University of Wisconsin, the years from 1982 to 1984.

WID Education at the University of Wisconsin

The support of a number of people made possible the activities described above, and below as well. All of them gave me the freedom to work on WID without niggling or complaint. It would be nice to say that I was relieved of other duties to have the time to work on WID, but that was not the case. In effect, I was given the freedom to work sixty rather than fifty hours a week for as long as I wanted. Phones, supplies, and computers came freely and were certainly welcome. Time was my own problem.[3]

And an increasing amount of time it took. In the early 1980s under the firm leadership of Elinor Barber, at the Ford Foundation, the Research Center of the Women's Studies Program at the University of Wisconsin, directed by Elaine Marks, and the WID groups in the College of Agricultural and Life Sciences, discovered one another. Not a simple process, it required a good deal of effort by Marks and myself. She had to convince her women's studies colleagues that even though the WID group had received funding from USAID, we were not all CIA operatives and traitors to good causes. I had to convince my male agriculture colleagues that not all Women's Studies scholars were totally ethnocentric, mad bra burners. But the effort led to a series of important events.

With Ford support, we collaborated in 1982 and 1983 on two regular University of Wisconsin courses, one at the undergraduate and the other at the graduate level, whose content was the broad scope of women's activities in developing countries. In the summers of 1983 and 1984, Ford support allowed us to conduct two three-week sessions attended by students (mainly but not exclusively women) from developing countries. They came to Wisconsin to live together and study the most current feminist and development theory under the direction of Drs. Marja-Liisa Swantz of Finland and Neuma Aguiar of Brazil. Swantz and Aguiar were leaders of WID activities in Europe and Latin America. They had a great deal to teach about working in settings different than our own.

Around these activities, there was also a series of seminars on such topics as household-level research with participants from both on and off the University of Wisconsin campus. The purpose of these was very broadly educational. All were open to students, staff, and the general public. Each was designed to introduce the university faculty and staff to colleagues from other institutions, to showcase what university people were working on, and to try to engage local community activists in WID work on campus by, for example, bringing them in to share their experiences with the students in the summer programs. The Ford Foundation support was, of course, temporary, and despite our best efforts, the university's central administration could not be convinced to maintain the level of activity the Ford monies had allowed. Women's Studies was successful in creating a new faculty position, one-half of which was devoted to WID activities. African Studies secured support from the Department of Education to cover the costs of a staff member to work with the community at large, especially the public schools, informing them about WID. Marks and I continued to look for broader support, but like so many other WID activities, this one had a short if successful life.

To close the Wisconsin story, support from Title XII grants allowed the growing WID group in UW-CALS to sponsor a series of faculty, staff, and student colloquia during 1983 on the methodological problems of household-level research in developing countries. The colloquia were organized on a regional basis (Africa, Asia, and Latin America) and encouraged use of the talents of representatives of other campuses in the University of Wisconsin system.

Title XII provided funds for other WID activities in the 1980s. With USAID assistance, some attention to WID became institutionalized in the very large basic grants that provided ongoing support to the Land Tenure Center (the only institution of its kind in the United States, supported by USAID for decades), and in the major projects implemented in Gambia and Zambia by the Office of International Agricultural Studies and Programs. Universities are after all, among the most conservative institutions in any society. It is their function to transmit received culture and knowledge to future generations, not a task that encourages revolution. It is often argued that colleges of agriculture are among the most conservative influences within these conservative institutions. That may well be true, probably even at Wisconsin where the college is that of Agricultural and Life Sciences and includes such basic and cutting edge science departments as bacteriology, biochemistry and genetics, and where the entire university is set up administratively to encourage cross cultural programs of research and education. In any case, revolutionary change is better played out on a different stage, in this case a national one with universities as only one element.

Organizing the Association for Women in Development

From at least the beginning of the 1980s, small groups of women began to talk about the possibility of a national association that would somehow include all of us: university scholars, policy makers, and what we came to call practitioners, the people who actually ran multi-million-dollar development projects at the universities and the consulting firms around the Washington Beltway. None of us had much independent travel money, but we managed to hold sessions within sessions, as at the second national Title XII Women in Development Workshop in Washington, D.C., in 1980 and the National Association of State Universities and Land Grant Colleges (NASULGC) annual meeting in 1981, also in Washington. From gatherings like these as well as endless telephone conversations, correspondence, and the beginnings of e-mail, a proposal was put together and presented to the Johnson Foundation of Racine, Wisconsin. In early 1982 the foundation, with the strong support of its vice president, the late Rita Goodman, agreed to fund a conference at its Wingspread Center in Racine.

Wingspread became the birthing place of the Association for Women in Development (AWID). Some thirty women, each representing a constituency, met for three days. We were from university consortia networks, several USAID offices, long-established groups like the professional home economists and NASULGC, the scholarly community, and the private sector. All of us had a strong interest in enhancing the situation of women in developing countries. Over three days we hammered out, sometimes painfully, the beginnings of an organizational structure for AWID. We established some preliminary goals, tentative plans for an inaugural national meeting, and the concept of the trialogue—echelons, practitioners, and policy makers—to hold the disparate elements together.

Then came the time of begging as AWID gathered its limited forces to plan a 1983 conference. The Southeast Consortium for International Development, through the generosity of its WID officer, Ellen Fenoglio, offered us secretariat support. Ellen served as the association's first treasurer, a task demanding a very cool head and strong nerves. A Washington lawyer, Marcia Wiss, helped us, on a pro bono basis, to incorporate and acquire tax-exempt status. Marcia forced us to focus on such organizational issues as bylaws, terms of officers, and dues structure. Those of us with university appointments drew on our institutions for time, telephone charges, postage, and so on. Never have I been more grateful for the University of Wisconsin's strong tradition of support for public service by its faculty and staff.

Without the support of Margaret Fahs, Jim Cowan, and Bob Clodius of NASULGC, AWID would not have survived its first year. Margaret and Jim gave us office space to organize the first conference, helped us recruit an organizer, began our newsletter, shared their Washington expertise with unparalleled generosity, and smoothed over our inevitable gaffes. What did all this volunteer work produce? More work to begin with. A lot of it was provided by our first paid employee, conference organizer Virginia Hamell. An enormous amount of further volunteering was done by a conference program committee and a fund-raising committee, co-chaired by Kate Cloud and Francille Firebaugh. All of us wracked our brains for sources of support and wrote begging letters. There was an organizational group and a group to identify possible developing country participants. Eventually, it all came together.

The conference was scheduled for the fall of 1983 in Washington to celebrate a decade of experience, and the tenth anniversary of the Percy Amendment to the Foreign Assistance Act. Within that rubric, the focus of the program was food and energy. Funds from the Rockefeller Foundation, thanks to Joyce Moock, and from the World Bank, thanks to Gloria Scott and Paula Valad, allowed the participation of women from developing countries. Participation by U.S. minority women and developing country women had been considered vital from the organization's first days.

Part of the conference involved the first formal election of AWID officers and a board of directors, with terms to start at the first annual membership meeting. Board members were to be equally divided among representatives of policy-oriented individuals, those representing private voluntary organizations and foundations, and university representatives—the trialogue—with the nominations for president of the association to rotate among the three constituencies.

The organization had five stated goals and purposes: increasing the awareness of the interdependence of nations, institutions, and individuals in development; ensuring that women participate as full and active partners in a more equitable development process and that they share in its benefits; strengthening research and action in the women in development field by increasing interaction among scholars, practitioners, and policy makers in both the private and public sectors; improving the practice of multilateral, bilateral, and private institutions in the integration of women as both agents and beneficiaries of development; and providing improved communications to a widening audience on problems and solutions relating to women in development.

In the end, success certainly crowned our efforts. By early 1983 AWID had something under 500 paid members. Conference organizers hoped that at least 300–400 of them would join us in Washington. In fact, the conference drew more than 850 paid registrants, overwhelming our rather shaky secretariat and the hotel facilities. The tone of the meeting throughout was one of almost joyous celebration. U.S. senator Charles Percy addressed the opening banquet. There were more workshops than any one person could attend. A reception on Capitol Hill enabled conference participants to express WID concerns to members of Congress and their staff and a seminar organized at USAID by Jean Weidemann, on the staff of the Board for International Food and Agricultural Development, was an opportunity to explain its operations.

The conference closed with what has become an AWID tradition, the annual business meeting, with all the trappings of a real organization. This was the time, too, to hear from the disenchanted, those who feel left out or under-represented. In 1983 these were not many. (Their numbers and the diversity of complaints had increased sharply by 1985, another mark of AWID's success in my judgment.) It was agreed that our next conference would be the spring of 1985. I agreed to continue to serve as AWID president for calendar year 1984, thus setting a precedent by which no one individual had to oversee two conferences. Much of 1984 was spent in reviewing the 1983 conference for lessons we could use in 1985. We also focused a good deal of energy on organizational issues. Our election procedures were refined; a more rational dues structure was established; efforts were made, with the active help of Vivian Derryck, to strengthen our membership in the American minority community; and when new officers were elected, Paula Goddard of USAID was chosen as president.

Leaving AWID

My own role in AWID began to wind down. I continued as editor of the newsletter through 1985, but I had become distracted by the end of 1984 by both personal and professional decisions. My husband and I spent 1984 and 1985 in Washington, where I worked as a senior analyst and operations coordinator for a major USAID project at the consulting firm of Abt Associates. When I returned to Wisconsin in mid-1985, I took a conscious decision to move away from an administrative connection with WID so as to revive intellectual interests largely suppressed for nearly twenty years. I did two WID-related consulting tasks for USAID, editing a series of case studies of USAID-funded projects involving women which demonstrated that in agricultural projects at least some progress on involving women was being made. I also edited a summary paper of lessons learned and did an evaluation of WID-related projects undertaken by members of the Organization for Economic Cooperation and Development/Development Assistance Committee. I then turned my attention to research and writing on women's access to land and agricultural productivity in a range of agricultural systems, including, prominently, that of the United States.

It was a good time to move on. Like many others, I saw an event of 1984 as a strong hint of changes to come. In that year the organization DAWN—Development Alternatives with Women for a New Era—was founded by a significant group of Third World scholars. Its intellectual platform was set forth in *Development Crises and Alternative Visions: Third*

World Women's Perspectives, by Gita Sen and Caren Grown, and was marked by very provocative arguments about how women had fared in such developed countries as the United States. The playing field was both broadening and leveling as our colleagues from around the world found the resources to institutionalize the work in which they had been engaged for decades.

Kathleen Staudt

Kathleen Staudt, a professor of political science at the University of Texas at El Paso, received her Ph.D. from the University of Wisconsin at Madison. She teaches courses on women, the border, policy, and comparative politics, and she has been an insider critic of the political science discipline, co-authoring, with William Weaver, *Political Science and Feminisms: Integration or Transformation*, published in 1997.

Her research agendas have gone through several phases. The first addressed gender bias in agricultural policies and programs for Kenyan farmers. Her 1990 volume, *Managing Development*, examined politics and policies in a way that wove gender throughout the text.

The second phase examined women's political activities, initially in Africa and then from comparative perspectives. With co-editors Sue Ellen Charlton, Jana Everett, and Jane Parpart, she published two volumes on women and the state. For the *Human Development Report* of 1995, she prepared a background paper on women and political representation worldwide. She also analyzed gender in bureaucratic politics in the USAID experience in *Women, Foreign Assistance, and Advocacy Administration* (1985) and comparative international and national organizations in *Women, International Development, and Politics: The Bureaucratic Mire* (1991, 1997). In the third phase Kathy focused on political economy at the U.S.-Mexico border in *Free Trade? Informal Economies at the U.S.-Mexico Border* (1998) and, with co-editor David Spener, in *The U.S.-Mexico Border: Transcending Divisions, Contesting Identities* (1998).

Currently, her research focuses on public schools, democratic education, and cross-border organizations, and she has two co-edited books forthcoming. Mother of a daughter and a son, she serves on several civic boards in the El Paso, Texas–Juarez, Mexico region.

Straddling Borders: Global to Local

The daughter of working-class parents, I grew up in Milwaukee, Wisconsin, in the industrial heartland of the United States. In the mid-1960s I responded to the idealistic call to serve in the Peace Corps, an experience that forever internationalized me. My mother worried about me and my father thought I was either gullible or crazy. Extensive service in the cause of social justice and the pursuit of knowledge is rare for people like him, people who are compelled to bring home paychecks from the mind-numbing work they do to survive. My father got his lifelong job during the Great Depression at an outboard motor factory (ironically, one that went "offshore" to Ciudad Juarez in the 1970s, just ten miles south of where I now live). My mother gave up paid work in a munitions factory during World War II for unpaid work in the postwar baby boom era and that factory also moved to Juarez later.

For eight years my education was Lutheran parochial, and the tough public junior and high schools were a shock to me. Though stifling, parochial education created a rock-solid foundation of idealistic values. The everyday experience of female economic dependency in my family also etched a deep impression in my soul. My mother's allowance from my father's salary set the stage for unhealthy social dynamics in our household. This cultural baggage still had no name or intellectual framework within which to grow and flourish.

In 1966 I took my first plane trip, going to Washington, D.C., for three months of Peace Corps training, including intensive Tagalog language immersion, after which I went to the Philippines. Women's liberation had yet to permeate my being, so I did little critical reflection about gender structures beyond the United States or within its borders in making my own life choices. The university was not yet in my future, but I would be the first in my extended family to attend. The few girls who pursued higher education in my neighborhood became teachers and nurses; the majority worked for pay as secretaries or as homemakers in an era and class where child care centers were not the norm.

After two years in the Philippines I returned to the United States in culture shock, as many former Peace Corps volunteers called it. At the University of Wisconsin in Milwaukee, I chose political science as my major because it directly addressed the policies and collective action issues so central to my budding student activism regarding U.S. foreign policy—especially the Vietnam War—welfare rights, and women's liberation. We undergraduates made unrealistic demands on institutions, especially universities that had no authority to respond to those demands, but it was good practice, however ineffective. My professors in the nearly all-male departments were wonderful mentors. Only in graduate school at the

University of Wisconsin in Madison did I begin to comprehend academic political science as a huge male bastion with its own historical baggage and demographics and its mainstream research agendas.

Few women pursued graduate studies or served in faculty positions in those days. Just one in seven political science Ph.D.s were awarded to women in the early 1970s, and political science faculties were overwhelmingly male. The disciplinary mainstream was devoted to American politics and to men in politics, except in political behavioral studies that included women as the demographic variable called "sex." Although women's studies programs were beginning to develop, political science was a latecomer. I remember Jane Jaquette's criticism concerning how inhospitable the discipline was to research on women, feminism, and women students and faculty. At the University of Wisconsin, the lone female political science faculty member had no interest in these topics. As pioneering students we had to figure out how to build support among men with only lukewarm interest in topics outside their disciplinary mainstream.

Kenya and Agriculture

At the time, the study of Africa offered inspiration and hope, given the emergence of the continent's newly independent countries. My early graduate coursework, emphasizing the state's role in activating development strategies, contained shockingly few references to women farmers, who were and are the major food producers in many parts of Africa. With only a footnote here and a paragraph there, it seemed irrational to me to exclude, in both research and policy terms, analytic attention to women producers. When I proposed a Ph.D. dissertation topic on the distribution of agricultural services to Kenyan men and women farmers, faculty advisers wondered was this *really* political science? Shouldn't I be in anthropology? And who was this Ester Boserup anyway? To academics and activists who would soon identify their work as women in development, or WID, economist Ester Boserup's *Women's Role in Economic Development* was the godmother treatment of the field; to my male advisers, she was no political scientist. My proposed dissertation, straddling comparative politics and public administration, involved sampling men and women farmers, but policy impact studies back then either did not differentiate gender or, more commonly, excluded women. In this context my commitment to the incipient WID research and action movement was born.

In Kenya I met women who had an interest in the research for the sake of knowledge and for its potential influence on policy. In 1974 and 1975 Achola Pala (who later added the surname Okeyo) and I affiliated as dissertation researchers with the Institute for Development Studies at the University of Nairobi. We were the only two researchers at the time focusing on women, and most of the other researchers treated us as irrelevant.

However, in Nairobi I met women who took an interest in us and our research: Peg Snyder who, with Mary Tadesse, worked in the African Women's Training and Research Centre of the United Nations Economic Commission for Africa; women with the Ford and Rockefeller Foundations; and women in various UN agencies such as the United Nations Children's Emergency Fund (UNICEF). Only later would I learn that many of these women were operating from marginal spaces with meager resources in their own institutions, an experience I later shared when I joined the small women in development enclave of the United States Agency for International Development (USAID). We all learned the importance of forging ties both inside and outside the institutions for which we worked from the tenuous insider enclaves we occupied.

The University of Nairobi's Institute for Development Studies put affiliated researchers through a useful exercise that required personal discipline and writing with speed. Before ending the usual yearlong research experience, affiliates were expected to produce a working paper with policy recommendations. I tabulated my 212 farmer household surveys by hand in order to write my paper and deliver it before departure for the United States. This modest, hand-typed and mimeographed research paper got on the Institute's distribution list and thus in the hands of many activists in the region.

My paper compared the forty percent of female-managed farms to jointly managed farms, showing that all farms depended on female labor and that women managers adopted new crops as fast as men, despite their systematically inferior access to government agricultural extension services, training, and credit. Much data was mined from my dissertation, which was later published in academic journals and assigned as readings in university courses. My approach fueled a variety of other WID research agendas. More importantly, my paper was used to justify program changes in the Kenyan Ministry of Agriculture to focus more resources on women farmers, reduce the bifurcation of agriculture and home economics, and recruit more female extension officers. It was also used to influence policies and programs of the United Nations and bilateral development organizations such as USAID.

Politics and Power Struggles

Back home, my experiences were mixed. Dissertation advisers now viewed my research as credible, rigorous, and even pathbreaking, but earlier struggles in political science impelled me to ground the theoretical frameworks, methods, and analysis deeply in that discipline. When I completed my Ph.D. work in 1976, only thirteen percent of political scientists were female and few departments had a women in politics course in their curricula. In addition to myself, only one woman who had entered the Ph.D. program at Wisconsin in 1971 survived the grueling but stimulating experience. We struggled and knew we had to continue struggling in whatever institution of higher education we would join. However, I was invited to teach the first course on women in politics in the University of Wisconsin's political science department. That opportunity helped ground me in U.S. women's studies. My dissertation had attributed women farmers near exclusion from government benefits to their political powerlessness. The Wisconsin course on women and politics increased my expertise on women's political powerlessness in U.S. politics.

The search for a full-time academic position was hard for women in the 1970s, and especially hard for those seeking to teach women's studies or women in politics. These subfields received no respect and limited visibility. Mainstream journals rarely published the research in these new areas. I remember waiting to see how the African Studies Association would classify my dissertation in its annual listing, given the word "women" in my title, but it didn't seem to fit their categories and just fell through the cracks without any listing at all. One of the first thoroughly mainstream journals to which I submitted a revised dissertation chapter didn't even bother to send it out to peer reviewers. I recovered from the trauma, sent it to another journal, and eventually, it was published. I reflect back on all this as fortifying and strengthening my resolve and skills. I expected to work twice as hard as my colleagues so I wrote scores of refereed articles to develop a record that could never be used to justify the denial of academic tenure and promotion.

In 1977 I was one of 250 applicants for a Third World Politics–Women in Politics position at the University of Texas at El Paso. Many Ph.D. holders then were driving taxis, but I got the job. With a faculty line in women and in comparative politics, I created a new course, Women, Power, and Politics. It became a core course in the new women's studies minor at El Paso because with English department colleagues, I maneuvered it through the highly political university curriculum committees.

At USAID: A New Turn

In 1978, having worked only a year in my tenure-track position at El Paso, I took a risk. I applied, under the Intergovernmental Personnel Act, to be on loan to the Women in Development Office at USAID (USAID WID) as a social science analyst. I sought this position because of the opportunity to work with powerful political women such as Arvonne Fraser and Elsa Chaney. I'd met Arvonne at the National Women's Conference in 1977 and had long admired Elsa's research on women and politics in Latin America. I also realized that the job offered me a rich opportunity to challenge bureaucracy from the inside.

My expertise in agriculture and public administration proved useful to the WID Office. I dove with great relish into procedural manuals, served on oversight committees, and communicated daily with the complex individuals who were in strategic positions to approve, revise, or deny projects and funds with gender consequences. I understood the overwhelming mission our office had: to implement a congressional mandate that was virtually ignored within USAID. True implementation of that mandate to integrate women into its development programs would involve transforming USAID, with its staff of over 5,000, its approximately sixty field offices abroad, and its project budgets in the millions of dollars.

USAID WID was an egalitarian, mostly female office of from five to seven professionals with a daunting mission to challenge a bureaucracy almost one thousand times larger. We all drew on past strengths for our twelve-to-fourteen-hour days with incredible workloads. One of our tasks was to try to define women in development in a way that differentiated it from the equal employment opportunity office, where it had originally been situated, and from the traditional population and family planning initiatives that most of the agency thought was its contribution to women.

Then as now, I was amazed at the power of staff, including mid-level staff, to advance or undermine policy and program initiatives. A desk officer, for example, assigned to note taking at a meeting, could remember (or forget) to make women farmers visible when writing summaries of the meeting consensus during the project proposal process. I felt that my time was best utilized applying expertise followed with relentless persistence and follow-up with the people who make things happen in paper-pushing everyday bureaucracies.

The year I spent in USAID transformed my primary research agenda from agricultural policy to gender politics in bureaucracy. I witnessed and analyzed the bureaucratic resistance to women's programs, treating my year on loan as a research experience. I believed that if I didn't write about it after this experience, it would take years before these patterns would have a name and an analysis. I wrote daily, evenings, and weekends, ethnographic style, filling six fat notebooks. My first publication returning to academia was on this bureaucratic resistance. In later years, people working in or interacting with development institutions who had read my publication would write to me from different parts of the world about how their everyday bureaucratic problems now had a name.

Staff members in the WID Office had assignments in the oversight work of USAID's major mission: creating fundable projects implemented in sixty-some countries around the world. One of my first assignments involved tackling the huge procedural manuals in the incredibly bureaucratic process of bringing a project idea through its various stages of development and approval. I didn't view this task with disdain, understanding that procedures are the tools and levers by which policies such as women in development become visible, are addressed, and incorporated into the everyday work of all staff. Systems can be changed. The trick is to figure out how.

Given my research and writing on agricultural programs, I was assigned liaison work with the Africa Bureau. (One never had credibility as a "one-agenda [that is, a women's agenda] person.") One of my most vivid memories is of an absurd Project Identification Document Review that illustrated staff ignorance of women's agricultural labor in a West African country.

"Women farmers in West Africa?" a man inquired incredulously. "Ha! Just like when women worked in factories during World War II? Let's not get into a war about this!"

I handled the conversation seriously but pleasantly, knowing that insults rarely are a basis for alliance building. The country desk officer summarized our WID concerns in the widely disseminated telegram-like memo that is the means for communication throughout the agency USAID, with the State Department, and country missions. "We got an inch in the cable traffic," we cheered back in the office, since the memo meant that WID expertise was brought into the preparation of a complex project proposal. Eventually, when the project was finally designed and approved this meant resources for women farmers, recruitment of female agricultural staff, and higher-education training and curriculum development in that country.

Yet detailed oversight, country program expertise, and personal follow-through were all difficult to sustain, considering that our office was hard-pressed to review the great piles of project materials we received. Our supposed allies and liaison officers in other agency bureaus often wore multiple hats. Some had the WID assignment added to too many other assignments; others lacked interest or expertise. At times our struggles to transform the bureaucracy seemed overwhelming, but I was sustained by the opportunity to collect and document information on women's institutional advocacy.

Our WID Office tried to get a handle on what the whole agency was doing, where it was being done, and with what budgetary amounts. We called this the "tracking system." However, we had to depend on field staff—many of whom were either clueless or hostile to the idea of integrating women into the development process—to report activities and provide financial data for our system. I remember the shock, when we compiled the report, in finding that the agency allocated just two percent of its budget to women in development (thus ninety-eight percent to men!). This reporting tool was, however, a useful way to bring visibility to the problem and to build rationales for allocating more resources for women-specific and women-integrated projects. Using our tracking system and the report, the network of constituents in the Coalition for Women in Development, an outside group, could use both the data and the report as they made their rounds inside the agency and out. But the many diverse constituencies within USAID also prompted inevitable competition as scarce resources were prioritized and divided up among those seeking consulting opportunities or funds for their projects in various sites around the world.

Connecting Scholars and Activists with Government

Arvonne and Elsa pursued policy strategies with a political sense. They understood the importance of collaborating with scholar activists and developed a network among them. Most agency bureaucrats had neither time nor inclination to engage in the sort of lifelong learning that makes one's work effective, but they had a grudging respect for scholarly research. Thus, networking with scholars and activists who had done methodical analysis and research on development topics and shared an interest in women's issues was in the interests of our office. Many in our scholar-activist network were at land grant universities with USAID contractual relationships, particularly on agricultural projects whose contractors did little to respond to the WID mandate. People such as Kate Cloud and Helen Henderson at the University of Arizona and many others worked with our office to try to influence the male-dominated contractor groups. Each university WID group had unique relations with U.S.-oriented women's studies groups ranging from positive to neutral to negative.

At the 1979 National Women's Studies Association (NWSA), our WID Office at USAID sought to connect with the members of that organization. Our goal was to interest them in the field of women in development, which meant broadening their perspectives to include women internationally. We were not successful. NWSA was a large, highly charged group of diverse women—academic researchers, and activists—many marginalized in their own male-dominated institutions. Many nonpolitical people pay little attention to the complexities, fragmentation, and contradictions of government agencies. Others, still remembering painfully the Vietnam War, mentally merged all foreign policy institutions. Some probably thought USAID and the CIA—the Central Intelligence Agency—were one and the same. Our women in development group and we, as individuals, were viewed as tainted, as affiliates of the enemy because we worked in a government agency. Some NWSA members got so exercised that our exhibit was almost trashed, and a resolution was passed that banned USAID participation in the association along with what were labeled as other imperialist, classist, racist, and sexist organizations. Alas, this culture of confrontation within the association began to unravel it from the inside out over other "diversity" issues in future years.

Our unsuccessful attempt to build a bridge with the NWSA, or even to converse about our struggles as we worked every day in our obviously male-dominated organization, was a low point in my life. It illustrated the difficulty at that time of connecting U.S. feminists, occupying marginal space within a country containing just five percent of the global population, with those in the other ninety-five percent of the world. What made matters worse was my follow-up attempt to explain why our office was represented at the meeting in a short essay for a NWSA publication. I was horrified when the editor imposed a new title, "In Defense of AID," that did not reflect the content of my essay.

Influencing International Institutions

While many of my USAID experiences were grim, others were packed with insights and, ultimately, influence. One vivid example involved preparations for the UN Food and Agricultural Organization's (FAO) World Conference on Agriculture and Agrarian Reform and Development in 1979, informally known as WCAARD. With Elsa, incoming WID Office deputy director Paula Goddard, scholar-bureaucrat-anthropologist Emmy Simmons, and Charlie Paolillo, deputy director of the agency's policy bureau, we supplied recommendations and intensive training for U.S. representatives who advocated successfully for progressive positions on women's land ownership, income-generating activities, and credit in the conference resolutions. Our work was printed and distributed to delegates to that conference and to others in a *Background Documents* collection that put me at some ease, for I rarely relax until words are on paper.

We were all delighted when the final report of the conference contained a whole section on the integration of women in rural development. It urged governments to consider repealing laws that discriminated against women in inheritance, ownership, and control of property and effectively inhibited women's economic participation, and called for providing women access to rural services. The report also urged the establishment of recruitment and training programs in the extension services and for increased education and employment opportunities for women by, among other things, promoting income-generating opportunities for women and guaranteeing equal rights. It also noted the importance of women's organizations in facilitating women's participation in the economic, political, and social activities of a nation. It called for establishing or revising data collection systems to recognize women's participation in economic development and urged the establishment of day care and other services to ease the burden of women's household work so they could participate in educational, economic, and political activities. Finally, the report called attention to the section on rural women in the Plan of Action adopted at the world women's conference.

Of course, to implement these recommended policies meant insiders and outsiders would have to engage in struggles, but at least we had the right words on paper with the UN imprimatur. One insider, Natalie Hahn of FAO, with the collaboration of women's groups lobbying the UN Commission on the Status of Women, was successful. She was instrumental in getting all of these recommendations inserted in a special article in the Convention on the Elimination of Discrimination Against Women that was adopted by the UN General Assembly later in 1979.

Globalizing the Local

Toward the end of my tenure at USAID, the election of Ronald Reagan in 1980 brought doubts about the survival of the WID Office. That under-lined for me the importance of long-term work in academia: teaching, research, and writing about women and gender. Returning to the University of Texas at El Paso, I became engaged in organizing at mid-institutional levels, building coalitions for change, and connecting my research-teaching mission to practice. With a critical mass of just five female faculty members, we built a women's studies program that continues to sustain itself. We val-ued each other enough to avoid the splits previously encountered in women's studies.

After my two children were born in the mid-1980s, I focused on global-izing the local on the U.S.-Mexico border but continued work with interna-tional organizations bent on empowering women. Living and teaching in El Paso, at the international border with Mexico, global-local connections are always obvious. With the support of Partners for the Americas for the women's health activists who head many Planned Parenthood offices, I worked with El Paso health activist Patti Pagels and with Mexican family planning workers. Sally Yudelman of the Inter-American Foundation—a rare grassroots-oriented institution—and I worked with a women's advo-cacy organization in Ciudad Juarez, just next to El Paso in the nearly two-million-person metropolitan area that spans the border. Then, with Beatriz Vera, Gay Young, and the late Guillermina Villalva Valdez, we addressed women workers' problems in the foreign export processing factories known as *maquiladoras*. (Cuidad Juarez is the maquiladoras capital of Mexico.)

For all the praise about Mexico's "transition to democracy," civic activists still have great difficult obtaining political accountability, professional response from the criminal justice system, or even respectful acknowledge-ment of public problems, particularly those affecting women and families from poverty backgrounds. In late 2001 the cross-border Coalition Against Violence was born at a solidarity conference that brought together labor and anti-violence organizers consisting of students, teachers, and represen-tatives of anti-violence service centers. Our focus is on the murders of girls and women over the last decade and on the organized interests that are stakeholders in government accountability. Cross-border actions are politi-cally complicated, but we have developed a series of recommendations that include short- and long-term actions for Mexico and the United States through the executive, legislative, and judicial branches of governments.

My interests in women's acquisition of political power in national set-tings and within institutional spaces remain my research passions and activist agenda. In the mid-1980s Jane Jaquette and I made presentations at the National Democratic Institute for International Affairs conference on women and politics organized by Vivian Derryck and Arvonne Fraser. It was exciting to be present among the increasingly powerful political women leaders from around the world. But we all knew there was much more to be done if women were to achieve any kind of political parity with men and if women's interests were to be adequately addressed. Strategically placed women—and a few men—within United Nations institutions also shared these concerns, though their voices were often constrained behind bureaucratic doors. The UN Division for the Advancement of Women sought to put women's political representation on the UN agenda and regularly to collect and report data on obvious gender inequalities.

In 1989 I was asked to write a monograph called *Women in High-Level Political Decision Making* for a UN-sponsored conference in Vienna. It was one of the first comprehensive studies to examine women's proportional representation in different ideological and political institutions. The monograph contained data not only on parliaments, legislatures, presidencies and prime ministers, but also on cabinets and cabinet portfolios. In a room of women representatives who wrote country case studies, we hammered out recommendations on political power and decision making that would inform the division's strategies and later the Fourth World Conference on Women at Beijing in 1995.

The division's deputy, John Matthiason, was a skilled veteran in the complexities of crafting language for ideologically diverse participants and we created strong language regarding data collection and for subsequent recommendations on women's political power. Later I analyzed UN agencies for their women and gender strategies. Kristen Timothy, another skilled UN veteran, worked with me to formulate concrete recommendations for the Beijing conference out of occasionally vague institutional documents. In another opportunity to influence international thinking, I prepared a monograph on women's political power and representation for the United Nations Development Program's 1995 *Human Development Report*, a special issue devoted to gender. It was republished in UNDP's *Background Papers* for 1996.

Meanwhile, back at the border, I brought another international development concept home—informal work, or income-generating self-help initiatives operating outside official regulation on both sides of the U.S.-Mexican border. The comparative laboratory was a perfect one, and thanks to the National Science Foundation I obtained support for a team in which students could acquire research expertise. As faculty coordinator for the university's Institute for Community-Based Teaching and Learning, known as Community Partnerships, we connect university courses, community organizations, and public schools so that students' coursework includes action research and experience, thereby deepening their learning and making them responsive to community needs. Community partnerships are in place with the local Industrial Areas Foundation (IAF), which organizes parental engagement in historically neglected public schools, and with immigration advocacy organizations and cross-border NGOs like the Federación Mexicana de Asociaciones Privadas, an organization with chapters in 45 Mexican cities, under the leadership of Guadalupe de la Vega and Enrique Súarez. IAF organizing, with teachers and mothers (many of the latter from Mexico), resembles a women's movement, but one based on practical interests such as schools, water, and job training for displaced workers. This seems like WID in action, working through educational institutions.

Have I lost my way, diverting from research and action on women internationally and on politics and gender? I think not. My local community is international. My strategic location, at the front lines of global economic change and at an international border, embraces many current development issues. Unlike USAID in the late 1970s, whose leaders defined its mission apart from women and gender, my university now views community outreach, regional research, and innovation as congenial with its mission. With ten percent of our student body from Juarez, Mexico, I work enthusiastically in cross-border coalitions, straddling institutions and building bridges among diverse stakeholders with a deep commitment to justice and the rule of law. I believe it imperative to connect activists, practitioners, and policy makers. Early involvement in the women in development movement offered inspiration, mentors, and organizing strategies for the border-straddling work I now do with other women and some progressive men.

Eddah W. Gachukia

Eddah Wacheke Gachukia is an educator and women's development and rights activist whose work spans four decades. Born and reared in rural colonial Kenya, her parents belonged to the first generation of Kenyans to acquire education. Eddah attended the only high school for African girls, studied at Makerere University, and obtained her Ph.D. in literature from the University of Nairobi in 1981, where she has also taught. In Kenya's women's movement, she held leadership positions in several organizations, including Maendeleo Ya Wanawake and the National Council of Women of Kenya.

She served two terms (1974–83) as a member of Parliament, led the Kenyan delegation to the International Women's Year Conference in Mexico, was a delegate to the second women's conference at Copenhagen in 1980, and was elected leader of the Kenyan NGO Committee that hosted the NGO Forum at Nairobi in 1985. Founding chair of the African Women's Development and Communication Network in 1992, she helped to found the Forum for African Women Educationalists (FAWE), and was its first executive director.

She has served on the boards of many organizations, including Kenya Airways, the National Housing Corporation, Uchumi Supermarkets, the Population Council, the United States International University, and Civicus. She chairs the board of the Collaborative Centre for Gender and Development and has served as a consultant to many international organizations including UNICEF, the United Nations Development Program, the World Bank, and UNESCO.

Together with her husband Daniel, a former diplomat and company director, she manages the Riara Group of Schools that provides preschool, primary, and high school education. They have four children and Eddah longs to spend time with her nine grandchildren.

Education, Women, and Politics in Kenya

I was told that she ran away from home. She had heard of a new school for girls at a time when she was also in the process of being married off to an elderly man with five wives and children older than herself. So she decided to run away. The elders met to discuss her behavior. "Her mother was all to blame," they said, "for letting a girl ripe for marriage, whose dowry had already been delivered, out of her sight." There were rumors of a white man who was luring girls away from home for a so-called education that ruined them. News from another ridge was that a girl who had gone to the white man's school had refused to marry the man earmarked for her and instead had gone to the town to become a "bad woman" in the name of a course in nursing.

She would have been ostracized by the clan, except for what happened eight months later, just before her case was due for review. She came home carrying huge baskets full of maize on her back. That was not all. She needed the help of her younger sister to collect her entire harvest. The young woman who had nearly faced a curse from her people had ended up filling her mother's granary. The elders could hardly believe what they were seeing. Any education that resulted in filling a mother's store when other people's stores were only half full should be given a chance. What if the whole thing was a trick by the white man? Not believing what they saw, two emissaries were sent off to spy around the school. Their report confirmed the school girls were taught not only the virtue of hard work, but had been allocated a parcel of land each for practical work. What more could the elders say? Come the next term, she was actually allowed not only to return to school, but also to take her younger sister with her. All this happened in the 1920s.

"She" was my mother, Wanjiku. Although she died when I was six, I still remember certain things about her that other mothers in our village did not do, such as reading the Bible to us. The Bible was the only book in the house, but my mother taught me the elementary aspects of reading and writing before I entered school. She gave me a head start others did not have. Having tasted education, mother wanted her children educated, too. Our home was almost an island among a conservative people to whom educating girls was a waste of money and time. What would girls do with education? The whole goal of a girl's life was marriage. All a girl needed was to learn hard work from her mother.

Standard Five was the last class in my primary school. The nearest school offering the next level was sixteen miles away. Distance alone was not as bad as being the only girl in the class for a whole year, with older men and boys who were male chauvinists and did not understand what a girl was doing in their class. This was a challenge for me and I worked very hard to beat them. It was a very lonely year.

Boarding school was much better. Since we were all girls, we were protected from long journeys to and from school, hard labor before and after school, the vagaries of weather and dangers of crossing swollen rivers, teasing from boys especially for scoring higher marks, and men who were now hunting for literate girls to marry. The school curriculum, however, was heavily biased toward the teaching of home-based skills in the name of "housewifery." After every holiday the school lost several girls who had either been forced into marriage or voluntarily opted for marriage rather than continuing their education.

A frequent source of conflict that bothered me was female circumcision. Some girls who had undergone the rite, believing in their own superiority, demanded respect and special treatment from the uncircumcised. Unknowingly, I longed to go through this traditional rite that was supposed to confer maturity and dignity on me, but my staunch Christian father would hear none of it.

High school was most enjoyable. We lived and learned with girls from all over Kenya and had a library with books, British magazines, and newspapers. I found school easy and led my house in singing competitions. I was also a sharp shooter in net ball and remember creating a small organization of girls from my district, Kiambu, and organizing an entertainment program for the school on the weekends.

From there it was on to Makerere University, then a college of London University. My grandmother was upset. When would all this education end? Was it not time for marriage? Yet the name Makerere earned you a lot of respect, and being a teacher coming from Makerere meant being well regarded because we were well taught. It was at Makerere that I met Daniel, my husband, father of my children, but above all, my intellectual companion. I enjoyed total support from him in all the work I have undertaken, whether within the family, as a student through the post-graduate level, as a teacher and university lecturer, as a parliamentarian, in national and international leadership, and in all my work with women and girls and for them.

I am a staunch believer in God. How else would a child who had lost a mother at the age of six not only survive but live to do the things I have been involved in? The significance of my mother's and my own story is that many girls in Africa and developing countries elsewhere face the same constraints in education that both my mother's generation and my own suffered, some of which still persist in some African communities at the beginning of the twenty-first century.

The irony of these two stories—my mother's and my own—is that many girls in Africa and other developing countries face the same constraints in education that both my mother's generation and my own suffered. For over eighty years, we have struggled with the same issues and problems. Only recently, the press in Kenya narrated a story of a sick man who tried to sell off his daughter for 22,000 Kenya shillings, a mere U.S. $300, to raise money for his medical treatment. The significant difference is that those involved in this case were arrested. Three people were jailed. After several decades of advocacy and intensive awareness building, the law now supports girls' education as a basic right.

We have certainly come a long way. In July 2001, three girls from different communities in Kenya sought refuge at different centers, most of them religiously based, to escape forced marriage. All three were given special protection to continue with their education. What is new, in addition to the legal protections that now exist, is the young girls' higher level of knowledge and their awareness of their right to education.

Introduction to the Women's Movement

Early in my life, one did not question the African tradition. It was a given. It was clear even to young children that although all children were loved, boys were preferred. As a young person living under the colonial system, one was initiated early into a world characterized by injustices, inequalities, and open discrimination. As a high school girl I could not fail to notice the superior facilities enjoyed by European and Asian girls in their separate schools. On our way back from some tournament or other in these schools, we would sing songs decrying such blatant discrimination and promising ourselves that their days were numbered.

As we approached political independence, we were gaining sufficient courage to question the double standard. New houses were planned for teachers at the school where Daniel and I taught. One plan was for the Europeans and the other for Africans. My husband and I looked at the plans and noted the ridiculously minor, yet critical details that distinguished the two. Among these were a verandah, shelves, and cupboards, in the kitchen, electrical sockets for kettles, a cooker, a fridge and an iron-box. We raised the matter at the next staff meeting, wondering whether such discriminatory practice was dictated from government headquarters or from the school management. Needless to say, the issue thoroughly embarrassed the Head and his team but it marked the end of all such discrimination in that school.

The denial of admission for African and Asian children in the only good primary school in our town was another issue that provoked my conscience and spirit of activism to change the status quo. The school was reserved for European children, but since they were too few students it did not qualify for government support. Many Europeans were already leaving Kenya because they had no faith in an African led government. Later, the European parents preferred to close down the school and send their children to Europeans-only boarding schools, rather than admit African and Asian children.

Introduction to the Women's Movement

As Kenya approached political independence, we were gaining sufficient courage to question the gender double standard. My involvement in the women's movement stemmed from my protests against discrimination that targeted Africans in general. The European school in our town refused to admit African children. Deciding that something needed to be done to improve the local school primary school for African children, I convened the first group of African women in Thika town. Our small group grew into an active branch of the national Maendeleo Ya Wanawake Organization (Progress of Women), the ideal forum for the articulation of women's views as our country approached independence from colonial rule. In my leadership capacity I represented Thika District in the First and Second National Kenya Women's Seminars in 1962 and 1963 and interacted with women leaders not only from Kenya but the Eastern African region, along with Europe and America.

Among the women who influenced my thinking in the early 1960s was Margaret Kenyatta, the founder-chairperson of the National Council of Women of Kenya who later served as mayor of Nairobi and president of the UN Conference on Women at Nairobi in 1985. Another influential woman was Maria Nyerere. In her opening address to the Second National Kenya Women's Seminar, she expressed statements that were to guide my entire career as a leader of the women's movement in Kenya and Africa. There, she said:

> Many of the women present at this seminar are, or will be, leaders in their community. We must all recognize that leadership cannot be exercised in a spirit of pride, and should not have privilege attached to it. We shall only be effective leaders and teachers if we enter into this work because of a desire to serve our people and our country. We should not look for rewards, nor even for gratitude.

There was also Eseza Makumbi, member of the Ugandan Legislative Assembly who, in a memorable address, drew a contrast between the status of the African woman in the past and the present. She spoke of the woman of the past as being in an "inferior position as a wife" and as "an inferior being in marriage ready to serve, obey and love her husband as it suited him." In contrast, "the new woman [was] caught up in a situation of dynamic change, conscious of herself as an individual with needs and ideas to express, a partner in marriage, in the upbringing of children and in family decision making, and as a responsible citizen with important roles beyond the family." Mrs. Makumbi called on all women, especially the lucky few who had acquired education, to volunteer their services beyond their homes and jobs.

In 1963 I won a British Council scholarship to study language teaching at Leeds University in the United Kingdom. Already a mother of three, I decided there was no way I was going to leave my children behind in Africa. Friends in London arranged for the care of the children there. I would at least be able to visit them during vacations. My husband was already studying in France. I was not aware that I was raising a major gender issue that still haunts many African women. Many years later, as I evaluated donor support to women's education, I raised questions about scholarships for women to pursue higher education that did not include an allowance for family support.

The stint at Leeds University allowed me to specialize as a language teacher and also to make contact with the international women's movement. I was frequently invited to functions of organizations such as the University Women's Association, the Federation of Business and Professional Women, and the Girl Guides Association. Several times I addressed such gatherings on the situation of women and girls in Africa. In 1965 I went to my first international gathering when Maendeleo nominated me to represent Kenyan women at the triennial Conference of the Associated Country Women of the World (ACWW) in Dublin. I was then living in Paris as a diplomat's wife. Having no funds to send delegates all the way from Nairobi, Maendeleo officials decided to send two of us who were already in Europe. This trip turned out to be a turning point in my involvement in the women's movement in Kenya.

There were only three Africans at the ACWW conference, which placed the burden on us to clearly articulate issues affecting women on our continent. Women from Asia were more advanced in this process and we learned a lot from them. I attempted a bid for the next conference held in Nairobi, but Australia won. Still, my report back to Maendeleo at the next general meeting was so well received that I was elected—in my absence—as vice-president of the national organization.

Those were hard days in Maendeleo, with hardly any funding to facilitate program work. As volunteers we had to depend on our individual resources, since membership fees were not adequate for establishing a secretariat. In recognition of our work in mobilizing poor women for development and after a spirited petitioning campaign, the government did second an officer to assist in coordinating volunteer efforts.

Later, with the dynamic Jane Kiano as Maendeleo's president and me as national secretary, we undertook a national mobilization campaign to recruit members. We also sent petitions to the government and appeals to President Mzee Jomo Kenyatta for the inclusion of women in decision-making positions. Then, in 1974, I represented Maendeleo at the next ACWW conference in Perth, Australia, in a two-women delegation. As in the previous conference, we found ourselves leading some sessions and being key speakers at others. With Maendeleo growing stronger in Kenya, the government supported our application to hold the 1977 conference in Nairobi. Our bid was successful and on arriving back home this captured serious media attention.

Meanwhile, we received a big surprise in October 1974 when President Kenyatta nominated me to Parliament to represent women's interests. I was frightened by the challenge. How did one combine politics with family life? What worried me was that this was not just another job. Rather, it was a very public role, always under the threat of censorship for statements made. Consulting with women's groups and organizations on pertinent issues was easy, but learning parliamentary procedures and practices was a challenge.

At that time we were in the process of preparations for the International Women's Year Conference 1975 at Mexico City. In my new capacity as the women's representative in Parliament, I was appointed leader of the Kenya delegation. Although the themes of the conference—equality, development, and peace—were and remain important, our priorities in Kenya were different. While for women from developed countries the issue that resonated most was equality, in most provinces of Kenya the priority was bringing water closer to homes.

Returning from Mexico City, we wrote a detailed report on what was expected of the government in implementation of the Plan of Action that came out of the conference. That was when we realized the danger of a low-key delegation, without top government representation. The effort to draw up concrete plans for the implementation of the Plan of Action was generally limited to the Women's Bureau, which the government established in 1976. But it was clear that despite our small number, we had listened to Kenyan women's priorities and were determined to respond to them.

Therefore, the National Council of Women in Kenya (NCWK), of which I was elected chairperson in 1976, launched the well-celebrated Kenya Water for Health Organization (KWAHO) initially known as the United Nations Children's Emergency Fund-NGO Water for Health Program. I recall an outstanding health expert, Dr Muringo Kiereine, led our think tank on the issue and the very community oriented Wambui Njenga who was the original coordinator. Margaret Mwangola took over the coordination in 1979 and the programme continues to be a successful, broader program of clean water.

Soon after its start-up of KWAHO, the National Council launched the Greenbelt Movement in an effort to stem the increasing rate of desertification in Kenya. Its think tank was led by the internationally celebrated environmentalist Wangari Maathai. The movement remains at the front line in the fight against public land grabs and environmental degradation motivated by greed.

I facilitated the birth of these two community-based initiatives, whose success in addressing felt needs have been well documented. Through these two activities we introduced the concept of community and women's ownership of development programs. An essential component of KWAHO projects is the training of women in the operation and maintenance of water pumps and other equipment. The two programs were also key to the establishment of very strong linkages between rural- and urban-based women's groups. My three years in the NCWK leadership also witnessed the acquisition of financial support from a donor partner, the Carnegie Corporation, which enabled us to establish a full-time secretariat and run a regular magazine, *Kenya Woman,* and even buy a vehicle for fieldwork. We established several sub-committees that were active on issues affecting women and children. Some of them later developed into autonomous organizations affiliated to the council. This specialization enhanced the quality of our work through contributions of professional and research experts.

The Political Front

My career as a member of parliament representing women's interests enabled me to scrutinize legislation to ensure its appropriateness for meeting the needs of women. We also had a great struggle to provide paid maternity leave in the Employment Bill, finally settling for two months only and the loss of annual leave for a woman during the year she uses maternity leave. The Pensions Amendment Bill of 1978, as tabled, assumed that only men served on permanent and pensionable terms in the civil service and that only men had dependents. I was able to move for the use of "spouse" in place of "widow." The original amendment also stated that a woman would receive her husband's pension only for as long as "she remained of good character," clearly a ridiculous provision. The amended bill referred to both women and men.

One needed to do a lot of homework and cover a lot of ground to ensure effective and informed participation in the House. I found many male colleagues to be patronizing. With only four women in a Parliament of one hundred and eighty, we did our best. I served a second term after my selection by President Daniel Arap Moi in 1979. As a women's representative I found myself traveling all over the country conducting fundraising drives for women's groups' activities that included revolving funds, raising livestock, bee and poultry keeping, making handicrafts, water, home improvement. It was a very exciting time for women's development, with international donor partners assisting women's organizations either directly or through the Women's Bureau. Together, women learned how to petition and demand their rights from extension services. Such was the dynamism of the women's movement in Kenya during the 1970s, and it was my privilege to be associated with it and to articulate its needs in the august House.

The 1970s also witnessed tremendous growth in the national women's movement, especially through the creation of specialized professional groups, stimulated by and affiliated to their international counterparts. I learned a great deal about financial and credit matters from Mary Okelo and Christine Hayanga, about law from Grace Githu, and about the health of women and children from Florence Manguyu. I believe networking with women in strategic positions was the women's movement's greatest strength.

Among my disappointments in Parliament was the shelving of the proposed Marriage Bill in 1982 that would have harmonized the various marriage laws still in force, especially the ambiguity and potential conflicts characterizing marital relationships. While providing for the mandatory registration of all marriages, the proposed bill sought to recognize as marriage any cohabitation lasting over three years. It also demanded that a man declare before a first marriage whether there was any possibility of future polygamy, a provision meant to protect women who did not wish to be drawn into polygamy against their will. The proposed bill would have also outlawed wife beating—allowed by African tradition—and made it a criminal offense. The overwhelmingly male parliament, however, rejected the bill. Ironically, soon after its rejection, Tanzania adopted a law similar to the one we proposed, entrenching women's rights in marriage and outlawing polygamy.

The failure of the bill in Kenya sparked an outcry from all women's organizations to deny votes for those who had slighted women during the debate. A male member of Parliament who had argued that wife beating was part of African culture never saw Parliament again. We have no doubt women's votes had something to do with it.

My years in Parliament were also a time of pressing for women's representation in public affairs. When an all-male commission was appointed to look into the terms of service of civil servants around 1981, I called the head of the Civil Service to remind him that the service was the largest employer of women in Kenya and that therefore women should sit on the commission. He told me point-blank that no qualified woman could be found to sit on it. I offered several names on the phone and he agreed those were qualified women. I then sent him a list of twenty names in an effort to prove that the issue was not qualifications but outright discrimination. That list was appreciated in official circles and led to further searches for women, who normally work efficiently but quietly, focusing on their immediate mandate and not likely to attract outside attention.

I thank God I lived to witness the tabling of a motion on affirmative action by Hon. Phoebe Asiyo. In 2000 the Affirmative Action Bill by Hon. Beth Mugo and the Equality Bill by Hon. Martha Karua were tabled. Both bills have generated a lively public debate without the hostility generated earlier.

From Copenhagen to Nairobi

In contrast to the Mexico City conference in 1975, Kenya sent a high-level delegation, led by the minister in charge of women's affairs, to the second conference at Copenhagen five years later. This was a clear indication of the government's commitment to women's interests, especially since—at the same time—Kenya was bidding to host the third conference in 1985. I recall the significant support from donor agencies that facilitated the inclusion of a good number of NGO representatives in the Kenya delegation and the delegations of other Third World nations. This ensured that the committees and workshops at both the UN conference and especially at the parallel NGO Forum had fair representation from the Third World, unlike the 1975 conference. The second conference was also important as the platform for launching the all-important Convention on the Elimination of All Forms of Discrimination Against Women. It was also important for the way it recognized the role of NGOs as complementary partners to governments in the promotion of women's development, especially in advocacy.

The year 1983 saw the end of my parliamentary career. I had just settled into the teaching of language and literature at the University of Nairobi when I heard of my election as the chairperson of the NGO Organizing Committee for FORUM 85. Key among the urgent tasks was an assessment of women's gains during the United Nations Decade for Women (1976–85) and the charting of a path for future action. The level of women's consciousness was remarkably high. They were determined to capitalize on the momentum of the conference and NGO forum of 1985 to secure commitments to the mainstreaming of their issues and concerns in all development programs. As I continued to spearhead women's issues after the conference, I focused my energies on two non-governmental organizations of which I am proud. These are the Forum for African Women Educationalists (FAWE) and the Collaborative Center for Gender and Development (CCGD).

Forum for African Women Educationalists

My pride in the Forum for African Women Educationalists is based on the determination of African women ministers of education and vice chancellors of universities make a significant difference in challenging the obstacles to girls' education in their countries. As FAWE's founding executive director, it was my pleasure to work with dynamic women politicians, academicians, and key allies in donor partner organizations. We created FAWE as a unique Pan African organization to move countries towards education for all, a UN goal, and within that context to address the issues affecting girls and women in education. Alarmed by the low participation rates of African girls and women in education and recognizing the crucial roles of women in development, FAWE identified its mission as that of helping assure that women and girls were an integral part of the intellectual and technical resource base needed for the survival and prosperity of Africa. We were aware of our comparative advantage as senior policy makers in education and as credible role models demonstrating the benefits of girls' education.

FAWE worked—and continues to work—with ministries of education and creates inter-sector partnerships to ensure two things: first, that gender equity is built into all educational policies and in all national development programs, and that where gender imbalances in education persist, positive and specific short-term affirmative action is taken to redress them; second, that there is continuous and rigorous debate about, and review of, all social policies that impinge on how education policy is developed and implemented.

FAWE's success is evident in the creation of a policy environment that is friendly to girls' education and the establishment of an impressive network in support of girls' education at national, regional, and international levels. Winning over male ministers of education to support girls' education in their countries was a great achievement. Creating essential linkages between research, policy making, and practice, we demonstrated successful strategies for accelerating girls' education and promoted women's leadership and policy-making skills within education through targeted capacity-building programs.

Since retiring from FAWE in 1998, I have derived great satisfaction from the way the media in Africa have assumed a central role in promoting girls' education. I am also sincerely complimented by the many invitations from FAWE national chapters, now numbering thirty-five, all over sub-Saharan Africa. I delight in joining them in celebrating their successful activities at the country level and found it a privilege working with the dynamic women in the chapters to translate their dream into reality.

Collaborative Center for Gender and Development

In 1994, concerned that a systematic analysis of how gender impacts all aspects of development still remained elusive, a group of us in Kenya founded the Collaborative Center for Gender and Development, commonly known as The Center. It contributes to understanding the gender perspective as a key imperative in change through training, research, advocacy, and publishing. As a nonprofit voluntary organization, the CCGD serves as a resource base for programs geared towards mainstreaming gender in all development processes. The Center's mission is to contribute, in a nonpartisan manner, to a gender-responsive transformation of society, to ensure the upholding of equity issues, to promote the well-being of individuals and communities, and to advance the development of democratic and gender-responsive cultures and institutions.

Its activities are aimed to promote gender-responsive policy formulation, programming, and implementation in all aspects of development by facilitating development of gender analysis skills and capacity for responsive organizational management. We address and attempt to redress the discriminatory practices that hinder development and perpetuate oppression by building capacities for gender training in development and training institutions using materials and information we either develop or acquire. At national, regional, and international levels our aim is to facilitate networking, collaboration, and program sharing and to lobby governments and nongovernmental organizations to assure gender fairness in all development programming and implementation. My greatest source of pride in The Center lies in its expanding scope and membership. Its impact on engendering Kenyan economic and parliamentary policies and processes is a dream come true for me.

We in the African women's movement have come a long way, but we still have a long way to go. The good news is that we have sharpened our tools; that there are many more of us; and that with improved communication channels, our networking has assumed remarkable efficiency, even within Africa. Women continue to respond to emerging challenges with tremendous energy. Among the responses are networks of widows, networks for peace, and networks of women living with HIV/AIDS. These represent the dynamism characterizing women's activities in Africa and ensure that African women will remain key participants in shaping our continent's destiny and that of the world.

Endnotes

Irene Tinker, "Introduction: Ideas into Action"

1. For summary of the economic debate and a discussion of its impact on women see chapters by Amartya Sen, Senauer, and Papanek in Tinker, *Persistent Inequalities.*

2. The distinct roles of activists, scholars, and practitioners is explored in my "The making of a field" in *Persistent Inequalities: Women and World Development.* Edited by Irene Tinker. New York: Oxford, 1990.

3. Amrita Basu expounds this variety in her edited book *The Challenge of Local Feminisms: Women's Movements in Global Perspective.*

4. Official documents from the four UN conferences for women and the text of the Convention on the Elimination of All Forms of Discrimination Against Women may be found in *The United Nations and the Advancement of Women: 1945-1995.* For commentary on the documents see Fraser, *The UN Decade for Women* and Pietila and Vickers, *Making Women Matter.*

5. An excellent source book on the history of women and the United Nations, including the UN Decade for Women, is Winslow, *Women, Politics, and the United Nations.*

6. Boserup in *My Professional Life and Publications 1929-1998* p. 49.

7. Ester Boserup condenses her ideas about women in her chapter in a book honoring her contributions, in Tinker, <u>Persistent Inequalities</u>. A full discussion of her work may be found in "Utilizing interdisciplinarity to analyze global socio-economic change: a Tribute to Ester Boserup," 2003, in *Global Tensions: Challenges and Opportunities in the Economy*, Lourdes Beneria, ed. London: Routledge Press. For her own presentation of the evolution and import of her ideas, see *My Professional Life and Publications 1929-1998* .

8. A summary of the goals and actions of the UN world conferences may be found in John W. Foster and Anita Anand, eds., *Whose World is it Anyway?* In one chapter of this book, Anand reviews women's issues within the context of other world conferences. See also Martha Chen, "Engendering world conferences: the international women's movements and the UN." in Weiss and Gordenker, eds., *NGOs, the UN, and Global Governance.*

9. The U.S. official position has once again reversed itself under the Bush administration. Political pressures against abortion has led the U.S. government to oppose the use of condoms despite their efficacy in preventing HIV/AIDS.

10. For example, the U.S. delegates were reprimanded in Copenhagen for attending a reception given by the Cambodian government-in-exile at a time the U.S. supported Pol Pot.

11. For greater detail about the policies and politics of the first three women's conferences, see Tinker & Jaquette, "UN Decade for Women: its impact and legacy," in *World Development*. Lucille

Mair provides an excellent view from the South in "Women: A decade is time enough," *Third World Quarterly*. West includes the 1995 conference in her "The United Nations women's conferences and feminist politics," in *Gender and Global Governance*, edited by Meyer and Prugl,1999.

12. The actions of women's organizations at these conferences and what were the implications for women are discussed in several chapters in *Gender and Global Governance*, edited by Meyer and Prugl, including my "Nongovernmental organizations: an alternative power base for women?" References are made to documents by women activists for the Human Rights (1993) and Population (1994) conferences.

Aziza Hussein, "Crossroads for Women at the UN"

1. This was my subjective assessment, but the official decision to nominate me had probably more to do with my previous experience as an official Egyptian delegate at the UN in 1955 when my husband, Dr. Ahmad Hussein, served as Egyptian ambassador to Washington.

2. Membership in the commission rotates every three years; states are elected according to a quota allocated to different geographical regions. The Arab countries left their seat vacant for a number of years, thus giving a Egypt a chance to be reelected from 1962 until 1977, when Libya was elected.

3. In Dublin I represented the Huda Shaarawi Association which had been a member of the International Alliance of Women since its establishment. Its founder, Huda Shaarawi, was the first Egyptian woman to remove her veil in public.

4. During my long tenure as Egypt's representative on the Commission on the Status of Women, from 1962 to 1977,

the government provided me with the highest-level diplomats as advisers while giving me maximum latitude in expressing myself on behalf of Egypt. I got practically no instructions on status of women's policy or substance. When I had to face a political situation like the Arab-Israeli question I had to be cognizant of official policy. My alternate to the commission was Mervat El Tellawi.

5. IPPF had been sending emissaries from Pakistan and India, via the Cairo Woman's Club, to advocate family planning among NGOs in Egypt since 1962. As president of the club, I was invited to attend an IPPF International Conference in Singapore in 1963. Soon afterwards, the Egyptian family planning association was started and launched the first family planning program in the country. In 1965 the government established its own family planning program.

6. I acted as an intermediary between Helvi Sipila and Dr. Aziz Bindari, the then head of the Egyptian Family Planning Board, who had been a proponent of development almost at the expense of women's right of accessibility to contraceptive services. I wanted to ensure a balance between demand creation and supply of services to cope with unmet needs and to prevent unplanned pregnancies.

7. For more detail on family law see my chapter "Recently Amendments to Egypt's Law on Personal Status," in *Religion and Politics in the Middle East*, edited by Michael Curtis, 1981, 125–28. Also see the chapter "Aziza Hussein: Family Law and Family Planning in Egypt," in Marion Fennelly Levy's book, *Each in Her Own Way*, 1988, 155–78.

8. I presented a paper on the UN Status of Women's Commission to the Arab League's women's committee and to a meeting of the Arab ministers of social

affairs. I recommended setting up a regional Arab Woman's Commission that would be represented at the UN Commission meetings on a par with the Inter-American Commission of Women. As a result of these efforts the Arab League established it first Arab Women's Commission in 1971.

Gloria Scott, "Breaking New Ground at the UN and the World Bank"

1. UN Headquarters staff supporting these meetings included another Jamaican, Angela King, who was at that time on the staff of the Social Development Division dealing with the annual report on the World Social Situation. Starting as a diplomat on the Jamaican delegation to UN, she later held many important UN posts and most recently served as assistant secretary-general responsible for the General Assembly Special Session for Beijing + 5. Held in June 2000, this special session assessed progress in meeting goals set by the Fourth World Conference on Women in 1995.

2. During this time Freda Paltiel of the Canadian delegation and I developed a very good working relationship that resulted in considerable support later from the Canadian International Development Administration (CIDA) and introductions to Canadian WID networks. In many of the UN's functional commissions, including those dealing with women's issues, the Canadian delegations played an important mediating role.

Leticia Ramos Shahani, "The UN, Women, and Development: The World Conferences on Women"

1. The full text of the Convention on the Elimination of All Forms of Discrimination Against Women is published by the United Nations Department of Public Information as

Reprint DPI/993. As of February 1993, 35,000 copies had been printed. It is available at United Nations publications and sales offices or from United Nations Publications, 2 UN Plaza, Room DC2-853, New York, NY 10017, USA. It is also available in the United Nations Blue Book Series, volume 6, *The United Nations and the Advancement of Women, 1945–1995,* as Document 69. For more information about the convention, see United Nations, *The Work of CEDAW: Reports of the Committee on the Elimination of Discrimination Against Women,* vol. 1. 1982–1985.

2. The full text of the Forward-Looking Strategies adopted at the Nairobi conference can be found in *The United Nations and the Advancement of Women* as Document 84. This volume also contains a comprehensive record of the actions of the Commission on the Status of Women through 1994 and the documents adopted at the first and second UN world conferences on women.

Margaret Snyder, "Walking My Own Road: How a Sabbatical Year Led to a United Nations Career"

1. C. Villa-Vicencio, *Spirit of Hope,* 259.
2. Margaret Snyder and Mary Tadesse, *African Women and Development: A History. The Story of the African Centre for Women,* 6.
3. Ibid., 196.
4. Ibid., 131.
5. Ibid., 112.
6. Snyder and Tadesse, 86
7. Snyder, 1999, 253.
8. Ingrid Reed, who was instrumental in my receiving the Rockefeller Public Service Award with Jesse Jackson and others in 1978, facilitated my application to spend a year at the Woodrow Wilson School of Public and International Affairs of Princeton University. The farsighted Susan

Beresford at the Ford Foundation and Joyce Moock at the Rockefeller Foundation enabled grants for travel worldwide to listen to partners of ACW and UNIFEM whose activities were long since off the UN books: grassroots women, organization leaders, MPs, and UN colleagues.

9. The books are *African Women and Development: A History* and *Transforming Development: Women Poverty and Politics, a History of UNIFEM.* My document collection, interview tapes, and photos found a home in my name in the archives of the Seeley G. Mudd Manuscript Library collection of Public Policy Papers at Princeton University.

10. *Women in African Economies: From Burning Sun to Boardroom.* The book presents business ventures and investment patterns of seventy-four Ugandan women.

Kristen Timothy, "Walking on Eggshells at the UN"

1. Adelman and Morris, *Economic Growth and Social Equity in Developing Countries.* Stanford, Calif.: Stanford University Press, 1973.

2. Moser, *Gender Planning and Development: Theory, Practice and Training.*

Irene Tinker, "Challenging Wisdom, Changing Policies: The Women in Development Movement"

1. Studies about women were elusive in the 1960s; when I began lobbying Congress on the need for affirmative action as president of the Federation of Organizations for Professional Women, I was embarrassed as a scholar by the thinness of data I was quoting. To address this problem, I met with Barbara Newell, then president of Wellesley College, who wanted the college to participate in the women's

movement. In 1974, we combined the Federation's policy approach with Wellesley's academic prowess to set up the Center for Research on Women in Higher Education and the Professions, in Wellesley.

2. Women activists tell their own stories about their efforts for women's equality in Tinker, ed., *Women in Washington: Advocates for Public Policy.*

3. The IWY conference was then scheduled for Bogota, Columbia; it was rescheduled after an election won by a right wing party unwilling to expend funds on women.

4. A report of the seminar proceedings and twelve essays appeared as *Women and World Development*, edited by Irene Tinker and Michele Bo Bramsen; *Women and World Development: An Annotated Bibliography* was produced by Mayra Buvinic with Cheri S. Adams, Gabielle S. Edgcomb, & Marttta Koch-Weser. Published in 1976 under the auspices of the AAAS by the Overseas Development Council, the two volumes were combined in 1980 by Praeger.

5. Originally I had planned to add an international dimension to the Wellesley Center but locate it in Washington. However, the strains between policy and scholarship caused the Federation to move back to Washington within two years; so I set up the International Center for Research on Women (ICRW) as a project of the Federation while we filed for tax exempt status. Coralie Turbitt was director until she became Peace Corps country director in Kenya.

6. Tinker, *Street Foods: Urban Food and Employment in Developing Countries* presents seven countries studies and traces the impact of the original projects after five to ten years. Policy implications are also included.

7. Tinker, ed., *Persistent Inequalities:*

Women and World Development; Tinker, *Women's Rights to House and Land: China, Laos, Vietnam*; "Beyond Economics: Sheltering the Whole Woman." in Blumberg and others, *Engendering Wealth and Well-Being*, NGOs: an alternate power base for women? in Meyer and Prugl, eds., *Gender Politics in Global Governance*.

Anna María Portugal, "Isis International: A Latin American Perspective"

1. Leti Boniol and Annie Calma, "Coming a Long Way Together: Chronicle of ISIS International-Manila and One of the Women Behind It," in *Women In Action*, vol. 2 (1999). Isis International, Manila, the Philippines. Available at the Web site www.isis-women.org.
2. Ibid.
3. *Isis International Annual Report 2000*, Highlights Section, 5–7. Isis International Latin American and Carribean Program, Santiago, Chile.
4. *Isis International* Latin American and Caribbean Program, *Annual Report 2001*, 6.
5. Ibid., 5.

Devaki Jain, "A View from the South: A Story of Intersections"

1. It is interesting that Ujaama in Tanzania and kibbutzim in Israel were post-liberation ideas around the same concept of attempting to replace inequality through collectivity—not through force, as in erstwhile Soviet Union, but as a form of "voluntary mobilization."
2. Nyerere had relinquished the presidency of Tanzania in 1985 and been invited by the chair of the Nonaligned Movement to convene such a commission.
3. South Commission, *Challenges to the South*.

4. My preoccupation with poverty and the importance of building solidarity amongst the like-minded propelled me to call a meeting of all those who had received the Right Livelihood Award, known as the Alternative Nobel Prize. Given to those who had worked at the grassroots on the basic issues of life and livelihood, my friends and I called it "Survival Strategies of the Poor and Traditional Wisdom."
5. Sreenivasan, M.A. *Of the Raj, Maharajas and Me.*
6. This volume, by Tara Ali Baig, was published by the government of India in the 1950s.
7. Political upheavals like the Jayaprakash Narayan movement occurred, starting with the Bihar Famine of 1966 and climaxing in 1975 with the declaration of emergency and suspension of the Constitution. The emergency was declared while many of us were at the First World Conference on Women at Mexico City in June 1975. I left Mexico before the conference ended for fear that India would be closed to returnees. Side by side were technical responses whether from the National Planning Commission, in the shape of the Fifth Five Year Plan (1971–76)—a marker in India's economic evolution, signaling consumption restraint, austerity, and transfer from the rich to the poor to various review committees like the Commission on Education, the Committee on the Status of Women, which was preparing the now famous report, "Towards Equality."
8. This was a fellowship for people like myself who had dropped out of the university and become housewives. It offered a support of 500 rupees per month in 1974.
9. Jain, *Women's Quest for Power: Five Indian Case Studies.*
10. Jain, "Valuing Work: Time as a Measure," in *Economic and Political*

Weekly.

11. Jain, "Impact on Women Workers: Maharastra Employment Guarantee Scheme," a study sponsored by the International Labour Organization, Geneva, December 1979 (mimeograph).

12. Devaki Jain and Mukul Mukerjee, *Women and Their Households: The Relevance of Men and Macro Policies: An Indian Perspective.*

13. The lecture was in honor of Padmaja Naidu, a woman who was both a poet and part of the Indian nationalist struggle.

14. Jain, *Indian Women Today and Tomorrow.*

15. *Integrating Women's Interest into State Five Year Plan,* vols. 1–2, issued by the Ministry of Social Welfare of the government of India.

16. Anisur Rehman,1982 Bhoomi Sena Study, Geneva: UNRISD, part of an evaluation of UNRISD's "Popular Participation Programme" funded by DANIDA.

17. Jain, *Income Generating Activities for Women: Some Case Studies.*

18. Eck and Jain, *Speaking of Faith: Cross-cultural perspectives on Women, Religion, and Social Change.*

19. Jain, "Valuing Women: Signals from the Ground." Prepared for the University of Maryland, June 2001.

20. Amartya Sen, "Population and Reasoned Agency: Food Fertility and Economic Development." Paper presented at the Population, Environment, Development Seminar at the Royal Academy of Sciences and the Beijer Institute, 1993.

Peggy Antrobus, "A Caribbean Journey: Defending Feminist Politics"

1. This chapter is adapted from my Lucille Mathurin Mair Lecture, sponsored by the Centre for Gender and Development Studies, University of the West Indies, Mona Campus, Jamaica, March 2000. See also Mathurin, *The Rebel Woman in the British West Indies During Slavery.*

2. Three factors are relevant: first, because of the dominance of the Roman Catholic Church in Latin America, most women lived in strongly patriarchal families, while Caribbean family structures were much more flexible and matrifocal; second, the rate of literacy for Caribbean women was higher than that for Caribbean men, the only region for which this was true; and third, related to both these facts, Caribbean women enjoyed one of the highest levels of female labor force participation in the world, while—according to official statistics—Latin American women had one of the lowest.

3. Snyder, *Transforming Development,* 144.

4. Structural adjustment programs (SAPs) required governments to reduce spending in order to release resources for debt servicing. The areas most commonly cut were in the social sectors of education, health, and welfare. Cuts in these services also meant a loss of jobs for women, since they predominated in these sectors. Women at home and in the community were expected to fill the gaps created by cuts in services. Latin American feminists described this as "super-exploitation."

5. Cebotarev, Teaching Notes, 1999. University of Guelph.

6. Ibid.

7. Susan Faludi's book, *Stiffed: The Betrayal of the American Man,* suggests a similar trend in the United States. At least Faludi's book, as I understand it, does not blame women for the betrayal of American men. She argues, as I do, that the source of the crisis lies in the undermining of our humanity, that of women no less than that of men, by corporate power and by its capture of the state.

8. DAWN, *Markers on the Way,* 21.

Vivian Lowery Derryck, "Searching for Equality: WID Needed at Home and Abroad"

1. See Thomas Friedman, *The Lexus and the Olive Tree,* for a thoughtful analysis of globalization and its potential consequences.
2. Margaret Snyder's *Women in African Economies* contains detailed documentation of Ugandan women's economic role and the options and potential of women in one African country.

Arvonne S. Fraser, "Seizing Opportunities: USAID, WID, and CEDAW"

1. Margaret Rogers, ed., *A Decade of Women and the Law in the Commonwealth.* This 300-page booklet was based on materials from the *Commonwealth Law Bulletin* documenting progress in women's rights from 1974 to 1985. It was distributed worldwide to women's and legal rights groups by the Commonwealth Secretariat and my Humphrey Institute project.
2. Isabel Plata went home and organized a very successful legal rights program in Profamilia and went on to become the director of Profamilia, the first woman to hold that position. Silvia Pimentel is a law professor at a São Paulo university who writes extensively on women's issues. Both were active IWRAW members.
3. The inheritance case involved Wambui Otieno, a Kikuyu woman in Kenya who married a man from the Luo tribe. When he died his tribe demanded his body under customary law. Married in a civil court and knowledgeable about law, she sued for the right to bury him. IWRAW gave international publicity to the case. For details, see especially chapters 8 and 9 in Otieno, *Mau Mau's Daughter: A Life History.* In the nationality case, Unity Dow, a Botswana woman married to an American man living in Botswana, sued to have her children hold the nationality of both parents as stipulated in CEDAW. She ultimately won, even though Botswana had not ratified the convention, because the court declared that under international customary law the children had a right to both nationalities. Dow is now a judge in Botswana.

Geertje Lycklama á Nijeholt, "Toward Empowerment: Influencing the Netherlands Aid Programs"

1. Ministry of Foreign Affairs of The Netherlands, Directorate General for International Cooperation (1980), "Women in Development Cooperation: A Policy Paper." Second Chamber, States General, 1980–1981, 16400 chapter 5, no. 9 reprint, The Hague.
2. Ria Brouwers, "Een tip van de sluier. Ontwikkelingssamenwerking & Vrouwenemancipatie" (A Tip of the Veil: Development Cooperation and Women's Emancipation). Institute for Political Science, Nijmegen: The Netherlands: 1983. p. 6–8.
3. Brouwers, 1983. pp 45–46.

Dorienne Rowan-Campbell, "Creating a Commonwealth Sisterhood"

1. We had hoped to have the Women and Development Unit of the University of the West Indies (WAND) also as a partner, but WAND's commitment to work on project management and influence skills did not make much sense to CARICOM.

Elise Fiber Smith, "Women Empowering Women Through NGOs"

1. The culmination of this early work was the publication by OEF of *Empowerment and the Law* (1986), a landmark in the field. Today, Women, Law and Development International (WLD) carries on the work of OEF

with Marge Schuler as its executive director. In 1989 OEF transferred its nonprofit status to WLD.

2. Other panels demonstrated the methodologies in OEF's Women Working Together and the Women Entrepreneur training series, giving these a multiplier impact far beyond the specific projects they were designed for.

Cornelia Butler Flora, "The Ford Foundation and the Power of International Sisterhood"

1. The book based on Cornelia Butler Flora's dissertation is *Baptism by Fire and Spirit: Pentecostalism in Colombia.*
2. Flora, "Religion and Change: Pentecostal Women in Columbia?" in *Journal of Inter-American Studies and World Affairs,* 17 (November): 411–25.
3. Flora, "The Passive Female: Her Comparative Image by Class and Culture in Women's Magazine Fiction" in *Journal of Marriage and the Family* 33 (August 1971) 435–44.
4. Ann Pescatello, ed. *Female and Male Latin America: Essays.* Pittsburgh: University of Pittsburgh Press, 1973. (In Spanish: in 1977, Mexico, D.F. Editorial Diana).
5. I received comments in the class evaluation suggesting that I should not be in school with my child, one student stating that "Mrs. Flora should stay home with the baby."
6. I describe these movements more fully in three publications: "Social Policy and Women in Latin America: The Need for a New Model" in *Journal of Third World Societies,* May 1982, pp. 191–205; "Socialist Feminism in Latin America" in *Women and Politics,* Spring 1984, pp. 69–93; and "Socialist Feminism and Political Structures in Four Latin American Countries" in *Women and Development Series,* Working Paper no. 14, Michigan

State University, November 1982.

Kathleen Cloud, "Hard Minds and Soft Hearts: A University Memoir"

1. Kathleen Cloud, "Sex Roles in Food Production and Distribution Systems in the Sahel," in *Proceedings of the International Conference on Women and Food,* University of Arizona: (Tucson, Ariz.: 1978.) Cowan, 1978.
2. The recommendations were adopted as formal policy by BIFAD in October, and with their endorsement, by the National Association of State Universities and Land Grant Colleges at their annual meeting in November 1978. See Cloud, "Gender Issues in AID's Agricultural Projects: How Efficient Are We?" AID Working Paper no. 85, United States Agency for International Development, Washington, D.C. 1979.
3. Catherine Overholt et al., eds., *Gender Roles in Development Projects: A Case Book.*
4. Hilary Feldstein and Susan Poats, *Working Together: Gender Analysis in Agriculture.*
5. Aruina Rao, Kathleen Cloud, and Kathleen Staudt, *Gender Training and Development Planning: Learning from Experience.*
6. Borooah et al., eds. *Capturing Complexity: An Interdisciplinary Look at Women, Households and Development.*

Jane B. Knowles, "Notes from the Middle Border: WID on Campus"

1. In the 1970s MUCIA consisted of seven universities: Illinois at Champaign-Urbana, Iowa at Iowa City, Indiana at Bloomington, Michigan State at East Lansing, Minnesota at Minneapolis–St. Paul, Ohio State at Columbus, and Wisconsin at Madison. Each member university elected two men to the Consortium's Board of Directors and

had the option of choosing a Liaison Officer who was paid to do the Consortium's business on his campus. All these choices were strictly the business of the member university, and all seven operated differently.

2. The MUCIA connection was very important here. The Consortium, with its well-established systems for sharing staff with particular skills, for handling funds, reporting to granting agencies, etc., was familiar both to our male colleagues and the financial administrators of all our institutions.

3. This is the place to acknowledge the support of a number of people without whom the activities described in this paper could not have gone forward. First and foremost was my family. Their tolerance of my absences and distractions was endlessly good-natured, despite the extra work it meant for all of them. The first and most important professional support came from Dr. John T. Murdock, Executive Director of MUCIA from 1976 to 1980, and Professor of Soil Science at UW. John hired me on the basis of my enrollment in a professional training seminar he valued. He gave me both permission and room to grow, never flinched at the difficulties I caused him with the MUCIA Board and was my first empowerer. Then there were Land Tenure Center colleagues Brown and Bruce, and Dr. David Stanfield. Finally, but certainly not least, there were Dean Leo J. Walsh of US/CALS whose strong support of international education in general, perhaps somewhat to his surprise, was broadly based enough to include me. Dr. Kenneth H. Shapiro, Associate Dean for International Programs in CALS and Professor of Agricultural Economics, was my immediate supervisor for the last several years of my career. Ken's quiet, sometimes necessarily very patient support ranged

from important small gestures (an enormous bottle of champagne delivered to me at the first AWID conference) to important large ones (forbearing from throwing me out the window when I played a major role in the UW's loss of an AID project). All of them provided me with the luxury of women staff members too numerous to mention who unstintingly supported my WID work.

Appendix I: Acronyms

AAAS	American Association for the Advancement of Science
AAI	African-American Institute
ACC	Administrative Committee on Coordination
ACW	African Centre for Women (formerly ATRCW) of the ECA
ACCW	Associated Country Women of the World
AED	Academy for Educational Development
AIDoS	Italian Association for Women in Communication
APC	Association for Progressive Communications
AWID	Association for Women's Rights in Development
AWLAE	African Women Leaders in Agriculture and the Environment
BIFAD	Board for International Food and Agricultural Development
CARICOM	Caribbean Community
CCGD	Collaborative Center for Gender and Development, in Kenya
CEDAW	Convention on the Elimination of All Forms of Discrimination Against Women, the women's human rights treaty adopted in 1979, ratified in 1981
CEPIA	Citizenship, Studies, Information and Action, in Brazil
CID	Consortium for International Development

CIDA	Canadian International Development Agency
CIDOC	Information and Documentation Center
CSD	United Nations Commission for Social Development
CSW	Commission on the Status of Women, UN body
CWGL	Center for Women's Global Leadership, at Rutgers
DAC/WID	Development Assistance Committee /Women in Development group of the OECD
DANIDA	Danish International Development Agency
DAW	United Nations Division for the Advancement of Women
DAWN	Development Alternatives with Women for a New Era, an organization of women of the South organized before the Nairobi conference
DFL	Democratic-Farmer-Labor Party of Minnesota
ECA	Economic Commission for Africa, UN regional body
ECE	Economic Commission of Europe, UN regional body
ECLAC	Economic Commission for Latin America and the Caribbean, UN regional group [previously ECLA]
ECOSOC	United Nations Economic and Social Council
ECWA	Economic Commission for West Asia, UN regional group
EPOC	Equity Policy Center

ESCAP	Economic and Social Commission for Asia and the Pacific, UN regional
EU	European Union
FAWE	Forum for African Women Educationalists
FAO	Food and Agriculture Organization, UN agency located in Rome
FGM	female genital mutilation
FLS	Forward-Looking Strategies
GDP	gross domestic product
GNP	gross national product
HDR	Human Development Report, published by UNDP
HIID	Harvard Institute for International Development
ICRW	International Center for Research on Women
ICT	Information Communication Technology
IDB	Inter-American Development Bank, located in Washington, D.C.
IFAD	International Fund for Agricultural Development
ILAV	International Archives for the Women's Movement
ILO	International Labour Organization, UN agency located in Geneva
INSTRAW	International Research and Training Institute for the Advancement of Women, UN agency located in Santo Domingo, Dominican Republic
IPPF	International Planned Parenthood Foundation
IPA	Intergovernmental Personnel Act
ISS	Institute of Social Studies, The Hague
ISST	Institute of Social Studies Trust
ITDG	Intermediate Technology Development Group
IWRAW	International Women's Rights Action Watch, organization dedicated to monitoring and implementation of CEDAW
IWTC	International Women's Tribune Center
IWY	International Women's Year
KWAHO	Kenya Water for Health Organization
KWFT	Kenya Women's Finance Trust
LACHWN	Latin American and Caribbean Women's Health Network
LDC	less-developed country
LSE	London School of Economics
MUCIA	Midwest Universities Consortium for International Activities
NASULGC	National Association of State Universities and Land Grant Colleges
NCRW	National Council for Research on Women
NCWK	National Council of Women, in Kenya
NCWR	National Council for Women's Rights, in Brazil
NDI	National Democratic Institute, of the National Endowment for Democracy, in United States
NGO	nongovernmental organization
NIEO	New International Economic Order
NWSA	National Women's Studies Association
OAU	Organization of African Unity
OECD/DAC	Organization for Economic Cooperation and Development/Development Assistance Committee
OEF	Overseas Education Fund
PNP	People's National Party, in Jamaica
PVO	private voluntary organization
SADC	Southern African

Development Community

SEWA   Self Employed Women's
Association, organization
located in Ahmedabad,
Gujarat, India. Founded by
Ela Bhatt.

SID   Society for International
Development

SIDA   Swedish International
Development Agency

UCLA   University of California, Los
Angeles

UNCTAD United Nations Commission
on Trade and Development

UNDP   United Nations Development
Programme

UNECA   United Nations Economic
Commission for Africa

UNESCO United Nations Educational,
Scientific and Cultural
Organization

UNFPA   United Nations Population
Fund, UN agency located in
New York City

UNICEF United Nations Children's
Fund

UNIFEM United Nations Development
Fund for Women (formerly
the UN Voluntary Fund)

UNITAR United Nations Institute for
Training and Research (no
longer exists)

UNRISD UN Research Institute for
Social Development

USAID   United States Agency for
International Development

UWI   University of the West Indies

UWT   United Tanganyika Women

UW/CALS University of Wisconsin
College of Agricultural and
Life Sciences

VFDW   Voluntary Fund for the UN
Decade for Women

VISTA   Volunteers in Service to
America

YWCA   Young Women's Christian
Association

WAND   Woman and Development

Unit, University of the West
Indies

WEAL   Women's Equity Action
League

WHO   World Health Organization,
UN agency located in Geneva

WID   Women in development

WWB   Women's World Banking

Bibliography

Adelman, Irma, and Cynthia Taft Morris. *Economic Growth and Social Equity in Developing Countries.* Stanford, Calif.: Stanford University Press, 1973.

John W. Foster and Anita Anand. Ottawa: United Nations Association of Canada, 1999, 65–108.

Africa Women and Peace Support Group, 2004-Liberian Women

Antrobus, Peggy. "Consequences and Responses to Social and Economic Deterioration: The Experience of the English-Speaking Caribbean." In *Economic Crises, Household Survival Strategies and Women's Work.* Edited by Lourdes Beneria.

———. "Development Alternatives with Women (DAWN)." In *Proceedings of theAssociation for Women in Development Colloquium on The Future of Women in Development,* October 19–20, 1990, Ottawa, Canada. Ottawa: North South Institute, 74–81.

———. "The Empowerment of Women." In *The Women and International Development Annual.* Vol. 1. Edited by Rita S. Gallin, Marilyn Aronoff, and Anne Fergusson. Boulder: Westview, 1984, 189–207.

———. "Gender Implications of the Development Crisis." *Development in Suspense: Selected Papers and Proceedings of the First Conference of Caribbean Economists.* Edited by George Beckford and Norman Girvan. Kingston, Jamaica: FES, 1987, 145–160.

———. "Gender Issues in Caribbean Development." In *Caribbean Economic Development: The First Generation.* Edited by Stanley Lalta and Marie Freckleton. Kingston, Jamaica: Ian Randle, 1993.

———. "Grassroots Strategies and Innovative Programmes for the Integration of Women in Development: The Caribbean Experience." *Development* (Society for International Development) 27, no. 2 (April 1984), 45–49.

———. "The Impact of the Debt Crisis on Jamaican Women." In *Development in Suspense.* Kingston, Jamaica: Friedrich Ebert Stiftung, 1989.

———. "Making Women Visible in Development: The Role of DAWN." *Proceedings of the International Forum on Intercultural Exchange,* Japan, September 30–October 2, 1992. Japan: National Women's Education Centre, 1993, 17–23.

———. "Structural Adjustment, Curse or Cure? Implications for Caribbean Development." *OXFAM Journal* 1, no. 3 (October 1993), 13–18.

———. "Women and Children's Well-Being in the Age of Globalization." *Development* (Society for International Development) 44, no. 2 (June 2001), 53–57.

———. "Women Organizing Locally and Globally: Development Strategies, Feminist Critiques." In *Feminists Doing Development. A Practical Critique.* Edited by Marilyn Porter and Ellen Judd. London: Zed Books, 1999, 175–89.

———. "Women's Defense of Local Politics in the Face of Structural Adjustment and Globalization." SID journal, *Development* (Society for International Development) 41, no. 3 (1998), 72–76.

Antrobus, Peggy, with Nan Peacocke. "Who Is Really Speaking in the Environment Debate?" *UNESCO Courier* (March 1991), 39–42.

Basu, Amrita, with Elizabeth McGrory, eds. *The Challenge of Local Feminisms: Women's Movements in Global Perspective.* Boulder, Colo.: Westview, 1995.

Borooah, Romy et al. *Capturing Complexity: An Interdisciplinary Look at Women, Households, and Development.* New Delhi: Thousand Oaks, London: Sage, 1994.

Boserup, Ester. *My Professional Life and Publications, 1929–1998.* Copenhagen: Museum Tusculanum Press, University of Copenhagen, 1999.

Boserup, Ester. "Economic Change and the Roles of Women," in *Persistent Inequalities: Women and World Development.* Edited by Irene Tinker. New York: Oxford University Press, 1990.

———. *Women's Role in Economic Development.* New York: St. Martin's, 1970.

Branch, Taylor. *Pillar of Fire: America in the King Years.* New York: Simon and Schuster, 1998.

Brouwers, Ria. "Een tip van de sluier. Ontwikkelingssamenwerking and Vrouwenemancipatie" (A Tip of the Veil: Development Cooperation and Women's Emancipation). Nijmegen, The Netherlands: Institute for Political Science, 1983.

Chaney, Elsa M. *Supermadre: Women in Politics in Latin America.* Austin, Tex.: University of Texas Press, 1979. In Spanish: *Supermadre: La mujer dentro la política en América Latina.* México, D.F.: Fondo de Cultural Económica, 1983.

Chaney, Elsa M., and Mary Garcia Castro, eds. *Muchachas No More: Household Workers in Latin America and the Caribbean.* Philadelphia, Pa.: Temple University Press, 1989. In Spanish: *Muchacha cachifa criada empleada empregadinha sirvienta y . . . más nada: Trabajadoras del hogar en América Latina, y el Caribe.* Caracas: Editorial Nueva Sociedad, 1993.

Chaney, Elsa M., and Martha W. Lewis. *Creating a Women's Component: A Case Study in Rural Jamaica.* Washington, D.C.: Office of Women in Development, Agency for International Development, 1980.

Chaney, Elsa M., and Aída Moreno Valenzuela. "The Difficult Path Toward Organizing Householdworkers." In *Emergences: Women's Struggles for Livelihood in Latin America.* Edited by John Friedmann et al. Los Angeles, Calif.: University of California Latin American Center Publications, 1996.

Charlton, Sue Ellen, Jana Everett, and Kathleen Staudt, eds. *Women, Development, and the State.* Albany, N.Y.: SUNY Albany Press, 1989.

Chen, Martha Alter. "Engendering World Conferences: The International Women's Movements and the U.N." *NGOs, the UN, and Global Governance.* Edited by Thomas G. Weiss and Leon Gordenker. Boulder, Colo.: Lynne Rienner, 1996, 139–55.

Chiappe, Marta B., and Cornelia Butler Flora. "Gendered Elements of the Sustainable Agriculture Paradigm." *Rural Sociology*, 63 (1998), 372–93. *http://www.ncrcrd.iastate.edu/pubs/flora/gendered/htm*

Cloud, Kathleen. *Consortium for International Development/Women and Development Project Bi-annual Report*, Submitted to AID/WID. Washington, D.C., 1984.

———. *Final Report: Actions and Strategies to Strengthen and Expand the Involvement of American University Women in Title XII Activities.* Washington, D.C.: Report submitted to AID/DSB/XII, 1980

———. *Gender Issues in AID's Agricultural Projects: How Efficient Are We?* AID Working Paper no. 85. Washington, D.C. U.S. Agency for International Development.

———. "Sex Roles in Food Production and Distribution Systems in the Sahel." *Proceedings and Papers of the International Conference on Women and Food.* Edited by Ann Cowan. Tucson, Ariz.: University of Arizona Consortium for International Development, 1978.

Commonwealth Medical Association. *Report of the International Roundtable on a Woman's Right to Health, Including Sexual and Reproductive Health.* London: Commonwealth Medical Association, 1996.

Conway, Jill Kerr. *When Memory Speaks: Exploring the Art of Autobiography.* New York: Random House, 1999

Cook, Rebecca, ed. *Human Rights of Women: National and International Perspectives.* Philadelphia, Pa: University of Pennsylvania Press, 1994.

Curtis, Michael, ed. *Religion and Politics in the Middle East.* Westview Press, 1981, 125–28.

DAWN. *Markers on the Way: The DAWN Debates on Alternative Development: DAWN's Platform for the Fourth World Conference on Women.* Barbados: DAWN, September 1995.

Faludi, Susan, *Stiffed: The Betrayal of the American Man.* New York: Morrow, 1999.

Feldstein, Hilary, and Susan Poats. *Working Together: Gender Analysis in Agriculture.* West Hartford, Conn.: Kumarian Press, 1990.

Flora, Cornelia Butler. *Baptism by Fire and Spirit: Pentecostalism in Colombia.* Rutherford, N.J.: Fairleigh Dickinson University Press, 1976.

———. "Domestic Service in the Latin American Fotonovela." In *Muchachas No More: Household Workers in Latin America and the Caribbean.* Edited by Elsa M. Chaney and Mary Garcia Castro. Philadelphia: Temple University Press: 1989, 143–59.

———. "Income Generation Projects for Rural Women." *Rural Women and State Policy.* Edited by C. Deere and M. León. Boulder, Colo.: Westview, 1987, 212–38.

———. "Incorporating Women into International Development Programs: The Political Phenomenology of a Private Foundation." *Women in Politics* 2 (Winter 1982), 89–106. Also published in *Women in Developing Countries: A Policy Focus.* New York: The Haworth Press (1983), 89-106.

———. "The Passive Female and Social Change: A Cross-Cultural Comparison of Women's Magazine Fiction." In *Female and Male Latin America: Essays.* Edited by Ann Pescatello. Pittsburgh: University of Pittsburgh Press: 1973, 59–86. In Spanish: Mexico, D.F.: Editorial Diana, 1977.

———. "Peasant Women and Agricultural Production in the Andean Countries of Colombia, Ecuador, Peru, Bolivia, and Chile." *Resources for Feminist Research,* 11 (1), 85–87.

Flora, Cornelia Butler (1975). "Pentecostal Women in Columbia: Religious Change and the Status of Working-class Women." *Journal of Inter-American Studies and World Affairs,* 17 (4), 411–25.

———. "Religion and Change: Pentecostal Women in Colombia." *Journal of Inter-American Studies and World Affairs* 17 (1975), 411–25.

———. "Rural Development." In *Latinas of the Americas: A Source Book.* Edited by K. Lynn Stoner. New York: Garland, 1989, 535–80.

———. "Servicio domestico en la fotonovela en America Latina." In *Muchacha Cachifa Criada Empleada Empregadinha Sirvienta y mas nada.* Edited by Elsa M. Chaney and Mary Garcia Castro. Caracas, Venezuela: Trabajadoras domesticas en America Latina y el Caribe, 1993, 131–146.

———. "Social Policy and Women in Latin America: The Need for a New Model."

Journal of Third World Societies (May 1982), 191–205.

———. "Socialist Feminism in Latin America." *Women and Politics* (Spring 1984), 69–93.

———. *Socialist Feminism and Political Structures in Four Latin American Countries.* Women and Development Series. Working Paper no. 14. East Lansing, Mich.: Michigan State University, 1982.

———. "Women and Development Projects: Planned and Unplanned Change." *Journal of Comparative Rural and Regional Studies* (Fall 1984), 86–94.

———. "Working Class Women's Political Participation: Its Potential in Developed Countries." In *A Portrait of Marginality: The Political Behavior of the American Woman.* Edited by Marianne Githens and Jewel L. Prestage. New York: David McKay, 1977, 75–95.

Flora, Cornelia Butler, ed. *Interactions Between Agroecosystems and Rural Communities.* Boca Raton, Fla.: CRC Press, 2001.

Flora, Cornelia Butler, and Jim Christenson, eds. *Rural Policies for the 1990s.* Boulder, Colo.: Westview, 1991.

Flora, Cornelia Butler, J. Flora, J. Spears, and L. Swanson et al. *Rural Communities: Legacy and Change.* Boulder, Colo.: Westview, 1992.

Flora, Cornelia Butler, and Margaret Kroma. "Gender and Sustainability in Agriculture and Rural Development." In *Sustainability in Agricultural and Rural Development.* Edited by G. E. D'Souza and T. G. Gebermedhin. Brookfield, Vt.: Ashgate, 1998, 103–16.

Flora, Cornelia Butler, and Sue Johnson. "Discarding the Distaff: New Roles for Rural Women." In *Rural Society in the United States: Current Trends and Issues.* Edited by Thomas Ford. Ames, Iowa: Iowa State University Press, 1978, 168–81.

Flora, Cornelia Butler,, and Blas Santos. "Women in Latin American Farming System." In *Women and Change in Latin America.* Edited by June Nash and Helen Safa. South Hadley, Mass.: Bergin and Garvey, 1985, 208–28.

Flora, Cornelia Butler,, and John Stitz. "Female Subsistence Production and Commercial Farm Survival Among Settlement Kansas Wheat Farmers." *Human Organization* 47 no. 1 (Spring 1988.), 64–69.

Flora, Cornelia Butler,, and Celia Jean Weidemann. "Making Women in Development Work on Campus." In *Women Creating Wealth: Transforming Economic Development.* Edited by Rita Gallin and Anita Spring. Washington, D.C.: Association for Women in Development, 1985, 79–84.

Flora, Jan L., and Cornelia Butler Flora. "Race, Gender, and Class in Rural America." In *Introduction to Sociology: A Race, Gender, and Class Perspective.* Edited by J. A. Belkhir and B. M. Barnett, with A. Karpathakis. Race, Gender, and Class Book Series. New Orleans, La.: Southern University Press, 1999, 369–83.

Francis, Charles A., Cornelia Butler Flora, and Larry King, eds. *Sustainable Agriculture in Temperate Zones.* New York: Wiley, 1990.

Fraser, Arvonne. "Becoming Human: The Origins and Development of Women's Human Rights." *Human Rights Quarterly* 21 (1999), 853–906.

———. "The Convention on the Elimination of All Forms of Discrimination Against Women." In *Women, Politics, and the United Nations.* Edited by Anne Winslow. Westport, Conn.: Greenwood Press, 1995, 77–94.

———. "The Feminization of Human Rights." *Foreign Service Journal* (December 1993), 31–34.

———. *The UN Decade for Women: Documents and Dialogue.* Boulder, Colo.: Westview, 1987.

———. "Women and International Development: The Road to Nairobi and Back." *The*

American Woman 1990–91. Edited by Sara E. Rix. New York: Norton, 1990, 287–300.
Freeman, Marsha, and Arvonne Fraser. "Women's Human Rights: Making the Theory a
Reality." In *Human Rights: An Agenda for the Next Century.* Edited by Louis Henkin and
John Lawrence Hargrove.Washington, D.C.: American Society of International Law,
1994, p. 103.
Friedman, Thomas. *The Lexus and the Olive Tree.* New York: Doubleday, 2000.
Galey, Margaret. "Forerunners in Women's Quest for Partnership" and "Women Find a
Place." In Anne Winslow, ed. *Women Politics, and the United Nations.* Edited by Anne
Winslow. Westport, Conn.: Greenwood Press, 1995, 1–28.
———. "Promoting Nondiscrimination Against Women: The UN Commission on the
Status of Women." *International Studies Quarterly* 23, no. 2 (June 1979), 273–302.
Gil, Leslie. *Precarious Dependencies: Gender, Class, and Domestic Service in Bolivia.* New York:
Columbia University Press, 1984.
Haslegrave, Marianne. *Beyond Cairo: ICPD Programme of Action.* Abridged ed. London:
Commonwealth Medical Association, 1994. *The Convention on the Elimination of All
Forms of Discrimination Against Women, The Reporting Process: A Manual for
Commonwealth Jurisdictions.* London: Commonwealth Secretariat, 1988.
Haslegrave, Marianne, ed. *User-friendly Guide to Health Issues in the Beijing Declaration and
Platform for Action.* Geneva: World Health Organization, 1996.
Hevener, Natalie Kaufman. *International Law and the Status of Women.* Boulder, Colo.:
Westview Press, 1983.
Hussein, Aziza. "Recently Amendments to Egypt's Law on Personal Status." In Curtis,
Michael, ed. *Religion and Politics in the Middle East.* Edited by Michael Curtis. Boulder,
Colo.: Westview, 1981, 125–28.
Isis International. *Los veinte años de Isis: Revista Mujeres en Acción.* (Twenty years of ISIS:
Special edition, nos. 2–3. Santiago, Chile: Isis International Latin American and
Caribbean Program, 1994. See especially Marilee Karl, "En el rancer del movimiento de
mujeres" (The Rebirth of the Women's Movement), and Jane Cottingham, "Un proyecto
visionario" (A Visionary Project).
———. *Annual Report 2000.* Santiago, Chile: Isis International Latin American and
Caribbean Program, 2000.
Jain, Devaki. "Impact on Women Workers: Maharastra Employment Guarantee Scheme." A
study sponsored by the International Labour Organization. Geneva: December 1979
(mimeographed).
———. *Income Generating Activities for Women: Some Case Studies.* New York: UNICEF,
1980.
———. *Indian Women.* New Delhi: Government of India, Ministry of Information and
Broadcasting, 1975.
———. *Indian Women Today and Tomorrow.* New Delhi: Nehru Memorial Museum and
Library, 1983.
———. "Valuing Women: Signals from the Ground." Unpublished paper prepared for the
University of Maryland, 2001.
———. "Valuing Work: Time as a Measure." *Economic and Political Weekly,* Oct. 26, 1996.
———. *Women's Quest for Power: Five Indian Case Studies.* New Delhi: Vikas, 1980.
Jain, Devaki, and Mukul Mukerjee. *Women and Their Households: The Relevance of Men and
Macro Policies: An Indian Perspective.* New Delhi: Institute of Social Studies Trust, 1989.
Jaquette, Jane. "Equality, Merit, and Need: Competing Criteria of Justice in Women and
Development." In *Persistent Inequalities: Women and World Development.* Edited by Irene

Tinker. New York: Oxford University Press, 1990, 54–69.

———. "The Family and Development Policy." In *Women at the Center.* Edited by Gay Young, Vidyamali Samarasinghe, and Ken Kusterer. West Hartford, Conn.: Kumarian Press, 1993, 45–62.

———. "Losing the Battle, Winning the War: The Political Dynamics of the UN Mid-Decade Conference." In *Women, Politics, and the United Nations.* Edited by Anne Winslow. Westport, Conn.: Greenwood Press, 1995, 45–60.

———. "Women and Modernization Theory: A Decade of Feminist Criticism." *World Politics* (January 1982), 267–84.

———. "Women and Power: From Tokenism to Critical Mass." *Foreign Policy* no. 108 (Fall 1997), 23–37.

Jaquette, Jane, and Kathleen Staudt. "Politics, Population, and Gender: A Feminist Analysis of U.S. Population Policy in the Third World." In *The Political Interests of Gender: Developing Theory and Research with a Feminist Face.* Edited by Kathleen Jones and Anna Jonasdottir. London: Sage, 1988, 214–33.

———. *Women in Developing Countries: A Policy Focus.* New York: Haworth Press, 1983.

Kabeer, Naila. *Reversed Realities: Gender Hierarchies in Development Thought.* London: Verso, 1994.

Lerner, Gerda. *The Creation of Feminist Consciousness.* New York: Oxford University Press, 1993.

Levy, Marion Fennelly. *Each in Her Own Way.* Boulder, Colo.: Lynne Reinner, 1988.

Lewis, Martha Wells. "Developing Income Generating Opportunity for Rural Women." *Horizons* 2, no. 1, (January 1983), 28–31.

———. "Did Beijing Make a Difference?" *Directions* 13 (September–October), 5–9.

———. *Women and Food: An Annotated Bibliography on Food Production, Preservation, and Improved Nutrition.* Washington, D.C.: Office of Women in Development, Agency for International Development, 1978.

Luce, Louise Fiber, and Elise C. Smith, eds. *Readings in Cross-Cultural Communication.* Boston: Harper and Row, 1987.

Lynn, N., Bustos Lynn, and Cornelia Butler Flora. "The Implications of Motherhood for Political Participation." In *Pronatalism: The Myth of Mom and Apple Pie.* Edited by Ellen Peck and Judith Senderowitz. New York: Crowell, 1974, 227–48.

———. "Societal Punishment and Aspects of Female Political Participation: 1972 National Convention Delegates." In *A Portrait of Marginality: The Political Behavior of the American Woman.* Edited by Marianne Githens and Jewel Prestage. New York: David McKay, 1977, 139–49.

Mair, Lucille. "Women: A Decade Is Time Enough." *Third World* Quarterly 8, no. 2 (April 1986), 583–93.

Mathurin, Lucille [Lucille Mair]. *The Rebel Woman in the British West Indies During Slavery.* Kingston, Jamaica: Institute of Jamaica, 1975.

Miller, Jean Baker. *Towards a New Psychology of Women.* Boston: Beacon Press, 1976.

Mohammed, Patricia, and Cathy Shepherd, eds. *Gender in Caribbean Development.* St. Augustine: University of the West Indies, 1988.

Moraga, Enrique Homariz. *Genero y Desastres: Introduccion conceptual y criterios operativos. La crisis del hurican Mitch en centroamerica.* San José, Costa Rica: Fundacion Genero y sociedad, 1999.

Morrison, Maria, and Loreto Biehl, eds. *Too Close to Home: Domestic Violence in the Americas.* Washington, D.C.: InterAmerican Development Bank, 1999.

Moser, Caroline O. N., *Gender Planning and Development: Theory, Practice and Training.* London: Routledge, 1993.

Myrdal, Gunnar. *Asian Drama: An Inquiry into the Poverty of Nations.* New York: Pantheon, 1968.

Netherlands Ministry of Foreign Affairs, Directorate General for International Cooperation. "Women in Development Cooperation: A Policy Paper." Second Chamber, States General, 1980–1981, 16400 chapter v, no. 9 reprint. The Hague.

Nussbaum, Martha C. *Women and Human Development: The Capabilities Approach.* Cambridge, U.K.: Cambridge University Press, 2000.

Overholt, Catherine, Mary Anderson, Kathleen Cloud, and James Austin. *Gender Roles in Development Projects.* West Hartford, Conn.: Kumarian Press, 1985.

Otieno, Wambui Waiyaki. *Mau Mau's Daughter: A Life History.* Boulder, Colo.: Lynne Rienner, 1998.

Papanek, Hanna, "To each less than she needs, from each more than she can do: Allocations, entitlements, and value," in *Persistent Inequalities: Women and World Development.* Edited by Irene Tinker. New York: Oxford, 1990.

Parpart, Jane, and Kathleen Staudt, eds. *Women and the State in Africa.* Boulder, Colo.: Lynne Rienner, 1989.

Pescatello, Ann, ed. *Female and Male Latin America: Essays.* Pittsburgh: University of Pittsburgh Press, 1973. (In Spanish: Mexico, D.F.: Editorial Diana, 1977).

Pietila, Hilkka, and Jeanne Vickers. *Making Women Matter: The Role of the United Nations.* London: Zed Press, 1990.

Portugal, Ana Maria, and Carmen Torres, eds. *Por todos los medios: Comunicación y género.* (By All Means: Communication and Gender.) Santiago, Chile: Isis International, 1996.

Rao, Aruna, Hilary Feldstein, Kathleen Cloud, and Kathleen Staudt. *Gender Training and Development Planning: Learning from Experience.* New York: Population Council, 1991.

Rodefeld, Richard D. et al., eds. *Change in Rural America: Causes, Consequences and Alternatives.* St. Louis: Mosby, 1978.

Rogers, Margaret, ed. *A Decade of Women and the Law in the Commonwealth.* Minneapolis, Minn.: Humphrey Institute of Public Affairs, 1985.

Safa, H. I., and C. B. Flora. "Production, Reproduction, and Polity: Women's Strategic and Practical Goals." In *Americas: New Interpretive Essays.* Edited by Alfred Stepan. New York: Oxford University Press, 1992, 109–36.

Schuler, Margaret. *Empowerment and the Law: Strategies of Third World Women.* Washington, D.C.: Overseas Education Fund, 1986.

Schummacher E. F. *Small Is Beautiful.* New York: Harper and Row, 1973.

Scott, Gloria L. N. "The Aging Female Population in the Caribbean Area: Some Economic Issues." In *Mid-Life and Older Women in Latin America and the Caribbean,* a co-publication of the Pan-American Health Organization and the American Association of Retired Persons. Washington, D.C.: PAHO/AARP, 1989.

———. "Health Needs of Caribbean Women: Challenges for the Nineties." In *Gender, A Caribbean Multi-Disciplinary Perspective.* Edited by Elsa Leo-Rhynie, Barbara Bailey, and Christine Barrow. Kingston, Jamaica: Center for Gender and Development Studies, University of the West Indies, 1997.

———. *Recognizing the "Invisible" Woman in Development: The World Bank's Experience.* Washington D.C.: World Bank, 1979.

———. "The UN Correspondence Training Programme in Social Planning." In *Correspondence Education in Africa.* Edited by Antoine Kabwasa and Martin Kaunda.

London and Boston: Routledge and Kegan Paul, 1973.

Scott, Gloria L. N., and Marilyn Carr. *The Impact of Technology Choice on Rural Women in Bangladesh: Problems and Opportunities.* World Bank Staff Working Paper no. 731. Washington, D.C.: World Bank, 1985.

Semler, Vicki J., Leonora Wiener, Tina Johnson, and Jane Garland Katz, eds. *Rights of Women: A Guide to the Most Important United Nations Treaties on Women's Human Rights.* New York: International Women's Tribune Center, 1998.

Sen, Amartya. *Development as Freedom.* New York: Knopf, 1999.

Sen, Gita, and Caren Grown. *Development, Crises, and Alternative Visions: Third World Women's Perspectives.* New York, Monthly Review Press, 1987.

Senauer, Benjamin, "The impact of the value of women's time on food and nutrition," in *Persistent Inequalities: Women and World Development.* Edited by Irene Tinker. New York: Oxford, 1990.

———. "Gender and Cooperative Conflicts." In *Persistent Inequalities: Women and World Development.* Edited by Irene Tinker. New York: Oxford University Press, 1990.

Shields, M. Dale, Cornelia Butler Flora, Barbara Thomas-Slayter, and Gladys Buenavista. "Developing and Dismantling Social Capital: Gender and Resource Management in the Philippines." In *Feminist Political Ecology: Global Perspectives and Local Experience.* Edited by Dianne Rocheleau, Barbara Thomas-Slayer, and Esther Wangari. London: Routledge, 1996, 155–79.

Snyder, Margaret. *African Women and Development: A History.* London: ZED, 1995.

———. *American Partnership with the New Africa: Questions of Power, Justice, and Gender.* New York: Phelps-Stokes Fund, 1999.

———. *Transforming Development: Women, Poverty, and Politics. A History of UNIFEM.* London: Intermediate Technology Publications, 1999.

———. "Women, the Neglected Human Resources for National Development." *Canadian Journal of African Studies* (1972).

———. *Women of Africa Today and Tomorrow.* Addis Ababa, Ethiopia: UNECA, 1974.

———. "Women and African Development" *Choice* 37, no.6 (2000), 1037–51.

———. *Women in African Economies: From Burning Sun to Boardroom.* Kampala, Uganda: Fountain Press, 2000.

Snyder, Margaret, and Mary Tadesse. *African Women and Development, A History: The Story of the African Centre for Women.* Johannesburg, South Africa: Witwatersrand University Press and London: Zed Books, 1995.

South Commission. *Challenges to the South: Report of the South Commission.* New York: Oxford University Press, 1990.

Sowa, Theo et al. *Liberian Women Peacemakers: To Be Seen, Heard and Counted.* Trenton, NJ: Africa World Press, 2004.

Sreenivasan, M. A. *Of the Raj, Maharajas, and Me.* New Delhi: Ravi Dayal, 1991.

Staudt, Kathleen. *Agricultural Policy Implementation: A Case from Western Kenya.* West Hartford, Conn.: Kumarian Press, 1985.

———. *Free Trade? Informal Economies at the U.S.-Mexico Border.* Philadelphia, Pa.: Temple University Press, 1998.

———. *Managing Development.* Newbury, Calif.: Sage, 1990.

———. *Policy, Politics, and Gender: Women Gaining Ground.* West Hartford, Conn.: Kumarian Press, 1998.

———. *Women, Foreign Assistance, and Advocacy Administration.* New York: Praeger, 1985.

———. *Women, International Development, and Politics: The Bureaucratic Mire.* Philadelphia,

Pa.: Temple University Press, 1991 and 1997.

Staudt, Kathleen, and David Spener. *The U.S.-Mexico Border: Transcending Divisions, Contesting Identities.* Boulder, Colo.: Lynne Rienner, 1998.

Sutton, Constance R., and Elsa M. Chaney, eds. *Caribbean Life in New York City: Sociocultural Dimensions, Staten Island.* New York: Center for Migration Studies, 1944.

Tinker, Irene. "Beyond Economics: Sheltering the Whole Woman." In *Engendering Wealth and Well-Being.* Edited by Rae Blumberg, Cathy Rakowski, and Michael Monteon. Boulder, Colo.: Westview, 1995, 261–83.

———. "Electoral quotas for women: Do they really empower women?" *Women's Studies International Forum,* 27: 4, 2004.

———. "NGOs: An Alternate Power Base for Women?" In *Gender Politics in Global Governance.* Edited by Mary K. Meyer and Elisabeth Prugl. Lanham, Md.: Rowman and Littlefield, 1999, 88–104.

———. "The Real Rural Energy Crisis: Women's Time." *The Energy Journal* 8 (1987), 125–146. Longer version originally prepared in 1984 for IDRC through Equity Policy Center and circulated by ILO is published in Ashok V. Desai, ed., *Human Energy,* New Delhi: Wiley Eastern, 1990.

———. *Street Foods: Urban Food and Employment in Developing Countries.* New York: Oxford University Press, 1997

———. *Persistent Inequalities: Women and World Development.* New York: Oxford University Press, 1990. Chapter titled on "The Making of the Field: Advocates, Practitioners, and Scholars." 27–53. Chapter undated and reprinted in Duggan, Lynn, Laurie Nisonoff, Nalini Visvanathan, Nan Wiegersman, eds. *Women, Gender, and Development Reader.* London: Zed Press, 1996, 32-42.

———. "Utilizing interdisciplinarity to analyze global socio-economic change: A tribute to Ester Boserup," in *Global Tensions: Challenges and Opportunities in the Economy,* edited by Lourdes Beneria. London: Routledge, 2003.

——— *Women in Washington: Advocates for Public Policy.* Beverly Hills, Calif.: Sage Publications, 1983. Chapter on "Women in Development." 227–37.

———. "Federal City College: How black?" in D. Reisman and V. Statan, eds. *Academic Transformation.* McGraw Hill, 1973, 95–126.

Tinker, Irene, and Michele Bo Bramsen, eds. *Women and World Development.* New York: Praeger, 1980.

Tinker, Irene, and Jane Jaquette. "UN Decade for Women: Its Impact and Legacy." *World Development* 15, no.3 (1986), 419–27.

Tinker, Irene, and Gale Summerfield, eds. *Women's Rights to House and Land: China, Laos, Vietnam.* Boulder, CO: Lynne Rienner, 1999. Chapter "Women's empowerment through rights to house and land," 9-26.

Tomasevski, Katarina. *Women and Human Rights.* London: Zed Books, 1993.

Torres, Carmen, ed. *Genero y comunicacion. El lado oscuro de los medios* (Gender and Communications: The Dark Side of the Media). Santiago, Chile: Isis International, 2000.

UNECA (United Nations Economic Commission for Africa). *The Data Base for Discussion on the Interrelations Between the Integration of Women in Development, Their Situation and Population Factors in Africa.* Addis Ababa, Ethiopia: UNECA, 1974.

———. *Factors Affecting Education, Training, and Work Opportunities for Girls and Women within the Context of Development.* Addis Ababa, Ethiopia: UNECA, 1971.

United Nations. *Covenant for the New Millennium: The Beijing Declaration and Platform for*

Action. Santa Rosa, Calif.: Free Hand Books, 1995.

———. *The United Nations and the Advancement of Women, 1945–1995.* New York: United Nations, 1995.

———. *The Work of CEDAW: Reports of the Committee on the Elimination of Discrimination Against Women, 1982–1985.* New York: United Nations, 1989.

Villa-Vicencio, C. *Spirit of Hope.* Johannesburg, South Africa: Skotaville Publishers, 1994.

Walker, Anne. "From Mexico to Beijing-1975-1995," In Anand, Anita with Gouri Salvi, eds. *Beijing! UN Fourth World Conference on Women.* New Delhi: Women's Features Service, 1998.

———. "How It Happened: From Day to Day, Excerpts from Global FaxNet Bulletins, April 3–September 25, 1995," and "Bringing Beijing Home: The Platform for Action and You." *Women's Studies Quarterly* 24, nos. 1 and 2 (Spring and Summer 1996), 18–39, 141–53.

———. "The Women's Movement and Its Role in Development." In *Theoretical Perspectives on Gender and Development.* Edited by Jane L. Parpart, M. Patricia Connelly, and V. Eudine Barriteau. Ottawa: Commonwealth of Learning and IDRC, 2000.

WEDO (Women's Environment and Development Organization). *Mapping Progress:Assessing Implementation of the Beijing Platform of Action.* New York, WEDO, 1998.

West, Lois A. "The United Nations women's conferences and feminist politics," in *Gender and Global Governance,* edited by Mary K. Meyer and Elizabeth Prugl. Rowman and Littlefield, 1999.

Winslow, Anne, ed. *Women, Politics, and the United Nations.* Westport, Conn.: Greenwood Press, 1995.

Resources

Food and Agriculture Organization (FAO). A list of more than fifty documents can be obtained by contacting FAO at *ftpp@fao.org* or can be seen on the FAO Forestry Department web site.

Human Development Report, published annually by UN Development Program, focuses on different topics each year.

The International Women's Tribune Centre, which issues newsletters and other publications, is headquartered at 777 UN Plaza, New York, NY, 10017. See its Web site at *www.iwtc.org.* Women's Ink, at the same address, sells books on women and development topics from many publishers around the world.

For more information in Spanish, contact Isis International's Resource Center and Information Program in Santiago, Chile at its Web site: *www.isis.cl.*

World Development Report, published annually by the World Bank, features a different subject each year. The 2000 report concerns world poverty.

World Resources Report, published biennially, contains data on housing, water supply, and urbanization.

Index

The Feminist Press at the City University of New York is a nonprofit literary and educational institution dedicated to publishing work by and about women. Our existence is grounded in the knowledge that women's writing has often been absent or underrepresented on bookstore and library shelves and in educational curricula—and that such absences contribute, in turn, to the exclusion of women from the literary canon, from the historical record, and from the public discourse.

The Feminist Press was founded in 1970. In its early decades, the Feminist Press launched the contemporary rediscovery of "lost" American women writers, and went on to diversify its list by publishing significant works by American women writers of color. More recently, the Press's publishing program has focused on international women writers, who remain far less likely to be translated than male writers, and on nonfiction works that explore issues affecting the lives of women around the world.

Founded in an activist spirit, the Feminist Press is currently undertaking initiatives that will bring its books and educational resources to underserved populations, including community colleges, public high schools and middle schools, literacy and ESL programs, and prison education programs. As we move forward into the twenty-first century, we continue to expand our work to respond to women's silences wherever they are found.

Many of our readers support the Press with their memberships, which are tax-deductible. Members receive numerous benefits, including complimentary publications, discounts on all purchases from our catalog or web site, pre-publication notification of new books and notice of special sales, invitations to special events, and a subscription to our email newsletter, "Women's Words: News from the Feminist Press."

For more information about membership and events, and for a complete catalog of the Press's 250 books, please refer to our web site: www.feminist-press.org, or call (212) 817-7925.